COOPERATIVE LEARNING

COOPERATIVE LEARNING

Theory and Research

Edited by
SHLOMO SHARAN

PRAEGER

New York
Westport, Connecticut
London

Library of Congress Cataloging-in-Publication Data

Cooperative learning : theory and research / edited by Shlomo Sharan.
     p.   cm.
   Includes bibliographical references.
   ISBN 0-275-92887-X (alk. paper)
   1. Group work in education. 2. Team learning approach in
education.   I. Sharan, Shlomo, 1932–
LB1032.C594   1990
371.1'48—dc20   89-36649

Library of Congress Catalog Card Number: 89-36649
ISBN: 0-275-92887-X

First published in 1990

Praeger Publishers, One Madison Avenue, New York, NY 10010
An imprint of Greenwood Publishing Group, Inc.

Printed in the United States of America

∞™

The paper used in this book complies with the
Permanent Paper Standard issued by the National
Information Standards Organization (Z39.48-1984).

10 9 8 7 6 5 4 3 2

To my mother,
SADIE J. SINGER,
and to the memory of my father,
MAURICE L. SINGER

Contents

Figures and Tables

FIGURES

TABLES

Preface

This volume seeks to provide a reply to the question, "What have recent theory and research to contribute to our understanding of cooperative learning and its effects on teachers and students?" As such, this volume concentrates on how that set of instructional methods generally included under the title of "cooperative learning" affects its practitioners and their clients, the students. As expected, the effects of any instructional method probably can be found over a broad range of dependent and mediating variables, and this is certainly the case for cooperative learning. Some investigators might feel that such diversity in the dependent variables discussed in a volume of this kind detracts from the theoretical unity of the book. By necessity, the theory and research related to a specific form of teaching lead in many different directions. Investigators interested, for example, in thinking patterns, inter-group relations, motivation, or teachers' verbal behavior, may find only one study or theoretical paper in this book to be of relevance to their work. Since investigators frequently focus on topics that often appear as dependent or mediating variables in educational settings rather than as part of the chief independent variable typical of schools, namely the process of instruction, some can claim that a book of this kind cannot be meaningful to the community of investigators concerned with education.

In light of this latter position, one that is often implicit in many volumes of collected papers on psycho-educational topics, it seemed desirable to make explicit the goal of this book. The goal here is to illuminate at least some of the major effects of cooperative learning methods as (part of) an independent variable. Clearly the concern of this book is how a set of particular instructional methods affects people in classrooms and what this form of instruction contributes to them, or fails to contribute. After all, it is the instructional process, perhaps more than any other major variable in schools, over which we exert a relatively large degree of control and which we can change more readily, despite the impediments, than many of the other personal or social variables found in classroom settings. Yet, the characteristics and procedures of teaching methods receive relatively meager attention in the research literature, compared with their role and significance in the process of schooling.

Investigators of cooperative learning methods and their effects appear to be expressing the position that significant improvement in the processes of teaching and learning in school can be achieved. In order to do so we must pay considerable attention to the manner in which instruction is conducted, no less than we attend to the contents of the curriculum. Curriculum development is traditionally considered to be a discipline in the field of education. Yet, relatively little attention is paid to methods or models of teaching beyond having prospective teachers learn the standard procedures of presenting material to students with a variety of techniques (lectures, audio-visual aids, demonstrations, etc.) and asking them questions about the material they heard or read about (which is how the teacher candidates themselves are prepared for their profession). The typical "methods" courses for teaching specific subject matter concentrate primarily on the subject matter and only very little on the "methods." Thus, course titles notwithstanding, models of teaching, in terms of the design of the process of instruction, receive only peripheral recognition in most university departments of education. This volume seeks to draw attention to cooperative learning as a model of teaching (actually a set of models) that produces a wide range of positive effects of the kind that schools claim they wish to generate. Therein lies one of its main claims on the attention of the readers of this book and to a central place in the professional skills of teachers, trainers of teachers, school administrators, and investigators of the instructional process.

It is my hope that the chapters of this volume are consistent with these goals, and I would like to express my appreciation to all of the authors who have contributed their efforts to this project.

1
Cooperative Learning and Achievement: Methods for Assessing Causal Mechanisms

GEORGE P. KNIGHT
AND ELAINE MORTON BOHLMEYER

The research on cooperative learning environments has generally focused upon several well-developed classroom structures. These environments substantially modify the nature of the classroom in an attempt to foster cooperation. Further, this research has focused upon the effects of cooperative learning on academic achievement and interpersonal relationships (cf. Sharan et al. 1980, 1984; Slavin et al. 1985). In the present chapter we will be concerned only with the influence of cooperative learning environments upon academic achievement; however, much of our analysis of the research and our recommended research directions may be applied to the effects on interpersonal relationships as well. We will briefly review, first, some of the most commonly used cooperative learning environments and second, the research on the hypothesized causal mechanisms through which cooperative learning environments may influence academic achievement. We will also discuss what we believe are critical limitations of this research which seriously limit our ability to make confident inferences regarding the causal mechanisms. Finally, we will describe an example research approach that we believe will dramatically improve our ability to infer the causal mechanisms through which cooperative learning affects academic achievement.

COOPERATIVE LEARNING METHODS

A number of cooperative learning methods have been developed and are being used. We will focus upon those cooperative learning methods that have been most widely adopted by educators and which have stimulated considerable research. Thus, our review of cooperative learning methods will be by no means exhaustive and some well-developed methods will be omitted. However, we believe the set of issues described in subsequent sections of this chapter is applicable to all cooperative learning methods.

Circles of Learning (Learning Together)

When Johnson and Johnson (1975) developed their method of cooperative learning, often called Learning Together, it was quite general in terms of implementation. A cooperative goal structure was described as one in which there is a group goal, sharing of ideas and materials, a division of labor when appropriate, and group rewards. In the research reports of this method, the typical description was that students worked as a group to complete a single group product, shared ideas and helped each other with answers to questions, made sure all members were involved and understood group answers, and asked for help from each other before asking the teacher, and the teacher praised and rewarded the group on the basis of group performance (Johnson and Johnson 1979; Johnson, Johnson, and Skon 1979; Johnson et al. 1983).

Recently, Johnson et al. (1984) have called their method Circles of Learning and have delineated the following 18 specific steps for implementation (some of which are optional):

1. Clearly specify instructional objectives.

2. Limit group size to no more than six. (Students new to cooperative learning should be in smaller groups to help ensure that everyone will participate.)

3. Structure groups to achieve heterogeneity in terms of ability, sex, and ethnicity. (Occasionally, homogeneous groups may be used to master specific skills.)

4. Arrange groups in circles to facilitate communication.

5. Use instructional materials to promote interdependence among students. Several alternatives are suggested, such as giving only one copy of the materials to a group so that students will have to share, giving each student in the group access to only one part of the lesson, and structuring competition among groups so that students will have to depend upon each other for their group to win.

6. Assign roles to ensure interdependence. Suggested roles are *summarizer-checker,* to summarize the lesson and to quiz group members; *encourager,* to solicit and encourage contributions from each member; *recorder,* to write down group decisions or a group report; and *observer,* to check for collaboration among group members.

7. Explain the academic task.

8. Structure positive goal interdependence. This can be accomplished by having the group produce a single product or by providing group rewards based on the individual performance of each group member.

9. Structure individual accountability for learning so that all group members must

contribute. For example, the teacher may give individual tests, randomly select members to explain a group project, have members edit each other's work, or randomly select one member's work on which to base a group grade.

10. Structure inter-group cooperation.

11. Explain criteria for success. Grading must be objective rather than on a curve. With heterogeneous groups, criteria for earning points for one's group may need to be individually determined.

12. Specify desired behaviors. Suggested beginning behaviors are to stay with the group, use each other's names, and take turns. More advanced behaviors include making sure each group member participates in discussions and understands and agrees with group answers.

13. Monitor students' behavior continually for problems with the task or with collaborative efforts.

14. Provide task assistance. The teacher will need to intervene at times to clarify instructions, answer questions, encourage discussions, and to teach academic skills.

15. Intervene to teach collaborative skills of effective communication, building a trusting environment, and constructive management of controversy.

16. Provide closure to the lesson, with summaries by students and teacher.

17. Evaluate the students' work. A variety of methods of evaluation are permitted. There may be only a cooperative incentive, with each person in a group receiving the same grade. There may be both an individualistic and a cooperative incentive, with individual grades for each student and a group reward based on the combined grades of group members, or students may receive individual grades with bonus points based on how many members of their group reached a criterion.

18. Assess group functioning through ongoing observation and discussion of group process.

Jigsaw Methods

In original Jigsaw, developed by Aronson and colleagues (1978), interdependence among students is promoted by giving each student in a learning group access to information comprising only one part of a lesson. Students are then accountable to their Jigsaw group for teaching that part of the lesson to the rest of the Jigsaw group members. In addition, the students from the different groups, each having the same material to learn, meet in counterpart groups to discuss and learn their part of the lesson before attempting to teach the material to the students in their Jigsaw groups. In this way, cooperation among students occurs not only within each Jigsaw group but also within the counterpart group.

Cooperative skills are emphasized and taught directly when using the Jigsaw method. In addition, students are encouraged constantly to evaluate group processes; however, there is no specific group reward for achievement or for the use of cooperative skills. The incentive structure in Jigsaw is individualistic: students' grades are based on individual examination performance. Therefore, students are individually accountable for learning the entire lesson, although there is no group incentive for doing so.

Jigsaw II (Slavin 1980) is an adaptation of original Jigsaw in which there is competition among groups called learning teams. There are both cooperative and individualistic incentives in Jigsaw II. The cooperative incentive operates as teams compete for specific group rewards such as group recognition in a class newsletter and special privileges provided to all members of a winning team. These group rewards are based on individual performance. Points are earned for one's team by improving performance relative to individual performance on previous quizzes. Each student, therefore, has an equal chance to contribute to the team score, and each student is individually accountable for performance. The individualistic incentives are grades based on actual scores obtained on the quizzes.

Jigsaw III, described by Kagan (1986), is a recent adaptation of Jigsaw developed by Gonzalez and Guerrero (1983). This adaptation is uniquely designed for bilingual classrooms to increase interaction among students of varying degrees of English proficiency. Each Jigsaw III group contains a student who speaks English, a student who does not speak English, and a student who is bilingual. All materials are bilingual. Team building and evaluation of group processes are particularly emphasized.

Student Teams—Achievement Divisions (STAD)

An essential component of STAD, developed by Slavin (1980), is competition among groups. Students work in their groups to drill and tutor each other to prepare for the competition. The competition factor has been advocated as a component of STAD that facilitates peer support and group norms for achievement (Slavin 1980). More recently, however, Slavin (1983a) has suggested that a specific group reward given for individual learning is the crucial factor in facilitating peer norms and sanctions for achievement. Slavin's more current view is that group competition is no more effective in providing a group reward than are other ways of providing team recognition.

In STAD the typical group reward for winning the competition is recognition in a class newsletter, but more tangible rewards may be given. Because of the competition it is essential that teams be matched evenly according to ability of team members. Slavin (1980) has outlined an objective procedure for group assignment that ensures even matching. Individual accountability to the group is accomplished in STAD by having each member's score on a quiz contribute to the team score. In order for each student to have an equal opportunity to contribute to the team score, students' scores are adjusted so that points contributed to the team are based on improvement over previous performance. The unadjusted scores are the basis for individual grades.

Teams–Games–Tournaments

TGT was developed by DeVries and Slavin (1978) and is similar to STAD except in the method of competition among teams and the resulting accountability to teams. Students of comparable ability from different teams compete face to face in tournaments. Comparable ability among competitors is maintained by having tournament winners compete with students of higher ability in the next tournament, while tournament losers compete with students of lower ability in the next tournament. Quizzes and tests are given to obtain individual grades for students.

Team-Assisted Individualization or Team-Accelerated Instruction

TAI (Slavin 1985) was designed to combine the motivational incentive of group rewards with an individualized instructional program appropriate for the level of skills possessed by each student. In this method, as in most other methods of cooperative learning, small learning groups are composed of students of varying ability. The unique aspect of this method is that each student works on an individualized unit of mathematics instruction. Team members use answer sheets to check each other's worksheets and practice tests, and are responsible for making sure that their teammates are prepared to take the final test for each unit. Discussion and peer tutoring occur because students are required to ask their team members for help before they ask for help from the teacher. The teacher, besides acting as a resource person for the cooperative learning groups, takes students out of their teams for five to six minutes daily to give instruction to groups of students who are at about the same level in the curriculum.

Both individual accountability and specific group rewards are built into TAI. Team scores are computed from the average number of units covered by team members in a four-week period and on their scores on their final unit tests. Teams whose scores meet an objective criterion receive a group reward in the form of a certificate.

Group Investigation

The Group Investigation method, developed by Sharan and colleagues (Sharan et al. 1984; Sharan and Hertz-Lazarowitz 1980; Sharan and Sharan 1976), emphasizes student self-regulation of learning activities. Group investigation includes both a cooperative group process, or what Sharan and Hertz-Lazarowitz (1980) call cooperation in means, and a cooperative goal structure. This emphasis is consistent with Slavin's (1983a, 1983b) conclusions that both a cooperative task structure and a cooperative incentive structure are necessary for improving achievement in a cooperative learning situation. There are four major dimensions characteristic of this method. First, the class is divided into a number of groups, with each group studying a different aspect of a general topic. Second, the topics for study are multifaceted for a meaningful division of labor that promotes interdependence among group members. Third, there is multilateral communication among students who, in addition to simply gathering information, must plan, coordinate, evaluate, analyze, and integrate their work with other students. Fourth, the teacher must adopt an indirect style of classroom leadership, acting as a resource person, providing direction and clarification as needed, and creating a stimulating classroom environment.

Group investigation is a highly structured method with six specific stages of implementation. Student involvement occurs in every stage, from selection of the topics for study to evaluation of student learning. The stages are as follows:

1. The teacher delineates a general topic area, and subtopics are identified through class discussion. Students then form small groups of two to six students. Group formation is based upon student interest in a particular subtopic, but heterogeneity of gender, ethnicity, and ability level is strongly encouraged. In this stage three types of goals need to be considered. First, instructional goals are pursued as students research the topic, delineate the most crucial subtopics for understanding the general topic area, and classify suggestions for group study. Second, organizational goals are pursued as students form groups and make decisions about how the various groups should maintain and exchange information. Third, social goals are pursued as students help each other to match subtopics to individualized interests and establish patterns of mutual assistance and support.

2. Students collaborate in planning how to carry out the investigation of their subtopic. Division of labor is encouraged to promote interdependence and individual accountability to the group. Students are taught to focus on the purpose of the investigation. There is an emphasis on possibilities for application of the knowledge acquired, as well as on what and how to study. A premise of this method is that focusing on the what, the how, and the why of an investigation will stimulate personal involvement and help students to perceive the relevance of learning.

3. Students implement their plans. The teacher arranges a wide variety of informational sources, both within and outside of school. Important sources of information are learning centers that the teacher has developed and which contain resources relevant to the general topic area. Frequent group discussions are promoted for social facilitation, cognitive stimulation, and clarification of information. This will probably be the longest stage of the investigation, and the allotted time may need to be adjusted so that students have sufficient opportunity to complete their work plans. In addition, the teacher may need to stop a group's work intermittently to teach necessary group process skills or study skills.

4. Students collaborate in analyzing and evaluating the information they have gathered. Groups must abstract the essential aspects of their investigation and plan a presentation that will be instructive as well as interesting to the rest of the class. To coordinate the presentations, a steering committee is formed that is composed of a representative from each group. The steering committee coordinates the time schedules

and the use of materials and provides recommendations to ensure that the content of each presentation is meaningful and stimulating.

5. Groups present a summary of the results of their investigation to the rest of the class. In this way, all students gain a broad perspective of the general topic. Students are encouraged to use audio-visual material, dramatizations, displays, and other creative ways to present the information they have gathered.

6. Reports, presentations, and individual learning are evaluated. Students may participate in the evaluation process by providing feedback to individuals and other groups and by submitting questions to the teacher for use on an examination. Teachers are encouraged to make individual evaluation an ongoing process by observing the investigative and collaborative skills used by students throughout the project. Group rewards consist of teacher and peer recognition and approval.

There is a major emphasis on social interaction among students in Group Investigation. According to proponents of this method (Sharan et al. 1984), the social interaction in cooperative learning groups provides a great deal of gratification to students. Because students enjoy working together, group norms of task-oriented interaction are developed; and students, thereby, are motivated to learn. Collaborative skills are taught directly and reinforced throughout a Group-Investigation project.

CAUSAL MECHANISMS

Considerable research has established an effect of cooperative learning on academic achievement. However, there is disagreement about what type of cooperative learning environment leads to enhanced academic performance. For example, Johnson et al. (1981) conducted a meta-analysis of 122 studies investigating cooperative learning. Their conclusions were that cooperation goal structures produce greater achievement than either competitive or individualistic structures, which do not differ in their effects upon achievement; and cooperative goal structures that do not create inter-group competition produce greater achievement than cooperative structures that do create inter-group competition.

Slavin (1983b) countered with an analysis of 46 studies that had examined the academic achievement of individual children rather than the achievement of the group. He clearly pointed out the need to differentiate between the task structure (i.e., working as a group or as an individual) and incentive structure. He noted that while all cooperative learning methods use some form of cooperative task structure, some use cooperative incentive structures for individual learning (e.g., group rewards based upon the average or composite performance of the group), some use cooperative incentive structures for group learning (e.g., group reward based upon a group product), and some use individualistic incentive structures for individual learning (e.g., individual rewards based upon the performance of the individual). After categorizing and evaluating these studies, Slavin concluded that cooperative learning enhances academic achievement only if the classroom involves a cooperative task structure and a cooperative incentive structure for individual learning. That is, the critical elements for cooperative learning to have a positive impact upon academic achievement are groups working together, group rewards, and individual accountability.

The debate apparent in these research programs is important. The potential impact is tremendous in light of the growing endorsements and adoption of cooperative learning methods in school districts. Knowing what cooperative learning method to use and when to use it is critical if we are to enhance academic achievement to the greatest extent. Indeed Slavin (1983b) was aware of this when he titled his review article, ''When Does Cooperative Learning Increase Student Achievement?'' Unfortunately, despite the importance of this issue and the large volume of research literature on cooperative learning, the complexity of this research issue leaves us in a relatively poor position to address the question of whether to use cooperative learning methods and which method to use in which situations.

Perhaps one reason for this current state is that the research on the mechanisms through which cooperative learning affects achievement has most frequently addressed this issue indirectly. This relatively indirect research approach has generally involved the comparison of the effects of different cooperative learning methods on achievement (e.g., Johnson et al. 1981; Slavin 1983b). While this research strategy has provided valuable information, the research and theoretical literature concerning cooperative learning appears to be in a position of readiness to advance towards more *direct* assessments of the causal mechanisms.

The central question is ''How do cooperative learning methods influence academic achievement?'' If we knew how each method influenced academic achievement, we would be in a position to predict when each method would influence academic achievement. That is, we would be in a better position to decide if we should use any cooperative learning methods; and, if so, which method should be used in which situations. Thus, the central issue that cooperative learning researchers must address is the mechanisms that mediate and moderate the relationship between cooperative learning and academic achievement. Further, we must be open to the possibility that there may be multiple and complex causal mechanisms for each cooperative learning method and that the different cooperative learning methods may have common and/or different causal mechanisms.

The notion that we need to understand how cooperative learning methods influence academic achievement has been addressed by several authors (e.g., Hertz-Lazarowitz 1985; Johnson and Johnson 1985a; Kagan 1986; Nijof and Kommers 1985; Slavin 1983b; Webb 1985). For example Slavin (1983b) suggested that group rewards and individual accountability enhance academic achievement by creating peer norms and sanctions that encourage children to learn. Slavin (1983b) also suggested that group rewards and individual accountability motivate students to take a more active role (i.e., high-quality assistance and elaborated explanations) in the learning process. A number of researchers have suggested that cooperative learning increases student involvement and interest in learning (Johnson and Johnson 1985a; 1985b; Kagan 1985; Sharan and Sharan 1976; Slavin 1978). Indeed, the latitude students are given in selecting and approaching a learning opportunity in methods like Group Investigation (Sharan and Hertz-Lazarowitz 1980; Sharan and Sharan 1976) would intuitively appear to stimulate interest. While this suggestion has been forwarded, little research has addressed this possibility *directly* by examining specific potential mechanisms in cooperative learning environments (cf. Hamblin, Hathaway, and Wodarski 1971; Slavin 1980) while also statistically verifying the likelihood of each mechanism. Further, because of the complexity of this issue and the somewhat uncertain classroom similarities and differences among cooperative learning environments, it is unlikely that comparing cooperative learning methods will convincingly identify the causal mechanisms.

Similarly, Kagan (1985) has suggested that minority children will benefit from cooperative learning because the reward structure is more consistent with their cooperative values than are the reward structures in a traditional classroom. The assumption is that the match between the student's values and the reward structure motivates the student and results in greater achievement. Indeed, this assumption is quite reasonable given the evidence of individual differences in cooperative, competitive, and individualistic values (e.g., Knight and Kagan 1977; Knight, Dubro, and Chao 1985; Chao, Knight, and Dubro 1986). However, research has not directly verified the moderating role of social values in either the cooperative learning–achievement relation or the relatively greater achievement gains among minorities in cooperative learning.

While the Slavin (1983b) and the Kagan (1985) hypotheses are clear examples of possible causal mechanisms that have not been *directly* assessed empirically, many other possible mechanisms have also been suggested. For example, Johnson and Johnson (1985a) have discussed 11 potential causal mechanisms, and Kagan (1986) has discussed 24 potential causal mechanisms. Variables characteristic of cooperative learning methods discussed by various authors and the corresponding potential mechanisms that may promote achievement are listed in Table 1.1.

The variables representing the hypothesized causal mechanisms listed in Table 1.1 can be grouped into five general categories represented by social influences, cognitive processing influences, academic task structure influences, reward structure influences, and participant role influences. It should be noted, however, that these five categories are interrelated and overlapping. Further, not only do cooperative learning environments differ from traditional classrooms on many of these dimensions, but the different cooperative learning environments are likely to vary among themselves on many of these dimensions.

The social influences involve processes through which students support, encourage, and give feedback to each other, as well as processes by which norms

Table 1.1
Variables Representing the Causal Mechanisms through Which Cooperative Learning May Promote Achievement

Variable	Mechanism
I. Johnson & Johnson (1985a)	
(Grouped into three clusters as suggested by Hertz-Lazarowitz, 1985.)	
A. Cognitive Process Variables	
1. Quality of Learning Strategy	Discussion in cooperative groups promotes use of high quality cognitive strategies during learning.
2. Controversy versus Concurrence Seeking	Constructively managed controversy promotes curiosity and active search for more information.
3. Cognitive Processing	Oral rehearsal of information promotes long-term retention.
B. Social Variables	
1. Peer Support, Encouragement, Regulation, and Feedback	These variables help to increase motivation and task engagement in students who need external agents to provide guidance and monitoring of progress.
2. Active Mutual Involvement in Learning	Mutual support among group members promotes willingness to present answers.
3. Psychological Support and Acceptance	Students in cooperative groups feel liked by their teammates and want to listen, help, and engage in learning with them.
4. Attitudes Toward Subject Areas	Students have more positive attitudes toward instruction and subject areas in which cooperative learning is used, thereby increasing their willingness to engage in learning tasks.
C. Instructional Variables	
1. Type of Task	Although different methods of cooperative learning may be better suited for different types of learning tasks, Johnson & Johnson have concluded that cooperation effectively promotes achievement with all types of tasks.
2. Time on Task	More learning time results in more learning. However, Johnson & Johnson concluded that there is little difference in time on task in cooperative, competitive, and individualistic goal structures, so this may account for only

a small portion of increased achievement over the other types of goal structures.

3. Ability Levels of Group Members

Interaction among students of diverse ability levels may be beneficial for learning. Low- and medium-ability members benefit from interaction with high-ability members, and high-ability members are not harmed.

4. Fairness of Grading

Students are motivated to work in cooperative groups because they judge that everyone has an equal chance to succeed.

II. Kagan (1986)

A. Academic Task Structure

1. Comprehensible Input

Students ask for clarification of communication from others and for communication to be adjusted so it is more comprehensible.

2. Complexity of Input

Controversy among students demands that they confront opposing points of view and reach higher levels of understanding.

3. Comprehensible Output

Cognitive activity involved in preparing for oral presentations improves understanding and retention.

4. Frequency and Type of Practice

Students drill and quiz teammates, resulting in repeated exposure to learning material, while receiving help and support from peers.

5. Clarity of Task Structure

High structure with clear goals and clearly defined steps for reaching goals is an effective method for teaching basic skills.

6. Subdivision of Learning Unit

Subdivision of lesson may help students experience learning tasks as less overwhelming.

7. Time-on-Task

Students enjoy interaction with peers, and peer interaction directs them toward learning tasks. Students are motivated by reward structure to keep peers on task.

B. Academic and Social Reward Structure

1. Frequent Immediate Rewards

Immediate reinforcement for learning from peers. Frequent periodic group rewards in some methods.

2. Peer Rewards

Peers support achievement.

3. Group-Based Rewards

Group rewards motivate students responsible for group score; peers may pull achievement from others upon whom they depend for rewards, and/or students may

Table 1.1 *continued*

		feel internal push to perform well when peers are depending on them.
4.	Rewards for Improvement	Students' individual contributions to team scores are based on improvement, thereby increasing sense of internal control.
5.	Equal Reward Opportunity	Either basing students' scores on improvement or having them compete against others of equal ability make rewards from classmates accessible to all students.
C.	Teacher Roles and Behavior	
1.	Attention and Expectation	Teacher's attention is focused on groups rather than on individuals, so teacher attention is distributed equitably among ethnic groups and low- and high-achievers.
2.	Discipline	Highly structured activities and peer norms for achievement result in less need for discipline, and more teacher time can be spent on academic content.
3.	Individual Consultation	Consultative role of teacher results in more time to give to individuals or groups needing help.
D.	Student Roles and Behavior	
1.	Activity	Students enjoy interaction and variety of activities, so they become actively engaged in learning and spend more time on task.
2.	Self-direction	Greater feelings of control over learning process lead to greater intrinsic motivation.
3.	Communication	Students need to formulate and organize their ideas in order to communicate them to teammates.
4.	Peer Tutoring	Group rewards and individual accountability encourages peer tutoring, which has been shown to promote achievement.
5.	Peer Norms for Achievement	Teammate approval is reinforcing.
6.	Equal Status	Contributions needed from all group members, so all students are responsible to the group for learning.
E.	Cultural Compatibility of Classroom Structure	
1.	Achievement Bias	Cooperative structure is compatible with achievement goals of cooperatively oriented students.

12

2. Ethnic-Relations Bias

3. Cultural Value Bias   Heterogeneous grouping prevents within-class segregation.
Cooperative structure is compatible with values of some minority groups who often feel alienated from school.

III. Nijhof & Kommers (1985).
Communication among Students with Diverse Levels of Prior Knowledge   Controversy and argumentation stimulate high levels of cognitive processing.

IV. Sharan & Shaulov (1986)
A. Self-Regulation of Learning   Active role in planning and implementing learning activities promotes enthusiasm, responsibility for learning, self-determination, and intrinsic motivation.

B. Opportunity to Work Cooperatively with Peers   Working together results in social facilitation whereby students help each other and generate optimism for success. Enjoyment of social interaction promotes motivation to persist at learning tasks.

V. Slavin (1983a&b)
A. Group Rewards Based on Individual Learning   Interdependence among group members promotes active role in learning process, i.e., high-quality assistance and elaborated explanations from peers, peer norms and sanctions for achievement, and immediate, positive reinforcement from peers striving by all students because they have equal access to rewards; and prevents diffusion of responsibility.

VI. Webb (1985)
Opportunity for All Students to Give and/or Receive Explanations   When group composition includes two distinct ability groups, or groups of only medium-ability students, and are evenly balanced between males and females, lower-ability students receive needed explanations, higher-ability students engage in high-level cognitive restructuring in order to give explanations, and medium-ability students both give and receive explanations.

for achievement are established in cooperative groups. Johnson and Johnson (1985a) have suggested that active support from peers motivates students to become and to remain engaged in learning tasks; a sense of cohesiveness and mutual involvement encourages students to risk volunteering their ideas; students who feel accepted and supported are more willing to help others in the group when they need help and reciprocal assistance becomes the norm; and the positive social experiences in cooperative groups is reflected by a more positive attitude toward learning tasks. Sharan and Shaulov (this volume) have suggested that the satisfaction students obtain from social interaction leads to increased persistence in those tasks that permit social interaction. Kagan (1986) has suggested that the enjoyment of social interaction with peers directs students toward learning tasks; there are social rewards obtained for achievement when group members are dependent upon each other for the success of the group; and students attempt to pull achievement from others upon whom they are dependent while also feeling an internal push to perform well for those who are dependent upon them. Slavin (1983a, and 1983b) has suggested that interdependence among group members promotes norms and sanctions for achievement.

The cognitive processing influences involve processes through which learning strategies are promoted by the need to give clear explanations to others, to process explanations received from others, and to constructively manage the controversy that arises within the group. Johnson and Johnson (1985a) have suggested that discussion and oral rehearsal promote the use of high-quality learning strategies and long-term retention while controversy promotes an active search for more information. Kagan (1986) has suggested that the required communication among students demands that such communication be clear and comprehensible and that the cognitive activity involved in this process improves understanding and retention, controversy leads to higher levels of understanding, and drill and practice among teammates result in repeated exposure to learning material. Nijof and Kommers (1985) have suggested that communication among students with diverse levels of prior knowledge stimulates high-level cognitive processing through controversy and argumentation. Webb (1985) has suggested that students who need help receive explanations, and students who give explanations are required to engage in high-level cognitive restructuring in an attempt to make the material more comprehensible to the peers.

The academic task structure influences involve processes through which the rules and procedures are followed in the cooperative learning classrooms. Johnson and Johnson (1985a) have suggested that cooperative learning increases time on task; the diversity of abilities among students within groups may benefit students of low and moderate ability through their interactions with students of high ability; and the grading system allows all students an equal chance for success and motivates students to strive for success. Kagan (1986) has suggested that the need for students to work and communicate with each other promotes repetition and high-level processing of information and skills; clarity of task structure promotes achievement through the use of clearly defined goals and detailed steps for attaining those goals; subdivision of the learning unit promotes achievement by breaking tasks into manageable parts that are less overwhelming to students; and the enjoyment of interaction with peers motivates students to stay on task.

The reward structure influences involve processes through which rewards are distributed among students. Slavin (1983a, 1983b) has suggested that cooperative learning promotes achievement through group rewards based on individual learning, primarily because of the creation of peer norms and expectations for achievement. Kagan (1986) has suggested that learning is stimulated by individual contributions to the group's rewards, based upon the individuals' improvement in learning, and the social rewards received from peers.

The participant's role influences involve processes through which both students and teachers function in ways different from those of traditional classrooms. Kagan (1986) has suggested that the teacher focuses on groups rather than individuals resulting in an equitable distribution of teacher attention among all students, and low achievers and minorities are not as likely to be the focus of low teacher expectations; the consultative role of the teacher and the lesser need for discipline allow the teacher to spend more time teaching academic content and helping those students who need help beyond what can be given by the group; and the students' active engagement in learning, self-direction, communication with peers, and peer tutoring establishes norms for achievement and the development of equal status among group members. Sharan and Shaulov (this volume) also emphasized the importance of students' self-regulatory activities in promoting enthusiasm, responsibility for learning, self-determination, and intrinsic motivation.

While these types of causal mechanisms have been hypothesized, the second-generation studies (Hertz-Lazarowitz 1985) designed to identify the true causal mechanisms have generally investigated the effects of cooperative learning environments on the hypothesized mediating variables while citing evidence (where available) of a relationship between these hypothesized mediating variables and achievement. While this experimental research clearly demonstrates that the cooperative learning environment causes variance in many of these hypothesized mediating variables, it is not necessarily the case that these variables in turn cause variance in academic achievement. In this case mediation is not occurring and one cannot infer the causal mechanisms. That is, cooperative learning may cause variance in many of the variables that Johnson and Johnson (1985a), Kagan (1986), Sharan et al. (1984), and Slavin (1983b) have suggested as internal dynamics of the cooperative learning environment, but these variables may not in turn be the mechanisms through which cooperative learning influences achievement. For example, some cooperative learning methods may causally influence peer norms and sanctions, but peer norms and sanctions may not be causally related to academic achievement in those cooperative learning environments. Indeed, peer norms and sanctions may be either unrelated to achievement or spuriously related to achievement because they are related to the actual causal variable.

It is also the case that the hypothesized moderating variables have not been investigated sufficiently. Knowing that groups of students differ on average on a hypothesized moderating variable and knowing that the independent variable affects the dependent variable differently for those groups is not sufficient to infer that moderation is occurring. For example, knowing that Mexican-American children on average prefer more cooperative reward distributions than do Anglo-American children and knowing that Mexican-American children on average experience more achievement gain in cooperative learning environments does not necessarily mean that the preferences for different reward distributions moderates the effects of cooperative learning on achievement. Indeed, Mexican-American children may differ from Anglo-American children in many other ways that may really create this moderation of the effect on achievement. For these reasons, we cannot at present argue with any conviction that any subset of the suggested mechanisms is indeed the mechanism through which cooperative learning influences academic achievement.

STRATEGIES FOR ASSESSING MEDIATION AND MODERATION

The issue, then, is what research strategy or strategies may be helpful in allowing us to identify with greater certainty which of the suggested variables represent causal mechanisms and which do not. One possibility is to conduct experimental studies in the classroom, where the experimenter can manipulate those variables that represent the potential causal mechanisms while controlling other potential mediating variables. While this research strategy could lead to considerable confidence in causal inference, it is unlikely that this type of experimental research is possible. Ultimately, experimental research of this nature is probably not totally feasible because the necessary variables are not manipulable or cannot be manipulated independently of other potential causal variables.

A second possibility is to conduct research and use data analysis strategies that have been specifically designed to examine causal relations, mediational relations, and moderational relations. Although this strategy might not allow as much confidence in causal inferences as would a more experimental strategy (if such were possible), it would allow much greater confidence than do the current second-generation research findings. That is, while these procedures may result in multiple, different causal possibilities (e.g., increased academic achievement may cause increased communication among students rather than increased communications causing increased achievement), they will allow increased confidence in the inference of causal influences by ruling out some noncausal relations. Perhaps the best strategy available at present is to assess the possibility of each of the potential causal mechanisms using appropriate causal analyses, and then to attempt to verify the causal relationship through more specific experimental research in the classroom if possible.

Although a number of possible approaches are available (e.g., path analysis, causal modeling with LISREL, etc.), we will summarize one set of procedures for assessing mediating and moderating effects (see Baron and Kenny 1986; Cohen and Cohen 1983; or Pedhazur 1982 for more detailed information). It should be noted that we are summarizing this procedure simply as one example of a generally more direct assessment of mediational and moderational relationships, and it is likely that a series of different approaches will ultimately be necessary to adequately investigate this rather complex issue. The procedures for assessing the possibility of a mediational relationship require either the manipulation or measurement of the independent variable and the measurement of the mediating and dependent variables within one sample. In order to infer that some variable mediates the causal relationship between an independent and a dependent variable, four relations must exist: (1) the independent variable must account for a significant percentage of the variance in the dependent variable; (2) the independent variable must account for a significant percentage of the variance in the mediating variable; (3) the mediating variable must account for a significant percentage of variance in the dependent variable; and (4) the percentage of variance in the dependent variable accounted for by the independent variable must drop significantly when the dependent variable has been residualized by the mediating variable (i.e., when the variance in the dependent variable shared with the mediating variable has been removed). That is, the first three events indicate that the independent variable is significantly related to both the hypothesized mediating variable and the dependent variable. The fourth event indicates that the relation between the independent and dependent variables is significantly reduced when the shared variance between the mediating and dependent variable is removed.

Unfortunately, the research investigating mediational effects has generally confirmed only the first three relations. Thus, there is uncertainty regarding whether the statistical control of the hypothesized mediating variable reduces the cooperative learning–academic achievement relation. This uncertainty dramatically limits one's confidence in causal inferences because the existence of the first three relations does not necessarily imply the fourth. That is, the learning environment can be related to achievement and the hypothesized mediating variable; the hypothesized mediating variable can be related to achievement, but statistically controlling for the mediating variable–achievement relation may not reduce the learning environment–achievement relation. In this case, the hypothesized mediation is not occurring.

For example, the *direct* assessment of Slavin's (1978, 1983b) active role hypothesis would require demonstrating that (1) students in cooperative learning classrooms have higher achievement scores than students in traditional classrooms; (2) students in those same cooperative learning classrooms take a more active role in their learning than do students in the traditional classrooms; (3) a more active role in the learning process among those students is related to greater achievement; and (4) the achievement difference between those students in the cooperative learning and traditional classrooms is significantly reduced, or eliminated, when the variance in achievement accounted for by role activity is removed.

The procedure assessing the possibility of a moderational effect and combined mediational and moderational effects (as in the Kagan (1986) structural bias hypothesis) requires either the manipulation or measurement of the independent variable and the measurement of the mediating, moderating, and dependent variables within one sample. In order to infer that a variable moderates the effect of an independent variable on a dependent variable it is necessary for the relation between the independent variable and the dependent variable to be significantly different at different levels of the moderating variable. However, the second-generation cooperative learning research investigating moderational effects has also not adequately examined the learning environment–achievement relation at different levels of the hypothesized moderating variable. Thus, the occurrence of moderation is uncertain and the inference of a causal mechanism is tenuous. For example, the assessment of Kagan's social values–reward structure match would require demonstrating that (1) students in cooperative learning classrooms have higher achievement scores than students in traditional classrooms; and (2) this effect is greater among those specific students who prefer cooperative reward distributions than among those students who prefer some other reward distributions. Again, however, the previously hypothesized mediating and moderating effects have not been directly tested.

We suggest that the third-generation cooperative learning research more directly assess the numerous possible causal mechanisms. It is apparent to us that the cooperative learning area is sufficiently advanced theoretically to warrant and allow a more direct assessment of the hypothesized causal mechanisms. It is also apparent to us that a more direct assessment of the causal mechanisms through which cooperative learning influences achievement will not be without its challenges.

In using causal modeling, path-analytic, or Baron and Kenney (1986) type procedures, several possibilities will represent particularly problematic challenges. First, different causal mechanisms may require the investigation of different units of analysis. For example, investigation of a teacher expectancy effect requires analysis of classroom units, while investigation of preferences for group activities requires analysis of individual student units. The difficulty will occur when one attempts to compare the relative importance of causal links, or to include variables in the investigation that are based upon different units of analysis.

Second, the multiple mediating and moderating variables that may be operating may change roles over time. For example, Sharan and Shaulov (this volume) suggested that cooperative learning enhances motivation to learn and, in turn, achievement; but that this effect is observed primarily among students who initially prefer cooperative activities. In this case, motivation to learn is a mediating variable while initial preference for cooperative activities is a moderating variable. However, cooperative learning may also cause increases in students' subsequent preferences for cooperative activities; therefore, subsequent preference for cooperative activities may function as a mediating variable. The difficulty will occur when one attempts to identify the appropriate use of a variable at different points in time.

Third, some of the variables specified by different causal models may vary together in inseparable ways, thereby preventing us from ruling out some possible causal mechanisms in favor of others. That is, many of the hypothesized mediating and moderating variables may covary either causally or spuriously. The difficulty will occur when one attempts to determine which covariations are causal and which are spurious and in turn which variables are causally related to achievement and which are spuriously related to achievement.

Finally, the different cooperative learning methods may or may not function in similar ways. That is, the various cooperative learning methods may function to enhance academic achievement through different causal mechanisms. Indeed, the variability in the methods, as well as the variability in the specificity with which the methods are described to teachers, suggests that much more detailed information is needed on exactly what the teachers and students are doing in the various types of cooperative classrooms, and it may be advantageous to review and organize findings around the research on each specific method rather than on cooperative learning methods in general.

Clearly the task at hand will not be an easy one. However, we believe that the theoretical and empirical position of the cooperative learning research area is such that this area is ready for new and additional research approaches. We also believe that this third-generation approach will allow researchers to rule out at least some of the numerous possible causal mechanisms through which cooperative learning may enhance achievement. As possible causal mechanisms are ruled out, one can begin to have greater confidence in the remaining causal mechanisms. Further, increased confidence in some of the possible causal mechanisms will have several positive effects. First, a greater understanding of the causal mechanisms will allow for more confident recommendations to educational personnel regarding which teaching method to use in different contexts and in varying circumstances. Second, evidence of the likelihood of different causal mechanisms may provide convincing information on the utility of cooperative learning approaches to those who are currently skeptical. Finally, evidence of the likelihood of different causal mechanisms may provide information necessary for improving the current cooperative learning methods. Given the potential created by a more thorough understanding of the causal mechanisms through which cooperative learning may influence achievement, it is important for researchers to utilize any and all means available in assessing these causal mechanisms.

REFERENCES

Aronson, E., Blaney, N., Stephan, C., Sikes, J., and Snapp, M. (1978) *The Jigsaw Classroom*. Beverly Hills, CA: Sage Publications.

Baron, R. M., and Kenney, D. A. (1986) "The moderator–mediator variable distinction in social psychological research: Conceptual, strategic, and statistical considerations." *Journal of Personality and Social Psychology* 51:1173–82.

Chao, C. C., Knight, G. P., and Dubro, A. F. (1986) "Information processing and age differences in social decision-making." *Developmental Psychology* 22:500–508.

Cohen, J., and Cohen, P. (1983) *Applied Multiple Regression/Correlation Analysis for the Behavioral Sciences*. Hillsdale, NJ: Lawrence Erlbaum Associates.

DeVries, D., and Slavin, R. (1978) Teams-Games-Tournaments: A research review. *Journal of Research and Development in Education,* 12, 28–38.

Gonzalez, A., and Guerrero, M. (1983) *A Cooperative/Interdependent Approach to Bilingual Education: Jigsaw Teacher's Handbook*. Hollister, CA: Hollister School District.

Hamblin, R. L., Hathaway, C., and Wodarski, J. S. (1971) "Group contingencies, peer tutoring and accelerating academic achievement." In *A New Direction for Education: Behavior Analysis,* edited by E. Ramp and W. Hopkins. Lawrence, KS: University of Kansas, Department of Human Development.

Hertz-Lazarowitz, R. (1985) "Internal dynamics of cooperative learning." In *Learning to Cooperate, Cooperating to Learn,* edited by R. Slavin, S. Sharan, S. Kagan, R. Hertz-Lazarowitz, C. Webb, and R. Schmuck, pp. 97–102. New York: Plenum Press.

Johnson, D. W., and Johnson, R. T. (1975) *Learning Together and Alone*. Englewood Cliffs, NJ: Prentice-Hall.

————. (1979) "Type of task and student achievement and attitudes in interpersonal cooperation, competition, and individualization." *Journal of Social Psychology* 108:37–48.

————. (1985a) "The internal dynamics of cooperative learning groups." In *Learning to Cooperate, Cooperating to Learn,* edited by R. Slavin, S. Sharan, S. Kagan, R. Hertz-Lazarowitz, C. Webb, and R. Schmuck. New York: Plenum Press.

————. (1985b) "Motivational processes in cooperative, competitive, and individualistic learning situations." In *Research on Motivation in Education, Vol. 2: The Classroom Milieu,* edited by C. Ames and R. Ames, pp. 249–86. Orlando, FL: Academic Press.

Johnson, D. W., Johnson, R. T., Holubec, E. J., and Roy, P. (1984) *Circles of Learning*. Alexandria, VA: Association for Supervision and Curriculum Development.

Johnson, D. W., Johnson, R. T., and Skon, L. (1979) "Student achievement on different types of tasks under cooperative, competitive, and individualistic conditions." *Contemporary Educational Psychology* 4:99–106.

Johnson, D. W., Johnson, R., Tiffany, M., and Zaidman, B. (1983) "Are low achievers disliked in a cooperative situation? A test of rival theories in a mixed ethnic situation." *Contemporary Educational Psychology* 8:189–200.

Johnson, D. W., Maruyama, G., Johnson, R., Nelson, D., and Skon, L. (1981) "Effects of cooperative, competitive, and individualistic goal structures on achievement: A meta-analysis." *Psychological Bulletin* 89:47–62.

Kagan, S. (1985) "Learning to cooperate." In *Learning to Cooperate, Cooperating to Learn,* edited by R. Slavin, S. Sharan, S. Kagan, R. Hertz-Lazarowitz, C. Webb, and R. Schmuck. New York: Plenum Press.

———. (1986) "Cooperative learning and sociocultural factors in schooling." In *Beyond Language: Social and Cultural Factors in Schooling Language Minority Students: Evaluation, Dissemination, and Assessment,* pp. 230–98. Los Angeles, CA: California State University.

Knight, G. P., Dubro, A. F., and Chao, C. C. (1985) "Information processing and the development of cooperative, competitive, and individualistic social values." *Developmental Psychology* 21:37–45.

Knight, G. P., and Kagan, S. (1977) "Acculturation of prosocial and competitive behaviors among second- and third-generation Mexican-American children." *Journal of Cross-Cultural Psychology* 17:783–90.

Nijhof, W., and Kommers, P. (1985) "An analysis of cooperation in relation to cognitive controversy." In *Learning to Cooperate, Cooperating to Learn,* edited by R. Slavin, S. Sharan, S. Kagan, R. Hertz-Lazarowitz, C. Webb, and R. Schmuck, pp. 125–45. New York: Plenum Press.

Pedhazur, E. J. (1982) *Multiple Regression in Behavioral Research: Explanation and Prediction.* New York: Holt, Rinehart, and Winston.

Sharan, S., Hare, P., Webb, C. D., and Hertz-Lazarowitz, R. (1980) "Life in schools and classrooms: Introduction." In *Cooperation in Education,* edited by S. Sharan, P. Hare, C. D. Webb, and R. Hertz-Lazarowitz, pp. 7–13. Provo, UT: Brigham Young University Press.

Sharan, S., and Hertz-Lazarowitz, R. (1980). "A group-investigation method of cooperative learning in the classroom." In *Cooperation in Education,* edited by S. Sharan, P. Hare, C. D. Webb, and R. Hertz-Lazarowitz, pp. 14–46. Provo, UT: Brigham Young University Press.

Sharan, S., Kussell, P., Hertz-Lazarowitz, R., Bejarano, Y., Raviv, S., and Sharan, Y. (1984) *Cooperative Learning in the Classroom: Research in Desegregated Schools.* Hillsdale, NJ: Lawrence Erlbaum Associates.

Sharan, S., and Sharan, Y. (1976) *Small-Group Teaching.* Englewood Cliffs, NJ: Education Technology Publications.

Sharan, S., and Shaulov, A. (1989) "Cooperative learning, motivation to learn, and academic achievement" (this volume).

Slavin, R. E. (1978) "Student teams and comparison among equals: Effects on academic performance and student attitudes." *Journal of Educational Psychology* 70:532–38.

——— (1980) "Student team learning: A manual for teachers." In *Cooperation in Education,* edited by S. Sharan, P. Hare, C. D. Webb, and R. Hertz-Lazarowitz, pp. 82–135. Provo, UT: Brigham Young University Press.

——— (1983a) *Cooperative Learning.* New York: Longman.

——— (1983b) "When does cooperative learning increase student achievement?" *Psychological Bulletin* 94:429–45.

———. (1985) "Team-assisted individualization: Combining cooperative learning and individualized instruction in mathematics." In *Learning to Cooperate, Cooperating to Learn,* edited by R. Slavin, S. Sharan, S. Kagan, R. Hertz-Lazarowitz, C. Webb, and R. Schmuck, pp. 177–209. New York: Plenum Press.

Slavin, R., Sharan, S., Kagan, S., Hertz-Lazarowitz, R., Webb, C., and Schmuck, R.
    (editors) (1985) *Learning to Cooperate, Cooperating to Learn.* New York: Plenum
    Press.
Webb, N. (1985) "Student interaction and behavior in small groups: A research sum-
    mary." In *Learning to Cooperate, Cooperating to Learn,* edited by R. Slavin,
    S. Sharan, S. Kagan, R. Hertz-Lazarowitz, C. Webb, and R. Schmuck,
    pp. 147–72. New York: Plenum Press.

2
Cooperative Learning and Achievement

DAVID W. JOHNSON
AND ROGER T. JOHNSON

INTRODUCTION

Social interdependence among students and the effectiveness of instruction are intimately related. Any learning task may be structured so that students compete to see who is best, work individualistically on their own, or work cooperatively in pairs, threes, or fours. There has been considerable debate as to which way of structuring learning situations is most desirable in terms of promoting student achievement (Johnson and Johnson 1974; Michaels 1977; Slavin 1977; Sharan 1980). In the process of examining this issue there are two major questions that have to be addressed:

1. What is the relative impact on achievement of competitive, individualistic, and cooperative efforts?
2. What are the variables mediating or moderating the relationship between cooperation and achievement?

Both of these questions will be discussed in this chapter.

COOPERATIVE LEARNING AND ACHIEVEMENT

How successful competitive, individualistic, and cooperative efforts are in promoting productivity and achievement is the first question pragmatists ask about social interdependence. And they have been asking this question for some

time. The investigation of the relative impact of the three types of social interdependence on achievement is the oldest research tradition within social psychology. It began with a research study by Triplett in 1897 and has extended
over 90 years. At least 323 studies with 1,691 findings on productivity and
achievement have been conducted. And that does not count the research on
social facilitation and other related areas where implicit competition may be
found.

The number of studies on cooperation and competition conducted in the last
30 years has increased dramatically. Of the 323 studies conducted, 90 percent
have been conducted since 1960 and two-thirds have been conducted since
1970. Through meta-analysis procedures the results of the 323 studies may be
reduced to a single analysis (Johnson and Johnson, in press). When all of the
studies are included in the analysis, the average cooperator performed at about
two-thirds of a standard deviation above average competitors (effect size =
0.67) and three-quarters of a standard deviation above the average person working within an individualistic situation (effect size = 0.75). This means that
students at the 50th percentile in a cooperative learning situation will perform
at the 75th percentile of students learning in a competitive situation and at the
77th percentile of students learning in an individualistic situation. Students in
a competitive learning situation attain a slightly higher level of achievement
than students in an individualistic learning situation (effect size = 0.15).

Not all the research, however, has been carefully conducted. The methodological shortcomings found within many research studies may significantly
reduce the certainty of the conclusion that cooperative efforts produce higher
achievement than do competitive or individualistic efforts. Thus, the results of
studies in which students were randomly assigned to conditions, in which there
was an unambiguous and well-defined control condition, in which teacher and
curriculum effects were controlled for, and in which it was verified that the
experimental and control conditions were successfully implemented, were analyzed. When only the high-quality studies were included in the analysis, students at the 50th percentile of the cooperative learning situation performed at
the 81st percentile of the competitive and individualistic learning situations (effect sizes = 0.86 and 0.88 respectively). Further analyses revealed that the
results held constant when group measures of productivity were included as
well as individual measures, for short-term as well as long-term studies, and
when symbolic as well as tangible rewards were used.

If cooperative learning does in fact promote higher achievement than do
competitive and individualistic efforts, it would follow that operationalizations
of cooperative learning that contained a mixture of cooperative, competitive,
and individualistic efforts would produce lower achievement than would "pure"
operationalizations of cooperative learning. The original jigsaw procedure
(Aronson et al. 1978), for example, was a combination of resource interdependence (cooperative) and individual reward structures (individualistic). Teams-
Games-Tournaments (DeVries and Edwards 1974) and Student-Teams-

Achievement-Divisions (Slavin 1980) were a mixture of cooperation and inter-group competition. Team-Assisted-Instruction (Slavin, Leavey, and Madden 1983) was a mixture of individualistic and cooperative learning. When the results of "pure" and "mixed" operationalizations of cooperative learning were compared, the "pure" operationalizations consistently produced significantly higher achievement.

INDICES OF ACHIEVEMENT

In addition to the mastery and retention of material being studied, achievement is indicated by the quality of reasoning strategies used to complete the assignment, generating new ideas and solutions (i.e., process gain), and transferring what is learned within one situation to another (i.e., group-to-individual transfer). A number of researchers have focused on the *quality of reasoning strategy* used within competitive, individualistic, and cooperative situations. Laughlin and his colleagues (Laughlin 1965, 1972; Laughlin and Jaccard 1975; Laughlin et al. 1968; McGlynn 1972) found that individuals working cooperatively used a *focusing* strategy in figuring out a concept underlying a set of numbers or words more frequently than did individuals working competitively or individualistically and, therefore, solved the problems faster. Dansereau and his colleagues (Spurlin et al. 1984; Larson et al. 1985) found that individuals in cooperative groups used elaboration and metacognitive strategies more frequently than did individuals working competitively and individualistically and, therefore, performed at a higher level. Numerous studies on Piaget's cognitive development theory and Kohlberg's moral development theory indicate that higher-level reasoning is promoted by cooperative experiences (see Johnson and Johnson, in press).

We and our colleagues (Gabbert, Johnson and Johnson 1986; Johnson and Johnson 1981; Johnson, Skon, and Johnson 1980; Skon, Johnson, and Johnson 1981) conducted a series of studies comparing student performance within competitive, individualistic, and cooperative learning situations on tasks that could be solved using either higher- or lower-level reasoning strategies. We found a more frequent discovery and use within the cooperative condition of such higher-level reasoning strategies as category search and retrieval, intersectional classification, formulating equations, sequencing, metaphoric reasoning, and conservation strategies. In the categorization and retrieval task, for example, first-grade students were instructed to memorize 12 nouns during the instructional session and then to complete several retrieval tasks during the testing session the following day. The 12 nouns were given in random order and students were told to (1) order the nouns in a way that makes sense and aids memorization and (2) memorize the words. Three of the words were fruits, three were animals, three were clothing, and three were toys. Eight of the nine cooperative groups discovered and used all four categories, and only one student in the competitive and individualistic conditions did so. Salatas and Flavell

(1976) found that even third-grade students had difficulty using category search procedures, yet in these studies first-grade students were able to do so after discussing the task within cooperative learning groups. Even the highest-achieving students failed to use the category search strategy in the competitive and individualistic conditions (that is, they benefited from collective induction).

Process gain occurs when new ideas, solutions, or efforts are generated through group interaction that are not generated when persons work individually. One of the most compelling studies of process gain was conducted by Ames and Murray (1982). They identified first- and second-grade children who were unable to understand conservation tasks. Subjects were randomly assigned to one of four conditions: individualistic work, being informed that a stranger had a different opinion, role playing the opposite of what they had originally answered, listening to a model peer answer conservation problems, and being placed in a cooperative pair with a partner who had different opinions (equally erroneous) and being required to reach consensus. Even when the two children did not know the basic principles of conservation, the cooperative condition resulted in the subjects spontaneously generating and sharing conservation judgments and explanations where none existed on the pre-tests. The conservation insights were sustained through both immediate and delayed post-tests and affected responses to items that were not part of the experimental session. The subjects in the cooperative condition outperformed the subjects in all the other conditions on the post-tests. While in the individualistic condition only 6 percent of the children gave conservation answers and explanations on the first post-test, 42 percent of the children in the cooperative condition did so.

Group-to-individual transfer occurs when individuals who learned within a cooperative group demonstrate mastery on a subsequent test taken individually. There are studies indicating that group-to-individual transfer does and does not occur after cooperative learning (Johnson and Johnson, in press). The studies that failed to find transfer of learning, however, suffered from a lack of positive interdependence, individual accountability, higher-level tasks, and discussion of the material being learned. Studies that carefully structured both positive interdependence and individual accountability within the cooperative condition, required students to discuss the material they were learning, and used higher-level tasks, consistently found group-to-individual transfer.

WHAT MEDIATES?

On the basis of the research conducted to date (which is considerable), it may be concluded that generally achievement is higher in cooperative situations than in competitive or individualistic ones and that cooperative efforts result in more frequent use of higher-level reasoning strategies, more frequent process gain, and higher performance on subsequent tests taken individually (group-to-individual transfer) than do competitive or individualistic efforts. These results beg the questions, "Why does cooperation result in higher achievement—what mediates?"

The critical issue in understanding the relationship between cooperation and achievement is specifying the variables that mediate the relationship. Simply placing students in groups and telling them to work together does not in and of itself promote higher achievement. There are many ways in which group efforts may go wrong. Less able members sometimes "leave it to George" to complete the group's tasks, thus creating a *free rider* effect (Kerr and Bruun 1983) whereby group members expend decreasing amounts of effort and just go through the teamwork motions. At the same time, the more able group member may expend less effort to avoid the *sucker effect* of doing all the work (Kerr 1983). High-ability group members may be deferred to and may take over the important leadership roles in ways that benefit them at the expense of the other group members (the *rich-get-richer* effect). In a learning group, for example, the more able group member may give all the explanations of what is being learned. Since the amount of time spent explaining correlates highly with the amount learned, the more able member learns a great deal while the less able members flounder as a captive audience. The time spent listening in group brainstorming can reduce the amount of time any individual can state their ideas (Hill 1982; Lamm and Grommsdorff 1973). Group efforts can be characterized by self-induced helplessness (Langer and Benevento 1978), diffusion of responsibility and social loafing (Latane, Williams, and Harkin 1975), ganging up against a task, reactance (Salomon 1981), disfunctional divisions of labor ("I'm the thinker and you're the typist") (Sheingold, Hawkins, and Char 1984), inappropriate dependence on authority (Webb, Ender, and Lewis 1986), destructive conflict (Collins 1970; Johnson and Johnson 1979), and other patterns of behavior that debilitate group performance.

It is only under certain conditions that group efforts may be expected to be more productive than individual efforts. Those conditions are:

1. Clearly perceived positive interdependence.

2. Considerable promotive (face-to-face) interaction.

3. Felt personal responsibility (individual accountability) to achieve the group's goals.

4. Frequent use of relevant interpersonal and small-group skills.

5. Periodic and regular group processing.

POSITIVE INTERDEPENDENCE

The first step in promoting cooperation among students is to structure *positive interdependence* within the learning situation. Positive interdependence exists when one perceives that one is linked with others in a way so that one cannot succeed unless they do (and vice versa) and/or that one must coordinate one's efforts with the efforts of others to complete a task (Johnson and Johnson, in press). Positive interdependence is the most important factor in structuring learning situations cooperatively. If students do not believe that they "sink or swim together," then the lesson is not cooperative. When students are placed in learning groups but no positive interdependence is structured, the learning situation is not cooperative, it is either competitive or individualistic. Under those conditions, there is no reason to expect groups to outperform individuals. In fact, the opposite may be true.

There are two major categories of interdependence: outcome interdependence and means interdependence (Deutsch 1949; Thomas 1957). How students behave in a learning situation is largely determined by their perceptions of the outcomes desired and the means by which the desired goals may be reached. When persons are in a cooperative or competitive situation, they are oriented toward a desired outcome, end state, goal, or reward. If there is no outcome interdependence (goal and reward interdependence), there is no cooperation or competition. In addition, the means through which the mutual goals or rewards are to be accomplished specify the actions required on the part of group members. Means interdependence includes resource, role, and task interdependence (which are overlapping and not independent from each other).

Positive interdependence has numerous effects on individuals' motivation and productivity, not the least of which is the fact that the efforts of all group members are needed for group success. When members of a group see their efforts as dispensable for the group's success, they may reduce their efforts (Kerr and Bruun 1983; Harkins and Petty, in press; Kerr 1983; Sweeney 1973). When group members perceive their potential contribution to the group as unique they increase their efforts (Harkins and Petty 1982). When goal, task, resource, and role interdependence are clearly understood, individuals realize that their efforts are required in order for the group to succeed (i.e., there can be no "free riders") and that their contributions are often unique. In addition, reward interdependence needs to be structured to ensure that one member's efforts do not make the efforts of other members unnecessary. If the highest score in the group determined the group grade, for example, low-ability members would see their efforts to produce as unnecessary, they might contribute minimally, and high-ability members might feel exploited and become demoralized and, therefore, decrease their efforts so as not to provide undeserved rewards for irresponsible and ungrateful "free riders" (Kerr 1983).

Within the literature on positive interdependence there are two controversies: whether goal or reward interdependence is the key to operationalizing outcome interdependence and whether resource interdependence is effective in the absence of outcome interdependence.

GOAL VERSUS REWARD INTERDEPENDENCE

There is a basic theoretical disagreement among researchers as to whether positive goal interdependence or positive reward interdependence mediates the relationship between cooperation and achievement. On one side of the controversy are Deutsch (1962) and Johnson and Johnson (1983), who state that positive goal interdependence results in a promotive interaction pattern among individuals, which increases their productivity and interpersonal attraction. From this perspective, given the perception of positive interdependence, individuals will act to facilitate each others' goal accomplishment, and increased achievement results. On the other side of the controversy are researchers such as Hays (1976) and Slavin (1983), who state that positive reward interdependence largely explains the relationship between cooperation and achievement. From this perspective, individuals will increase their achievement only if there is a specific academic group contingency reinforcing them for doing so.

Contrasting the two theoretical positions is complicated by the fact that while it is possible to implement positive goal interdependence without positive reward interdependence, reward interdependence cannot be implemented without goal interdependence. In order for group members to be motivated by a group contingency, they must first perceive that their goal accomplishments are positively interdependent. To contrast the two theoretical positions, cooperative learning groups with only positive goal interdependence have to be contrasted with cooperative groups with both positive goal and reward interdependence. In a series of recent studies, Deborah Mesch and Marvin Lew contrasted individualistic learning, positive goal interdependence alone, positive goal interdependence with an academic reward contingency, and positive goal interdependence with both an academic and a social skills reward contingency. They used an A-B-A reversal design in studies that lasted over 21 weeks, carefully observing conditions each week to ensure that they were being implemented correctly. Their studies took place in elementary, junior high, and high schools. They found that while positive goal interdependence is sufficient to produce higher achievement than individualistic learning, the combination of goal and reward interdependence is even more effective (Lew et al. 1986a, 1986b; Mesch et al. 1986). The impact of the two types of outcome interdependence seems to be additive.

GOAL VERSUS RESOURCE INTERDEPENDENCE

Although few research studies have attempted to differentiate between the effects of positive goal interdependence and positive resource interdependence, some distinction may be made theoretically. There are two basic positions, one represented by Deutsch and one represented by Aronson. From the theorizing of Deutsch (1962), it may be posited that when the cooperative situation is based on positive goal interdependence, individuals will act to promote each other's success out of recognition that they will benefit from doing so. When the cooperative situation is based on positive interdependence, however, there is mutual dependence on each other's resources, but individuals benefit only from obtaining resources from each other, not from giving their resources to each other. Aronson and his associates (1978) have conducted a set of studies in which they operationalized cooperation through a combination of positive resource interdependence and individual rewards, assuming that positive resource and goal interdependence were interchangeable and nonadditive.

To examine the relative impact of positive goal interdependence and positive resource interdependence on individual achievement and group productivity, Johnson et al. (in press) conducted a study using a computer-assisted problem-solving task. Forty-four black American high school seniors and college freshmen were randomly assigned to conditions, stratifying for ability, sex, and urban/rural background. Four conditions were included in the study: both positive goal and resource interdependence, positive goal interdependence only, positive resource interdependence only, and neither positive goal nor resource interdependence (i.e. individualistic). Positive goal interdependence promoted higher individual achievement and group productivity than did no goal interdependence. The combination of positive goal and resource interdependence promoted higher individual achievement and group productivity than did any of the other conditions, indicating that two sources of positive interdependence are more powerful than one. When used in isolation from positive goal interdependence, positive resource interdependence produced the lowest individual achievement and problem-solving success. Students may achieve more under individualistic conditions than under a combination of resource interdependence and individual rewards.

In addition, positive goal interdependence may promote substitutability among the actions of group members while resource interdependence may not. This may be seen in individual reactions to less able groupmates. Within a cooperative situation characterized by positive goal interdependence, when one member cannot do the work, group members will increase their motivation and effort in order to ensure joint success (because their actions can substitute for the actions of the less capable group member). Within a cooperative situation characterized by resource interdependence, when a member cannot provide his or her part of the required resources, the motivation and effort of the rest of the group members will decrease (because their actions cannot substitute for the actions of the less capable member).

PROMOTIVE (FACE-TO-FACE) INTERACTION

Promotive interaction may be defined as individuals encouraging and facilitating each other's efforts to complete tasks and achieve in order to reach the group's goals. Promotive interaction is characterized by students (a) providing each other with efficient and effective help and assistance, (b) exchanging needed resources such as information and materials and processing information more efficiently and effectively, (c) providing each other with feedback in order to improve their subsequent performance on assigned tasks and responsibilities,

(d) challenging each other's conclusions and reasoning in order to promote higher-quality decision making and greater insight into the problems being considered, (e) advocating efforts to achieve mutual goals, (f) influencing each other's efforts to achieve mutual goals, (g) acting in trusting and trustworthy ways, (h) being motivated to strive for mutual benefit, and (i) feeling less anxiety and stress (Johnson and Johnson, in press). The amount of research documenting the impact of promotive interaction on achievement is too voluminous to review here. Interested readers are referred to Johnson and Johnson (in press).

PERSONAL RESPONSIBILITY/INDIVIDUAL ACCOUNTABILITY

After positive interdependence and promotive interaction, a key variable mediating the effectiveness of cooperation is a sense of personal responsibility to the other group members for contributing one's efforts to accomplish the group's goals. This involves being responsible for (1) completing one's share of the work and (2) facilitating the work of other group members and minimally hindering their efforts, in other words, for doing as much as one can toward achieving the group's goals. There are a number of ways in which this personal commitment/responsibility may be inculcated. The first is through structuring positive interdependence among group members so that they will feel responsible for helping each other to achieve the group's goals. The second is through the teacher assessing each student's level of achievement, that is, holding each student accountable for completing assignments and learning the assigned material.

Students are not only accountable to the teacher in cooperative situations, they are also accountable to their peers. Learning groups should be provided with information about the level of mastery of the assigned material each student is achieving. Feedback mechanisms for determining the level of each person's achievement are necessary for members to provide support and assistance to each other. When groups work on tasks where it is difficult to identify members' contributions, when there is an increased likelihood of redundant efforts; when there is a lack of group cohesiveness, and when there is lessened responsibility for the final outcome, the less some members will try to contribute to goal achievement (Harkins and Petty 1982; Ingham et al. 1974; Kerr and Bruun 1981; Latane, Williams, and Harkins 1975; Moede 1920; Petty et al. 1977; Williams 1981; Williams, Harkins, and Latane 1981). If, however, there is high individual accountability and it is clear how much effort each member is contributing, if redundant efforts are avoided, if every member is responsible for the final outcome, and if the group is cohesive, then the social loafing effect vanishes. The smaller the size of the group the greater the individual accountability may be (Messick and Brewer 1983).

SOCIAL SKILLS

Placing socially unskilled students in a learning group and telling them to cooperate will obviously not be successful. Students must be taught the interpersonal and small-group skills needed for high-quality cooperation, and be motivated to use them. And all group members must engage in them (if only the most socially skilled group members engage in all the needed leadership and communication skills, they will increase their skills at the expense of their less active and less socially skilled groupmates—the ''rich-get-richer'' effect).

In their studies on the long-term implementation of cooperative learning, Lew and Mesch (Lew et al. 1986a, 1986b; Mesch et al. 1986) investigated the impact of a reward contingency for using social skills as well as positive interdependence and a contingency for academic achievement on performance within cooperative learning groups. In the cooperative skills conditions students were trained weekly in four social skills and each member of a cooperative group was given two bonus points toward the quiz grade if all group members were observed by the teacher to demonstrate three out of four cooperative skills. The results indicated that the combination of positive interdependence, an academic contingency for high performance by all group members, and a social skills contingency, promoted the highest achievement. The more socially skillful students are, and the more attention teachers pay to teaching and rewarding the use of social skills, the higher the achievement that can be expected within cooperative learning groups.

There is only so much that structure can do. Students need to master and use interpersonal and small-group skills to capitalize on the opportunities presented by a cooperative learning situation. Especially when learning groups function on a long-term basis and engage in complex, free exploratory activities over a prolonged basis, the interpersonal and small-group skills of the members may determine the level of student achievement.

GROUP PROCESSING

In order to achieve, students in cooperative learning groups have to work together effectively. Effective group work is influenced by whether or not groups reflect on (i.e., process) how well they are functioning. A *process* is an identifiable sequence of events taking place over time, and *process goals* refers to the sequence of events instrumental in achieving outcome goals. *Group processing* may be defined as reflecting on a group session to (a) describe what member actions were helpful and unhelpful and (b) make decisions about what actions to continue or change. The purpose of group processing is to clarify and improve the effectiveness of the members in contributing to the collaborative efforts to achieve the group's goals.

No direct evidence of the impact of group processing on achievement was available until a study was recently conducted by Yager (Yager, Johnson, and

Johnson 1985). He examined the impact on achievement of (a) cooperative learning in which members discussed how well their group was functioning and how they could improve its effectiveness, (b) cooperative learning without any group processing, and (c) individualistic learning. The results indicate that the high-, medium-, and low-achieving students on the cooperation with group processing condition scored higher on daily achievement, post-instructional achievement, and retention measures than did the students in the other two conditions. Students in the cooperative without group processing condition, furthermore, scored higher on all three measures than did the students in the individualistic condition.

Johnson et al. (in press) conducted a follow-up study comparing cooperative learning with no processing, cooperative learning with teacher processing (the teacher specified cooperative skills to use, observed, and gave the whole class feedback as to how well students were using the skills), cooperative learning with teacher and student processing (the teacher specified cooperative skills to use, observed, gave the whole class feedback as to how well students were using the skills, and had learning groups discuss how well they interacted as a group), and individualistic learning. Forty-nine high-ability black American high school seniors and entering college freshmen at Xavier University participated in the study. A complex computer-assisted problem-solving assignment was given to all students. All three cooperative conditions performed higher than did the individualistic condition. The combination of teacher and student processing resulted in greater problem-solving success than did the other cooperative conditions.

SUMMARY

In this chapter we addressed two key questions about the relationship between cooperation and achievement:

1. What is the relative impact on achievement of competitive, individualistic, and cooperative efforts?
2. What are the variables mediating or moderating the relationship between cooperation and achievement?

Over 323 studies have been conducted over the past 90 years comparing the relative impact of cooperative, competitive, and individualistic learning situations on achievement. On the basis of this research, it may be concluded that generally achievement is higher in cooperative situations than in competitive or individualistic ones and that cooperative efforts result in more frequent use of higher-level reasoning strategies, more frequent process gain and collective induction, and higher performance on subsequent tests taken individually (group-to-individual transfer) than do competitive or individualistic efforts.

The critical issue in understanding the relationship between cooperation and achievement is specifying the variables that mediate the relationship. Simply placing students in groups and telling them to work together does not in itself promote higher achievement. There are many ways in which group efforts may go wrong. It is only under certain conditions that group efforts may be expected to be more productive than individual efforts. There is evidence that cooperative learning will only be effective when teachers structure and promote:

1. Clearly perceived positive interdependence.
2. Considerable promotive (face-to-face) interaction.
3. Felt personal responsibility (individual accountability) to achieve the group's goals.
4. Frequent use of relevant interpersonal and small-group skills.
5. Periodic and regular group processing.

REFERENCES

Ames, G., and Murray, F. (1982) "When two wrongs make a right: Promoting cognitive change by social conflict." *Developmental Psychology* 18:892–895.

Aronson, E., Bridgeman, D. L., and Geffner, R. (1978) "The effects of a cooperative classroom structure on student behavior and attitudes." In *Social Psychology of Education: Theory and Research,* edited by D. Bar-Tal and L. Saxe. Washington; D.C.: Hemisphere Publishing, Halsted Press, Wiley.

Collins, B. (1970) *Social Psychology.* Reading, MA: Addison-Wesley.

Deutsch, M. (1949) "An experimental study of the effects of cooperation and competition upon group process." *Human Relations* 2:199–232.

———. (1962) "Cooperation and trust: Some theoretical notes." In *Nebraska Symposium on Motivation,* edited by M. R. Jones. Lincoln NE: University of Nebraska Press.

DeVries, D., and Edwards, K. (1974) "Student teams and learning games: Their effects on cross-race and cross-sex interaction." *Journal of Educational Psychology* 66, no. 5:741–49.

Gabbert, B., Johnson, D. W., and Johnson, R. (1986) "Cooperative learning, group-to-individual transfer, process gain, and the acquisition of cognitive reasoning strategies." *Journal of Psychology* 120, no. 3:265–78.

Harkins, S., and Petty, R. (1982) "The effects of task difficulty and task uniqueness on social loafing." *Journal of Personality and Social Psychology* 43:1214–29.

Harkins, S., and Petty, R. (in press) "The role of intrinsic motivation in eliminating social loafing." *Journal of Personality and Social Psychology.*

Hays, L. (1976) "The use of group contingencies for behavioral control: A review." *Psychological Bulletin* 83:628–48.

Hill, G. (1982) "Group versus individual performance: Are $N + 1$ heads better than one?" *Psychological Bulletin* 91:517–39.

Ingham, A., Levinger, G., Graves, J., and Peckham, V. (1974) "The Ringelmann effect: Studies of group size and group performance." *Journal of Personality and Social Psychology* 10:371–84.

Johnson, D. W., and Johnson, R. (1974) "Instructional goal structure: Cooperative, competitive, or individualistic?" *Review of Educational Research* 44:213–40.

—— (1979) "Conflict in the classroom: Controversy and learning." *Review of Educational Research* 49, no. 1:51–70.

—— (1981) "Effects of cooperative and individualistic learning experiences on interethnic interaction." *Journal of Educational Psychology* 73:454–59.

—— (1983) "The socialization and achievement crises: Are cooperative learning experiences the solution?" In *Applied Social Psychology Annual 4,* edited by L. Bickman. Beverly Hills, CA: Sage Publications.

—— (in press) *Cooperation and Competition: A Meta-Analysis of the Research.* Hillsdale, NJ: Lawrence Erlbaum.

Johnson, D. W., Johnson, R. T., and Stanne, M. (1988) "Impact of goal and resource interdependence on problem-solving success on a computer-assisted task." Manuscript submitted for publication.

Johnson, D., Johnson, R., Stanne, M., and Garibaldi, A. (in press) Impact of goal and resource interdependence on problem-solving success on a computer-assisted task. *Journal of Social Psychology.*

Johnson, D. W., Skon, L., and Johnson, R. (1980) "Effects of cooperative, competitive, and individualistic conditions on children's problem-solving performance." *American Educational Research Journal* 17, no. 1:83–93.

Kerr, N. (1983) "Motivation losses in small groups: A social dilemma analysis." *Journal of Personality and Social Psychology* 45:819–28.

Kerr, N., and Bruun, S. (1981) "Ringelmann revisited: Alternative explanations for the social loafing effect." *Personality and Social Psychology Bulletin* 7:224–31.

—— (1983) "Dispensability of member effort and group motivation losses: Free rider effects." *Journal of Personality and Social Psychology* 44:78–94.

Lamm, H., and Grommsdorff, G. (1973) Group versus individual performance on tasks requiring ideational proficiency (brainstorming): A review. *European Journal of Social Psychology,* 36, 886–93.

Langer, E., and Benevento, A. (1978) "Self-induced dependence." Journal of *Personality and Social Psychology* 36:886–93.

Larson, C., Dansereau, D., O'Donnell, A., Hythecker, V., Lambiotte, J., and Rocklin, T. (1985) "Effects of metacognitive and elaborative activity on cooperative learning and transfer." *Contemporary Educational Psychology* 10:342–48.

Latane, B., Williams, K., and Harkins, S. (1975) "Many hands make for light work: The causes and consequences of social loafing." *Journal of Personality and Social Psychology* 37:822–32.

Laughlin, P. (1965) "Selection strategies in concept attainment as a function of number of persons and stimulus display." *Journal of Experimental Psychology* 70, no. 3:323–27.

—— (1972) "Selection versus reception concept-attainment paradigms for individuals and cooperative pairs." *Journal of Educational Psychology* 63, no. 2:116–22.

Laughlin, P., and Jaccard, J. (1975) "Social facilitation and observational learning of individuals and cooperative pairs." *Journal of Personality and Social Psychology* 32, no. 5:873–79.

Laughlin, P., McGlynn, R., Anderson, J., and Jacobsen, E. (1968) "Concept attainment by individuals versus cooperative pairs as a function of memory, sex, and concept rule." *Journal of Personality and Social Psychology* 8, no. 4:410–17.

Lew, M., Mesch, D., Johnson, D. W., and Johnson, R. (1986a) "Positive interdependence, academic and collaborative-skills group contingencies and isolated students." *American Educational Research Journal* 23, no. 3:476–88.

——— (1986b) "Components of cooperative learning: Effects of collaborative skills and academic group contingencies on achievement and mainstreaming." *Contemporary Educational Psychology* 28:155–66.

McGlynn, R. (1972) "Four-person group concept attainment as a function of interaction format." *Journal of Social Psychology* 86:89–94.

Mesch, D., Lew, M., Johnson, D. W., and Johnson, R. T. (1986) "Isolated teenagers, cooperative learning, and the training of social skills." *Journal of Psychology* 120, no. 4:323–34.

Mesch, D., Johnson, D. W., and Johnson, R. T. (in press) "Impact of positive interdependence and academic group contingencies on achievement." *Journal of Social Psychology*.

Messick, D., and Brewer, M. (1983) Solving social dilemmas. In *Review of personality and social psychology,* edited by L. Wheeler and P. Shaver. Beverly Hills, CA.: Sage Publications.

Michaels, J. (1977) "Classroom reward structures and academic performance." *Review of Educational Research* 47:87–98.

Moede, W. (1920) *Experimentelle Massenpsychologie*. Leipzig: S. Hirzel.

Petty, M., Harkins, S., Williams, K., and Latane, B. (1977) "Effects of group size on cognitive effort and evaluation." *Journal of Personality and Social Psychology* 33, no. 4:579–82.

Salatas, H., and Flavell, J. (1976) Retrieval of recently learned information: Development of strategies and control skills. *Child Development,* 47, 941–48.

Salomon, G. (1981) *Communication and Education: Social and Psychological Interactions*. Beverly Hills, CA: Sage.

Sharan, S. (1980) "Cooperative learning in small groups: Recent methods and effects on achievement, attitudes, and ethnic relations." *Review of Educational Research* 50:241–71.

Sheingold, K., Hawkins, J., and Char, C. (1984) " 'I'm the thinkist, you're the typist': The interaction of technology and the social life of classrooms." *Journal of Social Issues* 40:49–61.

Skon, L., Johnson, D. W., and Johnson, R. T. (1981) "Cooperative peer interaction versus individual competition and individualistic efforts: Effects on the acquisition of cognitive reasoning strategies." *Journal of Educational Psychology* 73, no. 1:83–92.

Slavin, R. (1977) "Classroom reward structure: An analytic and practical review." *Review of Educational Research* 47, no. 4:633–50.

———. (1980) *Using Student Team Learning* (rev. ed). Baltimore, MD: Johns Hopkins University, Center for Social Organization of Schools.

———. (1983) *Cooperative Learning*. New York: Longman.

Slavin, R., Leavey, M., and Madden, N. (1983) *Combining Student Teams and Individualized Instruction in Mathematics: An Extended Evaluation* (Technical Report No. 336). Baltimore, MD: Johns Hopkins University, Center for the Social Organization of Schools.

Spurlin, J., Dansereau, D., Larson, C., and Brooks, L. (1984) "Cooperative learning strategies in processing descriptive text: Effects of role and activity level of the learner." *Cognition and Instruction* 1, no. 4:451–63.

Sweeney, J. (1973) "An experimental investigation of the free-rider problem." *Social Science Research* 2:277–92.

Thomas, E. (1957) "Effects of facilitative role interdependence on group functioning." *Human Relations* 10:347–66.

Webb, N., Ender, P., and Lewis, S. (1986) "Problem-solving strategies and group processes in small group learning computer programming." *American Educational Research Journal* 23:245–61.

Williams, K. (1981) "Developmental characteristics of a forward roll." *Research Quarterly for Exercise and Sport* 51, no. 4:703–13.

Williams, K., Harkins, S., and Latane, B. (1981) "Identifiability as a deterrent to social loafing: Two cheering experiments." *Journal of Personality and Social Psychology* 40:303–11.

Yager, S., Johnson, D. W., and Johnson, R. T. (1985) "Oral discussion, group-to-individual transfer, and achievement in cooperative learning groups." *Journal of Educational Psychology* 77, no. 1:60–66.

3
A Situational Identity Perspective on Cultural Diversity and Teamwork in the Classroom

NORMAN MILLER
AND HUGH JORDAN HARRINGTON

A fundamental question for educational institutions is: What is the most important thing for schools to teach students (or for students to learn in school)? In response, Johnson and Johnson (1978) state that it is "how to build and maintain positive relationships with other people." They argue that cooperation is the cornerstone to building and maintaining "stable families, career success, neighborhood and community membership, important values and beliefs, friendships, and contributions to society" and conclude that "[t]here is no aspect of human experience more basic and important than cooperating with others" (p. 11). Children with poor peer adjustment are at risk for later difficulty in life. The evidence is especially clear with respect both to high school completion and criminality (Parker and Asher 1987).

This chapter addresses this concern, namely, how can students learn to cooperate well with other students, particularly with those who are in some way different from themselves? Like anything else, it takes practice in a facilitating environment that provides guidance through a positive role model. It takes teachers who help students learn to cooperate, in the presence of barriers that can deter both teacher and students. In response to an increasingly multicultural society, the teacher who desires to help students learn to cooperate with those who are different and to value diversity must have a knowledge of conditions that inhibit and facilitate these goals.

There is a long history of theoretical attempts to understand the dynamics of tension, bias, and conflict between members of different social groups. In recent decades there has been a rapidly increasing body of experimental research to be integrated. The critical link between theory concerned with why there is conflict and practical interventions for resolving it, however, has not always been apparent. We will present a brief and limited review of theory about inter-group conflict that organizes the field, and then discusses the implications of our integration for the structuring of cooperative team activity in the classroom.

The first section reviews research on the development of racial awareness, preference, and attitudes in children. This section sets the stage for applying to children theories that have, for the most part, been based on research with adults. The second section summarizes major theoretical approaches to inter-group relations, introducing the variables that each theory has emphasized, their role, and empirical support for their influence. Then, in the third section, the approach taken by social identity theory and research related to it is presented. The theory, as reformulated here, is thereafter referred to as Situational Identity Theory and is used as the basis of the recommendations for structuring team-work activities in the classroom presented in the fifth and final section. The fourth section addresses the critical problem of the generalization of positive regard for specific outgroup members that is developed during an intervention to those same members when in other settings, to new outgroup members, and to the outgroup as a whole. The last section presents a set of recommendations derived from situational identity theory that will optimize inter-group coopera-tion in the school setting.

DEVELOPMENT OF RACIAL AWARENESS, PREFERENCE, AND ATTITUDES

Two general approaches have been taken to understand how a child develops awareness of racial differences, preferences, and racial attitudes—one based on reinforcement theory and the other on theory about cognitive development. Re-inforcement approaches have focused on such variables as the authoritarian parent and the fear of the unfamiliar to explain same-race preference, and chil-dren's fear of night and the cultural connotations of colors to explain white preference. Cognitive development theorists, on the other hand, have directed attention at the child's understanding of such concepts as physical conservation and racial constancy, the labeling process, and ethnic differentiation abilities.

To many persons' surprise, early studies demonstrated that nursery school children were aware of skin color differences. Researchers have consistently found that both black and white children have some awareness of racial char-acteristics at age three and high levels of awareness is firmly established by the age of six (Clark and Clark 1947; Goodman 1952; Horowitz 1936; Porter 1971). What was even more surprising was the frequent finding that both black and white children showed a preference for white persons. The former results led some researchers to pursue lines of investigation that examined causes of pref-erences for same-race others, whereas the latter prompted attempts to under-stand the preference for white as opposed to black colors.

Reinforcement Theories

An early approach toward understanding the development of racial prejudice assumed that racial attitudes of children were derived from their parents via observational learning and modeling. In particular, focus was directed at the characteristics of the "authoritarian personality" (Adorno et al. 1950). Circumstances in which a child is submitted to arbitrary and severe parental authority and never permitted direct expression, have the consequence, as a defense mechanism, of the child identifying with the idealized authority figure and displacing aggression toward outgroup persons (Katz 1976). Although mothers of less prejudiced elementary school children expressed a more permissive attitude in their child-rearing practices than did those whose children were highly prejudiced (Harris, Gough, and Martin 1950), Proshansky (1966) noted that other factors such as intelligence and educational as well as socioeconomic level are inversely related to authoritarian tendencies.

Allport (1954) proposed that children negatively evaluate persons of different races as an instance of a general fear of strange and unfamiliar things. Zajonc's (1968) research on "mere exposure" shows that repeated exposure to an unfamiliar stimulus increases the favorability of attitude toward it. Cantor (1972) documented the effect by exposing fourth- and fifth-grade white children to a period of familiarization with pictures of black and white boys. After the familiarization trials, the children gave more positive evaluations to the black boys than to the white boys, with highest ratings given to the most familiar black boys.

Williams and his colleagues hypothesized that early racial preferences of children reflect primitive feelings about day and night. They suggest that darkness is avoided by both human and nonhuman primates because it causes fear and disorientation. These reactions to light and darkness are presumed to generalize to the colors white and black first, and subsequently to skin colors. Children who were favorably biased toward the color white were similarly biased toward light-skinned persons (Williams and Robertson 1967), and children who had the highest level of pro-white bias also had the greatest aversion to night darkness (Boswell and Williams 1975).

In addition, the colors white and black are used as symbolic referents for positive and negative evaluations, respectively, and through stimulus generalization, children learn to categorize black persons as bad and white persons as good (Stabler et al. 1969). The fact that the color names "white" and "black" are the most frequently encountered in almost all languages and that in many cultures the color "white" connotes positive attributes and the color "black" connotes negative ones (Hays et al. 1972) supports this view.

Direct behavior modification techniques designed to provide positive reinforcement to the color black, however, have not always been successful in producing generalization to people of color (Katz and Zalk 1978; Parish and Fleetwood 1975; Parish, Shirazi, and Lambert 1976; Shanahan 1972). Al-

though it is not suggested that television is the source of children's racial preferences, it is increasingly being considered as a potentially important factor in
influencing children's racial awareness, preferences, and attitudes. Though exposure of children to members of different ethnic groups has increased over the
past two decades, it is not yet evident that proportional representation on television has been reached. Furthermore, press coverage of blacks is generally
negative (e.g., concentration upon crime news), reinforcing negative stereotypes (Wirtenberg 1978).

Cognitive Development Theories

The development of ethnic prejudice has also been attributed to natural shortcomings in cognitive development such as premature categorization, overge-
neralization, and rigidity of thought. Piaget (1928, 1957) described a type of
thinking called "transductive reasoning" in which a person makes the generalization that because two people are alike in one aspect (e.g., race) then they
must also be similar in other attributes (e.g., intelligence). Semaj (1981) investigated the relationship between impersonal classification and racial classification abilities and found the former to temporarily precede the latter. Semaj
(1980) also looked at the development of racial constancy (the irrevocability of
racial classification) and Piagetian tasks of physical conservation and found a
significant relationship as well as clear developmental trends for both cognitive
skills. The reduced level of positive white bias found in children with a higher
level of cognitive development (Clark, Hocevar, and Dembo 1980) supports
this view.

One form of intervention designed to thwart the development of stereotypes
or reduce their impact uses vicarious interracial contact. Written or audiovisual
materials present a story or information in which black and white children work
or play together harmoniously. Alternatively, multi-ethnic readers and discussions of ethnic groups that portray blacks (and other ethnic group members) in
a favorable manner have also been espoused. Studies of their effects, however,
have found either no change in racial bias (Best et al. 1975; McAdoo 1970;
Walker 1971) or short-term effects (Goldberg and Gorn 1979).

When white kindergartners and third-graders have an opportunity to experience prejudice and vicariously identify with the minority group member, they
increase their empathy toward the outgroup and subsequently their negative
attitudes are reduced (Hohn 1973; Weiner and Wright 1973). There may be
some legal difficulties with such an approach, but increased practice in empathy
and role-taking may facilitate attitude change.

Katz (1973) showed that differences between members of another race are
more difficult to discriminate than differences within one's own group. She
suggests that "racial labels may increase the perceptual similarity of faces of
another race . . . and facilitate the subsequent learning of stereotypes and negative attitudes" (Katz 1973:298). Among white children, those who were highly

prejudiced were significantly more aware of racial cues when differentiating faces and conversely less attentive to nonracial cues (e.g., presence of eyeglasses). In contrast, all black children found color cues salient, suggesting that white society does not permit blacks to ignore racial cues (Katz, Sohn, and Zalk 1975). Training white children either to label individuals or to individuate members of another race on the basis of perceptual cues (e.g., facial expressions) reduced racial prejudice for up to four months (Katz and Zalk 1978).

Katz (1976, 1981) proposes eight overlapping but separable steps in a developmental sequence of attitude formation that spans the first ten years of a child's life. These stages are summarized below (Albert 1983):

1. Early observation of racial cues—From the first year, a child's observation of cues associated with another race.

2. Formation of rudimentary concepts—By the age of four, the reinforcement (by parents or others) of the child's differential responses to an individual of another group by means of labels and evaluative comments; generalized from fear of the strange, fear of the dark, or already learned connotations to the colors black and white.

3. Conceptual differentiation—Once a group label is supplied, the child's learning of group boundaries, defining characteristics of groups, and evaluative connotations.

4. Recognition of the irrevocability of cues—The child's understanding that racial characteristics do not change over time.

5. Consolidation of group concepts—From the age of five, the ability to correctly label and identify both positive and negative instances of group membership and to understand racial constancy for different racial groups.

6. Perceptual elaboration—The accentuation or diminution of differences among members of ethnic groups during preschool and early school years.

7. Cognitive elaboration—The processes by which racial preference becomes racial prejudice as a result of school and other relevant experiences regarding other ethnic groups during the middle school years.

8. Attitude crystallization—The consolidation of ethnic attitudes in later grade school years as a result of cultural conditioning.

This theoretical framework takes into account parents, peers, the school, and interracial contacts and suggests that opportunities for attitude change are more promising at a time when the mind is more open to learning to see people as individuals rather than as members of a particular group or race.

Summary

In this section we have established that children enter the school system with a firm awareness of their own and others' ethnic identity. Further, racial labeling becomes a basis for learning stereotypes and developing negative attitudes toward those who are different from oneself. Stated differently, perception precedes cognition. Neither behavior modification techniques nor multicultural education programs have been especially successful in fostering positive attitudes that endure and generalize. In contrast, approaches that teach children to individuate members of another race seem to offer more promise for inter-ethnic harmony.

THE DEVELOPMENT OF INTER-GROUP RELATIONS THEORY

In this section we review several approaches to inter-group behavior, most of which have been based on observation of an experimentation with young adults. Table 3.1 summarizes the six theoretical perspectives reviewed in this section, along with situational identity theory, which is reviewed in the next section. Also listed are the principal causal variables that each emphasizes as leading to conflict, important moderator variables or conditions that either exacerbate or inhibit this conflict, and the variables that are stressed by each particular approach in an attempt to reduce or eliminate inter-group conflict. Although each of the first six theories have identified a key causal variable (as well as important moderator variables), we will later argue that none of these are necessary conditions for ingroup favoritism and/or outgroup rejection and that more basic processes operate to produce bias. Hence, we will also argue that strategies for intervention based on these approaches will not be sufficient in and of themselves for reductions of bias, although they may be components of the approach we recommend in the final section. The first two approaches we review are based primarily on motivational factors, the third emphasizes perceptual factors, and the latter three are cognitive in nature. In addition, the first three are more adequate in attempting to explain ingroup cohesion, whereas the latter three are oriented toward the explanation of outgroup rejection.

Realistic Conflict Theory

An early approach to inter-group relations was introduced by Sumner in 1906 under the concept of "ethnocentrism." His argument is that the basis of conflict between ethnic groups lies in the struggle for existence or for access to scarce resources. This conflict of interests produces cooperation and feelings of loyalty within one's own group and competition with and feelings of contempt for outsiders. These behaviors and sentiments serve "the dual functions of preserving in-group solidarity and justifying exploitation of out-groups" (Brewer 1979:307).

Competition does indeed heighten ingroup solidarity (Ryen and Kahn 1975; Worchel, Andreoli, and Folger 1977), even with just the expectation of competition (Kahn and Ryen 1972; Rabbie and deBrey 1971; Rabbie and Wilkens 1971). The mere presence of other ingroup members heightens competitive orientation because groups or even dyads tend to be more competitive than

Table 3.1
Causal Antecedent of Prejudice, Key Feature of a Beneficial Intervention, and Major Mediator of Reduction for Each of Seven Theoretical Approaches to Inter-group Relations

Theoretical approach	Causal antecedent of prejudice	Key feature(s) for an intervention	Mediator of reduced prejudice
Realistic conflict	Competition for resources	Cooperative means	Superordinate goal
Reinforcement	Absence of out-group reward	Cooperative reward structure	Intergroup success
Similarity-attraction	Perceived dissimilarity	Interaction	Increased similarity
Contact hypothesis	Isolation of groups	Equal status contact	Disconfirmed stereotypes
Ignorance model	Lack of familiarity	Increased familiarity	Reduced anxiety
Expectation states	Negative expectations	retrained outgroup	Reversed expectations
Situational identity	Social categorization: Undifferentiated outgroup Depersonalized members Competitive social comparison	Decategorization: Differentiation of outgroup Personalization of member(s) Differentiation of self from ingroup Personalization of self vis a vis outgroup member	Low situational salience of category boundaries

individuals in one-to-one contact (Dustin and Davis 1970; McCallum et al. 1985), especially when there is a single group product that is arrived at by group consensus.

Given this major assumption, that bias results from inter-group competition, the means to eliminate it is to restructure group relationships by using cooperative interdependence or superordinate goals. Such restructuring eliminates competition by requiring members of both groups to work together as a super-ordinate group. This approach of shifting the structure from competitive to cooperative interaction has therefore been a major impetus behind many of the inter-ethnic classroom techniques developed to promote acceptance and harmony among members of different ethnic groups. It should be noted that conflict of interest over scarce resources may apply to survival needs, such as food, supplies, or jobs, but it may also apply to other social needs, such as recognition, approval, or a teacher's attention.

Reinforcement Theory

A basic principle derived from reinforcement theory is that people like those who reward them (Lott 1961; Lott and Lott 1965, 1968). Homans (1961) discussed at great length the value of the group in providing social approval to its members and the consequent bonding to the group. One is rewarded for being similar to the ingroup, adopting their values, and cooperating toward their goals. Certainly, membership in groups that are successful provides a greater opportunity for reward. Even in ad hoc experimental groups, those that are successful are more highly valued than those that fail (Hoffman 1958; Shelley 1954; Steiner and Dodge 1956). In contrast, failure reduces ingroup cohesion, not only in comparison with successful groups, but also compared with those groups whose outcomes are ambiguous, as when no cues are provided about outcomes (Ryen and Kahn 1975; Worchel, Lind, and Kaufman 1975). These same effects are also found with second- and fourth-grade children (Heber and Heber 1957).

Group failure does not always lower ingroup cohesion if the group members perceive that the failure has been arbitrarily imposed by an outside source (cited by Pepitone 1958). In such cases this *shared threat* can actually increase cohesion. The effects of task outcomes, then, may be mediated by an attribution process (Streufert and Streufert 1969). One sees one's own group as responsible for positive outcomes; however, failure that occurs under ambiguous conditions can be attributed externally. Individual differences can also mediate the effects of failure on ingroup attraction. Within groups that fail, those persons with high self-esteem tend to like the ingroup more than those with low self-esteem (Stotland 1959).

Therefore, strategies for intervention derived from this approach focus also on cooperation toward a common goal, the achievement of which is rewarding to members of both groups. The positive affect associated with reward can then be generalized to members of the outgroup, who were presumably instrumental in obtaining the goal. To distinguish these first two approaches, the realistic conflict approach suggests that cooperation in means is important and relatively independent of the outcome of that cooperation. Reinforcement theory, on the other hand, suggests that the outcome of the interaction is more critical to altering evaluations of the outgroup and that the means (cooperation) are relatively less important. If cooperation increases the probability of success, then this is the preferred mode of interaction. From the reinforcement perspective, it is the perceived likelihood of success that determines whether cohesion is greater in cooperating or competing groups (Rabbie et al. 1974).

Similarity-Attraction

Studies of social attraction have long shown the tendency for people to prefer to associate with others who are similar in terms of interests, values, and personality traits (Byrne 1971). The assumption has been that similarity is intrinsically positive, or, in terms of reinforcement theory, it is rewarding or reaffirming. According to Heider's (1958) balance theory, one tends to like those who are similar or familiar, and whose behavior is consistent with the perceiver's values. Similar attitudes, nonetheless, must be toward valued objects, that is, those that are important and relevant (Newcomb 1958).

Friendships are often formed with those who are in close proximity, those with whom one lives or works. Proximity results in more frequent contact, lending more opportunity to perceive similar attitudes. Sharing similar values and attitudes thus implies a common fate—what may impact on one member of the group can impact on all of the group; and common fate serves as a basis for motivating cooperative behavior. Therefore, it is not surprising that persons tend to favor their own group, namely, those who are similar in social category and likewise, tend to avoid those who are different.

Hand in hand with the notion that perceived similarity leads to attraction, or as Rosenbaum (1986) emphasizes, that dissimilarity leads to rejection, is the idea that persons are more likely to see their own likable characteristics in those they like or believe that the other's likable characteristics are also descriptive of themselves (Byrne and Griffit 1973; Marks, Miller, and Maruyama 1981). Thus, the causal direction of the similarity-attraction hypothesis remains ambiguous. Nevertheless, it suggests that to the extent that contact increases familiarity and the likelihood of discovering similar interests, values, and attitudes, contact will promote inter-ethnic acceptance. Cooperation per se serves more of a moderator role in this model of inter-group relations, a means by which contact can be fostered, distinct from the strictly causal role it plays in the realistic conflict approach.

The Contact Hypothesis

The premise that contact results in familiarity and attraction is the cornerstone of the "contact hypothesis" (Allport 1954; Williams 1947). Much of the field research over the past 30 years that was directed at the improvement of relations between members of different social categories (principally racial groups) centered around the contact hypothesis. The underlying assumptions of this approach are that groups which are isolated (or segregated) from each other will display avoidance, and further that, in ignorance, they will assume that they are dissimilar and develop stereotypic views of each other's group and members. This in turn strengthens avoidance of the outgroup and maintenance of the groups' separation.

In its simplest form the contact hypothesis states that relations between members of groups who have not previously interacted will improve following direct interpersonal interaction. Mere contact between members of different ethnic groups, however, has not been sufficient to produce outgroup acceptance. What often happens, as noted by Gerard and Miller (1975) in their research during the process of desegregation in the Riverside school district, is that despite good intentions, supportive programs, and favorable administrative attitudes, "ethnic encapsulation" nevertheless increases. That is, within the social structure of the desegregated school, in the classroom, and on the playground, racial resegregation occurs (e.g., Oakes 1985; Rogers, Miller, and Hennigan 1981).

As a consequence of instances of this sort a number of contingencies for the promotion of outgroup acceptance have been added to qualify the nature of contact that will be beneficial. In addition to cooperation and common goals, as embodied in the realistic conflict approach, these contingencies include direct interpersonal interaction and high acquaintance potential, as might be derived from the similarity-attraction approach, as well as equal-status contact settings, disconfirmation of stereotypes, and normative support, for example, of legislators, teachers, parents, administrators, and employers (Cook 1978).

In distinction to the previously discussed approaches, the contact hypothesis has emphasized the importance of equal-status contact settings. Acknowledging that social groups frequently differ in social status, interventions have addressed the necessity of equalizing status in the interaction setting. It has been assumed by Cook (1978) and others that equal-status contact can be achieved by providing structurally and functionally equivalent roles in an interaction task (e.g., as would be found in work settings, equal-status sales clerk positions; in residence settings, equal-status apartment tenants; or in schools, equal-status as fifth-grade students). Emphasizing that equal-status contact is not sufficient to overcome differences in social status, alternative approaches have been developed, to which we now turn.

Stereotyping

Social representations of groups can be developed and operate in the absence of any personal experience with outgroups, typically as a consequence of the social learning of information about outgroups from one's own group. The structure and contents of the representations of various social categories comprise affect, imagery, and beliefs about traits, physical characteristics, preferences, behaviors, and values (Anderson and Klatsky 1987; Brewer 1988; Hymes 1986). The term *social representations* is relatively neutral compared with *stereotypes,* in that the former may serve a nonevaluative cognitive function and be independent of the prejudice commonly associated with stereotypes. The latter term implies both negative evaluations and biased beliefs. Like other cognitive biases, such as the primacy effect, stereotyping has been shown to increase when a judgment or prediction is made under time pressure (Freund, Kruglanski, and Schpitizajzen 1985; Kruglanski and Freund 1983) or under conditions of task difficulty or complexity (Bodenhausen and Wyer 1985; Bodenhausen and Lichtenstein 1987). Also, the tendency to generalize from a single instance, a hallmark of stereotypes, increases with greater task complexity (Reed 1983). Thus, stereotyping is inversely related to cognitive complexity; individuals who are more cognitively complex in their thinking are less likely to exhibit stereotyping (Linville 1982). Cognitive complexity is also inversely related to biases displayed in attribution patterns (Streufert and Streufert 1969).

A variant of the stereotype model of inter-group relations is the ignorance model (Stephan and Stephan 1984), in which lack of knowledge and familiarity with members of the outgroup are key mediators of prejudice. This approach emphasized the primary role of anxiety in inter-group contact. It is the anxiety aroused by the prospect of interacting with unfamiliar strangers that must be reduced before positive affect can be developed. Knowledge about them eliminates the anxiety that deters contact and acceptance. Thus, in inter-group relations that are characterized by stereotypes, one must first educate the participants in order to weaken the stereotypes. This is no easy task, given that negative traits are easy to confirm but difficult to disconfirm (Rothbart and John 1985) and are therefore more resistant to change than neutral or positive traits. When social groups also differ in social status, members often attribute this status difference to differences in the values that the groups hold. Status characteristics, and stereotypes associated with them, often influence the attributions made for different behaviors. Thibaut and Riecken (1955) report that high-status persons are given more credit for positive acts than are low-status persons. Likewise, negative acts are more often attributed to the situation for high-status persons compared with low-status persons. Biases in attributions have been demonstrated with ingroups and outgroups:—people tend to attribute desirable outcomes for ingroup members to dispositional characteristics of the ingroup member whereas the same outcomes are attributed to the situation for outgroup members. Conversely, undesirable outcomes are dispositionally attributed for outgroup members but discounted for ingroup members by attributing them to situational causes. Pettigrew (1979) has labeled this tendency to reinforce stereotypes with selective explanations as the *ultimate attribution error*.

Highly relevant is the fact that the substantive content of beliefs about an outgroup and the evaluative valence ascribed to it are orthogonal. The same trait when applied to the ingroup is given a positive evaluation, whereas when applied to the outgroup, it is depicted negatively. Similarly, when a true substantive difference between groups does exist, each group respectively views its own behavior positively and the outgroup's behavior negatively (Campbell 1963; Merton 1957; Sager and Schofield 1980).

Expectation States Theory

Status characteristics such as sex, race, and attractiveness are differentially evaluated at the societal level in terms of esteem, privilege, and desirability. This creates generalized expectations of competence in a wide range of tasks, much like a halo effect, according to expectation states theory (Berger, Cohen, and Zelditch 1972). Status characteristics serve as a basis for expectations that people have both toward themselves and toward others in the social interaction.

The status of a given characteristic is a function of the cultural evaluation of that characteristic. When status is salient group members behave as if the status characteristic is a relevant indicator of the skills involved in the task.

Both high- and low-status persons hold these expectations regarding themselves and each other. Cohen (1982) found that "high status members are seen as having better ideas and as having done more to guide the group . . . despite the fact that there is no logical connection between the status characteristic and competence on the task" (p. 213). Thus, equal-status roles in an intervention setting at the structural level are not likely to be paralleled by equal status at the psychological level if social status is salient. High-status group members (e.g., whites, males) dominate interaction and thereby, as a self-fulfilling prophecy, reinforce such expectancies in both high- and low-status persons. Thus, one of the less desirable consequences of desegregation is white dominance in activity and influence (Cohen 1972) and, conversely, black social inhibition (Katz and Benjamin 1960).

The intervention program Cohen has developed is designed to modify the expectations held by both high- and low-status members prior to the interaction task. She argues that the expectations of members of *both* groups must be altered if the interaction setting is to be equal in status and promotive of inter-group acceptance. Though many have focused on eliminating the low expectations whites hold for blacks, she cautions that "it is easier to modify the expectations for low status members' performance held by *high status members* than it is to change the expectations low status members hold for themselves" (Cohen 1982: 216, emphasis in the original). These expectations often parallel the social opportunities available to members of different social status.

In order to equalize the psychological status in the contact setting, the low-status group is given special advantage in this intervention. Advanced preparation is given to compensate for the external social disadvantage. By engineering equivalent psychological status in the setting, the intervention provides a context in which stereotypes, the driving force behind expectations, can be disconfirmed. Therefore, according to this theory, it is not status outside the contact situation per se that is critical but, instead, the cultural expectations this unequal status sets up for the participants. These, in turn, determine the quality of the interaction. Thus in viewing knowledge structures as the moderator of behaviors, this position is similar to the ignorance model, but it places special emphasis on the expectations that knowledge generates about group differences in competence.

Summary

In this section we have addressed the key variables that various theoretical approaches have focused on and the strategies for intervention that can be derived from them. It has been argued that people prefer their own group because other groups threaten the availability of resources; one's own group provides more reward to oneself; and one is more likely to perceive oneself as similar to other members of one's own group. Conversely, it has been proposed that outgroup members are, in some form, rejected because one believes that essential differences between groups offer little promise of positive interaction; lack of familiarity with the outgroup generates anxiety in anticipation of interacting with them and negative stereotypes function to perpetuate this cycle; or negative views are generalized to low expectations regarding the competence of outgroup members, who consequently will be less rewarding when one interacts with them. Each of these has been regarded as a sufficient condition to produce inter-group bias. All of these approaches tend to recommend cooperation as a strategy for intervention. Some do so on the assumption that cooperation in means will promote positive reactions as a result of discovered similarities. Others recommend cooperation in reward structure because the outgroup will become associated with positive reinforcement. Still others view cooperation as an opportunity in which information will emerge to disconfirm stereotypes or disrupt their cognitive role. Although each of these rationales for recommending cooperation may play a role in the reduction of prejudice, more fundamental processes concerned with the link between social categorization and identity needs must be considered.

SITUATIONAL IDENTITY THEORY

Mere categorization into two groups on the basis of trivial preferences (Tajfel et al. 1971) has been demonstrated to be sufficient to generate inter-group bias. This challenges the idea that discrimination must be a result of a realistic conflict of interest (Sherif 1967), isolation, preexisting stereotypes, expectations, or the anxiety these provoke. The dramatic impact of mere categorization in the "minimal group paradigm" has been amply demonstrated (cf. Brewer 1979; Tajfel 1982; Brewer and Kramer 1985; for reviews). When this method of assignment to groups is made explicitly meaningless it sometimes fails to produce ingroup favoritism (e.g., Rabbie and Horowitz 1969); more often than not it nevertheless functions to promote bias (e.g. Rabin 1985).

Assumptions

Social identity theory is based on several propositions about human nature
and behavior (Tajfel 1978; Tajfel and Turner 1979; Turner 1975, 1981). First,
people have *a basic need to establish and maintain a positive self-identity*—
people want to feel good about who they are. Self-identity, however, is highly
differentiated; it has many facets that are complexly related. The second assumption is that *one's identity includes both social and personal components*.
Social identity refers to those aspects of "who I am" that include the social
categories to which one belongs, either without choice such as gender, race,
age, physical/mental condition, or those to which one belongs by choice, for
example, religious, political, sexual preference, and so on. Personal identity
refers to those aspects of self that are more unique and idiosyncratic—the tex-
ture of traits, interests, values, and attitudes that are part of who one is and
differentiate oneself from similar others. Which components of identity are salient at any given time is a function of the situation. The third assumption is
that *one's attention can be focused on either social or personal identity in
either the perception of others or self-awareness*. Situational features will have
a powerful impact on (a) attention to a reference point to identity for both
oneself and others, (b) the manner in which information is processed during
the interaction, and (c) the consequent effects on behavior and affect.

Fourth, *orthogonal to the descriptive dimension* (the continuum of social-
personal identity) *is an evaluative dimension of identity*—the esteem attributed
to these characteristics. Components of identity have affective valence. In each
person's view, some demographic and personal characteristics are better than
others. Consequently, one's self-esteem and the esteem accorded to others is,
in part, a function of the social esteem, cultural desirability, or the level of
deference attached to certain characteristics. In some conditions it is appropriate to speak about a stable and general level of self-esteem; in addition,
however, self-esteem is a labile state that modulates with situations and during
interactions.

At the most basic level of processing information about others are observable, easily describable demographic categories. In their research with the "Who
Am I" questionnaire, Kuhn and McPartland (1954), who used the terms "con-
sensual" and "subconsensual" to refer to what we call social and personal
components, respectively, found that persons tend to begin with social characteristics to describe the self and, after exhausting these, proceed to personal
characteristics. We believe that the child's development of identity follows a
similar pattern, namely, labels for social characteristics before personal ones,
as meaningful descriptors of the self. In novel situations, that is, those in which
new persons are encountered, attention begins at the social category level—the
simplest processing position. Attention at the personal level, to be informative,
must be extended in time, in that it requires extensive processing in order to
come to know the unique constellation of personal as well as demographic

characteristics that comprise the depth and breadth of another. It takes more effort and interest than mere categorization. It is also a more cognitively sophisticated level of information processing.

Processes in Inter-group Relations

Two processes, one described as perceptual or cognitive in nature, the other motivational or affective, are central to the approach of social identity theory to inter-group behavior. The perceptual component of the theory involves a *categorization process* in which the similarity among objects within categories is exaggerated, as is the dissimilarity between categories (Campbell 1958). These basic perceptual processes apply to social categories as well. An inter-group situation is one in which persons are aware that there are members of more than one social category present. For example, in the classroom a student is aware that there are both boys and girls present. When the category membership of the self and others is salient, in effect, a unit formation is created between the perceiver and others in the same social category; they form a unit—"us." Likewise, a unit formation among those who are different from the self on this characteristic is also established—"them." This categorization, then, influences the manner in which information about the self and others is processed. Three tendencies are described as examples of the biases that occur in processing information when social categorization is activated. First, those who are similar on the salient characteristic are *assimilated,* that is, assumed to be similar on other characteristics (Heider 1958). These other characteristics are often unobservable, such as interests, attitudes, and traits (see Wilder 1986 for a review).

The second tendency or bias in processing that results from social categorization, opposite to the first, is *contrast*—the two groups, differentiated on the salient characteristic, are assumed to differ on other characteristics as well. This perceptual/cognitive part of the model, the assimilation-contrast effect, is a necessary but not sufficient condition for ingroup favoritism.

A third tendency is that, although assimilation occurs for both the ingroup (those who are like us on this characteristic) and the outgroup (those who are different), perceptions of the outgroup are relatively *undifferentiated*—the outgroup members are seen as relatively homogeneous in terms of traits and attitudes (Linville 1982; Linville and Jones 1980; Park and Rothbart 1982; cf. Quattrone 1986 for a review) compared with members of one's own group, who are more differentiated or distinguished. This greater differentiation of the ingroups is, at least in part, in order to distinguish the self from the ingroup. It has been argued further (Wilder 1978) that the perceived homogeneity of the outgroup deindividuates or *depersonalizes* its members. That is, they are not perceived as individuals but as representatives of the outgroup. This process, then, makes them ready targets for hostility (Zimbardo 1969).

Because persons strive to maintain a positive identity, a *competitive social comparison process* (the motivational component of the theory) operates to differentiate and distance oneself from members of other groups. People compare the self to others for a "reality check," in order to see how they are doing in comparison to others (Festinger 1954). Often others are the only standard one has for such evaluation. However, because there is affective significance attached to category membership, comparisons are made along any dimensions that are favorable to the ingroup and can thereby enhance one's positive social identity (Ng 1985). That is, group contrasts are selected in an ethnocentric (and thereby egocentric) manner. Alternatively, dimensions on which the ingroup is perceived as better than the outgroup may be given greater weight, that is, the importance attached to that dimension. The need for positive identity is thus satisfied by favorable comparisons between one's own social identity and the social identities of others. The extent of this bias is clarified by the tendency to maximize the difference in reward received by one's own and other groups rather than to maximize ingroup reward itself (Turner 1983a, 1983b). Social categorization is a perceptual process and is relatively neutral. Competitive social comparison adds the evaluative dimension—"we're better than they are." This process can then lead to biased attributions for the identical behavior of an ingroup versus outgroup member, what Pettigrew (1979) refers to as the ultimate attribution error.

When salient in the setting, category membership becomes an important part of one's (social) identity. It is for this reason that we prefer the term "situational" identity rather than "social" identity, which refers more specifically to one end of the continuum. Therefore, situational conditions that focus attention on group membership will have the consequence of inducing individuals to respond toward others in terms of their category membership and thereby exhibit ingroup favoritism over the outgroup—*categorical responding* (Brewer and Miller 1984). This bias has been found on measures of general evaluative ratings, specific trait evaluations, perceived similarity, satisfaction with task performance, memory for individual contributions to team efforts, evaluation of contributions to task performance, and reward allocations, even when there is no direct benefit to the person making the evaluations (cf. Brewer 1979 for a review).

Interventions in Inter-group Relations

To counteract the effects of social categorization and competitive social comparison processes, two intervention processes are necessary to reduce categorical responding. Brewer and Miller (1984) proposed that reductions in ingroup favorability and outgroup rejection are mediated by a *decategorization* process in which outgroup members are perceived and responded to as individuals rather than as representatives of a different social category. That is, an alternative process to inhibit or "undo" the social categorization process is necessary.

The first feature of this process is *differentiation,* which refers to the perceived distinctiveness of individuals within the outgroup social category—the realization, as it were, that "they don't all think (act, feel, etc.) alike." This thwarts the assimilation aspect of perception or weakens the assumption of homogeneity.

The second feature of this process is *personalization,* which is the perception of the uniqueness of an outgroup member. These unique characteristics can then take on hedonic relevance to the self, that is, these characteristics may reflect similarity to the self, for example, finding out common interests, shared beliefs, feelings, or desires. The theoretical roots of this relate to the similarity-attraction hypothesis—one tends to like those who are like them. One may also discover characteristics that are admired in the other, even if they are not similar to one's own characteristics (Newcomb 1960). It is this process that diminishes the contrast effect discussed earlier, as it applies to the self and other.

The elimination of categorical responding requires both differentiation and personalization. Bias can be reduced in *personal contact* if it is no longer necessary for the positivity of one's identity to be based on category membership and if the need for or threats to positive *social* identity are not salient. It is not assumed that personalization invariably results in liking or the development of a personal relationship. It is expected, however, that persons of different social categories will be given equal opportunity to be evaluated and responded to on the basis of their individual characteristics, unbiased by categorical responding. Neither is it assumed that biases of another nature cannot occur at the personal level.

To sum up, behavior toward members of an outgroup can, at one extreme, exemplify thoughtless automatic action driven by the crude perception that they are members of "that" social category, whatever it happens to be. At this extreme, information processing is shallow, highly efficient, and unelaborated. At an intermediate stage, although one may attend to information that makes outgroup persons distinct from one another, the basic distinction between one's ingroup and the outgroup is preserved, as is the basic dissimilarity of outgroup members to the self and other ingroup members. At an extreme opposite from the first, judgments about another's social category membership are absent or not salient and, instead, one responds to a person as someone who is unique, complex, characterized by inconsistencies as well as consistencies, and as one with both similarities as well as dissimilarities to the self. Thus, at this extreme, depth of processing is great. For the purpose of theoretical analysis and discussion, we have partitioned this continuum into three levels: (1) category-based; (2) differentiated; and (3) personalized responding (Brewer and Miller 1984).

The model as reviewed to this point, however, is incomplete. Decategorization is a necessary but not sufficient condition for eliminating categorical responding. Brewer and Miller (1984) focused on the social categorization process and changes in the perceptions of the outgroup member more than on competitive social comparison process and changes in the ingroup perceiver.

Their emphasis was on the perceptual component, but did not fully address the motivational component. In emphasizing the categorization component they focused on the ingroup member's role as "outgroup perceiver." Here we underscore the companion process in which the ingroup member acts as "self revealer." This, in turn, extends the process to one that is truly interpersonal, namely, "mutual or reciprocal decategorization." When an ingroup member takes an active, personal role in an interaction with an outgroup member, the ingroup member's attention differentiates the self from the ingroup and identification with the ingroup is diminished. This latter effect is as important as the differentiation of the particular outgroup member from other members of the outgroup. Likewise, personalization of the self in the interaction, or self-disclosure, is as important as personalization of the other. These are parallel and reciprocal processes.

In terms of situational identity theory, focusing on one's own personal identity changes the individual's relation to the ingroup (reducing its salience or relevance). A derivable hypothesis from this line of reasoning is that the more intimate the self-disclosure, the greater will be outgroup acceptance. Because individual members of groups are responded to more positively than the groups as a whole (Rothbart and John 1985; Sears 1983), dyadic interaction may often be desirable at a later stage in classroom activities. Deindividuated groups (all wearing the same uniform) are more hostile than groups whose members are individually identifiable (each wearing their own clothes) (Rehm, Steinleitner, and Lilli 1987). Therefore, teams that are created should allow individuals to maintain their unique identity.

To eliminate categorical responding, the basis of the social comparison process for the perceiver needs to shift from social characteristics to personal characteristics. Simultaneously, there needs to be a shift away from the competitive nature of the comparison, in which all characteristics must be better or worse than others (along the evaluative dimension), and toward the valuing of diversity, differences, and uniqueness. This latter orientation regards differences as a potentially valuable resource for whatever task must be confronted, rather than as a potential challenge to one's self-esteem (situational-identity).

Self-disclosure, the verbal presentation of the self to other individuals, is highly relevant to our approach. Research on the interactive nature of self-disclosure provides evidence that we tend to like others who disclose to us more than others who do not; we tend to like others as a result of having disclosed to them; and we tend to perceive that we are liked by others who disclose to us (see Cozby 1973; Chelune et al. 1979; Derlega and Berg 1987; for reviews). As Newcomb (1961) noted, in the early stages of an encounter, self-disclosure tends to be a function of similarity of demographic characteristics; at later stages of a relationship, the motivation to self-disclose is based on the discovered similarities in intimate areas of personal characteristics. This reciprocal give and take, proceeding gradually from the nonintimate to the intimate, has been described in terms of social exchange theory (Homans 1961), but dissonance (Festinger 1957) or self-perception processes (Bem 1972) are also likely to be involved. In essence, mutual disclosure is built upon and facilitates trust and respect between the two persons. Unless self-disclosure is facilitated by the structure of the interaction, social category boundaries will inhibit the development of friendships.

Summary

We propose that social categorization and social comparison processes are necessary and mutually sufficient to produce ingroup favoritism. This position does not deny that variables addressed by the other theoretical approaches, described in the first section of this chapter (namely, competition, group reward, stereotypes) also influence inter-group relations. Instead, we argue that these may be sufficient but are not necessary, and that more basic perceptual and motivational processes underlie ingroup favoritism. Consequently, interventions derived from these alternative approaches may not be sufficient to produce acceptance of outgroup members and generalization to the outgroup. We have argued that decategorization of the self and others is necessary for these positive attitudes to be developed. Only as a consequence of this process can one learn to value differences. Our focus on structural features of the situation is, in part, a recognition that these variables are more likely to be under the control of the interventionist. In the classroom this means that the educator can structure interaction in ways that reduce category salience, enhance personalization, and foster acceptance of uniqueness.

THE PROBLEM OF GENERALIZATION

The foregoing is an attempt to present a coherent theoretical understanding of inter-group relations. There remain several issues related to generalization that need to be addressed and are the subject of recent debate.

The Functional Role of Information

Cognitive schemata such as stereotypes operate and endure because of their affective significance and the consequent satisfaction of the need for self-esteem derived from them. Attempts to alter behavior by adding information that counters the stereotype are not likely to be effective. Furthermore, because they are group-specific, they are not likely to generalize beyond the target group. Learning to individuate others and personalize interactions is aimed at altering the affective component while simultaneously meeting individuals' need for self-esteem. The consequence is that individuals can learn to value differences and focus on their contribution to the achievement of task goals without experiencing threats to self-esteem. In personalized interaction, because identity becomes centered on the personal, differences are expected and boundaries cannot be sharply drawn. The shift is from stereotype-driven perceptions to an openness to the uniqueness of the other. If it is a generalized attitude of acceptance that one seeks to develop, then it is most important (and necessarily prior to behavioral changes) for a positive affect to occur. This individuating approach can promote an openness to multiple outgroups.

Stereotype models of inter-group intervention can place an unrealistic burden on both the interventionist (to provide credible, relevant, and disconfirming information) and on outgroup members (to display disconfirming behavior). Furthermore, negative encounters with outgroup members following some improvement in acceptance will reinforce the original stereotype and may even strengthen it beyond its original level. In the personalization approach, however, subsequent negative encounters with an outgroup member will be attributed to the personal characteristics of the outgroup member per se and not generalized to the group.

Two other issues have been debated among social identity theorists and others (e.g., Hewstone and Brown 1986): (a) should an outgroup member be regarded as typical and representative of the outgroup or be stereotype-disconfirming and counter-typical, or both? and (b) should class discussions address similarities or differences between ethnic groups, or both? From our perspective either response to either issue can be dysfunctional. In all these variations it requires that group distinctions (social identity) be salient and stereotypes operative in some way, that is, typical or counter-typical requires a group label to be the frame of reference; group similarities or group differences require group identities to be the basis of comparison. Our approach stresses that group labeling, by definition, creates boundaries. To build bridges on which *individuals* can meet will not be accomplished by reconfirming walls that *group members* must first scale.

Whereas we have argued that anything that minimizes the salience of social categories will decrease category-based responding and ingroup–outgroup bias, others take the view that social categories must be salient at the time that information counter to prejudicial beliefs is presented in order for it to be linked to the category and therefore to be effective (e.g., Rothbart and John 1985). Findings with respect to the typicality of outgroup persons who display stereotypically disconfirming information, which show that when such information is exhibited by an atypical outgroup member it has little effect (Wilder 1984), can be viewed as supporting this view. The subtyping of atypical outgroup members undoubtedly contributes to these results (Weber and Crocker 1983).

The elaboration likelihood model (ELM) of attitude change (Petty and Cacioppo 1986) distinguishes between central and peripheral routes to persuasion. Eagly and Chaikens (1984) make an essentially parallel distinction and point to heuristic responding to cues in the persuasion setting. These models provide useful theoretical tools for better understanding aspects of inter-group bias. They argue that under some circumstances external cues function to augment agreement with a persuasive message (positive evaluation of the attitude object) in the absence of careful processing of message content. Thus, a prestigious source speaking on a topic of little intrinsic interest to the audience would be persuasive, but not by inducing deep processing of the message.

Inter-group bias can be viewed from this same perspective, namely, as resting both on cue functions and on the processing of information about the outgroup. As we have argued, social category distinctions can exert strong cue functions. When cues to ingroup membership are salient and strong, and/or motivational impetus to ingroup–outgroup bias has been aroused (Katz 1981; Tesser 1986; Wills 1981) persons will respond to these cues and exhibit evaluative bias. Under these circumstances, if information contrary to a negative view of outgroup members is presented, it will not be processed well (deeply) and therefore will not be available to promote or justify positive behavior toward outgroup members on a subsequent occasion when category salience (ingroup–outgroup distinctiveness) or motivation for inter-group opposition is reduced.

This interpretation implies that high category salience will affect both encoding and response display (cf. Kulik 1983; Miller and Turnbull 1986). It will decrease processing of available information that disconfirms stereotypes of the outgroup, but will also affect the way in which whatever information has been processed and stored will be used when interacting with or evaluating outgroup members. When category salience is low, previously assimilated positive information about outgroup persons is more likely to be used, and/or neutral and negative information will be interpreted less pejoratively.

Returning to an opposing view—that category cues must be salient in order for stereotype-disconfirming evidence to exert a positive effect—assuming for the moment that it is true, it is important to note that in real-world settings category cues for racial/ethnic identity are almost never totally absent. Even in extreme situations like the military, where uniform dress codes eliminate some identity cues, language and other appearance cues remain available. This is not to deny that cues for making other category distinctions, such as those for occupation or religion, may be more ambiguous and difficult to detect. Anglos in an interracial marriage do not cease to notice that their spouse is black or Oriental. Instead, they give less weight to it than do others; it is less salient.

Thus, two points need to be made. First, the more ecologically valid comparison is not highly salient identity cues versus no identity cues (or irrelevant identity cues, as is the case when subtyping occurs); rather, it is highly salient versus moderately salient cues in that rarely does awareness of existing category distinctions such as those of race, ethnicity, or gender simply vanish. Second, motivational factors, such as those stemming from the inter-group dynamics of situational identity theory or those reflecting inclinations toward effort minimization or peripheral processing, as described in the ELM, make the role of substantive content less relevant. In most competitive inter-group situations, the beliefs that are acquired or displayed are more symptomatic than causal.

In sum, though we have argued that personalized interaction promotes inter-group acceptance, the mechanisms by which it does so await empirical evaluation. As is implicit for those who take the social cognition approach to stereotyping, the opportunity it provides for the processing of stereotype-disconfirming evidence may be critical. Alternatively, as we argue, the absence of group-generated motivational impetus to the display of antipathy, the motivational consequences of reciprocal self-disclosure, or weakened habits of responding to category cues may be more important. Thus, although application of ELM principles has implications for what (or how much) is processed, we question the ultimate functional role(s) of processed information as a causal factor and emphasize instead its diagnostic nature.

Taken together, these arguments suggest that interventions that contain features designed to reduce the salience of the category memberships of teammates (in contrast with those designed to augment them) will primarily affect the evaluative valence of attributions, whatever the nature of the real or attributed substantive differences between groups. Inter-group differences will be exaggerated and the attributes of the outgroup will be evaluated more negatively when category salience is high, irrespective of whether or not information is correctly recalled. This may in part account for the difficulty in finding memory effects that is sometimes seen in studies of actual inter-group interaction (Rogers 1982; Edwards 1984) or studies using members of real social categories (Taylor 1978). In addition, however, application of the principles of the ELM implies deeper, more thorough processing of substantive information when peripheral cues for responding (category membership) are less salient and sources of impetus to central processing (an interpersonal, in contrast to a task, focus) are strong.

The Intergroup–Interpersonal Dimension

Some (Brown and Turner 1981; Hewstone and Brown 1986), emphasizing Tajfel's (1981) distinction between the interpersonal and inter-group dimensions of social interaction, take the view that experience on the interpersonal and inter-group dimensions is not a "matter of degree." Instead, events and experience at one level are assumed to be independent of those at the other. Others take a related position on empirical grounds (Jackman and Crane 1986; Bobo 1983). Jackman and Crane (1986), in arguing that affective experiences such as those involved in personalized interaction will be less important when group-level phenomena are brought into play, stress the importance of differences in social power. In the presence of ongoing group relations, disparities in power contribute to a heightened salience of group self-interest.

Adherence to a strong form of the interpersonal–inter-group distinction implies that successful remedial interventions at the interpersonal level will have no (or little) effect on the nature of inter-group relations at a macro level, that interpersonal events are irrelevant to inter-group behavior. At the same time, it might imply that in school or work settings in which an intervention successfully alters attitudes toward individual outgroup members, reactions toward the social category of the outgroup members will ordinarily remain intact (e.g., Cook 1984).

In contrast, by assuming that ingroup–outgroup bias is most likely to be reduced when interaction with outgroup members is personalized as opposed to category-based, we take an opposing position. Presumably, repeated instances of such personalized interaction with outgroup members gradually weakens habits of category-based responding, habits normally strengthened by conformity to cultural norms (Pettigrew 1964). Indeed, this assumption was one of the cornerstones of the contact hypothesis (Allport 1954) and continues to enter most specifications of the conditions under which contact promotes inter-group acceptance (Ben-Ari and Amir 1986; Cook 1969, 1984; Rothbart and John 1985). This is not to deny that cues for group-level responding can be made strong enough to override tendencies toward inter-group acceptance. Rather we argue that in those circumstances where they are only of moderate strength, extensive prior personalized experience will have generalized benefit.

DESIGNING COOPERATIVE TEAM INTERVENTIONS

In this section we take principles derived from situational identity theory and apply them to settings in which one might want to maximize inter-group cooperation and acceptance. In schools the use of any among the array of cooperative team learning interventions that have been developed over the past decade is an obvious starting point (e.g., TGT, STAD, Jigsaw, Group Investigation, Learning Together, etc.). We move beyond this, however, to consider specific features that can be incorporated into the structure and implementation of these procedures in order to make them more constructive for the goal of maximizing inter-group acceptance than they might otherwise be. In our discussion it will be apparent that many of the variables invoked by the various theoretical orientations described at the outset of this chapter are routinely incorporated. In doing so, however, we implicitly emphasize their relation to the more basic processes of categorization and social comparison that form the fundamental elements of situational identity theory. First we discuss dysfunctional factors that perceptually enhance category salience. Then we focus on features of cooperative team procedures that are primarily dysfunctional because they augment divisive social comparison processes by creating a task focus to the exclusion of attention to personalized responding. This dichotomy is to some degree a heuristic for organizing the discussion in that, as will be apparent, the circumstances that influence the two processes are not independent.

Decreasing the Salience of Category Distinctions within Teams

Basis of assignment. When teams are formed it is obvious that when there is racial/ethnic heterogeneity in the classroom or work setting, the composition of teams should reflect this heterogeneity. To explicitly apply such a rule, however, is likely to perceptually and cognitively enhance social category salience. In the implementation of many existing cooperative team learning procedures teachers routinely attempt to construct teams that reflect in their composition the classroom ratios of racial/ethnic and gender categories. In contrast, random assignment of persons to teams would be better. In addition, when the task is multidimensional in terms of skills, knowledge, and ability that are relevant to its completion, assignments of persons to teams could be based instead on individual differences in such task-relevant skills, provided that such individual differences are uncorrelated with average group-level differences of the respective categories. Either procedure, however—random assignment or assignment based on individuals' unique attributes—is preferable to assignments that specifically and publicly acknowledge that teams were constructed to ensure that particular social categories occupy a position on each (or a particular) team. The latter calls attention to the social category of such individuals and instructs all that the teacher, or some other high-status person, uses social category membership as an important ingredient in his or her decision making.

Cross-cutting categories. When teams contain persons whose social category memberships cross, the salience of social category distinctions will be decreased. Thus, cross-cutting categories, as when a four-person team is composed of a black male, a white male, a black female, and a white female, should lessen category salience. In contrast, convergence, as when a team contains two black females and two white males, should augment category salience.

Multiple categories. In the same manner in which cross-cutting categories should reduce category salience, so too should the presence of multiple categories. Thus, social category distinctiveness should be lower in a team consisting of an Oriental, a Hispanic, an Anglo, and a black, than one containing two Orientals and two blacks. Consequently, it may be better to aggregate many diverse social categories within single workteams, thereby perhaps leaving other workteams homogeneous, rather than dispersing minority members as widely as possible among teams and as a result, sometimes having a single minority person on each team. This seems especially true in school settings wherein teams can be frequently recomposed over time and over different curriculum units within time blocks, thereby enabling students who happen to be assigned to a totally homogeneous team for one curriculum segment to be given numerous other assignments to heterogeneous teams. In addition, this principle applies in particular to settings in which interteam competition does not occur. When it must, the creation of some homogeneous teams (in order to maximize heterogeneity in others) should be avoided. With these caveats, however, the principle should be one of maximizing diversity within teams at the cost of some residual homogeneous teams.

Task roles. Often tasks require a division of labor such that subgroups of persons on the team work together to complete a particular aspect of the team task. Assignment of subgroups to specific task roles, in such instances, should cross-cut rather than converge with category membership. Again, the general principle of category-independent as opposed to category-based assignments should be applied when forming such subgroups. Here we differ with Brown and Turner (1981), who see convergent role assignment as preferable because it allows the members of each category to maintain their social identity more readily, whereas in their view cross-cutting assignments threaten members' social identity and thereby invoke negative comparison processes. This might be the case as long as the situation was structured in a way that makes social categories salient and relevant. The cycle of threat to identity, cross-category negative comparison and attribution, and increased inter-group prejudice, seems most likely in circumstances in which there is a potential for team or subgroup failure, which in turn seems more likely when there is interteam and/or intra-team competition. Later, we argue that the structuring of competitive relations between and within teams is to be avoided. When, as in most school settings, it is possible to avoid competitive group reward structures, the increased opportunity for personalized interaction with outgroup members that is implicit in cross-cutting as opposed to convergent role assignments, will make the former preferable. At the same time, it will eliminate the circumstances under which Brown's concerns are relevant.

Power and status. In addition to the fact that tasks often must be broken into subunits that require role specialization, as discussed in the preceding section, it is important to note that such roles often differ in status. Such cases can be divided into two types: those in which each individual has a unique or independent role and those in which multiple persons are formed into a subgroup and assigned a common role. (The latter case was discussed in the section on task roles.) In the first case, when individual roles vary in the degree of status associated with them, random assignment of team members to roles will ensure over the long run that category membership is not associated, on the average, with a low or high level of status. (Parenthetically, as is implicit in the approach of expectations states theory to team activity, when individuals are assigned roles for which they lack preparation, training, or ability, they may require special resources of one kind or another in order that they do not implicitly impose failure upon their team.)

In cases where subgroups are assigned to task roles that differ in status, the principle of cross-cutting versus convergent assignments should be applied. Parallel considerations apply of course to individual and subgroup assignments that differ in power or authority. Where decision-making power must be invested in individuals, levels of authority within the team should not covary with category membership. To be avoided in particular, however, are configurations that place solo majority members in a position of highest ascribed (as opposed to achieved) power or status.

Numerosity. That which is distinctive draws attention. Consequently, so-called *solo status* within a team, such that a particular social category is represented by a single person who is placed in a context in which another or other categories are represented by multiple others, is to be avoided. Such solo status enhances category salience.

Although solo status may particularly exacerbate category distinctiveness, other numerically unequal representations of categories may have similar effects. Thus, as was advanced with respect to multiple categories, it may be advisable to try to equalize the frequency of category representation in some settings or for some teams even if it means that others must be homogeneous.

Task Focus

Reward structures. Reward structures can be cooperative, competitive, or individualistic, and although existing cooperative team learning interventions do not provide examples of all possible permutations, these categorical distinctions in principle can be applied both to intra- and interteam arrangements for reward distribution. From our own theoretical perspective, competitive reward structures, either within or between teams, will be dysfunctional. This is not to dispute evidence that a competitive inter-group reward structure—irrespective of whether the competition is interactive—will augment within-team cohesion, even when the team is heterogeneous in composition (Druckman 1968; Samuels 1970). Such enhanced solidarity, however, is typically directed toward the task in which the teams compete. To the degree that within-team interaction is primarily task-focused it is less likely to be personalized. Consequently, the increased cohesion is less likely to be generalized to later occasions (Miller, Brewer, and Edwards 1985).

Our own evidence on this issue was replicated in a field experiment in desegregated classrooms. Over a ten-day period students participated in mixed-ethnic learning teams for 55 minutes a day. In the condition that imposed a cooperative inter-group reward structure, emphasis was placed on how well the entire class performed, and rewards were allocated on this basis. In the condition that implemented a competitive reward structure, emphasis was placed on which team exhibited the highest achievement and prizes were awarded competitively. Under the competitive condition, there was less evidence of cross-ethnic interaction, and this effect generalized into unstructured class, school, and home activities (Warring et al. 1985).

Individual versus team-level reward distribution. At first our earlier arguments might seem to suggest that within-team rewards should only be awarded at the team level and not to individual team members since the latter might invoke intrateam competition. Though such a view may have merit, especially when, for whatever reasons, receipt of rewards becomes correlated with category membership, it is important to note that needs for either social or individual identity are not likely to operate to the exclusion of each other. Individual identity needs and the quest for uniqueness (as opposed to needs for similarity to and identification with other group or team members) become salient when social identity needs are unthreatened and when one feels secure about one's group (social category) membership as well as one's acceptance on the heterogeneous workteam. In other words, in group settings, individual identity needs become salient when group identity is secure. When the team task is organized so that each individual's unique contributions are identifiable, as must be the case when rewards are dispersed on an individual basis, each team member can experience recognition as a unique contributor and thereby fulfill individual identity needs. Yet, at the same time, members can identify with the accomplishment and success of the entire team. Worst of all from this perspective is to distribute rewards to homogeneous subgroups as a unit within the team. Such common fate emphasizes the salience of subgroup category distinctions and invites competitive comparison. It is likely to be particularly disruptive if team performance is poor, on either a competitive or absolute basis.

Intrateam process. Cooperation and competition can also be conceptualized in terms of the nature or quality of the social interaction between team members. From this process perspective, too, competitive interteam interactions are less likely to produce personalization of outgroup members. Some cooperative team learning procedures place an emphasis on creating an awareness of the process events that underlie effective group performance, such as listening well to others and taking their perspective, helping rather than rejecting less motivated or less skilled team members, taking responsibility at the group as well as the individual level. Johnson and Johnson (1975) and Aronson et al. (1978) have incorporated attention to intra-group process events as important ingredients in their cooperative team learning interventions. When present, these features will promote the cross-category reciprocal self-disclosure processes essential to personalized interaction and at the same time impede and disrupt the dysfunctional social comparison and attribution processes that tend to arise when there are obstacles that interfere with completing the team task.

There are two approaches, however, to developing personalized interaction. One is exemplified by human relations training programs that emphasize the general development of sensitivity, receptivity, openness, and reciprocity. From this perspective the mastery of such skills is the focal point, constituting an independent substantive area of study. We emphasize instead the direct linking of group process skills to the team's task goals. In this sense they become instrumental. This has the effect of maximizing the quality of the team's task performance and thereby can act to build in reinforcement in terms of the team's outcome. In contrast to the more general group process skills described above, this latter approach might emphasize instead disclosure of how one successfully or unsuccessfully approached an aspect of the team task; direct requests for help with aspects of the team task; helpful, rather than demeaning responses to requests for help, in which a team member provided elaborative explanation rather than mere "answer giving"; constructive evaluation of one's own and teammates' task performance and group process behavior. It may well be the case that the development of such task-relevant interpersonal processes habits can be learned more readily in dyads than in larger teams, in that dyads may pose less threat to self-esteem. Whatever the case, however, these behaviors will not emerge automatically as a mere consequence of implementing team learning. The teacher can structure some aspects of these group processes skills into the teams' task, but formalizing them with response sheets and record keeping should not be a substitute for direct guidance and monitoring.

Threat. Like interteam competition, external threat of an impersonal nature will also focus team attention on task success. This in turn interferes with the development of personalized interaction. Within the context of school settings threat can best be conceptualized as expectations of task failure. In addition, school settings tend to intentionally promote internal attributions for failure. Where cooperative team activities are imposed, however, and a competitive reward structure is introduced, the stage is set instead for attributions of blame to low-status teammates whenever the team fails. All the factors that promote category salience will work to increase the likelihood of such negative bias. Potential solutions lie not just in minimizing category salience, but in eliminating competitive reward structures. Although social comparison is intrinsic to human interaction, in order to further curtail the negative effects of social comparison, human and instructional resources can be routinely made available at a level likely to ensure team task success. The routine use of criterion referenced testing, gain scores, and other procedures that individualize measures of performance will also be constructive with respect to this concern.

Multicultural educational programs as a curriculum task. The preceding discussion emphasized factors likely to augment or decrease social category salience, arguing that when augmented it is likely to be dysfunctional. Prominent in many schools that are ethnically heterogeneous in composition is the presence of multicultural curriculum components designed to make majority members aware of and accepting of outgroups. The presence of such programs can only enhance the salience of category distinctions. They may serve an instructional function that educates students about the diversity and unique attributes of human social groups, as might a college-level course on cultural anthropology, but more often than not they are implicitly aimed to promote the legitimacy of social identity needs of members of particular groups.

We would argue instead that in a pluralistic society, state-controlled educational institutions should not intentionally serve such functions. Here we emphasize the distinction between the social identity and knowledge function of such information. An emphasis on the latter would make substantive material on the characteristics, history, and customs of groups not represented by any single member(s) in the class or school as valid as that which concerns groups represented by individual class members. At the same time, we would emphasize the need for presentation in the curriculum of material that deals with the commonalities among humankind, commonalities that cut across the category boundaries of race, ethnicity, religion, and gender. Such material would explore instead the similarity in the problems and goals of members of these diverse categories.

Final Remarks

Recognizing that admirable strides have been made over the past decade with various cooperative learning methods, we have presented a model of intergroup processes that offers the opportunity to further refine these or other methods of intervention. Simultaneously, we acknowlege the many contributions that various theorists have made toward a greater understanding of human relations and have drawn extensively on their reasoning. The points of departure are few but we believe that they are critical. It is hoped that this chapter will serve as an impetus to the design of classroom interactions that focus on the personalization of the self and other and be instrumental in children learning to cooperate with one another and developing healthy relationships.

NOTE

The authors are grateful to Marcia Albert for preparing the information on children's development of racial awareness, preferences, and attitudes. She may be contacted for further information at California State Polytechnic Institute, Pomona, California.

REFERENCES

Adorno, T. W., Fenkel-Brunswik, E., Levinson, D. J., and Sanford, R. N. (1950) *The Authoritarian Personality*. New York: Harper.

Albert, M. (1983) *The development of racial attitudes in children*. Unpublished manuscript, Claremont Graduate School.

Allport, G. W. (1954) *The Nature of Prejudice*. Reading, MA: Addison-Wesley.

Andersen, S. M., and Klatsky, R. L. (1987) "Traits and social stereotypes: Levels of categorization in person perception." *Journal of Personality and Social Psychology* 53:235–46.

Aronson, E., Blaney, N., Stephan, C., Sikes, J., and Snapp, M. (1978) *The Jigsaw Classroom*. Newbury Park, CA: Sage.

Bem, D. J. (1972) "Self-perception theory." In *Advances in Experimental Social Psychology*, Vol. 6, edited by L. Berkowitz. New York: Academic Press.

Ben-Ari, R., and Amir, Y. (1986) "Contact between Arab and Jewish youth in Israel: Reality and potential." In *Contact and Conflict in Intergroup Encounters*, edited by M. Hewstone and R. Brown, pp. 45–58. New York: Basil Blackwell.

Berger, J., Cohen, B. P., and Zelditch, M., Jr. (1972) "Status characteristics and social interaction." *American Sociological Review* 37:241–55.

Best, D. L., Smith, S. C., Graves, D. L., and Williams, J. E. (1975) "The modification of racial bias in preschool children." *Journal of Experimental Child Psychology* 20:193–205.

Bobo, L. (1983). "Whites' opposition to busing: Symbolic racism or realistic group conflict?" *Journal of Personality and Social Psychology* 45:1196–1210.

Bodenhausen, G. V., and Lichtenstein, M. (1987) "Social stereotypes and information processing strategies: The impact of task complexity." *Journal of Personality and Social Psychology* 52:871–80.

Bodenhausen, G. V., and Wyer, R. S., Jr. (1985) "Effects of stereotypes on decision making and information processing strategies." *Journal of Personality and Social Psychology* 48:267–82.

Boswell, D. A., and Williams, J. E. (1975) "Correlates of race and color bias among preschool children."*Psychological Reports* 36:147–54.

Brewer, M. B. (1979) "In-group bias in the minimal intergroup situation: A cognitive-motivational analysis." *Psychological Bulletin* 86:307–24.

———. (1988) "A dual process model of impression formation." *Advances in Social Cognition* 1:1–36.

Brewer, M. B., and Kramer, R. M. (1985) "The psychology of intergroup attitudes and behavior." *Annual Review of Psychology* 36:219–43.

Brewer, M. B., and Miller, N. (1984) "Beyond the contact hypothesis: Theoretical perspectives on desegregation." In *Groups in Contact: The Psychology of Desegregation,* edited by N. Miller and M. B. Brewer. New York: Academic Press.

Brown, R. J., and Turner, J. C. (1981) "Interpersonal and intergroup behavior." In *Intergroup behavior,* edited by J. C. Turner and M. Giles. Oxford: Blackwell.

Byrne, D. (1971) *The Attraction Paradigm.* New York: Academic Press.

Byrne, D., and Griffit, W. (1973) "Interpersonal attraction." *Annual Review of Psychology* 24:317–36.

Campbell, D. T. (1958) "Common fate, similarity, and other indices of the stress of aggregates of persons as social entities." *Behavioral Science* 3:14–25.

———. (1963) "Social attitudes and other acquired behavioral dispositions." In *Psychology: A Study of a Science,* Vol. 6, edited by S. Koch. New York: McGraw-HIll.

Cantor, G. N. (1972) "Effects of familiarization on children's ratings of pictures of whites and blacks." *Child Development* 43:1219–29.

Chelune, G. J. (1979) *Self-Disclosure: Origins, Patterns and Implications of Openness in Interpersonal Relationships.* San Francisco, CA: Jossey-Bass.

Clark, K. B., and Clark, M. P. (1947) "Racial self-identification and preference in Negro children." In *Readings in Social Psychology,* edited by T. M. Newcomb and E. L. Hartley, pp. 169–78. New York: Henry Holt & Co.

———. (1950) "Emotional factors in racial identification and preference in Negro children." *Journal of Negro Education* 19:341–50.

Clark, A., Hocevar, D., and Dembo, M. H. (1980) "The role of cognitive development in children's explanations and preferences for skin color." *Developmental Psychology* 16:332–39.

Cohen, E. G. (1972) "Interracial interaction disability." *Human Relations* 25:9–24.

———. (1982) "Expectations states and interracial interaction in school settings." *Annual Review of Sociology* 8:209–35.

Cook, S. W. (1969) "Motives in a conceptual analysis of attitude-related behavior." In *Nebraska Symposium on Motivation,* Vol. 18, edited by W. J. Arnold and D. Levine. Lincoln, NE: University of Nebraska Press.

————. (1978) "Interpersonal and attitudinal outcomes in cooperating interracial groups." *Journal of Research and Development in Education* 12:97–113.

————. (1984) "Cooperative interaction in multiethnic contexts." In *Groups in Contact: The Psychology of School Desegregation,* edited by N. Miller and M. Brewer, pp. 156–85. Orlando, FL: Academic Press.

Cozby, P. C. (1973) "Self-disclosure: A literature review." *Psychological Bulletin* 79:73–91.

Derlega, V. J., and Berg, J. H. (1987) *Self-Disclosure: Theory, Research, and Therapy.* New York: Plenum Press.

Druckman, D. (1968) "Ethnocentrism in the inter-nation simulation." *Journal of Conflict Resolution* 12:45–68.

Dustin, D. S., and Davis, H. P. (1970) "Evaluative bias in group and individual competition." *Journal of Social Psychology* 80:103–8.

Eagly, A. H., and Chaikens, S. (1984) "Cognitive theories of persuasion." In *Advances in Experimental Social Psychology,* Vol. 17, edited by L. Berkowitz. New York: Academic Press.

Edwards, K. (1984) "The effect of category salience and status in intragroup and intergroup perceptions and evaluative attitudes." Dissertation, University of Southern California, Los Angeles.

Festinger, L. (1954) "A theory of social comparison processes." *Human Relations* 7:117–40.

Festinger, L. (1957) *A Theory of Cognitive Dissonance.* Stanford, CA: Stanford University Press.

Freund, T., Kruglanski, A. W., and Schpitizajzen, A. (1985) "The freezing and unfreezing of impression primacy: Effects of the need for structure and the fear of invalidity." *Personality and Social Psychology Bulletin* 11:479–87.

Gerard, H., and Miller, N. (1975) *School Desegregation.* New York: Plenum Press.

Goldberg, M. E., and Gorn, G. J. (1979) "Television's impact on preferences for nonwhite playmates: Canadian 'Sesame Street' inserts." *Journal of Broadcasting* 23:27–32.

Goodman, M. E. (1952) *Race Awareness in Young Children.* Cambridge, MA: Addison-Wesley.

Harris, D., Gough, H., and Martin, W. E. (1950) "Children's ethnic attitudes. II: Relationships to parental beliefs concerning child training." *Child Development* 21:169–81.

Hays, D. G., Margolis, E., Naroll, R., and Perkins, D. R. (1972) "Color term salience." *American Anthropologist* 74:1107–21.

Heber, R. F., and Heber, M. E. (1957) "The effect of group failure and success on social status." *Journal of Educational Psychology* 48:129–34.

Heider, F. (1958) *The Psychology of Interpersonal Relations.* New York: Wiley.

Hewstone, M., and Brown, R. (1986) "Contact is not enough: An intergroup perspective on the 'contact hypothesis'." In *Contact and Conflict in Intergroup Encounters,* edited by M. Hewstone and R. Brown, pp. 1–44. Oxford/New York: Basil Blackwell.

Hoffman, L. R. (1958) "Similarity of personality: A basis for interpersonal attraction?" *Sociometry* 21:300–308.

Hohn, R. L. (1973) "Perceptual training and its effect on racial preferences of kindergarten children." *Psychological Reports* 32:435–41.

Homans, G. C. (1961) *Social Behavior*. New York: Harcourt, Brace.

Horowitz, E. L. (1936) "The development of attitude toward the Negro." *Archives of Psychology* 194.

Hymes, R. (1986) "Political attitudes as social categories: A new look at selective memory." *Journal of Personality and Social Psychology* 51:233–41.

Jackman, M. R., and Crane, M. (1986) " 'Some of my best friends are black . . .': Interracial friendship and white racial attitudes." *Public Opinion Quarterly*, 50:459–86.

Johnson, D. W., and Johnson, R. (1975) *Learning Together and Alone: Cooperation, Competition and Individualization*. Englewood Cliffs, NJ: Prentice-Hall.

———. (1978) "Cooperative, competitive, and individualistic learning." *Journal of Research and Development in Education* 12:3–15.

Kahn, A. S., and Ryen, A. H. (1972) "Factors influencing the bias toward one's own group." *International Journal of Group Tensions* 2:33–50.

Katz, I. (1981) *Stigma: A Social Psychological Analysis*. Hillsdale, NJ: Erlbaum.

Katz, I., and Benjamin, L. (1960) "Effects of white authoritarianism in biracial work groups." *Journal of Abnormal and Social Psychology* 61:448–556.

Katz, P. A. (1973) "Stimulus predifferentiation and modification of children's racial attitudes." *Child Development* 44:232–37.

———. (1976) *Toward the Elimination of Racism*. New York: Pergamon Press.

———. (1981) "Development of children's racial awareness and intergroup attitudes." In *Current Topics in Early Childhood Education*, Vol. 4, edited by L. Katz, pp. 1–43. Washington, D.C.: National Institute of Education.

Katz, P. A., Sohn, M., and Zalk, S. R. (1975) "Perceptual concomitants of racial attitudes in urban grade school children." *Developmental Psychology* 11:135–44.

Katz, P. A., and Zalk, S. R. (1978) "Modification of children's racial attitudes." *Developmental Psychology* 14:447–61.

Kruglanski, A. W., and Freund, T. (1983) "The freezing and unfreezing of lay inferences: Effects of impressional primacy, ethnic stereotyping, and numerical anchoring." *Journal of Experimental Social Psychology* 19:448–68.

Kuhn, M. H., and McPartland, T. S. (1954) "An empirical investigation of self-attitudes." *American Sociological Review* 19:68–76.

Kulik, J. A. (1983) "Confirmatory attribution and the perpetuation of social beliefs." *Journal of Personality and Social Psychology* 44:1171–81.

LaPierre, R. T. (1934) "Attitudes versus actions." *Social Forces* 13:230–37.

Linville, P. W. (1982) "Self-complexity as a cognitive buffer against stress-related illness and depression." *Journal of Personality and Social Psychology* 52:663–76.

Linville, P. W., and Jones, E. E. (1980) "Polarized appraisals of out-group members." *Journal of Personality and Social Psychology* 38:689–703.

Lott, A. J., and Lott, B. E. (1965) "Group cohesiveness as interpersonal attraction: A review of relationships with antecedent and consequent variables." *Psychological Bulletin* 64:259–309.

———. (1968) "A learning theory approach to interpersonal attitudes." In *Psychological Foundations of Attitudes*, edited by A. Greenwald, T. Brock, and T. Ostrom. New York: Academic Press.

Lott, B. E. (1961) "Group cohesiveness: A learning phenomenon." Journal of Social Psychology 55:275–86.

Marks, G., Miller, N., and Maruyama, G. (1981) "The effect of physical attractiveness on assumptions of similarity." *Journal of Personality and Social Psychology* 41:198–212.

McAdoo, J. L. (1970) "An exploratory study of racial attitude change in black preschool children using different treatments." Doctoral dissertation, University of Michigan.

McCallum, D. M., Harring, K., Gilmore, R., Drenan, S., and Chase, J. P. (1985) "Competition and co-operation between groups and individuals." *Journal of Experimental Social Psychology* 21:301–20.

Merton, R. K. (1957) "The self-fulfilling prophecy." In *Social Theory and Social Structure,* edited by R. K. Merton, pp. 193–210. Glencoe, IL: Free Press.

Miller, D. T., and Turnbull, W. (1986) "Expectancies and interpersonal processes." *Annual Review of Psychology* 37:233–56.

Miller, N., and Brewer, M. B. (1984) *Groups in Contact: The Psychology of Desegregation.* New York: Academic Press.

Miller, N., Brewer, M. B., and Edwards, K. (1985) "Cooperative interaction in desegregated settings: A laboratory analogue." *Journal of Social Issues* 41, no. 3:63–81.

Newcomb, T. M. (1958) "The cognition of persons as cognizers." In *Person Perception and Interpersonal Behavior,* edited by R. Tagiuri and L. Petrullo, pp. 179–90. Stanford, CA: Stanford University Press.

———. (1960) "Varieties of interpersonal attraction." In *Group Dynamics: Research and Theory,* edited by D. Cartwright and A. Zander, pp. 104–19. Evanston, II: Row, Peterson.

———. (1961) *The Acquaintance Process.* New York: Holt, Rinehart & Winston.

Ng, S. H. (1985) "Biases in reward allocation resulting from personal status, group status, and allocation procedure." *Australian Journal of Psychology* 37:297–307.

Oakes, J. (1985) *Keeping track: How schools structure inequality.* New Haven: Yale University Press.

Oakes, P. J. (1987) "The salience of social categories." In *Rediscovering the Social Group: A Self-Categorization Theory,* edited by J. C. Turner, pp. 117–41. New York: Basil Blackwell.

Parish, T. S., and Fleetwood, R. S. (1975) "Amount of conditioning and subsequent attitude change in children." *Perceptual and Motor Skills* 40:79–86.

Parish, T. S., Shirazi, P., and Lambert, F. (1976) "Conditioning away prejudicial attitudes in children." *Perceptual and Motor Skills* 43:907–12.

Park, B., and Rothbart, M. (1982) "Perception of out-group homogeneity and levels of social categorization: Memory for the subordinate attributes of in-group and out-group members." *Journal of Personality and Social Psychology* 42:1051–68.

Parker, J. G., and Asher, S. R. (1987) "Peer relations and later personal adjustment: Are low-accepted children at risk?" *Psychological Bulletin* 102:357–89.

Pepitone, A. (1958) "Attributions of causality, social attitudes, and cognitive matching processes." In *Person Perception and Interpersonal Behavior,* edited by R. Tagiuri and L. Petrullo (Eds.), pp. 258–76. Stanford, CA: Stanford University Press.

Pettigrew, T. F. (1979) "The ultimate attribution error: Extending Allport's cognitive analysis of prejudice." *Personality and Social Psychology Bulletin* 5:461–76.

———. (1964) *A Profile of the Negro American*. Princeton, NJ: Van Nostrand.

Petty, R. E., and Cacioppo, J. T. (1986) "The elaboration likelihood model of persuasion." In *Advances in Experimental Social Psychology*, edited by L. Berkowitz, pp. 124–206. Orlando; FL: Academic Press.

Piaget, J. (1928) *Judgment and Reasoning in the Child*. New York: Harcourt, Brace.

———. (1957) *The Child's Conception of the World*. New York: Humanities Press.

Porter, J. (1971) *Black Child, White Child: The Development of Racial Attitudes*. Cambridge, MA: Harvard University Press.

Proshansky, H. (1966) "The development of intergroup attitudes." In *Review of Child Development Research*, Vol. 2, edited by I. W. Hoffman and M. L. Hoffman, pp. 311–71. New York: Russell Sage Foundation.

Quattrone, G. A. (1986) "On the perception of group's variability." In *Psychology of Intergroup Relations*, edited by S. Worchel and W. C. Austin, pp. 25–48. Chicago, IL: Nelson-Hall Publishers.

Rabbie, J. M., and deBrey, J. H. C. (1971) "The anticipation of intergroup cooperation and competition under private and public conditions." *International Journal of Group Tensions* 1:230–51.

Rabbie, J. M., and Horowitz, M. (1969) "Arousal of ingroup–outgroup bias by a chance win or loss." *Journal of Personality and Social Psychology* 13:269–77.

Rabbie, J. M., and Wilkens, G. (1971) "Intergroup competition and its effect in intragroup and intergroup relations." *European Journal of Social Psychology* 1:215–34.

Rabbie, J. M., Benoist, F., Osterbaan, H., and Visser, L. (1974) "Differential power and effects of expected competitive and cooperative intergroup interaction upon intragroup and outgroup attitudes." *Journal of Personality and Social Psychology* 30:46–56.

Rabin, I. (1985) "The effect of external status characteristics on intergroup acceptance." Dissertation, University of Southern California, Los Angeles.

Reed (1983) "Once is enough: Causal reasoning from a single instance." *Journal of Personality and Social Psychology* 45:323–34.

Rehm, J., Steinleitner, J., and Lilli, W. (1987) "Wearing uniforms and aggression: A field experiment." *European Journal of Social Psychology* 17:357–60.

Rogers, M. (1982) "The effect of interteam reward structure on intragroup and intergroup perception and evaluative attitudes." Dissertation, University of Southern California, Los Angeles.

Rogers, M., Miller, N., and Hennigan, K. (1981) "Cooperative games as an intervention to promote cross-racial acceptance." *American Educational Research Journal* 18:513–18.

Rosenbaum, M. E. (1986) "The repulsion hypothesis: On the non-development of relationships." *Journal of Personality and Social Psychology* 51:1156–66.

Rothbart, M., and John, O. P. (1985) "Social categorization and behavioral episodes: A cognitive analysis of the effects of intergroup contact." *Journal of Social Issues* 41, no. 3: 81–104.

Ryen, A. H., and Kahn, A. (1975) "The effects of intergroup orientation on group attitudes and proxemic behavior: A test of two models." *Journal of Personality and Social Psychology* 31:302–10.

Sager, H. A., and Schofield, J. W. (1980) "Racial behavioral cues in black and white children's perceptions of ambiguously aggressive acts." *Journal of Personality and Social Psychology* 39:590–98.

Samuels, F. (1970) "The intra- and inter-competitive group." *Sociological Quarterly,* 11:390–96.

Sears, D. O. (1983) "The person-positivity bias." *Journal of Personality and Social Psychology* 44:233–50.

Semaj, L. (1980) "The development of racial evaluation and preference: A cognitive approach." *Journal of Black Psychology* 6:59–79.

———. (1981) "The development of racial-classification abilities." *Journal of Negro Education* 50:41–47.

Shanahan, J. K. (1972) "The effects of modifying black-white concept attitudes of black and white first-grade subjects upon two measures of racial attitudes." Doctoral dissertation, University of Washington, Seattle.

Shelley, H. (1954) "Level of aspiration phenomena in small groups." *Journal of Social Psychology* 40:149–64.

Sherif, M. (1967) *Group Conflict and Cooperation.* London: Routledge and Kegan Paul.

Stabler, J. R., Johnson, E. E., Berke, M. A., and Baker, R. B. (1969) "The relationship between race and perception of racially related stimuli in preschool children." *Child Development* 40:1233–39.

Steiner, I. D., and Dodge, J. S. (1956) "Interpersonal perception and role structure as determinants of group and individual efficiency." *Human Relations* 9:467–80.

Stephan, W. G., and Stephan, C. W. (1984) "Intergroup anxiety." In *Groups in Contact: The Psychology of Desegration,* edited by N. Miller and M. B. Brewer. New York: Academic Press.

Stotland, E. (1959) "Peer groups and reactions to power figures." In *Studies in Social Power,* edited by D. Cartwright. Ann Arbor, MI: University of Michigan Press.

Streufert, S. and Streufert, S. (1969) "Effects of conceptual structure, failure, and success on attribution of causality and interpersonal attitudes." *Journal of Personality and Social Psychology* 11:138–47.

Sumner, W. G. (1906) *Folkways.* New York: Ginn.

Tajfel, H. (1978) *Differentiation between Social Groups: Studies in the Social Psychology of Intergroup Relations.* London: Academic Press.

———. (1981) *Human Groups and Social Categories.* Cambridge: Cambridge University Press.

———. (1982) "Social psychology of intergroup relations." *Annual Review of Psychology* 33:1–39.

Tajfel, H., Flament, C., Billig, M. G., and Bundy, R. F. (1971) "Social categorization and intergroup behavior." *European Journal of Social Psychology* 1:149–77.

Tajfel, H., and Turner, J. C. (1979) "An integrative theory of intergroup conflict." In *The Social Psychology of Intergroup Relations,* edited by W. G. Austin and S. Worchel. Monterey, CA: Brooks/Cole.

———. (1985) "The social identity theory of intergroup behavior." In *Psychology of Intergroup Relations,* edited by S. Worchel and W. Austin, pp. 7–24. Chicago, IL: Nelson-Hall.

Taylor, S. E., Fiske, S. T., Etcoff, N. L., and Rinderman, A. J. (1978) "Categorical bases of person memory and stereotyping." *Journal of Personality and Social Psychology* 36:778–93.

Tesser, A. (1986) "Some effects of self-evaluation maintenance on cognition and affect.'' In *Handbook of Motivation and Cognition,* edited by R. M. Sorrentino and E. T. Higgins, pp. 435–64. Chichester: John Wiley & Sons.

Thibaut, J. W., and Riecken, H. (1955) ''Some determinants and consequences of the perception of social causality.'' *Journal of Personality* 25:115–29.

Turner, J. C. (1975) ''Social comparison and social identity: Some perspectives for intergroup behavior.'' *European Journal of Social Psychology* 5:5–34.

———. (1981) ''The experimental social psychology of intergroup behavior.'' In *Intergroup Behavior,* edited by J. C. Turner and H. Giles. Chicago, IL: University of Chicago Press.

———. (1983a) ''Some comments on '. . . the measurement of social orientations in the minimal group paradigm'.'' *European Journal of Social Psychology* 13.

———. (1983b) ''A second reply to Bornstein, Crum, Wittenbraker, Harring, Insko, and Thibaut on the measurement of social orientations.'' *European Journal of Social Psychology* 13.

Walker, P. (1971) ''The effects of hearing selected children's stories that portray blacks in a favorable manner on the racial attitudes of groups of black and white kindergarten children.'' Doctoral dissertation, University of Kentucky, Lexington.

Warring, D., Johnson, D. W., Maruyama, G., and Johnson, R. (1985) ''Impact of different types of cooperative learning on cross-ethnic and cross-sex relationships.'' *Journal of Educational Psychology* 77:53–59.

Weber, R., and Crocker, J. (1983) ''Cognitive processes in the revision of stereotypic beliefs.'' *Journal of Personality and Social Psychology* 45:961–77.

Weiner, M. J., and Wright, F. E. (1973) ''Effects of undergoing arbitrary discrimination upon subsequent attitudes toward a minority group.'' *Journal of Applied Social Psychology* 3:94–102.

Wilder, D. A. (1978) ''Reduction in intergroup discrimination through individuation of the outgroup.'' *Journal of Personality and Social Psychology* 36:1361–74.

———. (1984) ''Intergroup contact: The typical member and the exception to the rule.'' *Journal of Experimental Social Psychology* 20:177–94.

———. (1986) ''Social categorization: Implications for creation and reduction of intergroup bias.'' In *Advances in Experimental Social Psychology,* edited by L. Berkowitz. Orlando, FL: Academic Press.

Williams, J. E., and Robertson, J. K. (1967) ''A method of assessing racial attitudes in preschool children.'' *Educational and Psychological Measurement* 27:671–89.

Williams, R. M., Jr. (1947) *The Reduction of Intergroup Tensions.* New York: Social Science Research Council.

Wills, T. A. (1981) ''Downward comparison principles in social psychology.'' *Psychological Bulletin* 90:245–71.

Wirtenberg, J. (1978) ''Cultural fairness in materials development.'' Paper presented at the skills workshop of the Women's Educational Equity Act Program, Washington, D.C., April. (Abstract)

Worchel, S., Andreoli, V. A., and Folger, R. (1977) ''Intergroup cooperation and intergroup attraction: The effect of previous interaction and outcome of combined effort.'' *Journal of Experimental Social Psychology* 13:131–40.

Worchel, S., Lind, A., and Kaufman, K. (1975) ''Evaluations of group products as a function of expectations of group longevity, outcome of competition, and publicity of evaluations.'' *Journal of Personality and Social Psychology* 31:1089–97.

Zajonc, R. B. (1968) ''Attitudinal effects of mere exposure.'' *Journal of Personality and Social Psychology Monograph Supplement* 9 (2, Part 2).

Zimbardo, P. (1969) ''The human choice: Individuation, reason, and order versus deindividuation, impulse, and chaos.'' In *Nebraska Symposium on Motivation,* Vol. 17, edited by W. Arnold and D. Levine. Lincoln, NE: University of Nebraska Press.

4
Teachers' Verbal Behavior in Cooperative and Whole-Class Instruction

RACHEL HERTZ-LAZAROWITZ
AND HANA SHACHAR

BACKGROUND AND RATIONALE

The classroom is a unique social, educational, and communicative environment (Jackson 1968; Dreeben 1968; Wheeler 1966; Thelen 1981). The role of the teacher and his/her verbal behavior in the classroom is one of the characteristics which distinguishes the classroom from other social settings. To understand teachers' speech in classrooms is to gain insight into one of the most essential features of instruction in schools. Teachers' verbal behavior, particularly their verbal interaction with the students in the class, has been studied primarily with the goal of relating it to pupils' achievement (Dunkin and Biddle 1974; Medley 1979). However, this process-product research has typically ignored many crucial elements of classroom life, such as the effects of different patterns of instructional methods on the processes that occur in the classroom (Good 1981). Moreover, such research frequently failed to include any assessment of the style of instruction. Little wonder that the value of such research has not gone unchallenged (Berliner 1976; Doyle 1978).

The complexity of the classroom setting requires an approach to research that is multidisciplinary and multi-issue. The first author and colleagues proposed an integrative model of the classroom that served as a guide for subsequent research (Sharan, Hertz-Lazarowitz, and Hare 1981). The general plan of these studies included the in-service training of an entire elementary school teaching staff to implement cooperative learning, mainly the group investigation method (Sharan and Sharan 1976; Sharan and Hertz-Lazarowitz 1980). In the transition from the traditional whole-class method of instruction to cooperative learning, teachers had to redesign the various dimensions of classroom teaching and learning according to the integrated model of the classroom. The model consists of four interrelated dimensions, as follows:

1. The organizational-structural features of the classroom.
2. The structure of the learning task.
3. The pupils' repertoire of social and academic skills.
4. The teacher's instructional and leadership style and communication patterns. Some of the various elements of this model were adapted from earlier work (Flanders 1970; Bossert 1979; Thew 1975; Steiner 1972).

The model proposes that there is a predictable relationship between these four dimensions. Lack of coordination between them during teaching will detract from the effectiveness of the classroom, while adequate coordination of these dimensions serves to improve classroom functioning. Teachers are perceived as instructional designers who can engineer classroom functioning in order to increase coordination among these four dimensions.

According to the model, when traditional-direct or cooperative methods of instruction are implemented in a given classroom, each instructional method affects all the dimensions of the classroom *simultaneously* and systematically. Thus, changing *one* dimension in the classroom should affect other dimensions in a predicted manner. To illustrate let us consider the following case. The traditional classroom is usually perceived as constituting one social system, "the class as a whole." Its organizational structure aims to maximize the isolation of students from one another (dimension 1). The teacher is the center of the activity. He/she controls all communication networks and presents the information to the pupils (dimension 4). Students are expected to be largely passive, to listen, and to respond to the teacher only when called upon to do so. Student–student interactions are expected to be minimal and each student should look after himself (dimension 3). In such a classroom the learning task is structured as individualistic or competitive according to the goal structure (Johnson and Johnson 1975). No cooperation is usually required or even tolerated in means, processes, or outcomes. Moreover, most of the learning tasks are unitary (indivisible) and the pupil will be expected to interact only with printed sources of information (dimension 2).

At the other end of the spectrum is a classroom that works according to the cooperative group investigation method. In such a classroom the same four dimensions exist but in different forms. The class functions as a set of small groups or "group of groups", more typical of a complex social system (dimension 1). The learning task is of a divisible and/or investigative nature. It deals with multifaceted problems rather than with indivisible tasks that can be solved by a single correct answer and that require a one-dimensional perspective only (dimension 2). The pupils use the social-interactive and cognitive skills required for carrying out such a learning task. They exchange information, generate ideas, actively gather information, and participate in multilateral communication. Students take on various social roles in the learning process: leaders, planners, and investigators. Pupil social cognitive behaviors will follow the active-constructivist approach to learning rather than the passive-receptive approach typical of the former example (dimension 3). The teacher in such a classroom offers guidance and assistance to develop the skills that pupils need as members of relatively autonomous groups. In this type of classroom the teachers act as facilitators of learning and as resource persons rather than dispensers of information (dimension 4) (Sharan, Hertz-Lazarowitz, and Shachar 1981; Sharan and Hertz-Lazarowitz 1980). Research that analyzed teachers' and pupils' perceptions of various types of classrooms tends to support this model.

Let's return to the present research question within the integrative model of the classroom. Teachers' verbal behavior is perceived to be affected by and related to the other three dimensions of the classroom. The prediction was that if a given teacher uses the traditional method of instruction (i.e., the whole class as one system) her verbal behavior should be significantly different from that of the teacher who instructs her classroom in the small-group method. A teacher addressing large groups employs primarily a unilateral form of communication, which means that the teacher speaks to the whole class during most of the lesson (Thew 1975). Flanders and his colleagues assessed teachers' verbal behavior mostly in traditional direct-instruction classrooms (Flanders 1970). When the open classroom emerged in the United States researchers studied different types of classroom organization and found different effects of classroom organization on teachers' verbal behavior. (Solomon and Kendall 1975; Bossert 1979).

In earlier research on student behavior it was found that when the teacher reduces her centrality, student–student interactions were more pro-social in academic activities, such as giving academic help and cooperating on task performances. (Hertz-Lazarowitz 1983, 1989; Hertz-Lazarowitz et al. 1984). Student–student verbal interaction increased dramatically in the cooperative classroom. These verbal interactions were more intimate and more related to personal, social, and academic aspects during on-task learning activities than in traditional classes (Fuchs 1983; Hertz-Lazarowitz et al. 1985; Hertz-Lazarowitz et al. 1989; Maskit and Hertz-Lazarowitz, in press; Webb 1985, 1988). For purposes of the present study it was predicted that a parallel pattern of verbal behavior would be found among teachers.

We adopted Irvine's (1975, 1979) distinction between formal and informal speech events to describe the predicted change in teachers' verbal behavior. Formality is generally described as including three elements: the communicative code, the social setting in which the communication is used, and the interpretation given to the communication. In the sociolinguistic literature formality is described in the sense of increased structuring and predictability of discourse. Formality in speech events reduced variability and spontaneity, while informality is perceived to include speech events that are characterized by spontaneity, intimacy, and creativity (Wilkinson 1982; Cazden 1986). Teachers' verbal behavior is generally perceived to be very formal in accordance with the culture and the overt rules that prevail in schools (Jackson 1968). In the traditional classroom setting the teacher's authority is a central feature. All messages are directed to maintain the teacher as the central figure who holds power over the students. In the classroom, organized as one group of 30 or 40 students, teachers used nonpersonal, highly rigid, and authoritative speech to demonstrate their status, power, and control over the classroom.

We predicted that in traditional whole-classroom instruction, teachers' verbal behavior will be mostly unilateral and formal. Teachers will do most of the talking, and the content of their model behavior will be characterized by formal speech events, with little spontaneity or variability, and with no intimacy and affection. Indeed, according to our integrated model of the classroom presented above, the physical distance that exists between teacher and student is reflected in their model behavior as well. In the physical arrangement of the traditional classroom, the space is structured to maximize territorial distinctions between teacher and student. Students are generally not allowed to move freely in the room. There is the teacher's territory and the students' territory. Teachers may enter the students' territory whenever they please, and intrude on a student's privacy. A student will be punished if he or she uses the same privilege. We predicted that the same pattern of relations will be reflected in verbal behavior. Distance will be expressed in the frequent use of commands, directives, and anonymous references to the "class" as opposed to specific individuals in the room. We also assumed that in traditional instruction, teachers will interrupt children's verbal expressions.

A very different pattern was predicted for the same teachers when they restructure their classroom for small-group learning. The change in the physical setting and the change in the nature of the learning task structure were predicted to affect drastically the behavior of the teachers. Recall that the teachers who participated in this study experienced a long period of training in the G-I method. They also displayed changes in the way they perceived their roles as teachers. As was shown in earlier research conducted in similar conditions as a result of such training, teachers acquired more progressive attitudes, liberalized their pupil control ideology, and practiced new instructional behaviors (Sharan and Hertz-Lazarowitz 1982; Sharan et al. 1984; Hertz-Lazarowitz and Sharan 1984). Thus, in this project, small-group teaching was predicted to reduce the centrality of the teacher and her controlling role so that she would adopt more of a role of guide and support figure, and subsequently, she would increase her use of informal speech events. It was predicted that in the small-group classroom, teachers will be more intimate and personal. They will increase the variability, spontaneity and creativity of their speech and will communicate more positive affective messages to their students.

The prediction that teachers will change their verbal behavior in their own classroom as a result of change in instructional practice enables us to test the integrative model of the classroom. The prediction assumes that teachers' verbal behavior, which is the most important feature of their professional behavior in the classroom, is significantly determined by structural variables of the classroom, and not merely by the teacher's personal characteristics. It was hypothesized therefore that reorganization of the classroom into a different instructional method by altering the classroom physical structure and the nature of the learning task would significantly affect teachers' verbal behavior. Their speech will change from more formal to more informal, and these speech changes will be evident from the analysis of teachers' verbal exchange with pupils and of their verbal messages.

METHOD

Twenty-seven female teachers in three elementary schools in Israel participated during the entire school year, in an in-service training project. They had similar educational backgrounds, usually 14 to 16 years of schooling. Twenty-four classes were involved in this project: first grade (four classrooms), second grade (six), third grade (six), fourth grade (four), fifth grade (two), and sixth grade (two).

The project introduced the teachers to the group investigation (G-I) model of cooperative learning (Sharan and Hertz-Lazarowitz 1980). Teachers participated in biweekly evening programs where they learned to change their classroom teaching from the traditional to the cooperative type. This change of program was based on a planned-experiential program utilized in Israel (Sharan, Hertz-Lazarowitz, and Reiner 1978; Sharan and Sharan 1987). The workshops were accompanied by weekly on-site consultations. Toward the end of the second semester (February) the teachers began to implement the G-I method in their daily instruction. The time and pace of implementation were left to the individual teacher. However, colleague support units of two or three teachers within the school planned the implementation and discussed the various issues related to classroom implementation (Sharan and Hertz-Lazarowitz 1982). Fifty observations were made between February and June in 22 classrooms (five teachers of the 27 were not homeroom teachers and they were not in the analysis to evaluate the implementation of the G-I method). The observation measures checked for various dimensions of cooperative learning such as the structure of the learning task presented to the group members, the level of interdependence, and the academic and social skills exhibited by the pupils engaged in group work. This intensive schedule of observations was necessary to avoid measuring the misimplementation of the new G-I teaching method, a phenomenon that occurs frequently in change projects where only superficial elements are adopted. In the G-I method, misimplementation might include a change in the pupils' seating arrangements without affecting other dimensions of the classroom. All the teachers participating in this study actually implemented the G-I methods at least 30 percent of the learning time, and the observation indicated that the implementation was satisfactory. Interjudge reliability was .92 for three pairs of observers (Shachar 1982).

At first each teacher was observed and her verbal interaction was coded using a pencil-and-paper technique. After the teacher became accustomed to the observer, data collection started by tape recording each teacher for 16 minutes in three different lessons of the first semester. All lessons dealt with content areas of language and social studies. In each classroom the first, middle, and final phases of the lesson were tape-recorded. In the first semester, September to December, all classes were instructed in the whole-class, traditional method. In the second semester, December to February, classroom observers checked and confirmed the implementation of G-I instruction. Finally, in the third semester, April to July, the same recording procedure was utilized. Between May and June three lessons were tape-recorded, 16 minutes each lesson, after ensuring that the instructional method in the classroom was indeed G-I at least 30 percent of the time. The total of six recordings of teachers' verbal behaviors were transferred to written transcripts. Fifteen percent of the teachers' verbal behavior was further selected for categorization definitions and reliability checking. The selection of the material was randomized for content and timing, but was controlled for the beginning, middle, and end of a given period.

Twenty-three categories of verbal behaviors were defined by two judges, one an educational psychologist and the other a linguist. Three categories with very low frequencies were excluded from the list. Finally, 20 categories of verbal behavior were defined with agreement between judges of .90. See Appendix A for a description of these categories.

After the categories were defined, clearly described, and amply exemplified, all the transcripts of total teachers' verbal behaviors were analyzed by two additional coders. The agreement between coders was .83. Out of the full transcripts of the recorded lessons, only teachers' verbal behaviors were coded and analyzed. Pupils' talk, silence, or quiet seatwork were excluded from the study. The final data for analysis included 40 hours of teachers' verbal behavior, which represented 5,183 verbal statements. From the whole-class instructions 2,632 statements were taken, and 2,551 statements were from teachers' verbal behavior in the G-I cooperative classroom. Frequencies and percentage of statements were calculated separately for each category for the two methods.

For example, teacher A had a total of 50 minutes of verbal behavior in the three observations: 28 minutes of her verbal behavior in whole-class instruction and 22 minutes for G-I. While the recording time in classrooms was equal, the amount of the net teachers' verbal behavior could be flexible. All teachers' statements were similarly coded and counted. The total sum of statements *per each recording* was considered as 100 percent of teachers' talks in this observation. The frequency of each category in each of the six recordings was divided by the total sum of statements, so that the percentage frequency score of each category, calculated separately for six observations, served as the unit for statistical analysis. In addition teachers were asked to answer attitude questionnaires regarding attitudes toward progressive education and their control ideology. Background variables were also collected.

RESULTS

The intercorrelations between the 20 categories were factor analyzed by the method of principal axis and varimax rotation. Four factors exceeding eigenvalues of 1.0 accounted for 56 percent of the variance. Table 4.1 presents a factor array of the four factors and lists items with loadings of .35 and above. Two categories loaded below .35 on the factors, and were excluded from the factors. The four factors were defined as follows: (1) teacher praises and encourages pupils in relation to task performance; (2) teacher interacts with pupils in an intimate-egalitarian orientation; (3) teacher stages herself as a central figure in the classroom; (4) teacher interacts with pupils in a rigid authoritarian orientation (see Table 4.1).

A series of t tests were conducted for each of the 20 categories. All the comparisons between categories for means were statistically significant at the .05 level, except categories 17 and 20. The t tests for the factor scores were significant at the .001 level for each factor ($t = -6.01; -10.12; -6.41; 10.51;$ respectively).

As can be seen from Table 4.2 the data clearly indicate that verbal behavior of teachers displays a completely different and oppositional pattern in the two instructional methods. In the whole-class direct instruction almost 90 percent of teachers' verbal behavior is in the formal communication networks. The teacher uses verbal categories such as lecturing, giving instructions, short questions, collective discipline, and giving general praise. In the subsystem classroom (G-I) most of the teachers' verbal behavior is informal. She uses verbal categories such as encouraging pupil initiatives, helping pupils in the learning task, facilitating communication among pupils, giving feedback on task performance, and praising individual pupils. The decrease in percentage means is sharp in the transition from the W-C to the G-I in categories loaded high and positive on factors 1 and 2, and negative on factors 3 and 4. Figures 4.1 and 4.2 illustrate the profiles of two lessons, one of a class taught with the whole-class method, the other of a class taught with the group-investigation method. In each figure, the five most frequent types of teacher behaviors found in that classroom are presented.

Finally, in order to test for the effect of teachers' background variables a multiple regression analysis was conducted. Teachers' verbal behavior was regressed in a stepwise procedure on the following predictors (independent vari-

Table 4.1
Factors of Categories of Teachers' Verbal Behavior
(n = 22 teachers, 5,183 verbal statements)

Category Number	Factor	Loading
Praise and encouragement in task performance(a)		
15	Helps in the learning task	.972
18	Gives feedback on task performance	.828
17	Refers to discipline, pragmatically	.770
13	Gives competitive praise	.615
Intimate-egalitarian(b)		
20	Demonstrates feelings	.749
14	Encourages pupils initiatives	.557
5	Interrupts pupils' verbalization	-.549
3	Asks known-information questions	-.504
4	Clarifies pupils' verbalization	.462
7	Uses collective discipline	-.434
Teacher Centralization(c)		
2	Lectures	.920
12	Gives technical praises	.719
16	Facilitates communication among pupils	-.402
Rigid authoritarian(d)		
11	Hurries pupils	.683
1	Gives instructions	.662
6	Disciplines individuals	.532
19	Praises individuals	-.453
8	Remarks on behalf of others	.392
9	Uses first person plural	x
10	Mediates between pupils	x

a - 20.8 of total variance; 40.9 of extracted variance
b - 14.2 of total variance; 24.6 of extracted variance
c - 11.4 of total variance; 20.1 of extracted variance
d - 9.5 of total variance; 14.5 of extracted variance
 - loading less than .350

ables), seniority (measured by years of teaching), grade taught by the teacher, and a summary score of attitudes measures (Zak 1976). The multiple regression was conducted separately for the W-C and for the G-I class method.

Table 4.3 presents the predictors' explained variance on each factor, separately for the W-C and the G-I instructional modes. From this table we conclude that background variables do not predict at all teachers' verbal behavior on factors 1 and 4 in the W-C. The beta weights of seniority and grade taught

Table 4.2
Teachers' Verbal Behavior in Two Instructional Methods
(*n* = 22 teachers, 5,183 verbal statements, means and SDs)

	Traditional Whole Class		Group Investigation	
	M	SD	M	SD
Praise and encouragement in task performance(a)				
15 Helps in the learning task	1.40	10.69	27.15	8.20
18 Gives feedback on task performance	1.55	4.02	12.19	6.20
17 Refers to discipline, pragmatically	2.00	2.96	2.22	3.60
13 Gives competitive praises	2.20	10.22	0.52	1.31
Intimate-egalitarian(b)				
20 Demonstrates feelings	0.85	1.79	1.15	2.05
14 Encourages pupils initiatives	3.48	6.06	11.63	7.01
5 Interrupts pupils' verbalization	2.85	3.02	0.33	1.27
3 Asks known-information questions	23.11	10.98	4.77	5.19
4 Clarifies pupils' verbalization	2.00	2.94	0.63	1.42
7 Uses collective discipline	8.74	4.71	2.22	2.55
Teacher Centralization(c)				
2 Lectures	9.70	6.64	1.63	2.00
12 Gives technical praise	6.48	16.93	1.30	2.54
16 Facilitates communication among pupils	0.22	0.64	11.52	7.92
Rigid authoritarian(d)				
11 Hurries pupils	2.0	4.82	0.11	0.58
1 Gives instructions	17.89	6.32	7.67	9.95
6 Disciplines individuals	10.44	9.87	2.48	2.33
19 Praises individuals	1.74	3.76	11.19	4.95
8 Remarks on behalf of others	0.78	1.31	0.07	0.39
9 Uses first person plural	2.30	2.31	0.81	1.94
10 Mediates between pupils	0.74	1.51	0.15	0.60

as predictor of factor 3 (intimate-egalitarian) were significant in the W-C instruction and accounted for 42 percent of the variance. Seniority accounted for 12 percent of the variance in factor 2, but the beta weight was not significant. None of the predictors had significant beta weights in the G-I classroom. In sum, background variables account for a larger share of criterion variance in W-C instruction and explain more of the teachers' verbal behavior in the W-C instruction than in the G-I method. On the basis of this analysis, it can be carefully suggested that the change in the classroom as presented in the implementation of cooperative group investigation reduces the salience of personal background variables and that the social learning organization variable effects a significant change in the teachers' verbal behavior.

Figure 4.1
Profile of a Lesson: Group Investigation Method

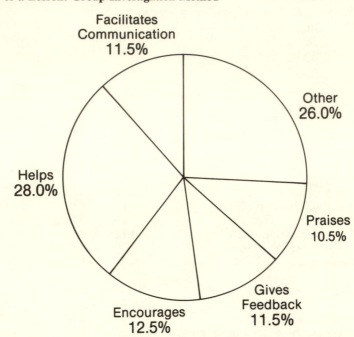

DISCUSSION

To sum up the results, we shall present the pattern of an average lesson in each of the two instructional methods by providing the profiles of each lesson. In whole-class instruction the teacher uses the following main five verbal categories: lecturing and presenting information, 10 percent; questioning known information, 23 percent; disciplining, 20 percent; instruction, 18 percent; encouraging and relating to individuals, 13 percent. In the group investigation method the teacher uses mainly the following five categories of verbal behavior: helping in the learning task, 28 percent; encouraging and relating to individuals, 45 percent; questioning known information, 5 percent; instructing, 8 percent; and disciplining, 7 percent. These two profiles demonstrate several significant changes in the teachers' instructional functions. The teacher in the group investigation classroom reduces drastically the use of lecturing, giving instructions and asking questions about known information, which are the core of the teachers' activity in the whole-class organization. In the traditional whole-class method these behaviors resemble clear characteristics of formal speech events in the classroom by being highly structured and addressed to collective audiences. These behaviors are, as predicted from the integrative model of the classroom, part of the ritualistic nature of the traditional classroom. The social

Figure 4.2
Profile of a Lesson: Whole-Class Instruction

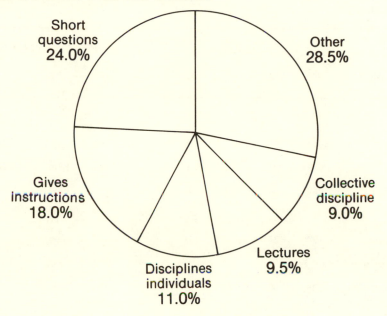

setting of the classroom, organized as one system, maximizes these formal verbal behavior events.

Some classroom researchers assume that instructing, lecturing, and asking are indeed the essence of the teaching profession (Good 1983) and advocate the increase of these behaviors by teachers. Teaching effectiveness is correlated with increased time spent in direct teaching. However, direct teaching to the whole class in the present study counted for about 50 percent of the time, while in the same instructional method we also found a relatively high percentage of time devoted to managerial strategies such as various forms of discipline. As much as 20 percent of the time was spent on verbal events related to discipline. We should recall that only some of the pupils in the classroom are involved in answering the teacher's questions and get them to try to answer them. As predicted, the teachers' speech patterns are strongly affected by the social organization of the classroom. In the cooperative learning classroom the most frequent verbal behavior was found to be interacting with groups or individuals within the group, to help them work on their learning task. In the course of this activity the teacher naturally uses direct teaching verbal behaviors such as instructing, explaining, and asking questions. However all these behaviors are addressed to small intimate systems, that is, groups of three to five pupils. It is this organizational factor that affects the verbal behavior of teachers. The data show that the amount of teacher talk (or instructional behavior) was similar in the two instructional methods under investigation. Thus the teacher remains

Table 4.3
Teachers' Verbal Behavior as Predicted by Seniority, Grade Taught, and Attitudes

PREDICTOR	WHOLE-CLASS				COOPERATIVE GROUPS			
	R^2	ΔR^2	r	β	R^2	ΔR^2	r	β
Factor 1								
Seniority	.032	.032	-.179	-0.18	.016	.016	-.127	-.10
Grade	.040	.008	.065	0.10	.022	.006	-.094	0.07
Attitude	.048	.008	.087	0.09	.026	.064	.093	0.06
Factor 2								
Seniority	.127	.127	.356	.31	.066	.066	.258	.25
Grade	--	--	--	--	.072	.005	.107	.08
Attitude	.206	.080	.328	.28	.073	.000	-.017	.03
Factor 3								
Seniority	.271	.271	.521	.46**	.094	.094	-.307	.25
Grade	.426	.155	-.459	-.38*	.157	.063	.301	.24
Attitude	.433	.006	.208	.07	.166	.008	.161	.09
Factor 4								
Seniority	.001	.001	.034	.04	.059	.059	-.242	-.25
Grade	.001.	.000	.023	.02	.098	.035	-.163	-.21
Attitude	--	--	--	--	.115	.016	.146	.13

* p < .05 ** p < .001

the central figure in the cooperative learning classroom, but he interacts mostly with subsystems of his classroom. The most fascinating finding is that when the teacher encounters a set of small systems instead of the whole class he radically increases positive pro-social instructional behavior and drastically decreases negative instructional behaviors such as disciplining, interrupting pupils' verbalization, and hurrying pupils when they work.

It is important to note that in the present study the group setting of the classrooms did not result in decreased teacher verbal behavior, as has been mentioned earlier, but in a noticeable change in the verbal behavior. The finding that background variables and attitudes explain less variance in teacher's verbal behavior than classroom learning organization is a striking finding that deserves more research. According to the theoretical framework suggested earlier, teachers switched from the use of formal speech events to the use of informal speech events and from nonintimate to intimate interaction with their pupils. This finding suggests that when teachers change their instructional style to cooperative learning they become involved in a complex process of linguistic change as well. This change constitutes an adaptation to the classroom setting (Labov 1972). One can assume that this process is a lengthy one for the teacher.

In another study that assessed the changes taking place in teachers who participated in a similar project, it was learned that the instructional change was accompanied by many reevaluations of teachers' personal and professional characteristics. The research indicates that teachers go through two stages in their adaptation to a change project. The first stage is accompanied by anxiety at losing control and being confused and disoriented because of the complexity of the social organization of the classroom; the second stage is followed by a feeling of greater ability to orchestrate classroom activities at a higher level of competence, as teachers claim "to reach out better to pupils in my classroom" (Sharan and Hertz-Lazarowitz 1982). The process of "reaching out" described by many of the teachers can be explained on the basis of the results of the present study. Teachers employed a new verbal repertoire that was related to both dimensions of their behavior, postulated in the integrative model of the classroom.

Teachers' instructional leadership style was focused on the contact with small groups and individual students, and on the encouragement and facilitation of their students' academic performance. In this fashion, teachers' communication patterns created a much more intimate and pro-social classroom context (Hertz-Lazarowitz 1983; Hertz-Lazarowitz and Sharan 1984).

The high frequency of categories such as "facilitating communications between students" and "encouraging student's initiatives" indicates that the teachers were indeed empowering their students in the cooperative classroom, while reducing their own centrality and power. We find this change in teachers' behavior to be a significant indication of their ability to change their behavior in the most crucial dimension of their professional activity. Teachers in the present study were representative of teachers in Israeli elementary schools in terms of their background variables. Thus we may conclude that given similar conditions of training and support, other populations of teachers could experience similar changes in their patterns of verbal interaction with pupils in their classrooms.

APPENDIX

Categories of Teachers' Verbal Behavior

1. *Instructing:* The teacher instructs the child what to do in a setup that does not allow the child to respond verbally but by action—by fulfilling or not fulfilling the instructions.

2. *Lecture:* The teacher instructs in a subject, and explains or clarifies any misconceptions relating to the material or to the tasks at hand.

3. *Short questions to elicit short answers* (ping-pong): The teacher addresses as many students as possible in a short time. This is described by many teachers as follows: "We talked about it in class," or "We have a class discussion."

4. *Translation:* Child says something and the teacher paraphrases it for the class.

5. *Interruption:* The teacher interrupts the student curtly for a variety of reasons.

6. *Disciplining one child:* The teacher addresses a specific child by name and scolds him in front of the class for some misbehavior. This episode is unrelated to the contents of the lesson.

7. *Disciplining the whole class:* The teacher scolds the whole class for some misbehavior. This episode is unrelated to the contents of the lesson.

8. *Discipline by proxy:* Authorizing a specific student or the whole class to act as the teacher's disciplining agent.

9. *Pluralizing:* The teacher uses vocabulary that implies cooperation, whereas communication is in fact unilateral.

10. *Prompting:* The teacher prompts and urges the students to perform learning motorial activities.

11. *Mediating:* The teacher mediates between children, and supervises the verbal-learning communication between them.

12. *Mechanical reinforcement:* Repeated verbal reinforcement using the same words and information (frequently performed without visual contact between the teacher and the child concerned).

13. *Competitive reinforcement:* Reinforcement expressing comparison between performance, initiatives, or behaviors of children.

14. *Spontaneous references to children's initiatives:* The teacher responds matter-of-factly to a child's initiative, inquiry, activity, comment, protest—unrelated to the course of the lesson.

15. *Helping the child in the course of learning:* Giving personal or group instructions relevant to the activity at hand.

16. *Encouraging interaction among children:* Transferring to the pupils the responsibility for proper communication among themselves and guiding their interactions.

17. *Referring matter-of-factly to problems of procedure and organization:* Reference to problems of order and procedure, attempting to solve the problem without punishing or imposing authority.

18. *Reference to students' performance:* The teacher refers to students' technical problems in carrying out their tasks.

19. *Individual personal reinforcement:* The teacher praises, encourages, admires, or expresses her approval at a specific student's activities.

20. *Revealing emotions:* The teacher spontaneously expresses verbally her emotions at that moment.

Examples of Teachers' Utterances for Each Category

1. *Instructing:* "Now quietly take out your books and your notebooks"; "Stop working for a minute"; "Put everything on your desks, and go out one by one."

2. *Lecture:* "In the process known as casting, we heat the metal in a big furnace at high temperature. The metal melts and . . .".

3. *Short ping-pong questions:* "Which letter is mute in this word?"; "Does the cylinder have any length? Width?"; "Did Moses live 130 years?"

4. *Translation:* "Sharon's question is, in what sphere do you criticize him?"; "To summarize what you are saying, Oren, a person who has everything is not necessarily happy."

5. *Interruption:* "Yes, there is something else here, I am interrupting Uri, but what do you add here?"; "Yes, but what do you do with the balcony? Add the digits"; "Stop that right away, don't shout! I'll ask each one of you in turn." Interruptions occur at a high frequency (84 percent) after ping-pong questions, which most children can answer. The question arouses them, and the interruption cools them down. In extreme cases of unruliness, the teacher scolds and rebukes.

6. *Disciplining the child:* "Kobbi, work quietly!"; "Ilan, do you have a hand? Raise it, then!"; "Maya, I beg your pardon!"; "Ron, sit down quietly!"; "Miriam, go back to your seat!"

7. *Disciplining the whole class:* "Stop it, stop it and fold your arms!"; "Now, stop it everybody, stop jumping!"; "Quiet!"; "Just a minute, just a minute! Everybody listen, everybody!"

8. *Disciplining by proxy:* "Excuse me, Yuval, Pnina would also like to hear Simon"; "You are not letting Zivit complete her reading."

9. *Pluralizing:* "O.K. We see that we have to work more on this issue" (referring to the teacher's decision).

10. *Prompting:* "What smell is this? Come on, what smell?"; "Come on, hurry up, take off your coats and take out your books—who's ready?"; "What's to be done now? Briefly, very briefly, Haim"; "Keren, faster, tidy up your desk!"

11. *Mediating:* "Did you hear what Sharon just said? So, what's the answer?"

12. *Mechanical reinforcement:* "So that's it? Wonderful"; "Yes, that's right"; "Fine, fine"; "Good, fine, we have heard that."

13. *Competitive reinforcement:* "Cyclamen Team is already settled down beautifully"; "Everybody look at Michael, see how he's folding his arms."

14. *Spontaneous references to children's initiatives:* "Have you finished everything? Let's see . . . this . . . and this one too . . . good!"; "Yes, Kobbi, did you call me? I'm coming"; "No, Gaddi, she simply made a mistake, because it was Saturday first, and Yom Kippur later."

15. *Helping the child in the course of learning:* "Try to see it with me, what permeated this piece of cloth"; "They are breathing, right? How do you think it affects them?"; "Well, that's not exactly so. Look here . . ."; "OK, so let's think what is the right order."

16. *Encouraging interaction among children:* "Did you complete one round? Did everybody say what he thought?"; "Yes, you can get along fine, I see you know how to get along"; "Gili, come sit next to Shlomo, he can help you write"; "Did you tell each other? Are you through? Fine."

17. *Referring matter-of-factly to discipline problems:* "What's happening here? Sit

down and let's see what's happened''; "Avi, I don't think that what you are doing is good, because Lili can't write this way."

18. *Reference to student's performance:* "I think that if you write a little faster you'll still make it''; "Don't you have any more space to write? You're right. Well, write here then''; "Do you think you can add on your own? Go ahead, then."

19. *Individual personal reinforcement:* "Now you see how well you can do when you try hard?''; "It's beautiful to look at, Maya. Your notebook is really something''; "Very good, Eyal. It's a pleasure to see how well you are doing."

20. *Revealing emotions:* "You know what? Now I'm really angry''; "I also do it this way in my mind. Both Hannah and I, who are adults, do it this way . . . with the face''; "What? I forgot! I forgot it's Yom Kippur! It slipped my mind completely! I'm so sorry!"

REFERENCES

Berliner, D. (1976) "Impediments to the study of teacher effectiveness." *Journal of Teacher Education* 27:5–13.

Bossert, S. T. (1979) *Tasks and Social Relationships in the Classroom.* New York: Cambridge University Press.

Cazden, C. B. (1986) "Classroom discourse." In *Handbook of Research on Teaching,* edited by M. C. Wittrock, pp. 432–64. New York: Macmillan.

Doyle, W. (1978) "Paradigms for research on teacher effectiveness." In *Review of Research in Education,* edited by L. S. Shulman. Itasca, IL: Peacock.

Dreeben, R. (1968) *On What Is Learned in School.* Reading, MA: Addison-Wesley.

Dunkin, M., and Biddle, B. (1974) *The Study of Teaching.* New York: Holt, Rinehart & Winston.

Flanders, N. A. (1970) *Analysing Teacher Behavior.* Reading, MA: Addison-Wesley.

Fuchs, I. (1983) "Prosocial reasoning and prosocial behavior of kibbutz and city children in two types of classrooms: Traditional vs. active organization." M.A. thesis, School of Education, Haifa University.

Good, T. L. (1981) *Research on Teaching* (Tech. Rep. No. 207). Columbia, MI: Center for Research in Social Behavior, University of Missouri.

———. (1983) "Teacher effectiveness research: A decade of progress." Paper presented at the annual meering of the American Educational Research Association, Montreal.

Hertz-Lazarowitz, R. (1983) "Prosocial behavior in the classroom." *Academic Psychology Bulletin* 5:319–39.

Herz-Lazarowitz, R. (1989) Cooperation and helping in the classroom; A contextual approach. *International Journal of Research in Education,* 13,113–119.

Hertz-Lazarowitz, R., and Sharan, S. (1984) "Enhancing prosocial behavior through cooperative learning in the classroom." In *Development and Maintenance of Prosocial Behavior: International Perspectives,* edited by E. Staub, D. Bar-Tal, J. Karylowski, and J. Reykowski. New York: Plenum.

Hertz-Lazarowitz, R., Baird, H., Webb, C., and Lazarowitz, R. (1984) "Student–student interaction in the science classroom: A naturalistic study." *Science Education* 68:603–19.

Hertz-Lazarowitz, R., Fuchs, I., Eisenberg, N., and Sharabany, R. (1985) "Student–

student interaction: Kibbutz and city children in traditional and active (Pealtani) classrooms." *Studies in Education* 42:91–110.

Hertz-Lazarowitz, R., Fuchs, I., Sharabany, R., and Eisenberg, N. (1989) "Students' interactive and noninteractive behaviors in the classroom: A comparison between two types of the classroom in the city and the kibbutz in Israel." *Contemporary Educational Psychology* 14:22–32.

Irvine, J. T. (1975) "Formality and informality in speech events." *Working papers in Socio-Linguistics* 52.

Irvine, J. (1979) "Formality and informality in communicative events." *American Anthropologist* 81, no. 4:773–90.

Jackson, P. W. (1968) *Life in Classrooms*. New York: Holt, Rinehart & Winston.

Johnson, D., and Johnson, R. (1975) *Learning Together and Alone*. Englewood Cliffs, NJ: Prentice-Hall.

Labov, W. (1972) "On the mechanism of linguistic change." In: *Directions in Sociolinguistics*, edited by J. Gumperz and D. Hymes. New York: Holt, Rinehart & Winston.

Maskit, D., and Hertz-Lazarowitz, R. (in press) "Cooperative learning: What is in the black box?" *Studies in Education* (Hebrew).

Medley, D. M. (1979) "The affectiveness of teachers." In *Research on Teaching: Concepts, Findings and Implications*, edited by P. L. Peterson and H. J. Walberg. Berkeley, CA: McCutcheon.

Shachar, H. (1982) *The Effect of Change in Classroom Structure on Teachers' Verbal Behavior*. M.A. thesis, University of Haifa.

Sharan, S., and Hertz-Lazarowitz, R. (1980) "A group investigation method of cooperative learning in the classroom." In *Cooperation in Education*, edited by S. Sharan, P. Hare, C. Webb, and R. Hertz-Lazarowitz, pp. 14–46. Provo, UT: Brigham Young University Press.

————. (1982) "Effects of an instructional change program on teachers' behavior, attitude and perceptions." *Journal of Applied Behavioral Science* 18:185–201.

Sharan, S., Hertz-Lazarowitz, R., and Hare, P. (1981) "The classroom: A structural analysis." *Changing Schools: The Small Group Teaching Project in Israel*, edited by S. Sharan and R. Hertz-Lazarowitz, pp. 21–53. Tel Aviv: Ramot Educational Systems (Hebrew).

Sharan, S., Hertz-Lazarowitz, R., and Reiner, R. (1978) "Television for changing teacher behavior." *Journal of Educational Technology Systems* 7:119–32.

Sharan, S., Hertz-Lazarowitz, R., and Shachar, H. (1981) "What children think about small group teaching." In *Changing Schools: The Small Group Teaching Project in Israel*, edited by S. Sharan and R. Hertz-Lazarowitz, pp. 21–53. Tel Aviv: Ramot Educational Systems (Hebrew; 2nd edn 1984).

Sharan, S., Kussel, P., Hertz-Lazarowitz, R., Bejarano, Y., Raviv, S., and Sharan, Y. (1984) *Cooperative Learning in the Classroom: Research in Desegregated Schools*. New Jersey and London: Lawrence Erlbaum Associates.

Sharan, S., and Sharan, Y. (1976) *Small Group Teaching*. Englewood Cliffs, NJ: Educational Technology Publications.

Sharan, Y., and Sharan, S. (1987) "Training teachers for cooperative learning." *Educational Leadership* 45:20–25.

Solomon, D., and Kendall, A. J. (1975) "Teachers' perceptions of and reactions to misbehavior in traditional and open classrooms." *Journal of Educational Psychology* 67:528–30.

Steiner, I. (1972) *Group Process and Productivity*. New York: Academic Press.

Thelen, H. (1981) *The Classroom Society: The Construction of Educational Experience*. London: Croom Helm; New York: John Wiley.

Thew, D. (1975) "The classroom social organization category system." *Classroom Interaction Newsletter* 11:18–24.

Webb, N. M. (1985) "Student interaction and learning in small groups: A research summary." In *Learning to Cooperate, Cooperating to Learn*, edited by R. Slavin et al. New York: Plenum.

———. (1988) "Peer interaction and learning in small groups." Paper presented at the annual meeting of the American Educational Research Association (AERA), New Orleans.

Wheeler, S. (1966) "The structure of formally organized socialization settings." In *Socialization after Childhood*, edited by O'Brim and S. Wheeler. New York: Wiley.

Wilkinson, L. C. (ed.) (1982) *Communicating in the Classroom*. New York: Academic Press.

Zak, I. (1976) *Non-Cognitive Factors of Teachers in Secondary Israeli Schools*. Tel Aviv: Ramot (Hebrew).

5
Creating Classroom Communities of Literate Thinkers

GORDON WELLS, GEN LING M. CHANG, AND ANN MAHER

Fri, Jan. 8, 1988. First day

Hi my name is Margarida and I live at 38 Redford St. Today at school we got assigned to an animal. We have lots of animals in are class room. She gave as numbers and I was number 5. I got to be a mely worm. I said I hated mely worms. But then I said to my self maybe it will be kind of fun!

Mon Jan 11 1988

Today I fil more better about the mealy worms and I studeyed it a lot and I did have fun I had lots of fun.

Tues Jan 12 1988–Wed Jan 13

Today I said I wonder if I feed the mealy worms some pizza and see if they will eat it. Anyway I tink thet they are going thro a stage my techer said she has a booklet and she is going to let me read it.

These are the first three entries in the learning log that Margarida kept over a six-week period, during which her whole grade four class made a study of animals, their habitats, behavior, and modes of reproduction. For some of the time, Margarida worked in a group of three, observing and recording the metamorphosis of mealy worms. For part of the time she worked more or less independently on a study of the panda, the results of which she presented to other children in a number of sharing sessions at the end of the project.

Throughout the six weeks Margarida also spent part of most days in discussions that involved the whole class. Some of these arose around books and objects related to the animal theme that were introduced into the classroom workshop by the teacher or by the children. Others involved a reflective consideration of the activities that the children were engaging in and of the strategies that they were developing for making sense of their experiences. The ways in which Margarida learned and collaborated were typical of the kinds of learning engagements and transactions her teacher encouraged and supported for all the children in the class.

During this period the authors of this chapter were also engaged in research in the same classroom. Maher, the teacher, wanted to discover whether children's skills as enquirers would be enhanced if the processes they engaged in were made explicit through class discussion. Wells undertook to videotape some of the activities that took place in order to provide evidence for Maher's inquiry. At the same time, the observations that were made contributed to a larger longitudinal inquiry in which both Chang and Wells are engaged. This study, which involves four schools and 72 Canadian children selected from four ethnolinguistic backgrounds, is concerned to explore the relationships between language, literacy, and learning and children's progress and academic achievement. Six of the 72 children were in Maher's class.

In this chapter we intend to examine some of the collaborative events that occurred during the project on animals. Our aim will be to explore in depth the sorts of learning they provided and, by relating these examples to issues of practice, to develop a rationale for the transformation of classrooms into communities of collaborative learners. But first we need to set out some of the principles that led us to propose this mode of organizing learning opportunities as a more effective alternative to the traditional mode of knowledge transmission.

KNOWING AND COMING TO KNOW

Let us start with *knowledge,* the acquisition of which is, by common consent, the major purpose of schooling. According to the *Shorter Oxford English Dictionary,* knowledge is "the state or condition of understanding [some matter], acquired by learning." Unfortunately, however, the provisions made in many schools for students' attainment of this state of understanding have been seriously hindered by misunderstandings among educators about the conditions under which it can best be achieved. These stem, in large part, from mistaken views about the nature of knowledge itself. Since, explicitly or implicitly, these misconceptions have been so pervasive in public education, it is important that we start by trying to achieve a clearer understanding of the way in which knowledge is constructed by individuals and within a community.

Because the outcomes of individuals' mental processes can be given external representations through symbolic systems such as language, music, or mathematics and because these representations can be stored in physical objects such as books, journals, maps, or floppy disks, it is easy to believe that these objects actually contain knowledge. And, from there, it is a short step to acting as if knowledge can be given to somebody in the same way as the book or map can itself be given. However, such a belief is entirely erroneous.

First, knowledge does not exist in packages that can be transmitted from one person to another. Being a state of understanding, knowledge can only exist in the mind of an individual knower. And it has to be constructed—or reconstructed—by each individual knower through a process of interpreting or making sense of new information in terms of what he/she already knows. Even when something is said to be "common knowledge," all this means is that, within a particular community, individual members have a representation of that event or state of affairs and believe that every other member of the community has a similar or equivalent representation. Furthermore, as well as occurring in individuals, the acquisition of knowledge is more appropriately conceived of as an organic process of making meaning than as one of passively receiving it. It is for this reason that those who have studied the acquisition of knowledge, such as Piaget (1977) or Bruner (1972), have emphasized its active nature, preferring to characterize the processing of coming to know in terms of "construction" instead of "accumulation."

Second, to emphasize the individual constructive nature of knowing and coming to know is not, however, to deny nor ignore the importance of the social dimension of the process. To be sure, certain types of knowledge arise mainly from an interaction between an individual and his or her physical environment, such as the acquisition of conservation, studied by Piaget. But for most types of knowledge, interaction with other people provides an essential input to the process of construction (Vygotsky 1978). In conversational interaction, participants formulate linguistic representations in light of the feedback they receive on the appropriateness of their formulations in the contributions of other participants. Conversation can thus provide a forum in which individuals calibrate their representations of events and states of affairs against those of other people, and realign and extend their existing mental models to assimilate or accommodate to new or alternative information. In this way, knowledge, although residing in individuals, can be exposed to social modification and undergo change and revision. As Bruner and Haste (1987) emphasize, what is involved is a *dialectical* relationship between the individual and the social.

Third, within such an account of the social context through which knowledge is constructed by the individual, there can be little place for an absolutist interpretation of the notion of "truth." If knowledge is true belief, as philosophers have argued, "true" must be taken to mean either verified against personal experience or as being in conformity with the beliefs of others, as these have been publicly expressed. It cannot mean true in an absolute and final sense since, as we have already seen, every individual's knowledge is open to revision and, as the history of science amply attests, even some of the most strongly held theories have been supplanted by others that have been judged to give a better explanation of the available evidence.

But what, it may be asked, does one's conceptualization of the nature of truth have to do with the provision of opportunities for learning in the class-room? Our answer is that even though they may remain tacit and unexamined, educators' beliefs about the relationships between truth, knowledge, and learning are of profound importance, because they underpin their concepts and expectations of schooling and of the orthodoxy by which school-based learning should be governed. Unfortunately, though, as is illustrated by one authoritative pronouncement after another, the methodologies of teaching at all levels of education are still to a large extent based on implicit beliefs in the absolute nature of knowledge and in the feasibility of the transmission of this knowledge from expert to novice. Such methodologies, furthermore, accord little significance to the active, constructive nature of learning or to the role of social interaction in the processes whereby each individual comes to know.

This brings us to the next issue that needs to be addressed: the relationship between individual learning and the modes of interaction that are practiced in the classroom.

LEARNING THROUGH INTERACTION

Wherever learning is dependent on the incorporation of information that cannot be obtained exclusively from the individual learner's transactions with the physical environment, linguistic interaction plays a crucial role in the process. Traditionally, and particularly in high school and university, the typical mode of interaction is that of the "lecture," that is to say of an extended monologic exposition of a topic, often interspersed with sequences of display questions (i.e., questions to which the questioner already knows the correct response). In this mode, an expert presents his or her knowledge to the learner, who is expected to be both willing and able to receive it. This can be represented diagrammatically as:

$$\text{Expert} \longrightarrow \text{[Knowledge]} \longrightarrow \text{Novice}$$

Although extended exposition has an important part to play in the totality of classroom life (in generating interest in, or providing a preliminary survey of, a topic to be addressed, or in summarizing or recapitulating what has been learned), it is totally inappropriate as the dominant mode of interaction. For, in this mode, little or no provision is made for students to contribute their interpretations and reformulations as well as whatever expertise they have, since the underlying orientation is typically that of knowledge transmission. Thus, it is not difficult to understand why frustration and boredom among learners are likely to occur when extended exposition is the dominant form of interaction in classrooms.

To give due recognition to the active and constructive role of the learner, a different mode of interaction is required—one in which the "expert" and the learner see themselves as fellow members of a learning community, in which knowledge is constructed collaboratively. Here, the underlying assumption is that each participant can make a significant contribution to the emerging understanding, in spite of having unequal knowledge about the topic under study. The relationship can be represented as follows:

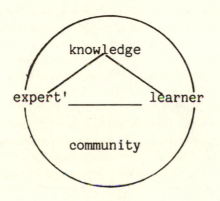

It is important to point out that the difference between these two modes of interaction—the transmission-oriented and the collaborative—does not lie in the spatial arrangement within which the expert and the learners find themselves, although there is a correlation between the spatial arrangement and the discourse generated. Rather, it lies in the nature of the discourse itself, which arises from the way in which the participants relate to each other and to the topic that they are addressing. In other words, in a situation in which the "expert" stands in front of a group of learners, collaborative learning can prevail; just as, in instances where "expert" and learner are seated side by side, a transmission orientation may characterize the ongoing interaction.

Within the collaborative mode, it is necessary to highlight two further characteristics. First, the teacher does not always assume expertise and authority about the topic under inquiry. One desirable consequence of this is that it opens up the class to pursuing topics that the students find challenging and intriguing but which may be beyond the teacher's knowledge repertoire. The emphasis, instead, is on encouraging students to discover and pool their expertise, and it is the teacher's adoption of such an emphasis that enables individual learners within the group to contribute meaningfully to the ongoing inquiry. Thus, in collaborative settings, the distinction between expert and novice is no longer statically maintained, but is subordinate to a concern for the cognitive and affective benefits of group learning for the individual learner. Second, whether or not the role of expert is filled by the teacher, and if so whether she or he is interacting in a group or with an individual student, the mode of interaction is that which is characteristic of talk between young children and their parents about a topic of mutual interest (Wells 1986). The adult's stance in this sort of talk is one of "contingent responsiveness," as he or she first listens to discover the child's topic and purpose, and then makes a contribution that will enable the child to extend and develop it.

On many occasions, however, such as when a topic is being addressed through group inquiry, the teacher will not be a participant. In such situations, collaborative interaction will occur among a group of students who may be of relatively equal expertise, and the role of expert will be distributed, with first one student and then another contributing on the basis of personal experience or of the information she or he has acquired. This brings us to another consequential characteristic within the collaborative mode that requires attention, that is to say the different kinds of learning that are being provided for when a teacher is part of the interacting group and when she or he is not.

Elsewhere (Chang and Wells 1988) we have contrasted the collaborative talk that occurs in these latter two contexts in terms of the different contributions they are likely to make to students' learning. Collaborative talk between peers, we suggested, *enables* one or more of the participants to complete a task as successfully as possible; this may be a practical task, such as making a model, or an intellectual task, such as understanding a phenomenon or composing a written document. Such talk, undoubtedly, provides many opportunities for learning, as well as enabling progress to be made with the task in hand. Yet, it would be naive to believe that the kinds of learning that are typically being provided for through peer collaboration, especially among children, would be the same as when an intentional teacher is present. For example, it is unlikely that peers would be explicitly concerned with facilitating intentional articulation and deliberate monitoring of the processes through which learning of content knowledge occurs or through which an assignment gets completed.

Where the collaborative talk is between teacher and individual learner, on the other hand, there is potential for these important benefits to occur.

Where one of the participants has greater expertise than the other, he or she can engage in interaction with the learner *with the deliberate intention of enabling* the learner to acquire some procedure, knowledge or skill that will be useful in other situations beyond that in which he or she is currently engaged. In these cases, collaborative talk not only facilitates the task, it also *empowers* the learner. Indeed, we do not think it would be too strong a claim to say that, under ideal conditions, it has the potential for promoting learning that exceeds that of almost any other type of talk. It is the ideal mode for the transaction of the learning-teaching relationship. (p. 97, emphasis added)

This, we believe, remains the responsibility of the teacher, particularly in the elementary grades. Equally, we believe it is important that teachers, in their practice, are sensitive to the distinctions discussed so far, and assume responsibility for ensuring that learners experience the various forms of collaborative interaction so that they may fully benefit from their potential.

Finally, it is essential to recognize that there exists another form of interaction that should be treated as having equal importance for learning—interaction with the internalized other. Briefly stated, this form of interaction occurs when we reflect on our own understanding—when we think, as it were, through dialogue with ourselves or with an "internalized other" (Mead 1934) in the dialectics of inner speech or writing, as we alternate between the roles of reflective writer and reflective reader. Besides creating a classroom climate that is conducive to collaborative interaction, it is equally essential to ensure that there is intellectual space for meaningful reading and writing within a school day. The intellectual space, however, is not merely a time provision to read and write on one's own. It should include attention to mechanisms within and beyond group-learning context that provide for individual expression and development of scholarship and intellectual interests, without their necessarily having to be constantly subordinated to a group agenda and negotiations. In classrooms where teachers are guided by this consideration, there are minimal problems of group dynamics, and learners find collaborative learning satisfying and beneficial rather than frustrating, as the movement between collaborative and individual learning is fluid but well integrated.

What we are suggesting, then, is that there are three modes of interaction that should be provided for in the classroom, in addition to the expert's exposition. First, the sharing of understanding—and ignorance—among learners, and between learners and experts, in order that they may mutually support and act as catalysts to each other in their knowing and coming to know; second, tutorial talk, in which individual students benefit from expert guidance that is responsive to their particular needs; and third, opportunities for reflecting and communing with themselves through inner speech, reading, and writing. As educators, we have to strike a conscious and thoughtful balance among all three, because overemphasizing one may cause a stifling of the benefits of another. To strike this balance we have to take a very sensitive view of what it means to learn through interaction, and realize the pitfalls associated with the common practice of defining interactive learning too narrowly. It is by going beyond a narrow and panacea-like definition of interactive learning that we can make it a means for effective learning instead of something that ought to be done.

This brings us to the third of our basic principles: the centrality of literacy in intellectual development.

LITERACY AND INTELLECTUAL DEVELOPMENT

Written language is a remarkable invention. Since the creation of the first graphic symbols more than 3,000 years ago, it has become a powerful instrument for the extension of human intellect (Goody 1977). Initially, writing provided a method for giving visual representation to speech, thus allowing practical information to be preserved over time and retrieved on a later occasion.

Then, over the subsequent centuries, formatting conventions developed, such as spaces between words, punctuation, pagination, and indexing, which made possible the systematic use of written language to accumulate and disseminate information, and this, in turn, transformed the cultures that institutionalized this powerful technology (Morrison 1987).

But the empowering potential of literacy, properly understood, goes beyond this archival function—literacy is more than an efficient means for communicating over time and space. In Bruner's words (1972), it is a cognitive amplifier that can empower individual minds. In writing, meanings are given a representation that has a permanence that is not possible in speech and this allows the distinction to be made between what is said—the text—and the various interpretations that can be derived from it.

For the reader this means that systematic and sustained attention can be given to the actual propositions that are asserted in the text in order to evaluate their coherence and consistency and to examine the evidence adduced to support them in light of one's own knowledge and experience. Through reading one can thus extend and sharpen one's understanding of the subject matter of particular texts and, at the same time, develop more generally a discriminating critical attitude to the ways in which ideas are given linguistic expression.

If reading promotes reflective and critical thinking, the same is even more true of writing. For the very act of composing requires one systematically to confront one's knowledge and attitudes in a critical and constructive manner in order to select, organize, and shape one's content appropriately for the purpose and audience one has in mind. Furthermore, unlike reading, which leaves no external trace of the mental processes in which one has been engaged, writing creates a visible record, which is the outcome of those processes. What one has written can be critically read, in the same way as a text by another person, in order to see what it means; it can also be revised and rewritten to develop ideas and attitudes that were initially vague, unclear, or incomplete. Thus by writing, reading, and revising, and by discussing one's text with others, one can extend and refine one's knowledge in a conscious and deliberate manner.

From the point of view of intellectual development, therefore, what is important about reading and writing is not so much their use to communicate information, important though this is, as the possibility that they provide for the development of a generalized way of using language as an intentionally controlled tool for precise and coherent thinking. However, although this type of *literate thinking* may have arisen historically as a result of the use of written text, it is not *dependent* on the activities of reading and writing. Once the power of this mode of thinking has been discovered through reflection on what was written, the same intentional processes can operate in spoken language and, when the appropriate conditions arise, speech can be given the same sort of careful attention as is given to print (Langer 1987). Indeed, among literate adults, such occasions occur in many areas of everyday life, at home as well as at work. And so, as Heath (1986) has suggested, children growing up in a literate community may have many opportunities to participate in literacy events, long before they begin to engage more formally in learning to read and write. The result is that, as recent research has shown (Ferreiro 1986; Ferreiro and Teberosky 1982; Goodman 1980; Heath 1986; Teale 1986), children come to school with some understanding of the forms, functions, and significance of literacy, although there is considerable variation in the extent of their under- standing and in their experience of the functions that literacy can serve (Wells 1987).

LITERACY AND LEARNING IN SCHOOL

Having reviewed these three principles independently, we shall now attempt to integrate them in an argument for the creation of classrooms as communities of literate thinkers.

As we said earlier, we concur with the majority of educators in considering the systematic construction of knowledge to be the major aim of education. This, we have argued, will best be achieved when it is recognized that knowl- edge has to be constructed by individual students through the progressive ex- tension and modification of their existing knowledge that occurs when they attempt to make sense of new information and experience.

This process goes on spontaneously simply as a result of encountering new experiences, but in a piecemeal and largely unconscious fashion. The function of schooling, however, is to bring the individual's knowledge, and the pro- cesses by which it is acquired, under conscious monitoring, so that she or he may take active and intentional control over her or his own learning and be able to make connections between knowledge acquired in school and that which is acquired in practical life situations outside the classroom (Barnes 1976). For the ultimate test of what is learned is the ability to exploit the knowledge to formulate and solve problems of a practical as well as an academic nature.

Literacy, understood as the conscious exploitation of the symbolic potential of language as an instrument for thinking, provides the means for achieving that intentional control over learning. As already suggested, careful attention to what was said and written, in order to decide what interpretations of a text are warranted, leads to the development of a critical and reflective attitude to the linguistic formulations in which knowledge is couched; it also encourages the development of the ability to engage in thinking that is disembedded from particular concrete situations (Donaldson 1978). Writing is potentially still more powerful in requiring one to confront what one knows and does not know, and to make warranted connections, as one attempts to orchestrate one's knowl- edge, and from it, compose a coherent text that will effectively communicate what one knows and feels. In addition, if writing is necessarily rewriting, it provides occasions for the socio-cognitive development of thinking about one's thinking.

But, as already argued, these skills of literate thinking can be acquired in speech as well as in reading and writing, if the participants have a clear end in view that demands that they attempt to express their point of view explicitly and with due attention to the justification of their opinions (Chang and Wells 1988). Furthermore, when working on written texts, as reader or writer, there is much to be gained from talking to other people—engaging in what we called above collaborative talk for the calibration of interpretations of the written text.

Our conclusion, therefore, is that to achieve most effectively the educational goal of knowledge construction, schools and classrooms need to become communities of literate thinkers engaged in collaborative inquiries.

INQUIRY IN ONE CLASSROOM

Having elaborated on the principles underlying our belief in the value of collaborative inquiry and literacy, let us now look at some episodes from the unit on animals in Maher's grade four class to see what are the literate consequences of an attempt to work out these principles in practice, through the creation of a classroom community of active learners. We will start with an episode that occurred during the first phase, that of observing a living creature.

There were several reasons for the choice of animals as the topic for this unit of study. How people and animals—and living things in general—get along in the world is a subject that Maher believes to be of central importance. Earlier in the year, the class had observed the metamorphosis of caterpillars into butterflies and in the previous year some of the children in the class had been involved in a study of newly hatched chicks. On this occasion, however, there was a choice of living creatures to study and so there was an opportunity for individual children to develop expertise that they could share with others who had studied a different animal.

Much of the research that the children carried out was library based, as they consulted reference books, naturalists' guides, and other printed and illustrated material. But an important part of the project involved first-hand observation. Maher wanted the children to have the opportunity to use all their senses—touching, smelling, looking at, and listening to a particular creature as well as just reading about it. So she assembled a collection that included a crayfish, some crickets, a Mexican land crab, and a rat, as well as the guinea pig and gerbil, which were regular members of the classroom community. The collection also included a colony of mealy worms. For the children to share the responsibility for looking after these creatures was a further objective of this project.

The first task then, was to spend some time each day observing one of these creatures either in groups or individually, and to enter the results of these observations in a log. The children were free to select what in particular they would attend to, but to get them started Maher had them spend the first morning in self-selected groups finding out as much as they could about one of a number of key terms such as "food-chain," "ecology," and "conservation."

Then, because she wanted them to interact with children with whom they did not typically choose to work, and to avoid the wide variation in group size that might have resulted from free choice, she had the children draw lots to determine which creature they would observe.

Observing the Mealy Worms

Margarida drew the mealy worms and, as her first entry in her log makes clear, her initial reaction was one of disgust. By the time she was observed in her group on the second day of the project, however, she had begun to feel differently.*

Margarida, Barbara and Pauline have a tray of mealy worms. M has put one in a small plastic beaker and is examining it intently.

1 M: Look how it's moving its head and crawling.
       Look, look! And over there it doesn't move hardly nothing.
2 B: Maybe it doesn't like it *there*.
       (Linh, a Chinese girl, is walking by and stops to look.)
3 L: *Could you* tell me something what you're doing?
4 B: We're helping each other—and thinking and observing.
5 M: Maybe if we put some more—one more in maybe it will be a little bit happier.
6 B: Yeah, put one more in.
       Look at all the other ones that are dying.
       (Chung is passing. He stops to look.)
7 C: You're not scared to pick it up?
8 M & B: No.
9 M: Look how it's curling all over each other and making a shape of a P.
       (B looks.)
10 M: I wonder how they die.
11 B: I guess they're not happy and they die.
12 M: No.
13 B: Why don't—why don't we go ask Mrs. Maher why this one died?
14 M: No.
15 P: One just went out of its shell.
16 B: They don't have shells.
17 M: Yes they do.
        Why are they going out of their shells?
18 B: They want to die?
19 P: No, they're losing the skin.
20 M: Yes, probably—like caterpillars.
        (Several boys including Chung stop to look.)

*In this and the following extracts, the following conventions apply: * = a segment of word length which was inaudible; < > = uncertain transcription; *italicized words or asterisks* = spoken simultaneously.

21   M: They like each other.
22   C: They don't even look like they have any legs.
23   M & B: They DO!
24   M: Watch (she tips the mealy worm out of the beaker and onto her hand).
25   C: They all look so ugly.
26   M: See, they have feet.
          Oh, my god! They all have feet on top of their head!
27   B: They have feet on top of their head?
28   M: Yeah, look. They're walking on it.
29   B: I'm going to call Mrs. Maher.

Watching this group at work, the strongest impression is of the intensity of their involvement, as they observe, react to, and speculate about the apparently dying mealy worms. Even the ringing of the bell for recess, which occurs at this point, does not interrupt their concentration, and it is several minutes before the teacher is finally able to persuade them to break off to go out to play. As soon as they return, they pick up the discussion as if there has been no interruption. The next extract starts a few minutes after they have resumed work.

46   M: But out of a hundred, let's see how many are alive.
47   P: Are there a hundred?
48   M: Yes.
49   B: Some of them are dying.
50   M: See those black stuff they're die—they're dead.
          (Tomas stops to look.)
51   T: You picking all of them up?
52   M: They do—we have to see how they kill each other—if they kill each other or what they do.
53   B: Yeah.
54   T: That one's dead.
55   M: No it isn't.
56   B: (to P) Can I take some? I never did this before—I'm kind of scared.
57   M: It's not dead, Tomas, it just moved. But it's getting dead.
          Let's watch this one first cos it's dying.
58   B: (to M) OK, pick up this one right there.
          (B and P show some reluctance to touch the mealy worms.)
59   B: This one, he's dying. . . . You can even see he's got the black spot.
          Call Gordon, I want to show him it.
          (Gordon joins them.)
60   M: This one's—this one is starting to die because the other ones are black and he's starting to get black.
61   B: Look, they—they're all black.
62   G: Why are those ones black?
63   M & B: 'Cos they're dead.
64   M: And this one's starting to get black as well because it's starting *to die*.
65   G: *D'you think* they go black before they die or after?

66 M: I think that's how they die.
67 G: How long have you been observing them? How many days?
68 B: Um—this is our first day.
69 G: OK. Now have you thought how you could—you could observe the same one each day?
70 M: Well . . .
71 G: Is there a way you could know which ones you were looking at?
72 B: Put them in a cup.
73 P: Yes, that's what I said.
74 M: See, they're *crawly*.
75 G: Perhaps you could think about that because if you don't know that you're looking at the same one each time you won't know how . . .
76 M: (to G) We could put one—these ones that we're looking at in a cup for a day **** or we could . . .
      (turning to P as G moves away) Because these are the ones we're watching we want to watch them every day to see how they're growing.
77 P: Look at this one.
78 M: I know. Isn't it AMAZING!

Two aspects seem worth singling out for attention. The first is the way in which observation leads to speculation and the beginnings of more systematic inquiry. On a number of occasions (e.g., 15, 27, 51) an observation by one child sets off a disagreement, which leads to a more careful observation by all of them. For example, Chung's comment that they do not appear to have any legs (22) leads to Margarida's discovery that they have "feet on top of their head" (26). Or, more significantly for the understanding that they eventually achieve, Pauline's observation that "one just went out of its shell" (15) is countered by Margarida's assertion that they do not have shells; this in turn leads Pauline to look again and observe that it is a skin that is being shed and this reminds Margarida of the caterpillars they had studied earlier in the year (20). At this stage, the girls are working on the hypothesis (discovered later to be erroneous) that the dark-coloured worms are dead, and much of their speculation is concerned with the supposed processes and causes of death (60–66). Quite early on, Pauline suggests that they separate them into two groups and, following Gordon's prompting, this becomes the basis for Margardia's more systematic proposal (76) to separate them "because these are the ones we're watching. We want to watch them every day to see how they're growing."

The spirit in which the children build upon each other's speculations about the changing colors of their mealy worms is quite remarkable. Their observations and interest in extending their understanding are so intimately linked that they generate a spontaneity to utilize their projection abilities, focusing upon making meaning of an observable phenomenon rather than arguing about the factual accuracy of each other's contributions. If the latter had occurred, it could easily have led to issues of group dynamics—which are noticeably absent among the children. The exchanges between Margarida and her peers demonstrate that to achieve a classroom climate that disposes children to engage in literate behavior, one must understand more than the learning activities that contribute to it. One must understand how the teacher's goals, collaborative interactions, and the classroom as a whole come together to create a curriculum of opportunities for literacy development.

The second notable aspect is the affective tone to so much of the talk. There seem to be two sources. First, the apparently sickly state of the worms arouses their concern: "I guess they're not happy and they die" (11); "Maybe if we put one more in maybe it will be a little bit happier" (5). The anthropomorphic attribution of affective states to other living creatures, even mealy worms, seems to be a natural response of children of this age. The second source is to be found in their own conflicting reactions to these creatures. The initial reaction, strongly expressed in Margarida's journal entry, is one of disgust; but this is counterpointed by the empathy already referred to and by the fascination that is aroused by the close observation of any living creature. The latter wins out, as is clear from their desire to share their observations with the adults in the room and from Margarida's last comment, "Isn't it AMAZING!"

Margarida's group was by no means unique; the same sort of involvement was to be seen in all the other groups. We have quoted this episode at length because, at first sight, mealy worms might seem unlikely to arouse such a response. Too often, when we are selecting curriculum topics, we consider them only in terms of their cognitive content or the skill-learning they promote. These are important matters, of course, but they ignore the affective dimension. Our observation of Margarida and her friends reminded us how important this is in providing the energy that enables children to become absorbed in a topic and stay on task for extended periods of time. Once we had been alerted to this dimension of their activities, we began to notice how the children's expression of their feelings about the topics they were working on acted like the warp on which the more cognitive weft was woven in all the discourses they were creating in speech and writing.

Here are two more examples, taken from Kathryn's journal, entitled "The Newt Study":

Tues. Jan 12, 88.

The newt only goes up when nobody is looking at it. The newt never realy pays attention to the guppies. When the newt goes up he wiggles up. When he moves he really moves but when he stayes still he's like a statuw. The newt dosen't like to be watched but when he is he dosen't care. We feed shrimpt to eat. The newt likes to stay at corner at the bottom of the aquarium. He also likes going throgh rocks witch is daingres because the crayfish is there. We put the basket in to see how the newt would react. It looks like the newt is smelling the basket. Soon it claimed [climbed] on the basket and started swimming up to the top then suddenly swam to the bottom of the aquarium.

Thurs. Jan 14, 88.

Today a very sad thing happened in our class. Wendy found the newt in the molded pumpkin box. It was very dry. And another thing. . . . It was dead. We decided to leave it there for now. We hadn't even thought up a name for it. Uma, Barbara and I felt like crying. He was just geting use to being held too. It had allredy loved to be peted. I'll miss him.

There is no doubt about Kathryn's involvement or about the sense of loss that she feels at the death of this little creature that she was getting to know through careful observation and through the sense of touch: "We hadn't even thought up a name for it." At the same time, in communicating her response to the event, she is clearly also intent on creating a dramatic effect for her audience in the way she delays the revelation of the nature of the "very sad thing that happened." At first the details of where and how the newt was found do not seem to merit the gravity of her characterization of the event and this effect is further reinforced by the way in which she appears to be introducing another detail of the same kind. However, the four periods that follow create a sudden feeling of anticipation—all the greater for having been preceded by the disarming "And another thing"—so that when the truth is finally revealed a much stronger effect is produced than would have been the case if it had been announced in the first sentence.

Kathryn's journal, like those of many of her classmates, is a window onto the child's observational abilities, among other skills. But more significantly, it is primarily a forum within which she, the learner, can explore her observations in detail and with involved projection as she "re-observes" the newt through writing. The journal thus affords, within the collaborative activity of adopting a living animal to study, an opportunity for individual exploration of various personal meanings and emergent learning goals by each learner. And, in the case of Kathryn at this stage of her observations, it is her interest in the newt's behaviour in response to its environment and other creatures around it. Thus, it is of little surprise that the following day Kathryn's writing expresses her strong sense of loss at its death at a time when she was just beginning to discover that "he was just geting use to being held too. It had allredy loved to be peted." Indeed, the keeping of a journal is a practice that encourages children to utilize their literate skills to discover what they are enthusiastic about, and from there to develop further new-found knowledge and learning interests.

Reporting on the Frog

Alongside the observation of one of the living creatures in the classroom, each child was required to research from books an animal of his or her choice, either alone or in a small group. Having selected the animal, they were asked to identify a question to give focus to their research.

Kathryn had started by observing the newt with a group of friends and then had gone on alone to study the frog, focusing on the frog's method of reproduction. Having completed her book research on the frog, she had prepared a display on a small table to communicate the results of her inquiry to others. This consisted of a model of a pond with male and female frogs on it, a written description of the frog's method of reproduction, together with a diagram of the reproductive organs of the male frog. On either side of the model were the books that she had consulted, including a naturalist's guide to North American reptiles, an illustrated book about frogs, and one about reptiles. She also included a copy of the fairy tale "The Frog Prince."

In the following episode, Kathryn is teaching what she has learned about the frog to three boys from her class, Lionel, Justin, and Tomas. Kathryn is standing by the table using a ruler to point to the various parts of her display. The three boys are sitting facing her. As in the previous episode, the interest of all participants is very apparent. This can be gauged both from the interactive nature of the discourse and from the fact that, throughout the 20 minutes they are observed, they never deviate from the topic. An added zest is provided by the interplay between the interpersonal relationship between the presenter (female) and audience (male) and the question she has chosen to study (reproduction).

The episode starts by Kathryn placing the frog in relation to the newt: "I found this quite weird actually that they're in the same family but they're enemies" (7) and this leads to a discussion of some of the different varieties of frogs. At (17), Kathryn turns to her own written text and begins to read from it, referring also to her accompanying diagram. In the extract that follows, she refers also to one of the reference books she had used.

28   K: Millions of sperms are stored until ejected.***
          So this is like the—it comes right there (pointing to her diagram).
29   L: So you are saying like this—
          (K picks up the book from which she took the diagram and shows it to the
          three boys.)
30   K: In here . . . the picture . . . here's the picture.
31   T: Is this the female?
32   K: Yeah, I didn't draw it (i.e., the diagram of the female).
33   T: Yeah, I—I can see.
34   J: Oh, I get it. You see this is the picture over there (pointing to the diagram of
          the male frog in the book and then to K's diagram).
          This is the picture over there.
35   L: Yeah, this is the male . . . and that's the female (pointing to pictures in the
          book) *because it needs that . . .* it needs that for the eggs.
36   K: *This is where*—this is where the eggs are stored.
37   L: So this is like the pouch—the pouch and this is, um—
38   T: Yeah, these are eggs.
39   K: But this is not the whole body (pointing to diagram).
          This is the * part.

Although Kathryn is the "expert," the other children do not sit back, passively absorbing the information she has to present. This is truly a social activity, as the three boys bring their knowledge to bear in understanding what she has to tell them, asking questions and offering their interpretations of each other's contributions. This is what is meant by the social construction of knowledge. And, in the following extract, one can see very clearly how this construction is enacted in the very form of the discourse.

The sequence starts after a slight lull in the conversation that follows, and is perhaps induced by, Lionel's comparison between frogs and sharks (54).

54	L:	So then—then . . . you know what I think . . . what's different from other animals like the shark.
		When the shark mates it has a fight and it gets scars. But, like, I don't think the frog fights and gets scars.
55	K:	(laughs) No, I don't think it—
		But, um—
56	L:	Where—where do they go like—where do they go when um—like*
57	K:	*When they—when they mate?
58	L:	No. When they, um—when, like, there's a tornado?
59	J:	This is how they ⟨breed⟩?
60	K:	(laughs)
61	J:	Like—like—do they have—do they have a shelter?
62	K:	Yeah, I guess so. I *guess they* just, um—they go—
63	T:	*under water*
64	K:	Yeah, they go under water when they think something's wrong and, like, they—
65	J:	It sometimes happens that*
66	L:	*So.* How long do you think a frog can stay in the water?
67	K:	Well, I think quite a long time, because you know . . .
68	L:	They stay under *water.*
69	K:	*Yeah,* because they breathe when they stay under water.**

In 56, perhaps through association with his previous contribution, Lionel is trying to move the discussion to another important dimension of the ecological study of the frog—namely its strategies for survival in the face of danger. As he pauses to find an appropriate term for what he has in mind, Kathryn, assuming that he is making reference to the current topic of discussion, which is reproduction, offers a completion to his question (57). This is not, however, what Lionel has in mind. In an attempt to make himself understood, he offers an instance of a hazard: "when, like, there's a tornado?" (58). Justin's next utterance (59) seems to be trying to make a connection between "mating" and "tornados" but, judging by Kathryn's laughing response and his continuation, Justin's question was probably to check his understanding of Lionel's question. His follow-up query (61), in fact, represents another attempt, and at this point everyone in the group understands Lionel. As the "expert", Kathryn feels it incumbent upon her to provide an answer. However, she is clearly uncertain on this matter, until Tomas offers his suggestion (63). With Justin's and Tomas's participation, she formulates an answer that addresses Lionel's interest in frog behavior in the face of danger: "They go under water when they think something's wrong" (64). Very naturally, Lionel becomes curious about how long frogs can remain underwater, if that is the way they cope with danger. Implicit in his question (66) and its extension (68) is the active meaning-making behavior that children engage in when they encounter what perhaps is dissonant or implausible information in light of their own knowledge or experience—their tendency to search for answers.

Our point in discussing this extract at some length is to illustrate one part of the learning process *in action*. So often the process appears to be unidirectional: teacher or text tells, and the student is assumed to have absorbed the information. What is ignored, because it is not seen, is the internal equivalent of what is made external in the previous extract: that is to say, the process of bringing existing knowledge to bear in actively construing and interpreting the information that is made available through the posing of questions and, more important, the search for answers. Among peers, this process is made fully apparent, as the contribution of one student is extended, challenged, or modified by the contributions of the others.

Ideally, the same process should be encouraged when the teacher is one of the participants but, as has frequently been demonstrated, the inequality of status between teacher and student militates against the sort of collaborative construction of knowledge that has just been illustrated (Barnes 1969; Mehan 1979; Sinclair and Coulthard 1975). It is for this reason that we are urging that students should be given opportunities to engage in small-group learning; these situations encourage them to take a much more active role in making meaning than when they are expected to be relatively passive recipients of information transmitted by teacher or textbook.

It may be objected that, without a teacher present to monitor and direct the discussion, there is a risk that some of the information that is contributed will be inaccurate and that the knowledge that is constructed will therefore be incomplete or, worse still, false. There is indeed such a risk. But there is equally a risk that, when the information comes from teacher or textbook, the interpretation that the student puts upon it will be inaccurate. However, this goes undetected unless the student has the opportunity to externalize his or her own understanding in a variety of ways, such as commenting, questioning, providing answers, or reformulating a contribution through collaborative interaction. It is these opportunities that the group situation positively encourages (Sharan and Sharan 1976). Furthermore, where the students are themselves responsible for the meaning that is jointly constructed, they are much more likely to adopt a critical stance to the suggestions that are made in the "transmission" mode of learning, in which information from teacher or text is accepted uncritically because it comes with the stamp of the expert's authority (Olson 1980).

As was emphasized earlier in the chapter, the group learning situation is not only a natural but also a catalytic means of learning. Nevertheless, the actual construction of knowledge still remains the responsibility of the individual learner, and much of it goes on as unobservable tacit internal operations of the mind. It is for this reason that the externalizing or making "public" of students' thinking on a topic of inquiry needs to be encouraged. However, besides the oral mode, a written outcome of some kind should form an integral component of any group-learning situation. Because of the more stringent demands for explicitness and systematicity of exposition that are placed on a writer by the anticipated needs of the audience, writing provides the learner with an individualized opportunity to confront his or her own knowledge, and to learn to develop a self-conscious stance toward the completeness and coherence of his or her understanding. It is in this dialectical interplay between what Scardimalia and Bereiter (1985) refer to as the "rhetorical space" and the "problem space" that writing develops an individual's thinking and knowledge.

Thus, as the boys together read Kathryn's text on the frog's reproductive system and, at the same time, listen to her presentation, the children as a group utilize writing in this dialectical manner.

The femal frog can make as many as 2000 eggs inside its body. To make a egg into a tadpole and then into a frog is very difficult. The eggs have to go into alot of different tubes and passways in the mothers body befor they are ready to get out. The femal frog is fat and heavy while carring the eggs. This slowes it down and makes it hard to escape from its enamys. To make a frog one egg of the femal must first be fertilized by the sperm of a male frog. The male makes millions of sperm in testes. They pass to the kidneys though the sperm ducts into the sperm sac. Where millions of sperm are stored untill ejected though the cloaca.

At this point, Kathryn's written account represents what she knows. But it is noticeable that, as she makes her presentation and the three boys actively listen to her, the group naturally uses her written account as the fulcrum upon which they compare their understanding and the adequacy of Kathryn's composition of what she knows. And, in so doing—as the ensuing discussion among the children demonstrates—she has the opportunity to discover the limitations both of her knowledge and of the way in which she has presented it to her audience. Clearly, Kathryn's somewhat clinical account has failed to answer what is for Justin a really important point about reproduction.

84   J: When—when they mate—when they get on top of each other . . . like—
85   ?:   *No.*
86   J: *Does*—does the female get on top of the male or does the **
87   ?:   *****
88   K: They really just (laughing) go like that (demonstrating) *(laughs)*
89   L: *I know* hug each other **

90	J:	*But*—but do they um—is the male on top of the female or the female on top of the male?
91	K:	They don't really lie down and do it . . . kind of just sideways.
92	J:	Yeah, I know.
93	L:	I know they sort of *like*—
94	J:	**
95	K:	The male's right here, right? And the female goes over there and *he* hugs her because, um—
96	J:	*Yeah*.
97	L:	He hugs her?
98	K:	Yeah, like that (demonstrating putting her arms round an imaginary body).
99	T:	Yeah.
100	L:	He hugs her? (sounding unconvinced) I thought they—
101	K:	(laughs with embarrassment) I think ** different.
102	J:	How—how big can a frog get?

Although somewhat embarrassed, Kathryn struggles to convey what she has learned, making use of gesture when words fail. On this basis, Lionel obligingly offers the term "hugs" to describe the action of the male with respect to the female. But in the end it is he who questions its appropriateness in a tone of exaggerated scepticism that is impossible to transcribe. It would have been really worthwhile if, at this point, there had been an opportunity for Kathryn to attempt a revision of her written account of the mating habits of the frog.

For this group of children, then—as for the others in the class—literate behavior is not restricted to meaningful reading and writing, but embraces an intertextual space that includes the child's writing, books of reference, diagrams and illustrations, and the oral discussion that surrounds and interprets the various texts. If, as we have suggested, the hallmark of literate thinking is the exploitation of the symbolic potential of external representation as an aid to the construction of inner meaning, these children are clearly engaged in literate thinking, as they move between the written verbal formulation, the diagrams, and the illustration, in order to be sure that they have understood. As is so often the case, what is read needs to be reformulated in one's own words— orally or in writing—and checked against the formulations of others, in order that whatever new information is constructed from intersubjective perspectives may be integrated into one's personal knowledge.

CO-REFLECTING ON THE PROCESSES OF INQUIRY

Something that was noticeable in all the above episodes was the children's openness to new ways of thinking and feeling in the face of new questions. Although they themselves would probably not have used the term "revision," they had begun to be influenced by their teacher's growing awareness of the pervasive appropriateness of this attitude to tasks undertaken and decisions made. As when writing, the first attempt is rarely the best one can achieve; rather, it represents the struggle through the foothills of meaning-making to a plateau from which a clearer view can be obtained of the goal to be attempted and of the route by which it may be reached.

Topic choice is a case in point. Choosing a topic is an essential, but often one of the most difficult, parts of undertaking any inquiry. On this occasion, the project started with a class brain-storming session, in which the children were encouraged to consider which animal they would like to study and, equally important, what question in particular they wanted to try to answer. Following this initial discussion, they were asked, when they had reached a decision, to sign up on the "topic board" with their topic and question. However, it was also made clear that it was quite acceptable for them subsequently to change their topic or question, provided that they recorded the change. The teacher regularly monitored the entries on the board and used them as a basis for conferences with individuals and groups about their topic choices.

The following is the transcript of one such conference. The teacher has gathered a group of children around the topic board and, having noticed that Justin has changed his mind a couple of times, she invites him to talk about the reasons for his decision.

1   T: Justin, you've changed your mind a couple of times.
2   J: Yes.
3   T: D'you think you could talk about why you changed your mind?
4   J: Well, I dunno. The catfish, it just kinda sat there.
5   T: (laughs)
6   J: The catfish wasn't that exciting and the jellyfish, um—like I couldn't find much books about the jellyfish and it just didn't—
7   T: Fine. So I see you've got "lion" down here.
        You were talking on Friday—I know from your African experiences.
        So you might be a little familiar.
8   J: Yes, I did it because, um—I—I,er—already know something about it.
9   T: And have you remembered that most important part about "You must be interested in what you're doing"? (This emerged in the earlier brainstorming session about choosing a topic/question for a project and was written on the blackboard.)
10   J: Yes, I know.
11   T: You are . . . You haven't got a question here yet . . .
        Have you thought about a question in your mind about the lion?
12   J: Yes.
13   T: Are you able to talk about that yet?
14   J: Well, I haven't really got one yet.
15   T: You're still thinking, okay.
        While we're talking this morning in this little group for a few minutes, listen to what other people say. You'll probably get some good ideas.

The teacher then turns to some of the other children to listen to their accounts and to ask about their progress. Seth has decided to try to discover how fishes move and, after considering some possible avenues for exploration, the teacher says, "We'll all be really keen on hearing what you find out, Seth." Sarah plans to do her research on rabbits, where they live and what they eat. Wendy also wants to study rabbits ("What they like to eat, what they eat in the wild"), to which, after accepting the proposal, the teacher replies, "It would be interesting to see if you have to make that question bigger to keep yourself interested." Sarah and Wendy decide to work together and, interestingly, they do indeed expand their question to a study of the similarities and differences between members of the rodent family. The final outcome of their inquiry was a well-researched and attractively presented display entitled "Rodentland."

As the teacher discovered, the topic board became a point of reference for both her and the children. Frequently, a small group could be seen looking at the choices made by other children and changes in topic were noticed and remarked on; they also saw that the teacher made frequent reference to the entries on the board to help her in her planning, and that she too was interested in the reasons for the changes that were made. In this way, the acceptability of revising goals and plans was given implicit recognition, and explicitly brought to conscious attention through writing as well as group discussion. The jottings on the topic board thus constituted a visible trace of the teacher's and children's co-determination of the topic questions raised for consideration. More importantly, they formed a common text, around which justifications, planning, and reflections on the actions taken or not taken in the course of the children's inquiry were conducted. Indeed, the topic board served to make a very tangible and concrete link between each child's learning at any one point in time and her or his past decisions and future actions, thereby enabling the child to engage with the teacher in reflection about the processes through which her or his inquiry went.

The next example concerns an even more direct consideration of some of the processes involved in carrying out an inquiry, and it involved the whole class. At the beginning of the project, the teacher had asked the children to think about the sorts of learning the project might lead them to engage in and they had come up with a list that included the following:

observing

reading

writing about

thinking about

talking about

asking questions

experimenting

making models

creating

This list then became the basis for a "tracking sheet," a copy of which each child filled in at the end of each day, as a record of what he or she had been doing.

At the end of the project, in reviewing with the class what they had achieved and the sorts of activities in which they had engaged, the teacher invited the children to reconsider their original list of types of learning. For 20 minutes or so, the children worked in self-chosen groups, evaluating the categories on the list in the light of their experience, with a view to possible revisions. When the whole class regathered, there was further discussion of the reports from the various groups. In the end, one change was made to the list as a result of a suggestion from Lionel, who proposed the addition of "feeling," in the sense of learning by touching.

However, as argued earlier, the value of the revision process does not only lie in the changes that may be made, but also in the qualitative changes in understanding that may result from a focused scrutiny of the current text in order to discover what it means and to evaluate its internal coherence and its adequacy as a representation of the author's intention. Another important reason for the teacher's inclusion of such an exercise within the total collaborative inquiry on animals had been to provide the children with opportunities to learn from re-seeing their learning processes. This is as important as the learning that arises from re-seeing products as the outcomes of engaging in those processes. But all too often this is neglected or overlooked. We believe it is an extremely essential area of the curriculum, if children are to develop their strategic knowledge and become autonomous learners.

The following extract from a discussion between Kathryn and her two friends, Mani and Janice, demonstrates the value of providing such opportunities. It comes from the recording that was made while the children were engaged in their small groups in their attempt to re-see the list of intellectual processes in which they had been involved as they carried out their inquiries on animals.

1 M: But "created."
2 J: "Created." I don't really get that.
3 M: Do you know what "created" means?
4 K: Yeah. You made it. Like, er—
5 J: Then that's just like you made models (referring to the previous category).
6 K: I created an idea (trying out the collocation).
       You can say it with ideas but you can't model an idea.
       Like you can model things. But creating—
7 J: Yeah, but if you *have an idea about—*
8 K: *Creating a thought.*
9 J: *But if you have an idea of—*
10 K: *Like creating a story.*
11 J: But if you have an idea of a lion—you can model a lion.
       So that's part of the thing.
12 K: Yeah, so "created" also means "model." Almost the same thing.

As they engage in co-reflection to revise the tracking sheet, these three girls find themselves being challenged to test their understanding of the terms "creating" and "making models," and they attempt to clarify the relationship between them by relating the words to the particular activities in which they and their friends had been engaging. Through grappling in this way with the subtle conceptual distinctions coded in language, they are led, in turn, to reflect upon their recent experiences from a metacognitive perspective—a perspective that is rarely adopted in the course of actually completing a learning task.

CONCLUSION

In presenting and analyzing these episodes selected from one specific classroom project, we have tried to illustrate the quality of the intellectual life that can occur in a classroom that functions as a community of literate thinkers. We have also tried to show how such a community is created both by establishing working relationships, between all participants, that are collaborative rather than directive or competitive, and by organizing the structure of the overall task in such a manner that exposition, group work, and individual endeavor are integrated in goal-oriented and meaningful ways. As we have argued throughout this chapter, people learn most successfully when they have the freedom to make choices about the activities in which they engage and are given support through processes of co-determination of what to learn and how best to do so. At the same time, for all of us—children, teachers, and researchers—the construction of knowledge requires goal-directed engagement with new information through direct experience and exposition, through discussion and deliberation with others, and through communing with oneself in writing and reading.

Although less explicitly, we have also tried to communicate something of the intellectual life that went on beyond the classroom as we, the authors, collaborated with each other in our study of literacy and learning in the classroom, thereby forming another learning community. In doing so, we have made frequent use of analogies from writing. This is not accidental. Both as experienced teachers and as practicing researchers, we lean on our knowledge of what enables writers to inform our thinking about what enables learning and inquiry.

In a project carried out in the previous year, the similarity between the processes in which students and teacher engaged in carrying out their various inquiries and the processes involved in working on a written composition had been noted by the authors, and had provided the basis for the development of the first draft of a model for conceptualizing an inquiry-based and writing-oriented curriculum (Chang and Wells 1988, in press). In this model (see Figure 5.1) it was suggested that, within an overall theme, groups of students would select topics for systematic inquiry and that such inquiries would typically have three components: "research and inquiry," "composition and construction," and "presentation of outcomes." Each of these would require students to engage in a cyclical and recursive manner in all the major processes

Figure 5.1
Model of a Writing-Oriented Curriculum

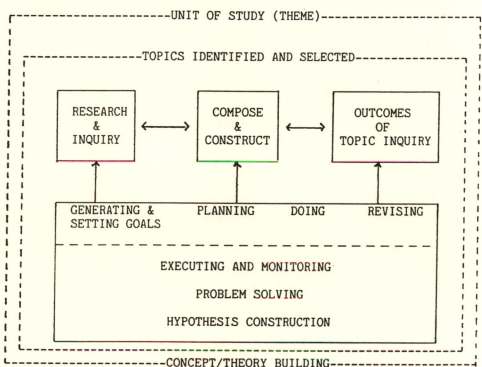

Source: Chang, G. L., and Wells, C. G. "Concepts of literacy and their consequences for children's potential as learners." In *Llengua de l'alumne i llengua de l'escola*, edited by M. Siguan (In press).

involved in writing: "generating and setting goals," "planning," "writing/doing," and "revision." During the present project on animals, the applicability of this model has been further explored by the researchers (Maher 1988) and, simultaneously, the children's attention has been drawn, both implicitly and explicitly, to the intellectual processes they have been engaging in as they pursued their inquiries. For all of us, the analogy has proved illuminating.

Finally, by way of a postscript, we should like to draw the attention of the reader to the cultural and linguistic heritage of the children in this classroom, which included Portuguese, Chinese, Vietnamese, Indian, and Caribbean, among others. By far the majority of the children are learning English as their second language or dialect. The message is therefore clear. Whether in monolingual or multilingual classrooms, equal outcomes for all children can be maximized, regardless of their cultural and linguistic background, by providing collaborative learning opportunities that integrate a wide range of uses of oral and written language. For the success with which children engage in literate thinking depends less on their competence in the specific language or languages they know than on the ways in which they use their linguistic resources to come to know and to communicate their understanding with others. Where learning is conceptualized in this way, children develop their thinking *and* their language as well.

NOTE

The research on which this paper is based was jointly funded by the Ontario Ministry of Education, under contract, by the Toronto Board of Education and by the Ontario Institute for Studies in Education. However, the views expressed are those of the authors and not necessarily those of the funding agencies.

REFERENCES

Barnes, D. (1969) *Language, the Learner and the School*. Harmondsworth, England: Penguin.

———— (1976) *From Communication to Curriculum*. Harmondsworth, England: Penguin.

Bruner, J. (1972) *The Relevance of Education*. Harmondsworth, England: Penguin.

Bruner, J., and Haste, H. (eds) (1987) *Making Sense: The Child's Construction of the World*. London: Methuen.

Chang, G., and Wells, G. (1988) "The literate potential of collaborative talk." In *Oracy Matters*, edited by M. Maclure, T. Phillips, and A. Wilkinson. Stony Stratford, England. Open University.

———— (in press) "Concepts of literacy and their consequences for children's potential as learners." In *Llengua de l'alumne i llengua de l'ascola*, edited by M. Siguan.

Donaldson, M. (1978) *Children's Minds*. London: Fontana.

Ferreiro, E. (1986) "The interplay between information and assimilation in beginning literacy." In *Emergent Literacy: Writing and Reading*, edited by W. Teale and E. Sulzby. Norwood, NJ: Ablex.

Ferreiro, E., and Teberosky, A. (1982) *Literacy before Schooling*. Exeter. NH: Heineman Educational Books.

Goodman, Y. (1980) "The roots of literacy." *Claremont Reading Conference Yearbook* 44:1–32.

Goody, J. (1977) *The Domestication of the Savage Mind*. Cambridge: Cambridge University Press.

Heath, S. (1986) "Sociocultural contexts of language development." In *Beyond Language: Social and Cultural Factors in Schooling Language Minority Students*. Los Angeles, CA: State University at Los Angeles.

Langer, J. (1987) "A sociocognitive perspective on literacy." In *Language, Literacy and Culture: Issues of Society and Schooling*, edited by J. Langer. Norwood, NJ: Ablex.

Maher, A. (1988) "Improving opportunities for literacy through teacher–researcher collaboration." Paper presented at the International Reading Association Convention, Toronto.

Mead, G. (1934) *Mind, Self and Society*. Chicago, IL: University of Chicago Press.

Mehan, H. (1979) *Learning Lessons: Social Organization in the Classroom.* Cambridge, MA: Harvard University Press.

Morrison, K. (1987) "Stabilizing the text: The institutionalization of knowledge in historical and philosophic forms of argument." *Canadian Journal of Sociology* 12:242–74.

Olson, D. (1980) "On the language and authority of textbooks." *Journal of Communication* 30:186–96.

Piaget, J. (1977) *The Development of Thought: Equilibration of Cognitive Structures.* New York: Viking.

Scardimalia, M., and Bereiter, C. (1985) "Development of dialectical processes in composition." In *Literacy, Language and Learning: The Nature and Consequences of Reading and Writing,* edited by D. Olson, N. Torrance, and A. Hildyard. Cambridge: Cambridge University Press.

Sharan, S., and Sharan, Y. (1976) *Small Group Teaching.* Englewood Cliffs, NJ: Educational Technology Publications.

Sinclair, J. McH., and Coulthard, R. (1975) *Towards an Analysis of Discourse: The English Used by Teachers and Pupils.* London: Oxford University Press.

Teale, W. (1986) "Home background and young children's literacy development." In *Emergent Literacy: Writing and Reading,* edited by W. Teale and E. Sulzby. Norwood, NJ: Ablex.

Vygotsky, L. (1978) *Mind in Society,* edited by M. Cole, J. Steiner, S. Scribner, and E. Souberman. Cambridge, MA: Harvard University Press.

Wells, G. (1986) *The Meaning Makers: Children Learning Language and Using Language to Learn.* Portsmouth, NH: Heineman Educational Books.

———— (1987) "Apprenticeship in literacy." *Interchange* 18:109–23.

6
Cooperative Learning and Students' Academic Achievement, Process Skills, Learning Environment, and Self-Esteem in Tenth-Grade Biology Classrooms

REUVEN LAZAROWITZ
AND GABBY KARSENTY

The need to improve methods of instruction to promote higher levels of academic achievement is one of the primary goals of curriculum development today. In the past two decades, emphasis has been placed on improving the level and content of textbooks by employing an inquiry approach to the study of science in high schools so students would acquire scientific knowledge and investigative skills (Mid-Continent 1969; Schwalb 1963). However, the emphasis in this latter work was on the cognitive domain exclusively. Subsequent approaches to the development of science curricula afford the student's learning behavior a more prominent role, and instructional methods seek to have students engage in the active pursuit of knowledge rather than having it presented to them verbally or through demonstration by the instructor. Such pursuit of knowledge should bear some of the critical features of true scientific investigation, such as the identification of research problems, the formulation of hypotheses, the systematic collection and organization of data, the interpretation of data, and drawing conclusions. Moreover, the discussion of the data among students should lead to the formulation of a new problem (Shulman and Tamir 1973). Even these advances concentrate on students' cognitive functioning and ignore their social and practical needs. More recently suggestions have appeared that strive to integrate a social with a science curriculum for study in high schools or that involve the students in selecting science topics of their choice (Baird, Lazarowitz, and Allman, 1984; Entwistle and Duckworth 1977; Hofstein and Yager 1982; Lazarowitz, Baird, and Allman 1985a; Lazarowitz and Hertz-Lazarowitz 1979; Tamir 1975; Yungwirth 1973).

It is generally acknowledged that, in addition to inappropriate curricular materials, low motivation to learn, low self-esteem, and a competitive classroom environment also contribute to low academic achievement. The goals of the present study were to develop and implement a learning unit in biology using a cooperative learning approach that combines peer tutoring with small investigative groups (PTSIG). The PTSIG method is a combination of jigsaw (Aronson et al. 1978), and group investigation (Sharan and Hertz-Lazarowitz 1980; Sharan and Sharan 1976). Cooperative learning in small groups encourages students to help one another and relate to one another as equals. The social interaction that occurs during the process of cooperative learning can exert positive effects on students' motivation to learn, on their self-esteem, and on the students' perception of their classroom environment as well (Sharan 1980; Slavin 1983).

Only a few studies have been reported thus far that employed a cooperative learning approach to the study of science in high schools. Generally the results have been encouraging (Humphreys, Johnson, and Johnson 1982; Lazarowitz, Hertz-Lazarowitz, and Jenkins 1985). We predict that students who study biology in cooperative small groups will demonstrate higher levels of academic achievement as well as improved inquiry skills and a higher level of self-esteem. These outcomes can be understood as resulting from greater student involvement in learning, a heightened sense of personal responsibility for learning, and the mutual assistance they experience during the process of learning as compared with their peers who study in classes conducted with the traditional whole-class method. In the present study, the traditional method for teaching biology, known as the classroom-laboratory mode of instruction (CLMI), constituted a second treatment. Thus, two instructional methods, PTSIG and CLMI, formed the independent variable in the experiment reported here.

The dependent variables evaluated in this study were academic achievement in biology, students' inquiry skills, perceptions of classroom environment, and students' self-esteem. The fundamental importance of process or inquiry skills for all citizens living in a science- and technology-oriented society have been pointed out by many educators (Bruner 1961; Schwalb 1963). Students' self-esteem has often been cited as critical for enhancing motivation to learn as well as for personality development (Aronson et al. 1978; Bloom 1975). Finally, students' perceptions of the classroom learning environment mirror the nature of peer relations and of teacher–student relations in the class, as well as reflecting the effects on the students of the methods and materials of instruction (Walberg 1969). These latter factors also appear to exert an impact on learning and learning outcomes (Fraser 1986a, 1986b; Hofstein, Yager, and Walberg 1982).

Process skills. Inquiry skills appear to help learners make decisions, to understand the nature of science, to become acquainted with the work of scientists and to develop logical thinking (Padila 1980; Tamir 1984).

According to Lawson, Nordland, and Devito (1975) and Tobin and Capie (1982), there is a positive correlation between formal reasoning and achievement on inquiry skills. Johnson (1976) found that students perceived inquiry-oriented science classes as more cooperative than classes where only textbooks were used. Students preferred cooperative science classes as settings for learning, and while students generally perceived school as a competitive enterprise, they still would prefer schools to be more cooperative. An inquiry approach to the study of science should show some kind of cooperation in the classroom or in laboratory work (Johnson 1976). This assumption is supported by Haukoos and Penick (1983), who reported that in classrooms that were characterized by an inquiry mode of learning, student interaction, and cooperation, the students demonstrated a higher level of achievement and their inquiry skills were better than those of pupils in other classrooms. In other studies it was found that where a cooperative mode of learning is combined with learning material that enables an inquiry approach, students' achievement is higher than those in the control group (Lazarowitz, Hertz-Lazarowitz, and Jenkins 1985). High school chemistry students who studied in small groups using an inquiry approach improved problem-solving skills (Ztadok 1983). Based on the above findings, it can by hypothesized that process-inquiry skills will be improved by small-group interaction.

Learning environment refers to the social aspects of the classroom and school where the learning process occurs, to the relations among teachers and among students, and between teachers and students. Thus, the learning environment refers to the social, affective, and learning facets of the classroom and has a reciprocal impact on academic achievement, motivation, and students' attitudes toward learning, subject matter, the classroom, school, and teachers (Hofstein et al. 1980; Hofstein, Yager, and Walberg 1982; Slavin, Madden, and Leavey 1982; Chavez 1984; Fraser 1981, 1986a, 1986b; Hofstein and Lazarowitz 1986). The classroom learning environment relates to students' achievement (Walberg and Anderson 1968), to students' affective acclimatization (Johnson and Johnson 1974), and to students' interest in learning (Walberg 1969). In the biology, chemistry, and physics classrooms, a strong relationship has been found between the learning environment and students' interest in those subjects. Moreover, this relationship was found to be stable over a long period of time (Lawrenz 1976, 1977; Hofstein and Ben-Zvi 1980). It is of interest to mention that the inquiry learning approach in science was perceived by students as creating a cooperative atmosphere in their classrooms (Johnson 1976; Lawrenz 1977; Hofstein and Lazarowitz 1986).

The learning environment of biology classrooms seems to be related to school educational policy and values (Sharan and Yaakobi 1981). On the other hand, cooperative learning contributed to positive social relationships among students (Johnson and Johnson 1974; Johnson 1976).

In high school biology it has been found that cooperative learning influenced three aspects of learning environment: positive attitudes toward science, students' cooperation, and active involvement in learning (Lazarowitz, Hertz-Lazarowitz, and Jenkins 1985: 241). Finally, it can be said that the learning environment is related to academic achievement, motivation to learn, and readiness to continue to study. The inquiry method had an impact on students' perception of the classroom climate, which was seen as more cooperative. The cooperative methods also contribute to positive social relations, which in turn enlarge the friendship circle among the heterogeneous population of students. The cooperative approach enables students to see common goals as their objectives in the learning process.

Self-esteem. The concept of self-esteem was defined by Aronson et al. (1978) as individual self-perception of attitudes, abilities, and assumptions held, which direct all the behaviors of a person. Researchers assert that cooperative learning may influence positively students' self-esteem, but research findings are not unequivocal. Improvement on social relations in the class and improvement on achievement have been found to increase students' self-esteem (Slavin 1980). When the cooperative mode of instruction was implemented in some studies, students' self-esteem improved (Johnson, Johnson, and Scott 1978; Slavin, Madden, and Leavey 1982; Lazarowitz, Hertz-Lazarowitz, and Jenkins 1985). However, DeVries and Slavin (1978) reported that students' self-esteem improved but not their learning self-esteem. According to Slavin (1983), the impact of the cooperative approach on students' self-esteem may last a short time, and depends on the way in which it was obtained. It is very difficult to expect such changes in a short time, and there is probably a need for prolonged treatment in order for the cooperative approach to have a positive impact on students' self-esteem.

RESEARCH DESIGN

Subjects. The subjects were 708 students from tenth-grade classrooms in ten schools. The experimental group consisted of 482 students in 19 classes—133 boys and 349 girls. The control group consisted of 226 students in ten classes—88 boys and 138 girls. Both groups studied photosynthesis from the BSCS Yellow Version (1975). The BSCS learning material advocates an inquiry approach as a mode of instruction, emphasizing the teaching of principles and concepts in science. Both groups made considerable use of laboratory experiments conducted by trained biology teachers in the BSCS approach. The experimental classes were instructed using a cooperative approach (peer tutoring in small investigative groups [PTSIG]), and the control group studied with the traditional classroom-laboratory method.

Schools. Two types of schools participated in the study: (a) urban schools, where students' parents were either factory workers or professionals; (b) rural schools, where most of the students' parents were farmers or lived in small towns.

Teacher sample. Seventeen high school biology teachers taught in the 19 experimental classes and ten in the ten control classes. All teachers had academic degrees (60 percent a BSc and 40 percent an MSc in biology), and 95 percent possessed a high school certificate of teaching. Their age ranged from 26 to 60 years, with a median of 35. Their range of teaching experience was from 3 to 40 years with a median of 7 years. These characteristics were equally distributed among teachers of both the experimental and control groups. All teachers participated in an eight-hour workshop in which they were trained in the cooperative method of instruction. Classrooms were assigned to either the control or the experimental group, in keeping with teachers' wishes. During the study, all teachers were visited every week by the investigators, who were also available upon request for consultation and clarification of problems.

The teachers' workshop included the following activities: (1) how to guide small group instruction, as suggested by Sharan and Hertz-Lazarowitz (1982); (2) performing games in which participants are encouraged to participate in a group discussion; (3) performing games in which speaking privileges were equally divided among group members; (4) getting acquainted with the role of group leader; (5) teacher behaviors related to class discipline and group problems; (6) how to construct small groups and to organize their learning; (7) learning about small cooperative group instruction in general and about PTSIG in particular; (8) listening to experts lecture; (9) experience in peer-tutoring in small investigative groups in which teachers performed a part of the learning unit in photosynthesis and became acquainted with the entire unit.

The learning material. The learning unit in photosynthesis was selected for several reasons. The content can be divided into independent subunits, so each subunit can be studied by a group member. This is a condition for selecting a topic for the cooperative approach (Aronson et al. 1978). Also, photosynthesis is important since it represents the process by which inorganic materials such as CO_2 and H_2O are bound into organic materials while the light provides the energy needed by the process. This energy is bound to the sugars that are the final product of the process, which occurs in the chlorophyll sites of the green plants. Thus, this is the link between the inorganic world and the biome.

Learning process. At the beginning of the study, a general outline of the learning material was presented to both groups by the teachers in a short lecture about the subject, and by using a 15-minute film about photosynthesis. This introduction served as an advanced organizer for all students. Then each group studied the subject according to the treatment to which it was assigned.

The experimental group. 1. The learning material was divided into the following five subunits: (a) The importance of green plants (an ecological approach); (b) the anatomical structure of the leaves; (c) chlorophyll, light, and photosynthesis; (d) the exchange of gases between the plant and the environment ($CO_2 + O_2$); (e) the chemical reactions that occur in the process of photosynthesis. Each subunit can be studied independently, but they vary in difficulty, the first two subunits being less demanding.

2. Each jigsaw group consisted of five students on a heterogeneous basis regarding gender and ability. Then each student received a different subunit to study. The teacher took care that every member of a group received a subunit

with which the learner would be able to cope. Distribution of the subunits to the students was directed by the teachers in order to match students' ability and learning task difficulty.

3. Each student then read to the other members of the jigsaw group the title of the subunit assigned to him or her, so all the group members became acquainted with the sequence of the learning material.

4. In this step, peers from different jigsaw groups who received the same subunit formed the counterpart or the specialists' group, consisting of five members. Their role was to study together the subject assigned to them.

5. The counterpart group conducted its study by means of an inquiry process (Schwalb 1963). The learning activities included readings, identifying problems to be investigated, performing experiments, collecting data, and arranging data results in tables and graphs. They explained and identified concepts and principles, and answered questions directed to them in the study materials. They then analyzed and discussed the experiments' results, making inferences and reaching conclusions.

6. The next step in the counterpart group, following the above activities, consisted of a group consultation regarding the points to be emphasized, how, and to what extent, in order to teach their jigsaw group peers when they returned to their original groups.

7. After making all these decisions (see 6), the counterpart group members checked each other for mastery of the learning subunit and how well each one was prepared for tutoring others, and made final decisions as to the method and materials needed in order to be able to teach.

8. Finally, following steps 5, 6, and 7, the counterpart group members returned to their original jigsaw groups for peer-tutoring.

9. In the jigsaw group, each member taught his/her part as it was studied in the counterpart group, so everyone served as a source of knowledge, while the group leader allocated to each student the necessary time for completing his/her task and for others to ask questions in order to clarify specific issues. That way, every group member had a feeling of contributing and participating in the group learning process.

10. To summarize the groups' activities: In the counterpart group, students investigated and learned the subject by seeking knowledge in an inquiry mode, performing experiments, and collecting data. In the jigsaw group the learning process was based on discussion in which students reported about their subject and experiments. They presented their group with data, tables, and graphs and raised questions; they guided the discussions in order to stimulate thinking and critiques.

11. Following the jigsaw peer-tutoring group, a mutual checking activity occurred, to see how well the group members understood and mastered the learning material. Each student tested the others regarding the subunit taught by him/her. Everyone knew that these activities would be followed by a test.

Hence, they wanted to be sure that the part for which he or she was responsible was taught well and that the rest of the group actually mastered the subject.

12. The topic of photosynthesis was divided into five subunits. Two tests were administered, the first one following the study of the first three subunits, and the second one at the end, covering the information provided in the fourth and fifth subunits only.

If every student performed at least one experiment in the counterpart group, he/she was allowed to present in the jigsaw group only the experiment performed, including the results, tables, and graphs, but not to perform it again.

Thus, students studied the subject in four ways: (1) everyone studied the subject individually, by reading and performing experiments in a group; (2) group discussion as to how to teach the subject, what to emphasize, how to overcome difficult issues, and how to present results, *et cetera;* (3) teaching his/her part in the jigsaw group; (4) self and mutual checking as to how well they mastered the subject and were prepared to teach (this activity being performed in the counterpart group), and how well they were prepared for the final test (in the jigsaw group).

As can be seen, every student went through a fourfold repetition, making sure that they mastered the learning material. It was assumed that these activities, in which everyone had to contribute and everyone's achievement depended upon how well one tutored the others, would generate a high level of responsibility for studying the material since all groupmates were dependent upon one another. The method was designed to promote cooperation and helping behavior among peers. Thus, one may assume that responsibility for one's own and for others' learning, mutual help, interdependence, and contribution to the group, are skills that can promote student self-esteem and positive feelings about the subject, classroom, teachers, peers, and school, and which can motivate learning for greater achievement.

The mode of instruction in the control group. The control group studied the same subject matter, photosynthesis, in a traditional classroom instruction-laboratory work setting, in which the material was presented to students by the teachers in a frontal approach. The teachers led the classroom discussion and introduced the subject to be investigated in the laboratory. While guided inquiry was widely used by the teachers, the main interaction was between teachers and students, rather than between the study materials and the students and among the students, as it was in the PTSIG. Learning pace was dictated by the teachers, as they went through the material and decided when an experiment was to be performed, when questions were to be answered, and tests were to be administered. It was the student's responsibility to master the subject and to be ready for a quiz. A competitive learning climate dominated these classrooms and every student worked alone during the learning process.

The topic of photosynthesis was taught to all classes with an emphasis on the existence of an ecological system that includes the physical-inorganic environment and the entire biome (plants, animals, microorganisms, etc.). The period of study was identical in both groups (three months, three periods per week, each period lasting for 50 minutes. Two additional weeks were used for testing, one test at the beginning and one at the end). Both groups used the same text, the BSCS Yellow Version (*An Inquiry into Life,* 1975). However, the experimental group received worksheets that directed them to a cooperative approach to learning as was described above. Both groups were visited weekly by the investigator or research assistants, who assisted the teachers and made sure they followed the methods of instruction as planned.

MEASURES

Pre-test on prior knowledge in biology. This test included three parts: (a) ten questions related to general knowledge in biology; (b) ten questions on learning material studied in the past, and which was prerequisite knowledge needed to study photosynthesis; and (c) ten questions related to the photosynthesis subject itself to learn if students had prior information on the subject to be studied. All questions were presented in a multiple-choice format, and were selected from BSCS (1968). The test was administered in order to assess students' entering behavior. The content validity of the test was ascertained by the BSCS developers, and a Cronbach alpha reliability of .88 was obtained from the analysis of students' answers in this study ($n = 708$).

Achievement tests on photosynthesis. Two post-tests were administered: Test 1 followed the completion of subunits 1, 2, and 3; Test 2 was administered at the end of the study (after subunits 4 and 5). Each test consisted of multiple-choice questions (BSCS 1968). Test 1 was related to the first three topics learned, and Test 2 included questions about the last two topics. Both tests have content validity established by the BSCS developers, as well as by a group of five high school biology teachers in Israel. A level of 85 percent of inter-judge reliability was reached among the biology teachers regarding content validity of the test. Based on students' answers ($n = 708$), the tests received Chronbach alpha reliabilities of 87 for Test 1 and .77 for Test 2.

Biology Test of Science Processes (BTSP). This test was developed by Royce (1979) and translated into Hebrew. It consists of 48 multiple-choice questions with five items each. The questions are related to the following nine science process skills representing nine subscales: measurement, classification, graph communication, interpreting data, prediction, evaluating hypotheses, controlling variables, selecting useful data, and designing an experiment. These skills can be considered as inquiry skills as well. Content validity was obtained by a group of five high school biology teachers who suggested language changes and adaptations to the curriculum taught in high school science in general. The reliability of the test and its nine subscales was obtained based on students' answers ($n = 708$), and a Cronbach's alpha value of .78 was obtained for the

Table 6.1
BTSP Subscales, Number of Items, Description of the Subscales, and Alpha Cronbach Values

Subscales	Description	No. of items	Alpha Cronbach
1. Measurement	Length, Weight Volume, Temperature	8	.76
2. Classification	Levels of Classification in Biology, Insects	6	.75
3. Graph communication	Graph reading	4	.77
4. Interpreting data	Selection of correct description of the graph	6	.75
5. Prediction	Ability to predict the results of an experiment	6	.75
6. Evaluating hypotheses	Rejection or acceptance of hypothesis	6	.76
7. Controlling variables	Identification of the experiment variables	4	.76
8. Data selection	Ability to infer what data to seek in an investigation	4	.77
9. Designing an experiment	Designing an experiment to test a hypothesis	4	.78

Table 6.2
Learning Environment Inventory Factors, Description, Number of Items, and Alpha Cronbach Reliability Values

Factors	Description*	No. of items in each factor	Alpha Cronbach Values
1. Cooperation	Students' perception of mutual assistance among peers in the class	9	.67
2. Satisfaction	Perception of peers' satisfaction with studies in the class	3	.71
3. Cohesiveness	Perception of friendly relations among classmates and degree of acquaintance with each other	5	.71
4. Cliqueness	Perception of class as consisting of closed circles of students	3	.73

5. Favouritisim	Perception of differential treatment of students by teachers	5	.70
6. Difficulty	Perception of students' ability to cope with classroom studies	5	.70
7. Competition	Perception of degree of competition for achievement and recognition by the teacher	6	.69
8. Apathy	Perception of extent to which peers care about academic and social aspects of classroom life	5	.68
9. Disorganization	Perception of extent to which classroom studies are orderly and planned	4	.70

*Description of the factors from Sharan and Yaakobi (1981).

entire test. Test question descriptions and Cronbach's alpha reliability values for the nine subscales are displayed in Table 6.1.

Learning Environment Inventory (LEI). The LEI was developed by Walberg and Anderson (1968) and used in science classrooms by Lawrenz (1976), Hofstein et al. (1980), Sharan and Yaakobi (1981), Fraser (1986b), and Hofstein and Lazarowitz (1986). This questionnaire uses a four-point Likert scale on all questions. In our study, the Hebrew translation made by Sharan and Yaakobi (1981) was used. By factor analysis, Sharan and Yaakobi (1981) identified nine factors: cooperation, satisfaction, cohesiveness, "cliqueness," favouritism, difficulty, competition, apathy, and disorganization. In her study, Lawrenz (1977) found that the test results were very consistent when the LEI was administered three times sequentially. Data obtained in this study yielded a Cronbach alpha reliability of .72 for the entire test. Test description of the nine factors identified by Sharan and Yaakobi (1981) and Cronbach alpha reliabilities for the test subscales obtained in this study with 708 students, appear in Table 6.2.

Self-esteem. Self-esteem was assessed by a questionnaire constructed from five items developed by Aronson et al. (1978) and five by Offer (1969). While eight questions were related to the students' self-esteem connected with the classroom climate, two questions reflected students' self-esteem in relation to the learning process. This test was used by Lazarowitz, Hertz-Lazarowitz, and Jenkins (1985) and was found as adequate for tenth-graders. Content validity was judged by five high school biology teachers. The test uses a scale of seven intervals from "strongly agree" to "strongly disagree." Data collected from the 708 students yielded a Cronbach alpha reliability value of .83.

METHOD

Research Procedure

The research design followed Campbell and Stanley's (1966) model in which experimental and control groups participate; both groups are pre-tested on the dependent variables, followed by a treatment given to the experimental group; and finally both groups are assessed for the dependent variables in the post-test. This model is presented in Table 6.3.

The model raises several problems: (1) The fact that the groups were not randomly selected (teachers' willingness to participate in this study was the deciding factor for classrooms' participation in either treatment group) may be a cause for differences in entry behavior found between students who belonged to the different groups. Thus, if the scores of the experimental group students were higher on the dependent variables at the beginning of the study, it is possible that a "ceiling effect" could occur on achievement scores at the end of the study. This effect, as well as students' socioeconomic and other uncontrolled factors, could distort the results from the impact of the treatment. Consequently, it was decided to treat the data with an analysis of covariance, where the pre-test scores served as covariates, in order to control statistically for var-

Table 6.3
Research Design Model

Pre-test	Treatment	Post-test
Both groups	Mode of learning "Photosynthesis"	Both groups
1. Pre knowledge in Biology	Experimental group: Peer tutoring in small investigative groups.	Test 1 and Test 2 in Photosynthesis
2. BTSP	Control group: Classroom-laboratory frontal-instruction.	BTSP
3. LEI		LEI
4. Self esteem		Self esteem

iation in students' initial level of knowledge. We were aware of the fact that while this analysis does not overcome the problem of the nonrandom assignment to treatments, it is the best approach available under the circumstances.

RESULTS

Students' Entry Behavior in Biology, Mathematics, and English

Scores on these subjects obtained from the previous semester were provided by the teachers for both groups, in order to compare students' entry behavior in the study. Table 6.4 displays two-way analyses of variance of the mean scores of the experimental and control groups and standard deviations in entry behavior in biology, mathematics, and English, and pre-test results on biology by groups and gender.

The results presented in Table 6.4 show that students' entry behavior in all subjects of both groups was equal and no significant differences were found between students in the two treatment groups, and no interaction was found between groups and gender. The low range of students' scores (51–55 points) on the pre-test of knowledge in biology (some questions were related to students' prior knowledge in photosynthesis) clearly indicated that their information on the subject to be studied in the experiment was minimal. These findings allowed us to assume that any knowledge of photosynthesis found in the study could be attributed to the treatment.

Students' Achievement

Students' mean scores on photosynthesis were categorized by treatment, Test 1, Test 2, and total score, and by type of school and gender. Data collected in the middle of the study and at the end were treated by an analysis of variance and two-way analysis of variance. The mean scores, standard deviations, and *F*-values are presented in Table 6.5.

In Table 6.5 one can see that the experimental group achieved significantly

Table 6.4

Means, Standard Deviations, and F-Values of Students' Scores on Entry Behavior Test in Biology, by Group and Gender

	Experimental group (N=482) X (SD)		Control group (N=226) X (SD)		F-Values
Entry Behavior In Biology		72.91 (12.61)		69.87 (13.50)	n.s.
Pre-test in Biology		54.63 (14.50)		53.70 (13.00)	n.s.
Mathematics		67.91 (15.18)		67.99 (15.38)	n.s.
English		70.47 (12.78)		68.58 (14.18)	n.s.
Pre-test in Biology	Boys (N=133)	53.58 (11.40)	(N=88)	55.45 (11.40)	Groups (A) = n.s.
	Girls (N=349)	54.46 (16.30)	(N=138)	51.54 (14.90)	Gender (B) = n.s.
					A X B = n.s.

SD = standard deviations
n.s. = non-significant

136

Table 6.5

Means, Standard Deviations, and F-Values of Students' Achievement Scores in Photosynthesis, by Group, Type of School, and Gender

	Experimental group (N=482) X (SD)		Control group (N=226) X (SD)		F-Values
Test 1	74.70 (13.53)		69.68 (16.68)		2.28**
Test 2	83.23 (7.60)		73.21 (18.30)		4.09**
Test 1 + Test 2	78.96 (17.88)		71.44 (14.86)		7.75**
Type of School					
Test 1 + Test 2					
Urban					
Boys (N=110)	81.36 (13.60)	(N=65)	68.22 (14.70)		groups (A) = 8.57*
Girls (N=300)	80.76 (15.80)	(N=103)	66.76 (11.90)		gender (B) = n.s.
					A X B = n.s.
Rural					
Boys (N=23)	75.00 (11.80)	(N=23)	64.65 (14.10)		groups (A) = 4.16**
Girls (N=49)	72.65 (15.00)	(N=35)	65.09 (10.90)		gender (B) = n.s.
					A X B = n.s.

* p < .01
** p < .05

Table 6.6
Students' Achievement on the Process Skills (MANCOVA, Adjusted Mean Scores, and F-Values)

| Sub-scales | Experimental group | | Control group | | F-Values | | |
	Boys (N=133) X*	Girls (N=349) X*	Boys (N=88) X*	Girls (N=138) X*	groups(A)	gender(B)	A X B
Measurement	97.00	92.39	86.84	86.65	16.38*	n.s.	n.s.
Classification	66.73	64.07	63.74	62.95	n.s.	n.s.	n.s.
Graph communication	74.51	73.60	65.27	67.36	13.46*	n.s.	n.s.
Interpreting data	78.31	79.35	68.57	73.92	9.44**	n.s.	3.9**

138

Prediction	68.65	69.90	66.60	67.10	n.s.	n.s.	n.s.
Evaluating hypotheses	64.38	64.49	64.06	64.26	n.s.	n.s.	n.s.
Controlling variables	65.40	64.54	65.31	65.50	n.s.	n.s.	n.s.
Data selection	58.33	58.90	62.79	59.90	n.s.	n.s.	n.s.
Designing an experiment	52.40	57.27	48.81	45.82	12.26*	n.s.	n.s.
Total test	63.06	66.71	58.52	59.88	7.04**	n.s.	n.s.

* $p < .01$
** $p < .05$
X* adjusted mean

higher scores in Test 1, Test 2, and on the combined scores. These differences were consistent regardless of the type of school (urban and rural). While differences in gender were not observed within the groups, they were significantly higher between the groups. Some pattern was found regarding type of school, where both boys and girls from the experimental group in both types of school performed significantly higher than their counterparts. No interaction was found between groups and gender.

Process Skills

Students' mean scores on the pre- and post-test on process skills were treated with a MANCOVA for both groups and by gender. The pre-test scores of both groups served as covariates and the adjusted means and F-values are displayed in Table 6.6.

The results in Table 6.6 indicate that the experimental group achieved significantly higher scores in the following four process skills: measurement, graph communication, interpreting data, designing an experiment, and in the total test scores. There were no significant differences between boys and girls within the groups, and no interaction was found between groups and gender in general, except on the subscale interpreting data.

Classroom Environment

Students' scores on the learning environment inventory from the pre- and post-test of both groups were treated by an analysis of covariance while pre-test scores served as covariates. The adjusted mean scores and F-values are presented in Table 6.7.

The results in Table 6.7 show significant differences between the experimental and control groups, where the former reported experiencing more cooperation and cohesiveness in their classrooms, and feeling more satisfied than the latter. Furthermore, the experimental group reported that their learning material was less difficult, their classes were less competitive and disorganized, there was less favoritism in their classes, and less apathy and cliqueness among their peers. No differences were found between boys' and girls' mean scores on any of the nine subscales.

Finally, the mean scores on the pre- and post-test on the self-esteem questionnaire are presented in Table 6.8. Data were treated by analysis of covariance with treatments and gender as between group variables.

It can be seen from Table 6.8 that, in general, the experimental group expressed a higher level of self-esteem than the control group. It is important to mention that in the cooperative mode of instruction girls emerged with higher self-esteem at the end of the study than their male counterparts, showing a higher net gain, while the girls in the control group who studied in a competitive climate expressed lower self-esteem than the boys in their group and the

Table 6.7
Learning Environment Inventory Subscales (Analysis of Covariance, Adjusted Mean Scores, and F-Values)

Sub-scales	Experimental group (N=482) X*	Control group (N=226) X*	F-Values
1. Cooperation	2.31	2.24	6.54**
2. Satisfaction	2.70	2.60	6.10**
3. Cohesiveness	2.40	2.31	7.36**
4. Cliqueness	2.26	2.47	3.47**
5. Favouritism	2.07	2.20	16.60*
6. Difficulty	2.12	2.25	19.30*
7. Competition	2.20	2.36	22.10*
8. Apathy	2.28	2.35	5.91**
9. Disorganization	2.14	2.30	27.90*

* $p < .01$
** $p < .05$
X* adjusted mean

girls in the experimental group. Thus, the results show significant differences between the groups, no main effect for gender, but a high interaction between groups and gender.

DISCUSSION

The goals of the study were to assess the impact of a cooperative mode of learning and instruction on tenth-grade biology students' achievement, process skills, their perception of the learning environment, and their self-esteem. The discussion will relate separately to each dependent variable, and it will consider also some teachers' views about cooperative learning as well as students' written comments about their experience while learning in small investigative groups.

Achievement in Biology

All students were pre-tested on their knowledge about general biology and specific information related to the subject to be learned. Since no significant

Table 6.8
Analysis of Covariance of the Mean Scores on the Self-Esteem of Tenth-Grade Biology Students, by Group and Gender

Groups (A)	Experimental		Control	
Gender (B)	Boys (N=133) X (SD)	Girls (N=349) X (SD)	Boys (N=88) X (SD)	Girls (N=138) X (SD)
Pre-test	4.23 (1.17)	4.41 (0.74)	4.54 (0.64)	4.47 (0.54)
Post-test	4.39 (1.21)	4.66 (0.74)	4.63 (0.49)	4.41 (0.51)
Adjusted means	4.58	4.67	4.52	4.37
Net-gain	+0.61	+0.25	+0.09	-0.06

	groups(A)	gender(B)	A X B
F-value	15.62*	n.s.	21.50*

* $p < .01$

differences were found between the experimental and control groups either in biology or in other subject matter, it can be assumed that the knowledge of the two groups at the beginning of the study was equal. This fact may partially overcome the issue of nonrandom selection of the group treatment, and any gain obtained in the study may be attributed to the treatment. The findings of this study clearly show that students who studied in a cooperative approach performed significantly better on Test 1, Test 2, and the combined tests.

Girls did as well as boys within each group treatment, and the differences found were again only between the groups. It appears that cooperative learning promoted conditions that enhanced students' learning by facilitating mutual help and cooperation among group members. These characteristics are well supported by the learning environment findings, which show that in the experimental classes there was a decrease in the competitive atmosphere during the learning process and an increase in cooperation among students. We may also surmise that the learning environment in the cooperative classroom was more flexible than in the frontal classroom, that it facilitated more interaction among students and with teachers, and thereby created a positive learning climate. The findings on the learning environment support this interpretation, since students perceived their classroom climate as positive, and they were more motivated to participate in reaching group goals due to positive attitudes toward the learning process. These features were expressed openly by students in the cooperative classroom. One student told the teacher: "This way of learning is very pleasant and effective and helps us to master the material," and a teacher said, "[T]he students worked nicely, they asked questions and have shown high interest in the learning material."

It seems that learning activities based on group discussion, along with the pupils' personal involvement in the learning process, contributed to their academic achievement. Students emphasized the fact that "the learning material studied that way was much easier and understandable." The small heterogeneous groups offered low-achievement students an opportunity to be helped by high achievers who explained and answered questions raised during the group discussion. Students mentioned the fact that "we checked our answers together and if there was a need we corrected them." It should be remembered also that the PTSIG encouraged students to examine different sources of information, to read, to learn, to prepare the learning material so they would be able to teach it to their peers, to check each other for their knowledge and readiness to teach, as well as asking them to find and to decide about the best ways of teaching. All these activities were aimed at having students rehearse the learning material in a variety of ways. These rehearsals probably helped students to master the learning material more effectively. Similar findings were reported by DeVries, Edwards, and Wells (1974), Johnson, Johnson, and Scott (1978), Sharan et al. (1984), and Lazarowitz, Hertz-Lazarowitz, and Jenkins (1985).

It should be mentioned that student achievement on Test 2 (experimental group) was higher than on Test 1. Test 2 was administered nine weeks after the study began, and students had more time to adjust to this mode of learning. This test dealt with more complex and difficult material. Students commented on this by saying that "this is the first time we are studying in such a way, and since we had more time to experience this method, we achieved more." Other investigators have also noted that students require time to adjust to cooperative learning methods (Slavin 1983).

The fact that no differences were found between girls and boys in the experimental group is encouraging. Cooperative learning seems to promote achievement in science equally well for boys and girls. In a learning environment where girls do not have to compete or to behave according to teachers' and students' social expectations, they are able to fulfill their academic potential. Thus, group instruction can be one of the avenues in which girls reach higher levels of achievement in science (Haukoos and Penick 1983; Lazarowitz, Hertz-Lazarowitz, and Jenkins 1985b).

Process Skills

The findings show that students instructed in PTSIG performed better in the following skills: measurement, graph communication, interpreting data, and designing an experiment, and on the total test. Although students in the experimental group did better than the control group, still there were some skills in which they achieved lower than 60 on a scale from 1 to 100. While these students' performance was better than those in the control group, their performance on questions about prediction, evaluating hypotheses, controlling variables, and data selection was not significantly different from that of peers in the control group. We do not have data here to explain why this occurred. We can only conclude that while cooperative learning positively affected the acquisition of some skills, its effect was less powerful on other skills. The process learning in the cooperative method required students to take measurements, to communicate and read about graphs, to interpret data, and to design experiments. Consequently, these skills were enhanced by exchanging ideas and cooperative discussion held by students in the group. Such strategies are not generally used in the frontal classroom approach, which may explain the difference between pupils' achievement in two groups. Students who studied chemistry in small groups were also found to achieve higher scores on some inquiry skills than students in the control groups (Ztadok 1983; Cohen 1987).

Learning Environment

Students in the experimental group perceived the learning environment as more cooperative and expressed more satisfaction. They perceived their learning material as less difficult, and their classrooms as less competitive. They expressed less apathy toward all aspects of the learning process, classroom, teachers, and school, and found more cohesiveness and less cliqueness in their classrooms. In their opinion, teachers displayed less favoritism in the cooperation classroom. Despite the fact that students in the cooperative classes had to move from jigsaw groups to the expert groups and back, or they had to seek additional study materials, they did not perceive their classroom situation as less organized. Rather, they perceived the class as a flexible and open situation that provided them with an opportunity for more diversified learning activities.

While findings on learning environment regarding gender were not presented in this study, the girls in the experimental group perceived their classroom as less competitive than did the boys, and in general expressed more positive attitudes toward the method. This evidence can explain the girls' achievement, which was equal to that of the boys'. The cooperative approach seems to create an environment for girls where they did not have to compete with boys. These positive findings can be explained due to the large variety of tasks offered by the method, which allowed students to study at their own pace. It also allowed them to be involved in planning and selecting their learning activities. Cooperative learning required teachers to relate individually and differently to students according to their needs and learning situation. Therefore, students found their learning tasks to be less difficult and more interesting, and perceived their classroom climate as more attractive and democratic. Those perceptions regarding their classroom learning environment were expressed by students in their attitude toward cooperative learning. Similar results were reported by Hofstein,

Gluzman, and Samuel (1979) in chemistry. While no significant differences in learning environment were found between boys and girls in the experimental group, the girls in the control group found their classes to be more competitive than the girls in the experimental one. These differences in the competitive domain may explain girls' relative satisfaction with the cooperative learning method as well as their achievement.

Self-esteem

Students' self-esteem was higher in the experimental group. Girls tended to gain more than boys, although not significantly. These gains in self-esteem can be explained by two factors: (1) students felt that they achieved more by learning through this method; (2) there was an improvement in social relations among students. Students felt responsible for their learning, and therefore they were more active and involved.

The present study appears to support Bloom's (1975) assumption that success and achievement are strongly linked to self-esteem. Small-group instruction encouraged cooperation and mutual help, which in turn had an impact on students' relations. Since every student was responsible for a small part of the learning material and had to teach it to other members of the group, this feeling of having a specific responsible role enhanced students' self-esteem. According to Allen (1976), students go through cognitive and behavior changes when assuming the role of teachers. Those changes are very positive in the high school student population. The small differences in self-esteem found between the groups can be explained by the short time in which students were exposed to the cooperative method, and probably by the self-esteem questionnaire, which might not have been sensitive enough to students' changes. A more specific study in which students' self-esteem is investigated during the cooperative learning process, for a longer time, and which includes a retention aspect, is needed in order to find more conclusive results.

SUMMARY

The four versions in this study were related to three domains: (1) the academic domain, in which academic achievement and process skills were assessed; (2) the learning environment of the classroom, which was investigated through students' perceptions of their learning climate, and (3) the students' self-esteem, as related to their classroom and learning experiences. The results show that academic achievement of students taught in a cooperative setting was superior both statistically and qualitatively, from a pedagogical point of view.

Students from the cooperative classes also achieved higher scores on measures of process skills. Scores on learning environment and self-esteem in the cooperative groups were also significantly higher than in the whole-class method, but they were not of the same magnitude as the scores on academic measures.

The differences between the mean scores of the experimental and control groups on learning environment ranged from .05 to .30 points, and the greatest gap was in the domain of "cliqueness," which was emphasized by students in the control group. The differences in self-esteem were small, too. Thus, the cooperative approach had a greater impact on the academic-cognitive than on the affective domain.

This project was one of the first attempts to implement PTSIG at the high school level in biology. It is difficult to have a significant impact on student learning environment and self-esteem in one experiment of short duration. A similar explanation was provided by Sharan and Yaakobi (1981). Another reason can be the instructional goals of the high school program, which aimed at preparing students for matriculation exams in which academic achievement plays a primary role. It is unreasonable to expect radical changes in the affective domain after one short treatment. In order to expect changes in the learning environment of schools and classrooms and in students' self-esteem, one may assume that more prolonged and extensive interventions are needed. Nevertheless, the significant improvement of students' academic achievement and process skills, as well as of the affective domain, suggests that the cooperative mode of instruction has considerable potential for promoting a better quality of instruction and learning in high schools. Society is concerned about student enrollment in science courses, their attitudes toward school and learning, as well as their achievement in science. Cooperative learning appears to provide a major alternative to the prevailing form of instruction, whose limitations are becoming glaringly apparent.

REFERENCES

Allen, V. (Ed.) (1976) *Children as teachers: Theory and research in tutoring.* New York: Academic Press.

Aronson, E., Stephan, C., Sikes, J., Blaney, N., and Snapp, M. (1978) *The Jigsaw Classroom.* Beverly Hills, CA: Sage Publications.

Baird, J. H., Lazarowitz, R., and Allman, V. (1984) "Science choices and preferences of middle and secondary school students in Utah." *Journal of Research in Science Technology* 21, no. 1:47–54.

Bloom, B. S. (1975) *Human Characteristics and School Learning.* New York: John Wiley and Sons.

Bruner, J. S. (1961) "The art of discovery." *Harvard Educational Review* 31:21–32.

BSCS, Biological Science Curriculum Studies (1968) *Resource Book of Test Items for Biological Science. An Inquiry into Life.* Boulder, CO: Education Programs Improvement Corporation.

BSCS—*Yellow Version* (1975—Israel adaptation) Jerusalem: Israel Center for Science Teaching, The Hebrew University.

Campbell, D., and Stanley, J. (1966) *Experimental and Quasi-Experimental Design for Research.* Chicago, IL: Rand McNally.

Chavez, R. C. (1984) "The use of high inference measures to study classroom climates: A review." *Review of Educational Research* 54:237–61.

Cohen, J. (1987) "The use of different strategies in teaching the subjects, chemical energy and chemical balance. Development, implementation, and evaluation." Ph.D. dissertation, Weizmann Institute of Science, Rehovot, Israel.

DeVries, D. L., Edwards, K. J., and Wells, E. H. (1974) "Team competition effects on classroom group process." Report no. 174b. Baltimore, MD: John Hopkins University, Center for Social Organization of Schools.

DeVries, D., and Slavin, R. (1978) Teams-Games-Tournaments: A research review. *Journal of Research and Development in Education* 12:28–38.

Entwistle, N. J., and Duckworth, D. (1977) "Choice of science courses in secondary school: Trends and explanations." *Studies in Science Education* 4:63–82.

Fraser, B. J. (1981) "Learning environment in curriculum evaluation." *Evaluation in Education: An International Review* (Oxford, Pergamon) Series 5:3–93.

—— (1986a) *Classroom Environment*. London: Croom Helm.

—— (1986b) "Two decades of research on classroom psychosocial environment." In *The Study of Learning Environments,* edited by B. J. Fraser. Salem, OR: Assessment Research.

Haukoos, G. A., and Penick, J. E. (1983) "The influence of classroom climate on science process and content achievement of community college students." *Journal of Research in Science Teaching* 20, no. 7:629–37.

Hofstein, A., and Ben Zvi, R. (1980) "The relationship between students' attitudes and achievement and classroom learning environment." Boston, MA: NARST Symposium.

Hofstein, A., Gluzman, R., and Samuel, D. A. (1979) "Classroom learning environment and students' attitudes toward chemistry." *Studies in Educational Evaluation* 5:231–36.

Hofstein, A., and Lazarowitz, R. (1986) "A comparison of the actual and preferred classroom learning environment in biology and chemistry as perceived by high school students." *Journal of Research in Science Technology* 23, no. 3:189–99.

Hofstein, A., and Yager, R. E. (1982) "Societal issues as organizers for science education in the 80's." *School Science and Mathematics* 82:539–47.

Hofstein, A., Yager, R. E., and Walberg, H. J. (1982) "Science classroom learning environment for improving instruction." *School Science and Mathematics* 4:343–50.

Hofstein, A., Ben Zvi, R., Gluzman, R., and Samuel, D. A. (1980) "Comparative study of chemistry students' perception of the learning environment in high school and vocational schools." *Journal of Research in Science Teaching* 17, no. 6:547–52.

Humphreys, B., Johnson, R. T., and Johnson, D. W. (1982) "Effects of cooperative, competitive and individualistic learning on students' achievement in science class." *Journal of Research in Science Teaching* 19, no. 5:351–56.

Johnson, R. T. (1976) "The relationship between cooperation and inquiry in science classrooms." *Journal of Research in Science Teaching* 13, no. 1:55–63.

Johnson, D. W., and Johnson, R. T. (1974) "Instructional goal structure: Cooperative, competitive, or individualistic." *Review of Educational Research* 44:213–40.

Johnson, D. W., Johnson, R. T., and Scott, R. (1978) "The effects of cooperative and individualized instruction on student attitudes and achievement." *Journal of Social Psychology* 104:207–16.

Johnson, D. W., Johnson, R. T., and Skon, L. (1979) "Student achievement on different types of tasks under cooperative, competitive, and individualistic conditions." *Contemporary Educational Psychology* 4:99–106.

Lawrenz, F. (1976) "Student perception of the classroom learning environment in biology, chemistry, and physics courses." *Journal of Research in Science Teaching* 13:315–23.

——— (1977) "The stability of student perception of the classroom learning environment." *Journal of Research in Science Teaching* 14:77–81.

Lawson, A. E., Nordland, F. H., and Devito, A. (1975) "Relationship of formal reasoning to achievement aptitude in preservice teachers." *Journal of Research in Science Teaching* 12:423–31.

Lazarowitz, R., Baird, H. J., and Allman, V. (1985) "Reasons why elementary and secondary students in Utah do and do not like science." *School Science and Mathematics* 85, no. 8:663–73.

Lazarowitz, R., and Hertz-Lazarowitz, R. (1979) "Choices and preferences of science subjects by junior high school students in Israel." *Journal of Research in Science Teaching* 16, no. 4:317–23.

Lazarowitz, R., Hertz-Lazarowitz, R., and Jenkins, J. (1985) "The effects of modified jigsaw on achievement, classroom social climate and self-esteem in high school science classes." In *Learning to Cooperate, Cooperating to Learn,* edited by R. Slavin et al., pp. 231–53. New York: Plenum.

Mid-Continent Regional Educational Laboratory and Biological Sciences Curriculum Study (1969) "Inquiry objectives for the teaching of biology." Kansas City, MO: Mid-Continent Regional Educational Laboratory.

Offer, D. (1969) *The Psychology of the Teenager.* New York: Basic Books/Harper Torch Book.

Padilla, M. J. (1980) "Science activities for thinking." *School Science and Mathematics* 80:601–8.

Royce, K. C. (1979) "The development and validation of a diagnostic criterion-referenced test of science processes." Ph.D. dissertation. University of Nebraska.

Schwalb, J. H. (1963) *Biology Teachers' Handbook.* New York: John Wiley & Sons.

Sharan, S. (1980) "Cooperative learning in small groups: Recent methods and effects on achievement, attitudes, and ethnic relations." *Review of Educational Research* 50:241–72.

Sharan, S., and Hertz-Lazarowitz, R. (1980) "A group investigation method of cooperative learning in the classroom." In *Cooperation in Education,* edited by S. Sharan et al., pp. 14–46. Provo, UT: Brigham Young University Press.

——— (1982) "Effects of an instructional change program on teachers' behavior, attitudes, and perceptions." *Journal of Applied Behavioral Science* 18, no. 2:185–201.

Sharan, S., and Sharan, Y. (1976) *Small-Group Teaching.* Englewood Cliffs, NJ: Educational Technology Publications.

Sharan, S., and Yaakobi, D. (1981) "Classroom learning environment of city and kibbutz biology classrooms in Israel." *European Journal of Science Education* 3, no. 3:321–28.

Sharan, S., Kussell, P., Hertz-Lazarowitz, R., Bejarano, Y., Raviv, S., and Sharan, Y. (1984) *Cooperative Learning in the Classroom.* Hillsdale, NJ: Lawrence Erlbaum.

Shulman, L. S., and Tamir, P. (1973) "Research on teaching in the natural sciences."

In *Second Handbook of Research on Teaching,* edited by R. M. W. Travers. Chicago, IL: Rand McNally.

Slavin, R. E. (1980) "Cooperative learning." *Review of Educational Research* 50:315–42.

————— (1983) *Cooperative Learning.* New York: Longman.

Slavin, R. E., Madden, N. A., and Leavey, M. (1982) "Combining cooperative learning and individualized instruction: Effects on the social acceptance, achievement, and behavior of mainstreamed students." Paper presented at the annual convention of the American Educational Research Association.

Tamir, P. (1975) "Evaluation, botany and zoology in the frame of biology learnings" (in Hebrew). *Biology Teachers' Leaflet* 45:23–32.

————— (1984) "An inquiry-oriented laboratory examination." *Journal of Educational Measurement* 11:126–36.

Tobin, K., and Capie, W. (1982) "Relationships between formal reasoning ability, locus of control, academic engagement and integrated process skill achievement." *Journal of Research in Science Teaching* 19, no. 2:113–21.

Walberg, H. J. (1969) "Social environment as a mediator of classroom learning." *Journal of Educational Psychology* 60:443–48.

Walberg, H. J., and Anderson, G. (1968) "Classroom climate and individual learning." *Journal of Educational Psychology* 59:414–19.

Yungwirth, E. (1973) "A study of the biological preferences of secondary school students in Israel." *Journal of Biological Education* 7:34–40.

Ztadok, N. (1983) "The evaluation of the subject chemical energy taught in small inquiry groups." MSc thesis, Weizmann Institute of Science, Rehovot, Israel.

7

Team Learning in German Classrooms: Processes and Outcomes

GÜNTER L. HUBER
AND RENATE EPPLER

Cooperation among students has always been an important issue in German pedagogy and didactics, although for very different reasons—ranging from the mere necessity to cope organizationally with the disproportion of the numbers of teachers and students, to educational goals that can only be realized by means of social interaction in classrooms (Meyer 1983). Despite theoretical interest in team learning and teachers' generally high appreciation of this didactic arrangement, learning teams are rare events in the average classroom (Rotering-Steinberg and von Kügelgen 1986). Everyday learning in schools seems to be mainly influenced by individualistic and competitive orientation. Teachers' objections to group activities in their classrooms center around three "detaining D's": delays, deficits (in achievement), and disruptions. However, as our analysis showed, these are no pretentions.

The traditional *Gruppenunterricht* gathers four to six students around one table, with a more or less complex task to solve, but usually without organizationally structuring their activities. Thus students frequently encounter experiences in group dynamics that often interfere with learning. Moreover, students regularly break down their task into less complex parts, and assign them individually to the group members. With this strategy the team makes best use of every team member's specific resources (e.g. reading or arithmetic skills, knowledge) for solving the task. However, this strategy may prevent students from coping with less familiar demands, and from enlarging their individual

Table 7.1
Dimensions of Team Learning

relation evaluation	interdependent	individualistic
interdependent	group-rallye	- (controls)
individualistic	Gruppenunterricht	individual seat-work

resources by learning. The unstructured *Gruppenunterricht* definitively fails necessary conditions for team activities (Slavin 1983).

Studies on team learning could not rely on students' (and teachers') social competencies for creating and maintaining supportive group processes. An analysis of carefully constructed models for structured learning in teams (Sharan and Sharan 1976; Slavin 1980a) suggested a taxonomy of social demands for teams. Though most teachers we asked to participate in our projects were more attracted by team learning models for obtaining or organizing knowledge (e.g., group investigation) than by models for "simple practice" (e.g., teams-games-tournament), we wanted to avoid overdemanding conditions that could spoil their interest. We started to experiment with STAD, which seemed to be a less demanding practice model, continued with jigsaw models for team-based processes of obtaining new information, and began a year ago with organizing learning by group investigation.

STUDY 1: STUDYING MATHEMATICS WITH "GROUP-RALLYE"

Taking into account the poor state of group activities in average classrooms, we decided to begin our field studies on team learning with a well-structured organizational model. This model strives to have students care about each other, and about each member's understanding and learning of subject matter, in contrast to unstructured approaches that invite "taylorism" in groups. Huber, Bogatzki, and Winter (1982) chose the STAD model (Slavin 1978), and introduced it as "group-rallye" to teachers and students.

Design. Following Slavin (1980b) we classified situational determinants for interpersonal processes by means of the following dimensions: (1) type of task, (2) mode of relation (between students), and (3) mode of evaluation/feedback. With condition (1) held constant for all participants, the remaining dimensions suggest a 2×2 design (Table 7.1) of teaching/learning arrangements.

Subjects. According to this design we organized a field study with 371 students in 22 classrooms (seventh grade) of the *Hauptschule* (lowest track of the

Table 7.2
Academic Achievement (Residual Gains)

	group-rallye	G.-Unterricht	ind. seat-work	control
mean	16.6	8.2	2.0	-28.9
sd	43.8	37.7	45.3	44.8

German school system). There were five classrooms in each condition, except for *Gruppenunterricht,* which took place in seven classrooms.

Procedure and materials. The content consisted of exercises in computing with fractions. The learning period lasted for three weeks. In control classes teachers did not teach fractions during this time. For every week the experimental groups received a booklet with tasks, mathematical explanations, hints for solutions, and three different types of advice for activities with teammates or for individualistic learning. At the end of each booklet there was a short achievement test. Feedback of test results was given according to the differing experimental conditions (interdependent/individualistic). Pre- and post-tests were administered one week before and after the learning period. At the same time the experimental classes answered two sociometric questions (preference/rejection of classmates as "co-workers").

Results. An ANOVA revealed significant pre-test differences in computing with fractions between the four conditions of our study. We therefore used the students' residual gain scores (Guthke 1972) for further comparisons. A MANOVA revealed that the group-rallye students achieved the highest gains (see Table 7.2), but their mean score differs significantly only from the means of individual learners and controls (results of Newman-Keuls' Q-test).

From the answers to the sociometric questions we derived the passive preference and rejection status of each student by relating the number of times he/she was named to the total number of positive or active votes in a classroom. Unfortunately pre-test levels of sociometric scores differed between the classrooms, a condition which, in a field study, cannot be remedied by randomization. In addition, an analysis adjusting the (dependent) post-test scores for pre-test differences was also inappropriate because of a lack of the necessary homogeneity of regression ($F = 6.23$; $p < .001$). A comparison of unadjusted means, however, revealed that sociometric choices changed due to interactive processes in the team learning conditions, but remained unchanged in the individualistic conditions (see Figure 7.1).

Discussion. The findings of Study 1 demonstrated the efficiency and practicality of a structured approach to team learning. By referring to these data we could dispel the doubts of many teachers. On the other hand, unexpected side effects in some of the groups aroused some doubts among members of the research team. We conducted individual and group interviews with the members of the most and the least successful teams in every classroom of the group-

Figure 7.1
Social Preference/Rejection

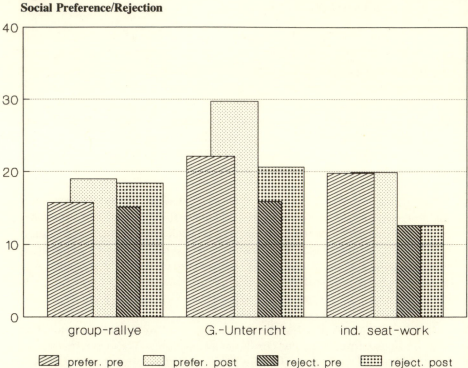

rallye condition. The students gave us important hints about undesirable interpersonal processes during team sessions. Though these critical remarks were few in number compared with the majority of positive comments, they must not be neglected. We need approaches that provide information about the ongoing processes in learning teams. For this purpose observational studies are needed that gather information about the subjective perspective of students.

STUDY 2: READING FOR COMPREHENSION IN JIGSAW CLASSROOMS

A primary purpose of Study 2 was to evaluate generally the jigsaw model (Aronson 1978, 1984; Slavin 1980a) for team learning. A secondary purpose was to evaluate the effects of different modes of feedback. Usually teams receive feedback only with regard to achievement. In this study feedback about achievement for half of the teams was accompanied by feedback about specific aspects of their cooperative processes. However, there is a possibility that the effects of team learning in academic and nonacademic areas are influenced by varying achievement levels and differences in heterogeneity between classrooms in different tracks of the German school system. We therefore included classrooms from two different tracks to answer the following questions:

• Does *jigsaw* learning affect academic and nonacademic variables?
• Which effects are a function of different modes of feedback?
• Do classrooms in *Hauptschule* and *Realschule* (the second track) respond differently to cooperative learning with the jigsaw method?

Design and subjects. Six classrooms (fifth grade) with a total of 131 students participated in this study, two from the *Realschule,* four from the *Hauptschule* of a large school center in southwest Germany. Usually students stay together in the same classroom for most subjects and for many years. Due to the tracking procedure, elementary school classrooms are disbanded after grade 4. Thus grade 5 creates a comparable social situation for all students; they have to establish social relations in their new classrooms. At the beginning of the school year we organized 30 heterogeneous teams that typically had four students per group. The students' personal preferences were considered as far as possible. Half of the teams received feedback about achievement only, the other half also received comments about their group's cooperative processes. Lack of funds prevented us from including control groups.

Procedure and materials. The students spent two weeks with team-building experiences with the jigsaw model (one training session every week). During the following five weeks the teams practiced reading for two hours per week in teams. We prepared texts from their regular reading books according to the specific demands of cooperative learning in the *jigsaw* "basic" teams and "expert" groups.

After each lesson all teams answered questions about the text. The correct individual answers were used to compute a team score for achievement feedback. Half of the teams rated their cooperative process by means of a six-point polarity scale called "Our team." We developed this instrument from students' free descriptions of positive and negative issues in team learning, which we acquired during an earlier pilot study. The scale contains 11 items for rating, for example, "noisy–silent," "friendly–hostile," "hard-working–careless," and so on. From the individual ratings we computed a team score for "process–feedback." We indicated some positive and the three most negative ratings on graph paper. Teams received this information, and were asked to discuss for five minutes what went wrong during the last session, and how they could improve their cooperation the next time.

Achievement effects were controlled for by means of a standardized test on "reading for understanding" (Anger, Bargmann, and Voigt 1965). Pre- and post-tests were administered with two parallel versions of this instrument.

In nonacademic areas we controlled for changes in (a) social classroom climate, using a modified version of Dreesmann's (1979) Instructional Climate

Figure 7.2
Academic Achievement

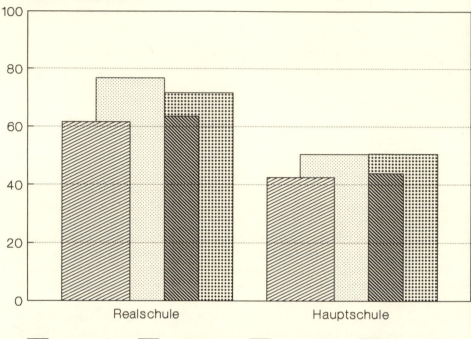

Questionnaire (ICQ), a rating scale for students comparable to Anderson and Walberg's (1976) Learning Environment Inventory. The ICQ contains nine subscales that assess relations between individual variables (e.g., learning motivation, cooperativeness) and situation variables (e.g., classroom discipline); and (b) students' style of dealing with social conflicts, using a sentence completion procedure (e.g., "When others do not agree with me . . .") from research in cognitive level/complexity (Schroder, Driver, and Streufert 1967; Huber and Mandl 1980).

Results. If not mentioned otherwise, the unit of analysis for the following data was teams, not individual students. As Figure 7.2 shows, the achievement levels (pre and post) are generally higher for the track *Realschule,* there are remarkable gains after five weeks of *jigsaw* learning, and no differences in achievement under the condition of process feedback (all effects controlled for by a $2 \times 2 \times 2$ MANOVA)—although the overall learning time for those teams was somewhat reduced by rating the cooperative process and discussing the results every session. This reduction of learning time for five team sessions adds up to a total of about 40 minutes spent with rating and discussing group processes "instead" of engaging in reading activities. Figure 7.3 shows the effects of feedback procedures (also controlled for by a 2×2 MANOVA) in

Figure 7.3
Social Climate Ratings (Gain Scores)

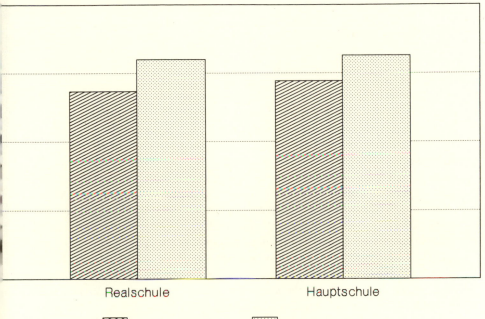

Realschule   Hauptschule

▨ achievement f.   ▦ process feedb.

terms of climate ratings on the ICQ's subscale for cooperation. The condition of process feedback improved students' experiences of cooperativeness in the classroom considerably; there was no difference between the tracks.

The individual style of handling social conflicts was assessed in two classrooms of *Hauptschule* only. These students continued reading practice after the end of this study, now using the model jigsaw II (Slavin 1980a) for another five weeks. The complexity level of their reactions to incomplete sentences signaling conflict was rated low (score 1) if they only described a specific situation, but was rated high (score 4) if they completed the sentences taking into account the perspective of other persons in the situation. This measurement of complexity level was administered three times: before the study, after five weeks, and after the additional five-week period of team learning in these two classrooms (see Table 7.3). The complexity of dealing with conflict situations is reduced after five weeks of team learning, then gradually the cognitive level in this area rises again. The differences between points of measurements are significant ($p < .004$). An interaction between point of measurement and mode of feedback indicates that mere achievement feedback seems to initially reduce complexity more than a combination with process feedback. The rise after five weeks is relatively smaller though also significant ($p < .05$) under the condition of achievement feedback alone.

Table 7.3
Individual Style (Complexity) of Dealing with Social Conflict

Hauptschule (2 classr.)	Pre-test	5 weeks	10 weeks
achievement feedback	3.13	2.53	2.72
process feedback	2.81	2.66	2.83

Discussion. Above all, the study proved positive achievement effects of the *jigsaw* technique, contrary to the claim of Moskowitz et al. (1985). From its inherent logic *jigsaw* seems best qualified for introductory sequences of learning, but it appears to be unsuited for the training of hierarchically organized skills, such as mathematics as in the studies by Moskowitz et al. During the relatively short period of expert group discussions within a jigsaw lesson, slow-learning members of a heterogeneous team will not become experts in applying a higher-order skill. When these students return from expert groups to their original teams, what can they teach that their faster-learning peers do not already know better? Jigsaw will produce achievement if applied to contents and phases of learning that give every team member a fair chance to become able to exchange knowledge and to foster the others' learning. The highly positive social climate ratings under the condition of process feedback should remind us that team learning is more than a means for stimulating student achievement.

The analysis of complexity levels under differing feedback conditions is impaired by the small number of classrooms and students in this study. Differing levels of prerequisites, especially differences in experiences with traditional *Gruppenunterricht,* may have interacted with those variables designed to be the independent ones in this study. Two alternatives seem to be helpful in this situation: (1) broadening the scope of research to include more subjects, more classrooms, or control groups, or (2) intensifying the analysis of team learning to study ongoing processes during team learning in a more detailed manner. In light of the limited resources available to us, we choose the second possibility.

STUDY 3: INTERACTION PROCESSES DURING
TEAM LEARNING

A starting point for this study was some of Webb's reports (1980a, 1980b, 1982, 1983, 1984) on interaction in learning teams without a specific social organization. With regard to McGrath's (1964) demand for a process-process-product approach in educational research, it seems to be indispensible to connect data about independent process variables (social organization, feedback, etc.) and dependent variables (achievement, social climate, etc.) with intervening variables (data about team interaction processes). After a review of recent publications on interaction processes during team learning (Eppler, Huber, and Winter 1984), and with some students' critical remarks (e.g., competitive behaviors; coercive "assistance" in learning) from Study 1 (above) in mind, we

Table 7.4
Design of Study 3

classroom	1	2	3
German (reading)	lecturing	jigsaw	jigsaw
mathematics	group rallye	group rallye	---

wanted to have a closer look at the organizational format of group-rallye (STAD). In addition we tried to compare this team model with *jigsaw*, in order to find out more about the positive changes in social climate ratings and self-evaluations of group processes during *jigsaw* sessions (see above, Study 2).

Design and subjects. Three classrooms (seventh grade; *Hauptschule*) with a total of 56 students participated in this study. Team learning in mathematics was arranged *(group-rallye)* in two classrooms and in German language *(jigsaw)* in two classrooms. In one classroom (no. 2) both organizational modes were used in both subject matter areas (see Table 7.4).

Procedure and materials. Groups of four were composed in accordance to students' preferences, controlling for heterogeneity of achievement level and gender. Team learning took place two hours per week in every subject over a period of eight weeks. The students practiced reading and/or fractional arithmetic. All teams received feedback about their achievement as well as process feedback (Study 2). In order to measure the independent and dependent variables we used the instruments described above in studies 1 and 2 except for the ICQ. In addition we included free descriptions of positive and negative experiences in team learning, and a personality questionnaire for children, both before and after the experimental phase.

The interactive behaviors of members in one team in each classroom were videotaped in every session. With the exception of the "expert" phase in the *jigsaw* model, where the team composition changes from one lesson to another, the activities of individual students in interaction with their team members could be traced through all team sessions. For a closer analysis we choose time samples (5 minutes each) from the beginning, the middle, and the end of mathematics lessons, and in German language lessons a sample of 5 minutes from the "expert" phase and of 7.5 minutes from the interaction in the "basic" teams (starting with the discussion of the worksheets). Within these periods every interval of 10 seconds was coded.

We developed a coding system for team interaction on the basis of our review (see above), relying especially on the suggestions by Peterson and Janicki (1979), Peterson, Janicki, and Swing (1981), Webb (1980a, 1980b), Wilkinson and Calculator (1982), and Wilkinson and Spinelli (1983). Verbal interactions thus were analyzed in terms of

- asking (for contextual conditions; for task information; for explanation of suggested solution strategies; for explanation of results; for results only);

answering (with the same subcategories as asking);

- directing (in the sense of giving orientation; telling one's opinion; organizing the work; demanding active participation);
- performing (with regard to directions).

In addition, positive and negative emotional remarks were coded.

As a necessary supplement to this observational approach we asked all students after the first and after the last team session to write down in their own words positive and negative experiences with team learning on prepared worksheets. All descriptions were sorted with regard to their general meaning. This interpretive process resulted in six broad categories, which encompass the students' subjective impressions. These were:

tasks and task-oriented behavior,

efficiency of teamwork,

control and influence within the teams,

group processes,

socio-emotional experiences, and

situational conditions for team learning.

RESULTS

Products of Team Learning

In general, the findings of studies 1 and 2 could be replicated. With regard to available space we therefore summarize the findings, elaborating only on the comparison of subjective ratings of process qualities under different conditions of team organization.

In the *group-rallye* condition (classrooms 1 and 2; mathematics) as well as in the *jigsaw* condition (classrooms 2 and 3; German; cf. Table 7.4) the differences between achievement before and after the study were significant. There were no achievement differences between the experimental groups and the control group (classroom 1; cf. Table 7.4) in the *jigsaw* condition.

It is necessary to take a closer look at the overall ratings of group processes under both conditions. The rating scale by which we obtained the data for process feedback is described above (Study 2). In this study we had the opportunity to compare how students from the same classroom rate their teams' interactions under two conditions of cooperative organization. The scores in Table 7.5 are arithmetic means of individual ratings over all items; the most positive score is 6. We concentrate here on classroom 2, where *jigsaw* and *group-rallye* were implemented every week. Figure 7.4 represents linear approximations of mean ratings under both organizational formats over eight weeks. The *jigsaw* scores clearly increase, whereas there is almost no change for *rallye* ratings. The difference is significant ($p = .02$). In all conditions the initial rating is at

Table 7.5
Subjective Ratings of Cooperative Processes (Classrooms 1, 2, and 3)

lesson no.	1	2	3	4	5	6	7	8
rallye/c. 1	4.5	5.5	5.1	5.5.	5.7	5.2	5.4	5.4
rallye/c. 2	4.8	4.5	4.4	4.2	4.4	5.5	4.4	4.5
jigsaw/c. 2	4.8	4.6	5.2	4.6	5.3	5.3	5.2	5.6
jigsaw/c. 3	4.8	4.9	4.8	4.8	4.8	5.4	5.5	5.2

the same level, and there are different tendencies within the *rallye* condition (classrooms 1 and 2) and the *jigsaw* condition (classrooms 2 and 3). Classroom 1, in contrast to classroom 2, showed higher ratings ($p = .003$), but both classrooms 2 and 3 did not differ in their appreciation for *jigsaw*. The difference may be due to the fact that in classroom no. 1 the co-author was present during teamwork, and she was more familiar with typical problems of *rallye* teams than the teacher in classroom no. 2. In the *jigsaw* condition, however, the alternation of teacher and learner roles for every student (if this organizational format is applied for phases of knowledge acquisition) compensated for individual differences insofar as a lack of social competencies (in this case, mutual

Figure 7.4
Rallye versus Jigsaw (Subjective Ratings in Classroom 2)

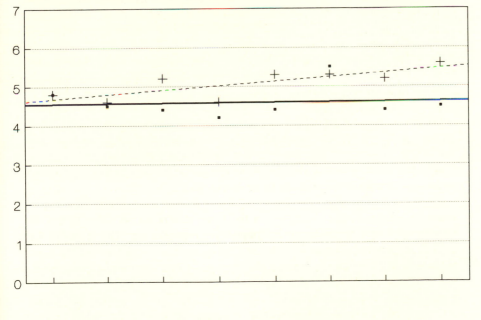

Table 7.6
Percentage of Individual Interactions in Mathematics (*Rallye*)

lesson no.	1	2	3	4	5	6	7	8
on task	66	87	91	93	83	58	87	86
student 1	31	31	35	43	32	30	28	31
student 2	29	25	29		26	30	38	39
student 3	5	14	18	31	23	32	25	23
student 4	21	14	11	19	15			

exchange and control of knowledge) seems to be "supplanted" (Salomon 1979) by structural characteristics of the organizational model.

Process of Team Learning

Observational data from group-rallyes. Table 7.6 presents the percentage of verbal interactions for every team session, in which every student participated either as sender or as receiver. The basis is the total of on-task interactions in every session (percentages are shown in the second row). The amount missing from 100 percent in every column is due to "extra team" interactions with the teacher or, in rare cases, with members of other teams. These internally "missing" interactions decrease over the period of eight weeks; interaction with the teacher is reduced from 24 percent at the outset to 7 percent at the end. Of particular interest are the different distributions of interactions among team members. The team of four appears to become divided into two pairs, whereas the distribution of activities is more balanced in cases when one member is missing. This result, which we find also in *jigsaw* teams (see Table 7.10), seems to support Johnson and Johnson's (1987) suggestion to have students work in pairs or triads instead of groups from four to six members, if group skills are not yet developed.

Table 7.7 displays the distribution of on-task interactions among the categories of interaction analysis described above. The difference between the total

Table 7.7
Percentage of Verbal Behaviors in Mathematics (*Rallye*)

lesson no.	1	2	3	4	5	6	7	8
asking	11	10	10	6	7	12	4	7
answering	8	4	7	7	7	16	7	21
directing	14	19	16	9	12	13	13	10
performing	36	34	36	49	43	30	25	28
emotions +	1	3	0	1	0	2	2	1
−	5	2	2	1	1	7	5	1

Table 7.8
Percentage of Interactions in German (*Jigsaw* "Experts")

lesson no.	1	2	3	4	5	6	7	8
on task	98	98	87	79	85	67	99	92
student 1	13	24		15	14	5	14	20
student 2	4	33	44	30	32	18	25	16
student 3	26	13	6	20	4	26	26	17
student 4	6	2	31	23	29	3	1	9
student 5	26	15	8		8	28	34	14

in every column and 100 percent are due to mere listening behaviors; on the average, listening accounts for about 25 percent of all interactional activities. Generally we see that asking questions decreases during the eight weeks.

A more differentiated analysis showed that this is due mainly to a reduction in questions about organizational conditions, task information, and so on. The category "answering" does not show a steady trend. There are sessions with relatively high percentages (nos. 6 and 8), perhaps as a result of task demands. Directing seems to be more equally distributed. The major part of interactions during all sessions is accounted for by the "performing" category. The percentages are higher at the beginning than at the end of the study, which seems to be an effect of growing routine and increasing self-directed learning activities. The socio-emotional area reveals more negative than positive emotional reactions. This does not seem to be the best condition for mutual support of team members. Clearly in these classrooms more attention should be given to ongoing interpersonal processes, and more training in interpersonal skills is necessary.

Observational data from jigsaw "expert" groups. In this condition it is impossible to compare individual students because the composition of "expert" groups is changed from one session to another (Slavin 1980a). From the differences from 100 percent in every column it is evident that contacts with the teacher were very high at the beginning. The role of group size for individual participation is also striking; in groups of five the imbalance is even more distinct than in groups of four (Table 7.8). The percentage of on-task behavior is impressive; the arithmetic mean over all sessions is 88 percent, though there is a high standard deviation of 11.3, probably due to the varying attractiveness of the texts for reading.

The distribution of activities among interactive categories is displayed in Table 7.9. It reflects clearly the task demands during the "expert" phase. Members from different basic teams come together in order to acquire specific knowledge about one part or aspect of a broader topic. Later, back in their basic team, they will have to teach this knowledge to their teammates who in turn have become specialists for other parts or aspects of their common subject

Table 7.9
Percentage of Verbal Behavior in German (*Jigsaw* "Experts")

lesson no.	1	2	3	4	5	6	7	8
asking	6	7	5	7	7	3	11	5
answering	9	8	9	7	5	7	20	7
directing	10	3	7	16	7	13	5	7
performing	35	64	45	17	41	5		14
emotions +	1	0	0	0	0	1	1	0
−	1	0	1	2	1	1	1	1

matter. So it is most important to work carefully through the text, to ask questions about difficult parts, give or get explanations and to listen to others' questions and suggestions. The discussion is a good model for those problems that one's teammates are likely to have with this text, and for ways of answering their questions efficiently.

Observational data from jigsaw basic groups. Characteristics of the group processes that occur later in the basic groups are represented in Tables 7.10 and 7.11. In comparison with the expert phase, the relatively low percentage of on-task behavior (arithmetic mean: 66 percent; sd: 13) may be surprising. If we look at Table 7.11, we get an important suggestion about possible causes: the percentages of questioning and answering were low. The team members' main effort seems to have been teaching others, and not so much learning from others, although everyone was following directions and listening much of the time, sometimes with many negative emotional reactions. Again, groups of three shared the activities more equally than larger groups (Table 7.10). Taken together, the jigsaw observations allow the following conclusions. The "expert" team was more concentrated on the task, the students listened more often to each other, whereas in the basic group the social climate was somewhat negative, above all more directive. There were no significant differences between these two types of groups with respect to asking and answering questions.

Table 7.10
Percentage of Interactions in German (*Jigsaw* "Basic" Teams)

lesson no.	1	2	3	4	5	6	7	8
on task	56	77	91	56	66	53	80	72
student 1	27	34	22	19	24	33	42	
student 2	39		24	26	22	38		29
student 3	12	19	28	11	18	11	35	26
student 4	18	31	17	16	16	15	24	36

Table 7.11
Percentage of Verbal Behaviors in German (*Jigsaw* "Basic" Teams)

lesson no.	1	2	3	4	5	6	7	8
asking	2	4	4	2	5	2	9	7
answering	4	7	6	4	7	3	7	5
directing	12	15	11	9	10	8	10	16
performing	18	27	66	46	25	48	60	35
emotions +	0	0	0	0	0	0	0	0
−	6	0	7	1	4	4	0	1

Subjective descriptions of team experiences. The first step in the process of analyzing the students' free descriptions of their experiences during team sessions led to the formulation of six categories described above. The *task* category includes on the positive side such experiences as other teammates giving help, that the person was able to explain something to others, or that there was mutual support. Frequent negative remarks state that some team members, especially during the first session, did not share the effort of finding a solution, but just copied the answers. Students also deplored the lack of help. The *efficiency* category contains a majority of positive comments which claim that team learning is easier, faster, more effective. The *control* category is highly problematic. Students complain of "dictatorial" tendencies in their teams, of competition, of patronizing. On the other hand there are students who had contradictory experiences. The *process* category includes complaints about noise and confusion. The *emotion* category is characterized by statements of working together, of a friendly atmosphere, of chances to become more familiar with each other. It encompasses also a great number of general comments to the effect that teamwork was fun. On the other hand students stated that they were teased or pestered by others. The *situation* category contains critical remarks that it was not possible to change the team's composition during the study, and some girls' negative remarks about the boys in their teams.

Figure 7.5 shows for every category the total number of positive and negative experiences expressed after the first and last week of the study: widely hatched (week 1) and dotted (week 8) columns represent positive experiences; narrowly hatched columns stand for negative comments. The most important results are a decrease of negative task statements, an increase of (positive) efficiency comments, and normalizing emotional reactions (decrease of an initial rapture). No less important, however, is the development within the three categories of control, process, and situation experiences. Negative control statements are still more frequent than positive ones after eight weeks of team learning; positive process experiences increase, but so do negative ones. Finally, since situational conditions are not influenced by team organization, there is no change within the situation category. When we compared the three classrooms we found that an overwhelming majority of negative statements came

Figure 7.5
Team Experiences (Subjective Descriptions)

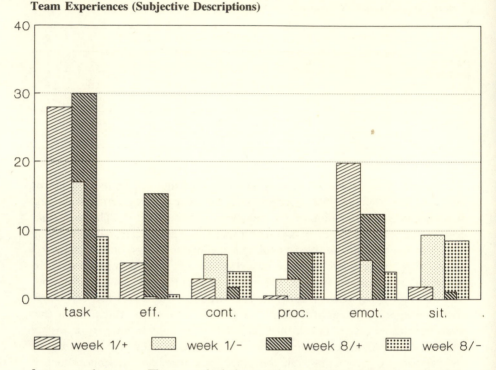

from one classroom. There, particularly negative control experiences were much more frequent from the start, and at the end this frequency had decreased only to the entry level of the two other classrooms.

Discussion

Observational data as well as qualitative data from the students' subjective perspectives complement the usual quantitative results in both a promising and a challenging manner. The students' ratings confirm the general results, which show that task orientation, achievement, and the socio-emotional climate are influenced positively by team learning. In addition, however, the data confirm the need for research not to be confined to achievement scores, but to control for interactive processes within the teams, and to look for possibilities of how to influence these processes. Without adequate pedagogical control and assistance the interaction of team members will continue to be unsatisfactory, from the perspective of team members, too. This applies especially for somewhat problematic teams. We strongly recommend evaluating not only students' achievement, but in addition their ways of interacting. If necessary, feedback about the cooperation process should be combined with remedial interaction tasks and exercises.

STUDY 4: LEARNING GEOGRAPHY THROUGH GROUP INVESTIGATION

This organizational model for team learning, described by Sharan and Sharan (1976), was introduced into geography teaching in a sixth-grade classroom of *Hauptschule*. The co-author herself was the teacher in this classroom from grade 5 on. So it was possible systematically to develop skills for team learning in this initially difficult classroom—difficult in terms of keeping discipline and negotiating controversies in nonaggressive ways, as well as in terms of achievement. In prior years in this classroom there was almost no other teaching style available other than the lecture method.

Team building. From the beginning of grade 5 the teacher offered possibilities to study with the traditional *Gruppenunterricht* in most subject matter areas. The *jigsaw* model was introduced first in German language, then in biology and geography. This was continued in grade 6, supplemented by *group-rallye* lessons in mathematics. Gradually the students learned to solve problems cooperatively. As a first step they learned not to beat up other students in cases of conflict, and they learned to plan and to organize teamwork. A method called "seating circle" played an important role in this process of team building. On these occasions the whole class discussed interpersonal difficulties and ways of coping with them. The teacher gave priority to these problems, so that afterwards tasks in subject matter areas could be handled more efficiently. This phase of preparation should not be neglected. *Group investigation* demands that the students have interactive competencies at their disposal. The teacher, on the other hand, should be ready to create learning situations for relatively autonomous teams. This should not prove to be too troublesome if she/he has developed an optimistic attitude toward the students and the readiness to reflect on her/his own teaching activities intensively.

The Process of Group Investigation

Step 1: Finding the topics for teamwork. For this study the teacher introduced to the students the general theme "The Black Forest," which is part of the geography syllabus. In their basic groups from former *jigsaw* sessions the students then collected and discussed all their ideas, questions, associations referring to this geographic region, which they wanted to elaborate during later lectures. The teams noted their key words on large pieces of wallpaper in order to share their results with the other teams. The topics covered aspects from topology, climate, biology, economics, and tourism, as well as from everyday life, including the Black Forest tart.

Step 2: Ordering the topics. The students reformulated their questions so that corresponding meanings were expressed in identical terms. The teacher wrote these formulations on index cards, which she distributed to the teams again, together with suggestions for six group themes: landscape, culture, economics, customs and local characteristics, communities, and history.

Step 3: Appointing of topics to group themes. The basic groups now tried to appoint their index cards to the proposed themes. They all met in the seating circle in order to discuss and modify these appointments. The aim was to consent to those questions and key words that should be treated under the specific headlines. The discussion resulted in a huge wall display, showing the different subtopics in relation to the more general topic headings.

Step 4: Forming of teams and planning. Now the students started to organize new teams, according to the topics they preferred for further elaboration. Within these thematically homogeneous teams they discussed the scope and subtopics of their theme, which resources were available or necessary, and in which way they should communicate the results of their work to the other teams. The immediate result of this step was a plan for further activities. However, most teams had to cope with many difficulties in planning.

Step 5: Exchanging plans. Using the organizational arrangement of the method of the seating circle again, the teams exchanged their project outlines and tried to avoid overlap and redundancies.

Step 6: Looking for resources. The institution of school libraries as found in North America is almost unknown in German schools. So this project was a good occasion to introduce the students to the city library. The teams gathered information about the services of a public library, and they got books, maps, and other materials that they needed for their specific tasks.

Step 7: Working in teams. The teams organized the study of the literature, and some of them successfully included additional sources of information. In a team that was occupied with the problem of ecological damage to the forests, some students used their families' weekend tours to collect specimens of branches and leaves.

Step 8: Sharing the results. During the final phase the teams shared the results of their work with each other. They not only reported about their work and their findings, but also tried to involve the other students in their process of knowledge acquisition. One team distributed a folder summarizing their findings about the "Black Forest as a secondary chain of mountains," together with materials like glue, paper, and stones. Guided by the team, the other students constructed models of a typical part of the Black Forest. A technique used by other teams was to supply the students with handouts and questions, which could be answered with the help of this material after the team's presentation of its findings.

Discussion

Though the students were highly active during this project and evidently enjoyed their work, there were some difficulties due to the demands of this organizational format. Compared with other models of team learning, *group investigation* calls for many interpersonal competencies as prerequisites, but also offers many opportunities to express those skills. The best preparation seems to be an extensive as well as intensive phase of team building and experiences with less demanding forms of cooperative learning. An important technique to ensure the development of interaction competencies (e.g., role-taking and role-making within teams, asking questions, giving explanations, empathy, and change of perspectives) is regular reflection about group processes. For this reason, teacher and students gathered every week in an additional seating circle and exchanged their experiences. They tried to identify characteristics of team processes that led to success or failure, to analyze and exchange individual ways of perceiving and evaluating the events, and to generalize subjective as well as intersubjective experiences to establish regulations or norms for future cooperative activities. This method obviously is both more demanding and efficient than the simple method of subjective rating and team feedback used in studies 2 and 3.

The lack of standards for assessing achievement and the absence of control classrooms limit the scientific yield of this study. However, it provided results that convinced teachers. This experience taught the authors to choose carefully the sequence of steps if the primary goal is the dissemination of cooperative learning. To begin with a small number of carefully documented case studies on different organizational models of team learning will supply us with the data (and lecture materials) necessary to make teachers eager to give team learning a try. With a larger number of *experienced* teachers and students further research in the area of cooperative learning should be easier and more reliable.

REFERENCES

Anderson, G. J., and Walberg, H. J. (1976) *The Assessment of Learning Environments: A Manual for the Learning Environment Inventory and My Class Inventory*. Chicago, IL: Office of Evaluation Research, University of Chicago.

Anger, H., Bargmann, R., and Voigt, M. (1965) *Verständiges Lesen 7–9*. Weinheim: Beltz.

Aronson, E. (1978) *The Jigsaw Classroom*. Beverly Hills, CA: Sage.

——— (1984) "Förderung von Schulleistung, Selbstwert und prosozialem Verhalten: Die Jigsaw-Methode." In *Kooperatives Lernen*, edited by G. L. Huber, S. Rotering-Steinberg, and D. Wahl, pp. 48–59. Weinheim: Beltz.

Dreesmann, H. (1979) "Zusammenhänge zwischen Unterrichtsklima, kognitiven Prozessen bei Schülern und deren Leistungsverhalten." *Zeitschrift für empirische Pädagogik* 3:121–33.

Eppler, R., Huber, G. L., and Winter, M. (1984) *Lernen in Kleingruppen: Wie interagieren die Lerner?* Bericht Nr. 11 aus dem Arbeitsbereich Pädagogische Psychologie am Institut für Erziehungswissenschaft I der Universität Tübingen.

Guthke, J. (1972) *Zur Diagnostik der individuellen Lernfähigkeit*. Berlin: Deutscher Verlag der Wissenschaften.

Huber, G. L., Bogatzki, W., and Winter, M. (1982) *Kooperation als Ziel schulischen*

Lehrens und Lernens. Bericht Nr. 6 aus dem Arbeitsbereich Pädagogische Psychologie am Institut für Erziehungswissenschaft I der Universität Tübingen.

Huber, G. L., and Mandl, H. (1980) "Differenziertheit und Integriertheit des Konstrukts der kognitiven Komplexität. Zum Problem der Operationaliserung des Konstrukts." In *Kognitive Komplexität,* edited by H. Mandl and G. L. Huber, pp. 219–47. Göttingen: Hogrefe.

Johnson, D. W., and Johnson, F. P. (1987) *Joining Together. Group Theory and Group Skills,* 3rd edn. Englewood Cliffs, NJ: Prentice-Hall.

McGrath, J. E. (1964) *Social Psychology: A Brief Introduction.* New York: Holt.

Meyer, E. (1983) *Gruppenunterricht. Grundlegung und Beispiel,* 8th edn. Oberursel: Finken-Verlag.

Moskowitz, J. M., Malvin, J. H., Schaeffer, G. A., and Schaps, E. (1985) "Evaluation of Jigsaw, a cooperative learning technique." *Contemporary Educational Psychology* 10:104–12.

Petermann, F., and Petermann, U. (1980) *Erfassungsbogen für aggressives Verhalten in konkreten Situationen.* Braunschweig: Westermann.

Peterson, P. L., and Janicki, T. C. (1979) "Individual characteristics and children's learning in large-group and small-group approaches." *Journal of Educational Psychology* 71:677–87.

Peterson, P. L., Janicki, T. C., and Swing, S. R. (1981) "Ability × treatment interaction effects on children's learning in large-group and small-group approaches." *American Educational Research Journal* 18:453–73.

Peterson, P. L., Wilkinson, L. C., Spinelli, F., and Swing, S. R. (1982) *Merging the Process-Product and the Sociolinguistic Paradigms: Research on Small-Group Processes.* Madison, WI: Wisconsin Center for Education Research.

Rotering-Steinberg, S., and von Kügelgen, T. (1986) "Ergebnisse einer schriftlichen Befragung zum Gruppenunterricht." *Erziehungswissenschaft—Erziehungspraxis* 2:26–29.

Salomon, G. (1979) *Interaction of Media, Cognition, and Learning.* San Francisco, CA: Jossey-Bass.

Schroder, H. M., Driver, M. J., and Streufert, S. (1967) *Human Information Processing.* New York: Holt.

Sharan, S., and Sharan, Y. (1976) *Small-Group Teaching.* Englewood Cliffs, NJ: Prentice-Hall.

Slavin, R. E. (1978) "Student teams—achievement divisions." *Journal of Research and Development in Education* 12:39–49.

——— (1980a) *Using Student Team Learning. The Johns Hopkins Team Learning Project.* Baltimore, MD: Johns Hopkins University, Center for Social Organization of Schools.

——— (1980b) "Cooperative learning." *Review of Educational Research* 50:315–42.

——— (1983) *Cooperative Learning.* New York: Longman.

Webb, N. (1980a) "Group process: The key to learning in groups." *New Directions for Methodology of Social and Behavioral Science: Issues in Aggregation* 50:77–87.

——— (1980b) "An analysis of group interaction and mathematical errors in heterogeneous ability groups." *British Journal of Educational Psychology* 50:1–11.

——— (1982) "Student interaction and learning in small groups." *Review of Educational Research* 52:421–53.

———— (1983) "Predicting learning from student interaction: Defining the interaction variables." *Educational Psychologist* 18:33–41.

Webb, N. (1984) "Stability of small-group interaction and achievement over time." *Journal of Educational Psychology,* 76:211–24.

Wilkinson, L. C., and Calculator, S. (1980) "Requests and responses in peer-directed reading groups." *American Educational Research Journal* 19:107–20.

Wilkinson, L. and Calculator, S. (1982) "Effective speakers: Using language to request and obtain information and action in the classroom." In *Communication in the Classroom,* edited by L. Wilkinson. New York: Academic Press.

Wilkinson, L. C., and Spinelli, F. (1983) "Using requests effectively in peer-directed instructional groups." *American Educational Research Journal* 20:479–501.

8
Cooperative Learning, Motivation to Learn, and Academic Achievement

SHLOMO SHARAN
AND ADA SHAULOV

Most authors of professional works and research studies on cooperative learning have asserted that this approach to classroom instruction enhances pupils' motivation to learn more than the traditional whole-class approach to instruction (Johnson and Johnson 1985; Slavin 1983a, 1983b; Slavin et al. 1985; Sharan et al. 1984; Sharan and Shachar 1988; Sharan and Sharan 1976). Yet, there are no empirical studies known to these authors that assessed directly the effects of cooperative learning on motivation to learn. In research published heretofore, enhanced motivation was deduced from improved achievement scores. Yet, improved achievement can stem from a variety of sources, motivation being only one of them. The primary aim of this study was to ascertain empirically if, in fact, cooperative learning contributed to pupils' motivation to learn more so than whole-class instruction, and to what degree. Consequently, this study focused directly on the assessment of pupils' motivation to learn and its relation to academic achievement. What we sought to ascertain was if the students' interest in the study material, or their actual participation in the pursuit of learning, was enhanced by cooperative learning, and if this enhanced motivation, in turn, contributed to their academic achievement.

What characteristics of cooperative learning are said to enhance pupils' motivation to learn? Why should it prove more motivating than whole-class instructional methods? We consider two sets of variables to be central in explaining the superior motivating effects of cooperative learning, namely: positive social facilitation and peer acceptance in small cooperative groups, and enhanced pupil involvement in decision making regarding one's work. We shall also consider the role of the pupils' social orientation as a personal character-istic that affects their adaptation to cooperative learning.

POSITIVE PEER INTERACTION AND ENHANCED
DECISION MAKING

Cooperative learning fosters positive social relations among classmates through peer collaboration and mutual assistance in small groups; it gives expression to the motivating effects of working together with others toward a common goal largely free from competition; and it cultivates the pupils' sense of acceptance on an equal footing with others in the group. An egalitarian division of labor within the group, in keeping with one's interests and abilities, where group members work on different aspects of the group topic, as well as the adoption of behavioral norms for equal status interaction within the group, enable each member to contribute to the group's goal without competing with others (Pe-pitone 1980).

On the other hand, whole-class instruction generally isolates pupils psycho-logically from one another in order to allow teachers to talk to everyone at the same time. Furthermore, by emphasizing public recitation in response to the teacher's questions, whole-class instruction also generates invidious social comparisons and competition for the teacher's praise and attention. Indeed, teachers using the whole-class approach frequently employ competition among pupils to stimulate their motivation to achieve. This competition augments stu-dents' fear of failure—someone inevitably loses in the competitive situation. Fear of failure, combined with the negative consequences of social comparison, would serve to reduce motivation to learn.

Moreover, the competition and reward system prevailing in whole-class in-struction makes students dependent upon extrinsic motivation to achieve. Con-sequently, this latter approach would not support intrinsic interest in the subject at hand. We would argue that teachers' calculated use of external rewards for improving student achievement might stimulate harder work for better grades but will not contribute effectively to pupils' inherent interest in the content and process of learning per se. The impact of these features of whole-class instruc-tion is greatly reduced, if not totally eliminated, in the cooperative learning classroom.

Cooperative learning also allows pupils a far greater degree of autonomy in respect to their classroom learning behavior than does whole-class instruction. The organization of pupils into small groups that regulate much of their own activity around the learning task decentralizes, to some extent, the decision-making process in the classroom and grants pupils considerable opportunity for self-regulation and independent decision making. Furthermore, the group in-vestigation method of cooperative learning enhances pupils' decision-making power by involving them in the selection of the learning tasks from a variety of alternatives, as well as in deciding who in the group will study which features of the group topic and how the group's work will be reported to the class as a whole (Sharan 1980; Sharan and Hertz-Lazarowitz 1980). By comparison, the whole-class instructional setting concentrates almost all decisions regarding teaching and learning in the hands of the teacher, minimizing opportunities for pupils to influence the learning process and to exercise personal control over their own work. Self-regulation, the power to make decisions affecting one's own work, and involvement with others in making decisions regarding both the process and products of one's work are considered to be critical components of high-level motivation in respect to carrying out learning tasks (Ames 1986; Ames and Ames 1985; DeCharms 1968, 1971; Deci 1975; Johnson and Johnson 1985; Ryan, Connell, and Deci 1985; Weisz and Cameron 1985).

In light of the above considerations we surmise that cooperative learning will have both a direct positive effect on pupils' achievement, as well as an indirect effect on achievement mediated by pupils' motivation to learn. We also hypothesize that cooperative learning will positively affect pupil motivation to learn and pupil academic achievement more than will whole-class instruction.

INSTRUCTIONAL METHOD AND THE PUPILS' PERSONAL CHARACTERISTICS

Much research has been devoted to the subject of the interaction between pupils' personal characteristics and the method of instruction in affecting learning outcomes (Cronbach and Snow 1977). Owens (1983) reported that pupils with a positive social orientation toward cooperation with peers in the learning process, such as willingness to share informational sources, to exchange ideas with others, and to make decisions collectively, preferred cooperative learning classes more than did those who expressed a competitive social orientation. Other investigators studied the relationship between academic achievement and the inclination to cooperate or compete with peers as a function of ethnic background (Kagan, Zahn, and Gealy 1977; Kagan et al. 1985). They reported that pupils from ethnic groups (Mexican background) with a more cooperative orientation enjoyed greater academic success in cooperative classes than they did in whole-class, competitive classrooms. An ethnic-cultural background or personal orientation that values cooperation with others will conflict with the instructional method employed in the traditional classroom. Consequently, the academic achievement of students from such a background or with a cooperative orientation will be affected negatively by comparison to the achievement of their ethnic peers who study in a classroom where the instructional method is more adapted to their social orientation.

In the present study we tested the hypothesis that the pupil's social orientation and the nature of the instructional method (cooperative learning or whole-class) affect academic achievement directly, as well as indirectly (i.e., is mediated by pupil motivation). In other words, pupils with a more cooperative orientation toward working with peers who study in cooperative learning classrooms will display greater motivation to learn and will achieve more academically than pupils with a less cooperative orientation.

Thus far we have examined the variables that could explain why cooperative learning can affect pupils' motivation to learn and their achievement. We turn next to consider two other critical variables that are acknowledged to affect pupils' motivation to learn and their achievement. These are the pupil's social status in the class and his/her level of academic achievement in the past in a given subject.

SOCIAL STATUS IN THE CLASSROOM

By the term "social status" we mean the degree to which a pupil is accepted by peers as someone with whom they wish to interact in various activities, both academic and social. The extensive literature on the importance of peer relations for adjustment and achievement in school has been discussed at length (Schmuck and Schmuck 1988). Clearly, pupils need positive peer relations to function optimally in school. We hypothesized that pupils' peer relations affect achievement directly as well as indirectly, through the mediation of their motivation to learn.

PRIOR ACADEMIC ACHIEVEMENT AS A PREDICTOR OF LATER ACHIEVEMENT

However we might improve pupil motivation to learn and improve the instructional method, the pupil's prior level of achievement will very likely play an important role in determining achievement in the future. Attribution theory has also emphasized the critical effect of prior achievement on pupils' expectations for achievement in the future, and on the role of these expectations in predicting actual achievement (Forsyth 1986). Some research has demonstrated the powerful role of the pupil's achievement history in predicting future achievement (Corno and Mandinach 1983). Hence we surmise that the pupils' achievement prior to the implementation of cooperative learning in the classroom will serve as a significant predictor of pupils' achievement in the future, both directly and indirectly, by affecting their motivation to learn.

METHOD

Subjects

This experiment was carried out in 17 sixth-grade classrooms located in four elementary schools in the larger Haifa, Israel, area. Ten classes were taught with the group investigation method, and seven classes were conducted with the traditional whole-class method. The principals of four schools agreed to have the experiment conducted in their schools, and no other schools were approached. The schools were chosen because they all had a relatively homogeneous population of middle-class students from both of Israel's main Jewish ethnic groups (Western and Middle Eastern backgrounds). All of the 553 children in this study were born in Israel, and Hebrew was their native language.

Another factor that determined the selection of these schools was that all of the teachers were participating in in-service training projects of various kinds. Hence, the fact that the sixth-grade teachers were asked to participate in a training program for cooperative learning did not constitute any special treatment not available to all of the other teachers in these schools. The cooperative learning project was offered for the same number of hours (a total of 35 hours, twice a month for a total of 5 hours per month, over a period of 7 months), as were other in-service training courses. However, it was not possible to assign all the sixth-grade teachers in the four schools at random to one of the two teaching methods. The principals insisted that the teachers be free to select the in-service training course of their choice.

The group investigation method was used in three subject areas: arithmetic, Bible, and (Hebrew) language (including literature). Teachers of the control classes continued to teach these same subjects with the whole-class approach as they had been accustomed to doing for years. There were no other fifth/sixth-grade teachers in these schools. All of the teachers taught the same classes of pupils for two consecutive years, that is, fifth and sixth grade. The in-service training course was held when the classes were at the fifth-grade level, and the measures were taken when the classes were at the sixth-grade level.

A total of 49 teachers participated in this study—28 teachers taught the ten cooperative classes and 21 taught the whole-class method (seven classes, three teachers per class). The sixth-grade homeroom teacher generally was the same person who taught language arts (reading comprehension), while arithmetic and Bible were taught by subject specialists. In two cases the homeroom teacher taught arithmetic instead of language arts, and in two instances the same arithmetic teacher taught more than one class.

Measures

Motivation to learn. Motivation is a construct that must be inferred from various behavioral manifestations and cannot be evaluated directly. Ames (1986) noted that the following behaviors indicated motivation to learn: serious attention to learning tasks, effort expended in learning activities, valuing learning for its own sake, deriving satisfaction from the process of learning, the quality of involvement in the learning process, attraction to learning, the extent of individual responsibility and independence in respect to one's own learning. In the present study we employed measures of the following three behavioral manifestations of motivation to learn: (a) perseverence in carrying out the learning task; (b) involvement in classroom learning, and (c) willingness to invest effort in preparing homework.

Task perseverence. This measure was defined here as the pupil's decision to remain in the classroom and continue to work on the task at hand rather than leave the class to play on the playground during a special recess. This required that the pupil relinquish participating in an activity highly valued by most pupils and choose to remain in the classroom to continue work on school tasks. This measure could reflect several of the types of behavior mentioned by Ames (1986) as indicative of motivation, such as: serious attention to the task, the investment of effort, valuing learning, and deriving satisfaction from performance of the task.

Implementation of this measure took place as follows. An observer entered each of the classes twice during the academic year, once before and once after the conclusion of the experiment. That means there was a total of three pre-test visits, one for each subject class, and three post-test visits, for a total of six recordings per pupil. The observers' visits were unannounced. Toward the end of the lesson the teacher told the pupils that whoever wished could go outside and play for 20 minutes, or they could remain in the room and continue to work on what they were doing at that time. The observers indicated the names of those who left the room on the day's attendance sheet. Visits by observers to the various subject classes of the same pupils were conducted with intervals of two weeks between each visit. Note that each observation of a given class (language, arithmetic, and Bible) was carried out by a different observer. Thus, each pupil could receive a score from 0 to 3 on the pre-test visits, and the same range of scores on the post-test visits.

Recording of the pupils' names was done as unobtrusively as possible so the pupils would not notice that their behavior was being recorded. In order to reduce the possibility that pupils would guess what was being done, we decided not to conduct any interviews with them and to rely exclusively on their overt behavior. Admittedly, this decision precluded the possibility of determining more precisely why the pupils chose to remain in the classroom, but we felt it was more important not to convey to them any message that might influence their behavior.

Involvement in classroom learning. This measure refers to the degree to which pupils take an active role in classroom learning activities as evaluated by the teacher. At the end of each trimester, homeroom teachers in Israel rate each student on classroom participation. We used teachers' evaluations from the last trimester report card of the previous year (fifth grade) and from the last trimester evaluation of the year in which the experiment was conducted (sixth grade).

Investment of effort in homework. Homeroom teachers rate each student on the effort invested in homework preparation and record their ratings on report cards. Once more we employed the teachers' ratings from the last trimester report card of the previous year and from the year of the study.

Pearson correlations between the three measures of motivation to learn were as in Table 8.1. These moderate correlations indicate that the three measures referred to a common phenomenon and that it was reasonable to employ them together as an index of motivation to learn. It is noteworthy that our measure

Table 8.1
Pearson Correlations between Three Measures of Motivation to Learn

	Effort	Participation
Perseverence	.59	.56
Participation	.58	

of task perseverence correlated at the same level with the two teachers' ratings as the correlation between the two ratings themselves.

Pupils' social orientation. A scale of six questions was adopted from a questionnaire developed by Owens and Straton (1980) called the Learning Preference Scale for Students. The scale consists of statements expressing an attitude or opinion about various features of studying in a cooperative small group, such as: "When I'm in school I like to work in a group," or "When I work in a group I like to help other people." Cronbach's alpha for internal consistency of the six questions was .70. Each question was placed on a 4-point Likert scale, with 1 being the lowest level of interest in cooperating with others in a group and 4 the highest level, that is, most interest in cooperating with others in a group. The pupils were told by the examiners that this questionnaire was part of their studies in the university. Each pupil was asked to indicate which response corresponded most to their own opinion about working together with others in a group. The pupils were not informed that this questionnaire had any connection with their actual experiences in their classes (see Table 8.2).

Pupils were categorized into three groups of high, medium, and low inclination for working in groups. Those with a mean score of 3 or more on all items constituted the most appropriate group for cooperative learning and the least appropriate group for the whole-class method; those with a mean score of 2 constituted the medium group for both instructional methods; those with a mean score of 1 on all six items constituted the least appropriate group for cooperative learning and the most appropriate group for the whole-class method. The distribution of subjects in the three levels using this questionnaire is shown in Table 8.3. The percentage of subjects at each of the three levels of inclination to work in groups was almost identical in the classes taught with each of the two instructional methods.

Academic achievement in the past and future. The measure of achievement was the pupil's grade in the particular subject for the third trimester of the previous year (past level of achievement or pre-test) and the grade for the last trimester of the year the experiment was conducted (future level of achieve-

Table 8.2
Pearson Correlations between Six Items on the Social Orientation Scale, and between Each Item and the Entire Scale

item	item-scale	6	5	4	3	2
1	.50	.27	.32	.39	.13	.36
2	.44	.20	.22	.27	.21	
3	.26	.15	.14	.14		
4	.42	.22	.30			
5	.38	.24				
6	.34					

ment, or post-test). The homeroom teachers spent more time with their classes than any other teacher, and they evaluated the students' motivation, while the subject teachers determined the students' grades in their subjects. Thus, students' grades in arithmetic and Bible were given by different teachers than those who evaluated the students' motivation.

In the sixth grade, teachers ascertain students' grades by giving 40 percent

Table 8.3
Distribution of Subjects at Three Levels of Inclination to Work in Groups in Classes Taught with the Group Investigation and Whole-Class Methods

Inclination to work in groups	Group-Investigation		Whole-Class	
	N	%	N	%
Low	81	26	64	27
Medium	134	42	94	40
High	102	32	80	33

Table 8.4
External and Internal Variables

External

T.M.	Teaching method
O.T.C.L.	Orientation toward cooperative learning
A.T.T.M.	Appropriateness to teaching method (Note that this variable indicates an interaction of method × social orientation)

P.C.	Playing companions
St.C.	Study companions
Se. C.	Seating companions
Total: S.S.	Social status

A.I.A.-Pre	Achievement in arithmetic (pretest)
A.I.B.-Pre	Achievement in Bible (pretest)
A.I.R.C.-Pre	Achievement in reading comprehension (pretest)
Total: A.A.I.P.	Academic achievement in the past

Internal

P.I.T.P.	Perseverence in task performance
P.I.C.D.	Participation in class discussion
P.H.	Effort invested in preparing homework
Total: M.T.L.	Motivation to learn

A.I.A.-Po.	Achievement in arithmetic (post-test)
A.I.B.-Po.	Achievement in Bible (post-test)
A.I.R.C.-Po.	Achievement in reading comprehension (post-test)
Total: A.A.I.F.	Academic achievement in the future

weight to approximately three quizzes administered during the trimester, and 60 percent of the grade is determined by the students' scores on two tests. The report card grades are clearly not a subjective evaluation by the teacher. Students who received grades of 50 or 60 were assigned a value of 1, those with grades of 70 or 80 were assigned a 2, and those with 90 or more were assigned a 3.

On the basis of the foregoing theoretical positions and the data supporting them we constructed a model that includes all of the relationships hypothesized heretofore. First we present a complete list of all the variables in the model, exogenous external variables, and endogenous internal variables dependent upon the variables that precede them in the model (Table 8.4).

Procedures

Implementation of the independent variable. Twenty-eight teachers, each of whom taught one of three subjects (Bible, Hebrew language and literature, which is equivalent to reading comprension, or arithmetic), participated in the in-service workshops devoted to the acquisition of cooperative learning techniques (the group investigation method). The topics emphasized in these workshops were: how to develop the pupils' discussion skills (including listening, distribution of speaking privileges, mutual assistance, etc., often called "team building"), how to help pupils plan their study projects cooperatively, the organization and processes relevant to group investigation of study topics, and the design of learning stations in the classroom (Sharan and Sharan 1976). The workshops were conducted in a manner consistent with the principles of experiential learning where teachers carried out the very processes and procedures they were to implement later in their classrooms (Sharan, Hertz-Lazarowitz, and Reiner 1978; Sharan and Sharan 1987).

The training workshops were also accompanied by collegial classroom consultation through the medium of mutual assistance teams. Three or four teachers collaboratively planned a lesson to be taught with the new cooperative learning techniques. They agreed on a short list of criteria by which to observe how the new procedures were being implemented, and they observed one another instructing their classes. A feedback session was conducted after each class session. In this fashion the teachers helped each other adapt the curriculum in each of the three subject areas to the needs of cooperative learning with the group investigation method and improve their use of the cooperative methods.

In order to ascertain the extent to which the two teaching methods were in fact implemented in the appropriate classrooms, direct observations were made three times during the academic year by objective observers not related to this project and uninformed about the goals of the project. Obviously they could notice immediately the difference in classroom structure between the different classes, but they were unaware of the reasons for this difference. Observations were made at the beginning, middle, and toward the end of the year using Thew's observation schedule (Thew 1975). Twenty subcategories of student and teacher behavior were collapsed into five main groupings: (a) unilateral communication (the teacher talks and pupils listen); (b) bilateral communication (question-and-answer interchange between teacher and pupils); (c) class as a unit (all pupils simultaneously engaged in the same task); (d) small groups of pupils, each engaged in its own task without relation to other groups, with the teacher assisting the groups (noncoordinated groups with multilateral communication within groups); (e) small groups of pupils engaged each in a different aspect of the same classwide project, with the teacher assisting the groups (coordinated groups).

Observers registered their scores on an observation sheet for the first ten minutes, middle ten minutes, and last ten minutes of the class session. During each ten-minute period each observer recorded one observation every 30 seconds for a total of 20 observations per ten-minute period. Hence, a total of 540 observations were recorded for each classroom during the three observations carried out during the year in each of the three subjects..

Table 8.5
Summary of Observations in Sixth-Grade Classrooms Taught with Group Investigation (N = 10) and Whole-Class (N = 7) Methods (Percentages of Total Number of Acts Recorded)

Category	Group-Investigation	Whole-Class
1.unilateral communication:		
teacher to pupils	28.0	47.5
2.bilateral communication:		
questions and answers	31.0	31.0
3.class as a single unit:		
identical individual tasks	5.0	19.0
4.uncoordinated groups	11.7	2.5
5.coordinated groups	24.3	----

The data gathered by the observers regarding the implementation of the two teaching methods are summarized in Table 8.5.

Teachers in the cooperative learning classes demonstrated behaviors that were distributed in all of the five major categories in this schedule, but less than a third of their behavior was devoted to whole-class lecturing. Or, one could phrase it differently, to the effect that even the teachers implementing cooperative learning in the classrooms continued to lecture 28 percent of the observed time. This proportion of time devoted to lecturing must be compared with the lecture time taken by teachers in whole-class instruction who lectured to their classes fully 47.5 percent of observed time. A 20 percent decrease in lecture time is a substantial change and is close to the extent of the change observed in earlier projects (Sharan and Hertz-Lazarowitz 1982). There was also a substantial decrease of 14 percent of observed time in the extent to which the teachers in the cooperative classrooms asked all the pupils in their classes to work simultaneously on the same task. Thus, the cooperative learning teachers were free to have their pupils devote fully 36 percent of observed time to learning in small groups compared with the use of small groups for 2.5 percent of observed time in classrooms taught with the whole-class method. These data

Table 8.6
Pearson Correlations between All of the Dependent Measures in This Study
(N = 553)

Variable	SS	ATTM	PITP	PH	PICD	AIRC	AIB
AIA	.06	.33	.55	.53	.48	.53	.56
AIB	.12	.31	.61	.57	.53	.59	
AIRC	.08	.37	.58	.56	.52		
PICD	.09	.23	.56	.58			
PH	.12	.22	.59				
PITP	.16	.20					
ATTM	.08						

document the degree to which the independent variable was in fact implemented in the cooperative learning and whole-class method classrooms in keeping with the basic principles of these two methods.

RESULTS

Before reporting the results obtained from the measures of the dependent variables in this study, the Pearson correlations between all of these variables appear in Table 8.6.

Motivation to Learn and Achievement

The first question to be answered in this study is: Does motivation to learn affect students' achievement and to what extent?

A stepwise regression analysis was performed with the three measures of motivation to learn as the predictor variable and pupils' grades in mathematics, Bible, and reading comprehension as the predicted variables. Table 8.7 displays the findings from this analysis.

The students' decision to remain behind in the class instead of going outside to play proved to be the single most powerful predictor of achievement of the three measures employed in this study, accounting for 30 percent of the variance in the pupils' grades in mathematics. All three measures of motivation to learn taken together accounted for a very substantial 38 percent of the variance in the students' grades in mathematics. The three measures of motivation ac-

Table 8.7
Stepwise Regression Analysis of Pupils' Grades in Arithmetic, Bible Studies, and Reading Comprehension, Using Three Measures of Motivation to Learn as Predictors

Measures of Motivation	Arith R^2	beta	Bible R_2	beta	R.C. $R2$	beta
1. Task perseverance	.30	.32	.37	.33	.34	.30
2. Effort preparing homework	.37	.26	.44	.26	.41	.27
3. Participation in class discussion	.38	.15	.46	.18	.43	.18

All R square values significant at the $p < .001$ level

counted for even larger proportions of the variance in the students' achievement in Bible (a total of 46 percent) and in reading comprehension (43 percent). In each of the latter two subjects, task perseverence was the most powerful predictor of achievement.

Motivation to Learn as a Mediating Variable

A path analysis was performed using all of the variables appearing in the list of variables presented above (Table 8.4). "Motivation to learn" served as a mediating variable, with (1) students' appropriateness to the teaching method, (2) students' social status, and (3) pre-test achievement as exogenous variables on the one hand, and the students' achievement scores on the post-test in each of the three subjects as the predicted variables on the other hand. The path coefficients for the direct and indirect effects of the exogenous variables on achievement appear in the following three figures (Figures 8.1, 8.2, and 8.3). (A coefficient of .05 is statistically significant.)

The three figures present all of the path coefficients for all of the variables in the model, as well as the values of the residuals and the correlations between the independent (exogenous) variables. The latter are, as assumed, very low (between .05 and .08). Examination of the findings from all three path models, and of the residuals, shows that the independent variables alone explain be-

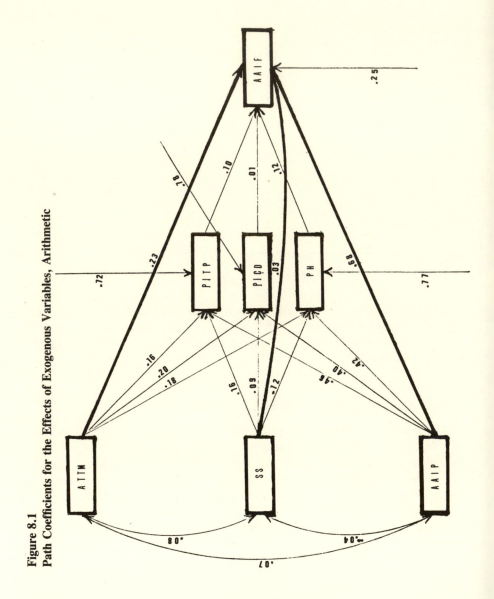

Figure 8.1
Path Coefficients for the Effects of Exogenous Variables, Arithmetic

186

Figure 8.2
Path Coefficients for the Effects of Exogenous Variables, Bible Studies

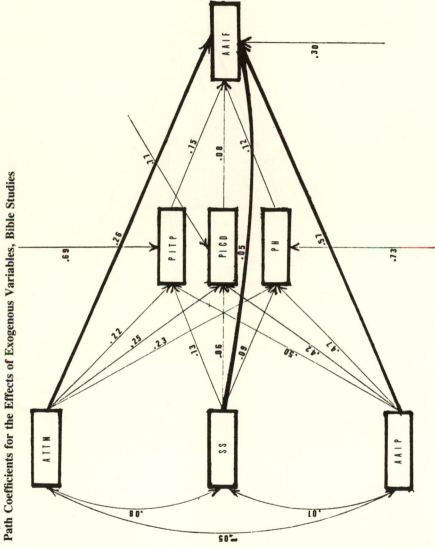

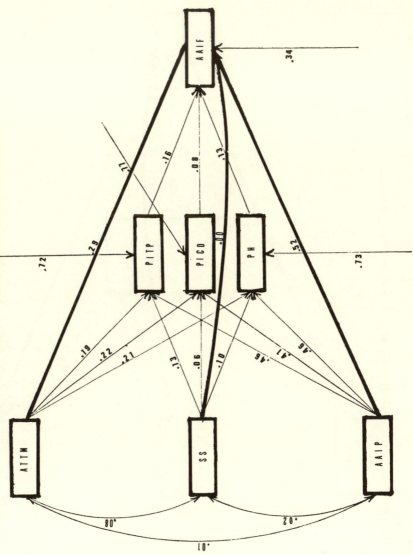

Figure 8.3
Path Coefficients for the Effects of Exogenous Variables, Reading Comprehension

Table 8.8
Path Coefficients* of Direct and Indirect Effects of Three Exogenous Variables on Student Achievement in Arithmetic, Bible Studies, and Reading Comprehension

Subject	Variable	Direct effect	Indirect effect
Arithmetic	ATTM	.23	.10
	SS	.03	.03
	AAIP	.68	.12
Bible	ATTM	.26	.05
	SS	.05	.07
	AAIP	.57	.14
Reading	ATTM	.29	.08
Comprehension	SS	.00	.08
	AAIP	.52	.16

* coefficients of .05 or more are statistically significant for direct effects

tween 22 and 31 percent of the variance in students' motivation to learn in the three subject areas, and they explain between 66 and 75 percent of the variance in students' achievement scores in the three subjects. Achievement in the past was the single most powerful predictor of student motivation and of student achievement; the student's appropriateness for the teaching method affected achievement directly to a substantial degree (23–29 percent of the variance) as well as indirectly (5–10 percent of the variance mediated by motivation).

The students' social status did not affect achievement in arithmetic directly or indirectly when participation in class discussion is the measure of motivation to learn. Nor did social status exert direct influence on achievement in reading comprehension. Hence, the data from arithmetic and reading comprehension do not fit the hypothetical model (see Figure 8.1), which must be modified. The modified model would exclude the path indicating a direct or indirect effect of social status on arithmetic achievement, and a direct effect of social status on achievement in reading comprehension. All other path coefficients were statistically significant and fit the hypothetical model.

All three measures of "motivation to learn" were significantly affected by all of the exogenous variables. Except for the direct and indirect effects of social status on achievement in arithmetic, motivation to learn mediated significantly between the exogenous variables and achievement in each of the three subjects. The path coefficients of the direct and indirect (i.e., mediated by "motivation to learn") effects of the three exogenous variables appear in Table 8.8.

The two exogenous variables of appropriateness to teaching method and academic achievement in the past exerted large direct effects on post-test scores in achievement in each of the three subjects. They also exerted significant, though less substantial, indirect effects on achievement as mediated by motivation to learn. The students' social status exerted significant direct and indirect effects on achievement in Bible studies. In arithmetic and reading comprehension, social status affected achievement indirectly, through motivation, but not directly.

Effects of Instructional Methods on the Dependent Variables

A series of analyses of variance was carried out to assess the effects of the two instructional methods on the mediating and dependent variables in this study, namely academic achievement in mathematics, Bible, and reading comprehension, on three measures of motivation to learn (task perseverence, participation in class discussion, and preparation of homework), and on the pupils' social status measured by three sociometric questions. The two instructional methods were a between-group factor (2) and the pre- and post-test scores were a within-group repeated measure (2). The classroom was used as the unit of analysis. The range of scores is from 1 (lowest score) to 3 (highest score). The *F*-values reflect interactions between treatment group and time (pre- or post-test). These data appear in Table 8.9.

Motivation to learn. The group investigation method was more motivating for students on all three measures, by contrast with the effect of the whole-class method. The data reveal too that not only did the cooperative learning method affect students' motivation more positively than the whole-class method, but also that the students who studied with the latter method did not display any change in their level of motivation to learn over the course of the year. But neither did their motivation scores decline.

Academic achievement. Students in the group investigation classes achieved higher scores in all three subjects than their peers who studied with the whole-class method. Almost invariably, the students in the group investigation classes received lower pre-test scores in each subject than those in the whole-class method. Nevertheless, the GI students reached a higher level on the post-test than the students in the W-C classes. Again, the classroom served as the unit of analysis.

Students' social status. On the pre-test and post-test, each pupil could make up to five choices on each of three questions. The mean scores reported here consisted of the mean number of choices received by each student, and they were derived from combining scores from all three sociometric questions.

DISCUSSION

This study yielded several findings that bear emphasis since they have not been reported in research thus far, namely:

1. Students' motivation to learn and their academic achievement are enhanced when their orientation toward cooperating with others in a group is appropriate for the method of instruction employed in the classroom, that is, when students who are inclined to work with others, or not to do so, have the opportunity to study according to the method most appropriate for them (cooperative learning or whole-class instruction).

2. Motivation to learn mediates to a substantial degree between several major independent variables, such as the appropriateness of the students' orientation toward groupwork for the instructional method used, their social status, and their prior level of achievement on the one hand, and students' academic achievement at the end of the year on the other.

3. The group investigation approach to cooperative learning affects students' achievement, motivation to learn, and social relations more positively than does whole-class instruction. Students in classes conducted with the latter method did not display any change in their level of motivation to learn over the course of an academic year. These results support the hypotheses regarding the mediating role of motivation to learn and its effects on achievement, and regarding the positive influence of the group investigation approach to cooperative learning on students' motivation to learn. The mediating role of motivation to learn was determined here by fulfilling the methodological requirements discussed by Knight and Bohlmeyer (Chapter 1 of this volume).

What Accounts for Student Achievement?

The hypothetical model suggested here was found to be appropriate in most of its elements for explaining the achievement of sixth-grade students in three academic subjects. The models explained fully 74 percent of the variance in the achievement scores in arithmetic, 65 percent in Bible studies, and 69 percent in reading comprehension. We noted that the model for predicting achievement in arithmetic must be modified by eliminating the direct effect of social status on achievement and by eliminating the mediating role of "participation in class discussion," which was found not to fulfill a mediating function. The

Table 8.9
Means, SDs, and F Statistics of Data Obtained with Three Measures of Achievement, Three Measures of Motivation to Learn, and Sociometric Questions (Social Status) in Classes Taught with the Group Investigation (N = 10) or Whole-Class Method (N = 7)(df = 30)

Measure		Group-Investigation		Whole-Class		F
		Pretest	Post-test	Prestest	Post-test	(df=30)
Motivation						
1. Task Perseverence	M	1.96	2.50	2.02	2.10	80.14*
	SD	.08	.05	.05	.06	
2. Participation in Class Discussion	M	1.80	2.40	1.80	1.80	63.12*
	SD	.14	.05	.12	.14	
3. Effort Doing Homework	M	1.90	2.40	1.90	2.00	74.83*
	SD	.09	.04	.09	.12	

Achievement

1.Arithmetic	M	1.84	2.08	1.88	1.91	
	SD	.07	.08	.10	.12	12.15*
2.Bible	M	1.96	2.39	2.00	2.03	
	SD	.15	.09	.16	.15	25.57*
3.Reading Comprehension	M	1.90	2.40	2.01	2.03	
	SD	.11	.09	.15	.14	55.03*
Social Status	M	4.07	4.61	4.07	4.03	
	SD	.59	.42	.65	.71	18.08*

*p .001

path indicating a direct effect of social status on achievement in reading comprehension also must be eliminated. The predictive power of the models would be improved without these latter elements.

Regression analyses showed that "motivation to learn" explained more than half of the variance in achievement in three academic subjects explained by the complete path model for each subject (Table 8.7). Therefore, the two factors of (1) the appropriateness of the student's social orientation for the teaching method (cooperative or whole-class) and (2) the student's social status in the classroom, both affect student learning above and beyond the effect of the student's prior level of achievement. Also, cooperative learning was found here, as in other studies (Sharan 1980; Slavin 1983a), to affect students' social status in the classroom more positively than the whole-class method. Since social status also affects motivation it follows that cooperative learning influences pupils' motivation to learn and their academic achievement through the social network of the classroom, as well as by providing many students with learning experiences consistent with their social orientation.

It is noteworthy that motivation to learn was found to mediate between the pupils' prior achievement and their achievement at the end of the year, despite the fact that these two sets of scores were obtained from the same students only months apart and are highly correlated. Of course, attribution theory and other motivational theories as well account for this finding. A student's earlier level of achievement predicts later achievement not only because it testifies to students' ability or prior knowledge, but also because it affects their motivation to invest effort in the pursuit of learning (Forsyth 1986; McClelland 1965). The present study adds to this explanation the impact of the instructional method and of the students' social status among their peers, on the students' level of motivation to learn and, in turn, on their later achievement. Motivation to learn is decidedly affected by the manner in which classroom learning is conducted. It is not exclusively a function of the curricular materials or of the students' earlier level of achievement, although the latter plays an important determining role. This conclusion suggests that even those students whose achievement heretofore was not very high, can be motivated to learn if the instructional method is appropriate for them and engages them in learning.

In order to better clarify this interpretation of our findings, we wished to examine more closely the academic achievement levels of the students whose motivation and achievement improved from the pre-test to the post-test period. Who were the students most affected by the instructional methods, in terms of their level of achievement? The students were divided into three levels of achievement, as explained above (those with grades 50 and 60 were assigned a 1, those with 70 or 80 were assigned 2, and those with 90 or above were assigned 3). The following histograms indicate the shift in the proportion of students at each of the three achievement levels from the pre-test to the post-test in the classes conducted with the two teaching methods (see Figure 8.4).

The histograms illustrate unequivocally that the relative proportion of high,

Figure 8.4
Distribution of Pupils from Three Levels of Achievement in Two Teaching Methods

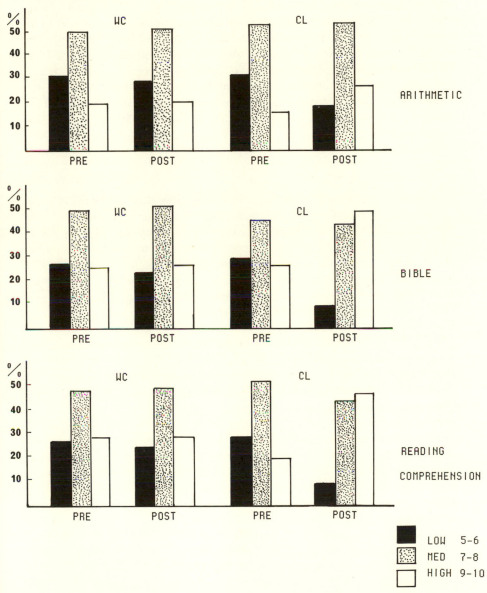

medium, and low achievers did not change in the classes taught with the whole-class method. The students' prior level of achievement is almost a perfect predictor of their achievement at the end of the year. In the cooperative learning classes, on the other hand, the number of low achievers declines markedly (in Bible studies and reading comprehension the percentage drops from 30 to 10 percent low achievers, in arithmetic the number dropped by 10 percent). The number of high achievers increases dramatically in Bible studies (from 35 to 50 percent) and reading comprehension (from 22 to 50 percent) and it increased noticeably, albeit less dramatically, in arithmetic as well (from 18 to 28 percent). The number of medium-range achievers in both the whole-class and cooperative learning classes remains virtually unchanged (though the different categories are not populated by the same students in the pre-test and post-test).

Motivation to Learn

Students' motivation to learn was assessed here by three measures of overt behavior in the classroom. These measures reflect a person's investment of time and energy in dealing with learning tasks, and were not inferred from grades or scores on tests of achievement. It appears reasonable to conclude, therefore, that cooperative learning promoted students' intrinsic interest in learning tasks by comparison with students in classrooms taught with the whole-class method. It should be emphasized that no specific individual or group rewards were employed in this study other than the usual grading system ordinarily used by the teachers.

On the basis of the data gathered in this study, we are not able make any assertions about the specific components of the group investigation method that constitute the primary motivating factors in this method. To identify those components requires a research program that will vary the main components systematically. The group investigation method provides learners with considerable support from peers and with a far greater degree of decision-making power over their own work in school than most other approaches to classroom instruction. It attributes importance to, and provides specific procedures for, giving students an important role in planning the topic and subtopics of their group's study and in helping their groupmates carry out their collective task (Miel 1952; Sharan and Hertz-Lazarowitz 1980; Sharan and Sharan 1976). Working toward a common goal with peers and involvement in deciding one's own course of work are generally considered to be critical factors for arousing intrinsic motivation in a task and a sense of personal responsibility for its completion (Ames 1986; DeCharms 1976; Ryan, Connell, and Deci 1985; Weisz and Cameron 1985) (see Fig. 8.5). These same factors are singularly absent from most classroom teaching and learning. Oddly enough, instruction is still largely viewed as a vast delivery service whose task it is to deliver a completed manufactured product to the consumer.

Another set of histograms presents the relative number of low-, medium-,

Figure 8.5
Distribution of Pupils from Three Levels of Motivation in Two Teaching Methods

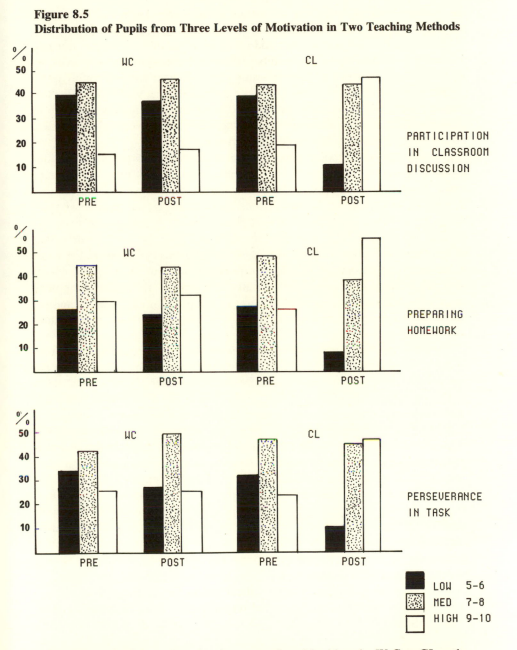

and high-motivation students in classes taught with either the W-C or GI methods. A different picture emerges on each of the three measures of motivation to learn. On the measure of participation in class discussion, there is no change from pre- to post-test in the W-C classes. In the cooperative learning classes the change is striking: only about 7 percent of the students are assessed as low participants in the class discussion, while almost 60 percent of the class are considered to be high participants. One might say that this finding is not remarkable because cooperative learning procedures almost necessarily involve the students in discussions of the learning task, and these findings simply document the implementation of the instructional procedures. While that explanation has truth, the finding also shows that cooperative learning does involve a majority of the students in the process of learning whereas whole-class instruction does not. That fact should not be overlooked.

Less obvious is the finding obtained with the second measure of motivation to learn, preparing homework. This measure refers to an activity carried out when the students were not in class and, hence, cannot be attributed to the demand characteristics of the instructional procedures. In the group investigation classes, both the medium and high categories of investing energy in the preparation of homework account for about 88 percent of all the students at the end of the year, up from about 64 percent in these two categories at the time of the pre-test. That leaves only 12 percent in the category of low investment of energy in homework compared with about 31 percent at the time of the pre-test. In the whole-class method at the time of the post-test about 28 percent of the students were considered to be in the low category in terms of preparing homework.

The third measure of motivation, task perseverence, is a "transfer" measure in the sense that it reflects the effect of the instructional method at a time when the students were not engaged in regular classroom work, when formal class work was suspended and the students were free to decide on their own what they wished to do. It is also noteworthy that this was a behavioral measure not dependent on teachers' evaluations. Here the number of students in the GI classes who consistently decided to continue to work on their studies and not go out and play increased 30 percent (20 to 50 percent) from the pre-test (average of three trials) to the post-test (average of another three trials). The relative proportions of the students from the whole-class method who decided not to go out to play remained unchanged from the pre-test to the post-test. In both methods, the medium category remained the same. These data about motivation also show that pupils at all levels of motivation to learn are positively affected by cooperative learning, including students who are initially considered to display low motivation to learn.

Social Status

This study also yielded findings consistent with the results of other studies of cooperative learning that reported improved social relations among students in cooperative learning classes (Sharan 1980, 1984; Slavin 1983a). It should be pointed out that cooperative learning studies have not always yielded increased scores on sociometric measures, although the general tendency among studies using this measure is quite positive (Slavin 1983a:115–17). Slavin (1983a) noted that most of the studies that failed to find improved sociometric selection of friends were conducted in elementary schools and that the lack of change could stem from a ceiling effect because most elementary school students report that they like their classmates. However, an experiment with two methods of cooperative learning conducted in Israeli junior high schools also failed to produce change in sociometric scores (Sharan et al. 1984:118–21). It was noted in the latter study that the social network of the classroom is not easily affected by the instructional method, even one that involves marked changes in peer interaction typical of cooperative learning. The relatively limited effect of sociometric choices (social status) on student achievement found in the present study could also stem from the restricted variation in these data generated by the instructional methods, even though the two teaching methods were found to differ statistically in favor of group investigation.

Many factors, in addition to the prevailing pattern of peer interaction determined by the instructional method, could affect pupils' sociometric choices, such as: the prior history of social relations in given classrooms, general school climate, or the intensity with which cooperative learning is employed with a given class. And if elementary students generally report liking each other, it could be that changes in sociometric selections would be more evident in response to negative questions rather than to positive ones. No negative questions were employed in the present study. Another distinction between items is the degree of intimacy in the relationship requested by the particular sociometric question (close or casual contact, for example). Such items have been found by students of sociometric evaluation to result in very different findings about interpersonal and inter-group relations (Schwarzwald, Laor, and Hoffman 1986), as would the positive–negative character of the questions used. The intimate–casual continuum was not examined in the present study. We have no information as to whether the three items employed here constitute different degrees of intimacy as perceived by sixth-grade students. The investigators had the impression that all three questions requested the same degree of intimacy. These latter differences in the content of the sociometric measure could also account for different results in sociometric data reported in the cooperative learning research literature.

Orientation toward Groupwork

A significant conclusion to emerge from this study is related to the "trait by treatment interaction" hypothesis (Cronbach and Snow 1977) to the effect that students are differentially oriented toward cooperative groupwork, and that their motivation to learn and subsequent achievement are enhanced when they study in a classroom conducted with a teaching method most consistent with their social orientation. This means that cooperative learning should be an instructional alternative available to students who are inclined to cooperate with their peers on learning tasks. It also means that not all students are so inclined and they should have the option of studying with the whole-class method. This is, in essence, the same conclusion reached by Kagan in his research on students from ethnic backgrounds that stressed cooperation rather than competition (Kagan 1980; Kagan et al. 1985). In many elementary schools today several instructional methods are practiced simultaneously, but many elementary schools, and almost all secondary schools, are still "one-mission organizations" in terms of their instructional technology. Also, not many teachers master a range of teaching methods and employ them as circumstances and goals dictate. Most schools still behave as if there is one best way to teach, and that is usually the same way, i.e. through the whole-class method. The results of the present study show that this state of affairs reduces students' motivation to learn and their actual academic achievement.

However, it must be made clear that the group investigation approach to cooperative learning was found to produce superior effects to those generated by the whole-class method in all of the domains evaluated here, namely: achievement, motivation to learn, and social relations with classmates. All students benefited from studying with the GI method, even those whose expressed social orientation was not directed toward cooperation with peers. Accommodation of student to instructional method according to the student's personal characteristics may produce more optimal adjustment and learning in school, but cooperative learning still emerges as a superior approach for all students compared with the traditional whole-class method, in terms of the measures employed in this study.

REFERENCES

Ames, C. (1986) "Effective motivation: The contribution of the learning environment." In *The Social Psychology of Education,* edited by R. Feldman, pp. 253–56. Cambridge: Cambridge University Press.

Ames, C., and Ames R. (eds) (1985) *Research on Motivation in Education: Vol 2: The Classroom Milieu,* Orlando, FL: Academic Press.

Corno, L., and Mandinach, E. (1983) "The role of cognitive engagement in classroom learning and motivation." *Educational Psychologist* 18:88–108.

Cronbach, L., and Snow, R. (1977) *Aptitudes and Instructional Methods: A Handbook for Research Interactions.* New York: Irvington.

DeCharms, R. (1968) *Personal Causation,* New York: Academic Press.

———— (1971) "Motivation in the classroom." In *Psychology and Educational Practice,* edited by G. Lesser, pp. 380–407. Glenview, IL: Scott Foresman.

———— (1976) *Enhancing Motivation: Change in the Classroom.* New York: Irvington (Halsted-Wiley).

Deci, E. (1975) *Intrinsic Motivation,* New York: Plenum.

Forsyth, D. (1986) "An attributional analysis of students' reactions to success and failure." In *The Social Psychology of Education*, edited by R. Feldman, pp. 17–38. Cambridge: Cambridge University Press.

Johnson, D., and Johnson, R. (1985) "Motivational processes in cooperative, competitive and individualistic learning situations." In *Research on Motivation in Education, Vol. 2: The Classroom Milieu*, edited by C. Ames and R. Ames, pp. 249–86. Orlando, FL: Academic Press.

——— (1987) *Learning Together and Alone*, Englewood Cliffs, NJ: Prentice-Hall.

Kagan, S. (1980) "Cooperation-competition, culture and structural bias in classrooms." In *Cooperation in Education*, edited by S. Sharan et al., pp. 197–211. Provo, UT: Brigham Young University Press.

Kagan, S., Zahn, G., and Gealy, J. (1977) "Competition and school achievement among Anglo-American and Mexican-American children." *Journal of Educational Psychology* 69:432–41.

Kagan, S., Zahn, G., Widaman, K., Schwarzwald, J., and Tyrrell, G. (1985) "Classroom structural bias impact of cooperative and competitive classroom structures on cooperative and competitive individuals and groups." In *Learning to Cooperate, Cooperating to Learn*, edited by R. Slavin, S. Sharan, S. Kagan, R. Hertz-Lazarowitz, C. Webb, and R. Schmuck, pp. 277–312. New York: Plenum.

McClelland, D. (1965) *Toward a Theory of Motive Acquisition*, New York: Van Nostrand Reinhold.

Miel, A. (1952) *Cooperative Procedures in Learning*, New York: Teachers College.

Owens, L. (1983) "Learning mode preferences and perceptions of classroom atmosphere by primary school students in Sydney and Perth." Paper presented at the conference of the South Pacific Association for Teacher Education, Brisbane.

Owens, L., and Straton, R. (1980) "The development of a cooperative, competitive and individualized learning preferences scale for students." *Journal of Educational Psychology* 50:147–61.

Pepitone, E. (1980) *Children in Cooperation and Competition*, Lexington, MA: Lexington Books.

Ryan, M., Connell, J., and Deci, E. (1985) "A motivational analysis of self-determination and self-regulation in education." In *Motivation in Education: Vol. 2: The Classroom Milieu*, edited by C. Ames and R. Ames, pp. 13–51. Orlando, FL: Academic Press.

Sarason, S. (1983) *Schooling in America: Scapegoat and Salvation*, New York: The Free Press.

Schmuck, R., and Schmuck, P. (1988) *Group Processes in the Classroom*, 5th edn. Dubuque, IA: Brown and Co.

Schwarzwald, J., Laor, T., and Hoffman, M. (1986) "Impact of sociometric method and activity content on assessment of intergroup relations in the classroom." *British Journal of Educational Psychology* 56:24–31.

Sharan, S. (1980) "Cooperative learning in small groups: Recent methods and effects on achievement, attitudes and ethnic relations." *Review of Educational Research* 50:241–71.

Sharan, S., and Hertz-Lazarowitz, R. (1980) "A group-investigation method of cooperative learning in the classroom." In *Cooperation in Education*, edited by S. Sharan, P. Hare, C. Webb and R. Hertz-Lazarowitz, pp. 14–46. Provo, UT: Brigham Young University Press.

――― (1982) "Effects of an instructional change project on teachers' behavior, attitudes and perceptions." *Journal of Applied Behavioral Science* 18:185–201.

Sharan, S., Hertz-Lazarowitz, R., and Relner, T. (1978) "Television for changing teacher behavior." *Journal of Educational Technology Systems* 7:119–31.

Sharan, S., Kussell, P., Hertz-Lazarowitz, R., Bejarano, Y., Raviv, S., and Sharan, Y. (1984) *Cooperative Learning in the Classroom: Research in Desegregated Schools*. Hillsdale, NJ: Lawrence Erlbaum.

Sharan, S., and Shachar, H. (1988) *Language and Learning in the Cooperative Classroom*. New York: Springer.

Sharan, S., and Sharan, Y. (1976) *Small Group Teaching*. Englewood Cliffs, NJ: Educational Technology Publications.

――― 1987 "Training teachers for cooperative learning." *Educational Leadership* 45:20–25.

Slavin, R. (1983a) *Cooperative Learning,* New York: Longman.

――― (1983b) "When does cooperative learning increase student achievement?" *Psychological Bulletin* 94:429–45.

――― (1987) "Developmental and motivational perspectives on cooperative learning: A reconciliation." *Child Development* 58:1161–67.

Slavin, R., Sharan, S., Kagan, S., Hertz-Lazarowitz, R., Webb, C., and Schmuck, R. (eds) (1985) *Learning to Cooperate, Cooperating to Learn*. New York: Plenum.

Thew, D. (1975) "The classroom social organization category system." *Classroom Interaction Newsletter* 11:18–24.

Weisz, J., and Cameron, A. (1985) "Individual differences in the student's sense of control." In *Motivation in Education: Vol. 2: The Classroom Milieu,* edited by C. Ames and R. Ames, pp. 93–140. Orlando, FL: Academic Press.

9
Treating Status Problems in the Cooperative Classroom

ELIZABETH G. COHEN, RACHEL LOTAN, AND LISA CATANZARITE

Cooperative groupwork has a strong potential for engaging students, improving friendliness and trust between students and, under some conditions, producing superior achievement gains in comparison to traditional individualistic modes of education (Johnson et al. 1981; Sharan 1980; Slavin 1983). There are, however, some important problems that remain to be solved in connection with designing classroom settings for cooperative learning. One of these problems arises from status differences between students in the classroom. It has been repeatedly shown that mixed-status groups engaged in collective tasks are dominated by high-status members and do not receive the benefit of the contribution of some low-status members (Berger, Rosenholtz, and Zelditch 1980). Research on mixed-status groups of classmates shows the same pattern of high-status dominance and low-status withdrawal (Rosenholtz 1985). If cooperative learning techniques depend on interaction for their desirable effects on learning, then access to interaction that differs according to the status of the student is of practical concern.

WHAT IS A STATUS PROBLEM?

Status characteristics are social rankings in which it is generally believed that it is better to be in the high state than the low state. The process by which status characteristics come to affect interaction and influence is described by expectation states theory (Berger et al. 1966, 1972).

Race and ethnicity are examples of diffuse status characteristics that can have an impact on the behavior of schoolchildren as they interact on collective tasks. When, for example, a racial status characteristic becomes salient in the situation, the prestige and power order of the small group working on a collective task comes to reflect the broader social status ranking of the races in a kind of self-fulfilling prophecy. Whites turn out to be more active and influential than blacks. (For a full description of this process, see Berger, Rosenholtz, and Zelditch 1980.) Using a standardized game task, it has been shown repeatedly in the United States, Canada and Israel that race and ethnicity can act as characteristics so that high-status students are more active and influential than low-status students (Cohen 1982).

When a status characteristic is diffuse, there are general expectations for competence and incompetence that are attached to the characteristic. The status organizing process is related to these expectations for competence held by the self and the other in collective task groups. It bears no relationship to feelings of friendliness. Theoretically, the use of cooperative interracial groups in desegregated classrooms can, at one and the same time, confirm stereotypes concerning the lesser competence of some races and, simultaneously, generate increased feelings of friendliness between the races.

There are other status characteristics at work in the classroom that have an impact on interaction in collective tasks. The most powerful are academic status characteristics (Hoffman and Cohen 1972; Rosenholtz 1985; Tammivaara 1982). When the educator gives a group a collective, cooperative task, status differences based on academic ability become activated and relevant to the new situation. The high-status students will then expect and will be expected to be more competent. The net effect is a self-fulfilling prophecy whereby the high-status student is more active and influential than the low-status student. When students see themselves and are seen by classmates as having more or less academic ability or reading ability, those who are seen as having more ability will be more active and influential than those who are seen as having less ability.

The classroom is a multi-characteristic situation. Students vary on three different types of status characteristics: social, academic, and peer. Social status characteristics are those ascribed characteristics brought into the classroom from the outside society (race, ethnicity, and sex). Academic status characteristics are created and maintained in the classroom setting. Peer status characteristics are created in the informal relationships between students. There are very few studies that have specifically tested the operation of peer status on behavior. One of the studies that has done so is that of Webster and Driskell (1983) on attractiveness as a status characteristic. Maruyama and Miller (1981), in reviewing the literature on physical attractiveness, conclude that physically attractive individuals are seen as more capable in short-term interactions. This generalization would also suggest the operation of attractiveness as a status characteristic.

From a practical point of view, these status effects constitute a significant problem to those who work with cooperative learning situations. Theoretically, the introduction of interdependence in a group task is sufficient to activate differential expectations for competence based on status characteristics. Once these expectations have become activated and relevant to the new cooperative task, low-status students will interact less than high-status students. If one argues that interaction is of great benefit to the student, then the net effect of the process of status generalization is that low-status students receive less of the benefit of interaction than high-status students.

This line of reasoning is not inconsistent with the research findings that in cooperative learning in desegregated situations, blacks make even greater achievement gains than whites (Slavin 1983). Cooperative groupwork will engage students who are ordinarily disengaged and will assist those who cannot read the curricular materials. Thus low-achieving students are often better off in the cooperative group than they would be in the traditional class. However, it can still be the case that these students are less active and influential than their high-status classmates. Furthermore, it is still possible that low-status students could show even greater gains if their expectations for competence were raised and if they were more active in the group.

Expectation states theory has been used to create various interventions that modify the operation of status characteristics. These interventions have been successful in the laboratory and in controlled classroom settings (Cohen 1982; Cohen, Lockheed, and Lohman 1976; Rosenholtz 1985). Despite these successes, the classroom is one of the most difficult places to produce lasting equal-status behavior because of the strong relevance of academic ranking as a status characteristic. Many features of conventional classrooms help to create an agreed-upon status order, running from the smartest students to the "dumbest." The evaluation system of most classrooms lets everyone know who are the winners and who are the losers in this academic ranking process. (For a full review of this literature see Cohen 1986.)

THE TREATMENT OF STATUS PROBLEMS: PLAN FOR ANALYSIS

Analyses of two comparable data sets are reported in this chapter. Initially, we will review research documenting status problems of children in classrooms as they interact cooperatively on learning tasks. This research demonstrated that the learning gains of low-status children can be inhibited by their failure to have as much access to interaction as high-status children (Cohen 1984b).

The data collected in 1979–80 on 307 children in nine classrooms is referred to as data set I. The instructional approach implemented in these classrooms was *Finding Out/Descubrimiento,* a bilingual approach to the development of thinking skills developed by Edward De Avila. Classrooms contained multiple learning centers, each with different materials and activities. The centers operated simultaneously; four or five children worked at each. They were assigned challenging tasks requiring repeated use of the same mathematics and science concepts in different ways and with different media. Over a period of 15 weeks, four days a week, for 45 minutes per day, children had to complete the task at each learning center and fill out the worksheet that accompanied the task.

In 1982–83 several important changes were introduced to the implementation of *Finding Out/Descubrimiento*. These changes included a new classroom management strategy, longer teacher training, and a special emphasis on the use of treatments designed to moderate the effects of status on interaction in cooperative classroom groups. Despite these strategic changes, the curriculum materials and the pattern of multiple materials and learning centers described above were identical in the two years. In the second part of the paper, the comparison of this second set of data (referred to as data set II) with the 1979–80 data (referred to as data set I) allows us to investigate the answers to several research questions concerning the possibility of moderating status effects in cooperative learning.

Research Questions

Of particular interest is an examination of the effects of the new classroom management system. Did it increase interaction? Did it reduce the effect of status on interaction as well as the effect of status on learning gains in comparison to the effects observed in data set I? These questions are investigated by correlating measures of status gathered from sociometric data with observed rates of behavior among a set of selected "target children" and with standardized test scores on the children's achievement in the fall and spring of each school year studied. The strength and nature of the observed relationships are compared for the two data sets.

The focus of a second set of research questions is an examination of shifts in status at the classroom level as measured by sociometric questions between fall and spring in data set II. In absolute terms, is there evidence of some improvement in the standing of low-status children during the school year? In relative terms, did the standing of low-status children in comparison with that of high-status children improve over the school year? Is there any evidence that classrooms showing reduced effects of status on the distribution of sociometric choices are classrooms that experienced superior implementation of the program? And finally, what is the relationship of status differences as measured by sociometric data to status differences as measured by talk between peers?

Measurement

Measures of status. The instrument used for both data sets consisted of sociometric questions, each of which was followed by a list of names of the students in that particular classroom. The sociometric questionnaires were administered in the fall and spring of each year. The students were asked, for example, to circle the names of those in their class who were "best at math and science,'' their "best friends,'' or "best at games and sports.'' Students then identified their choices by circling the appropriate names on the list following each question. There was an English and a Spanish version of the instrument. A group of trained test administrators tried to make sure that each child could understand the directions and could recognize the names of classmates on the questionnaire.

Since students could circle any number of names, the number of choices indicated for each criterion question varied between students and between classrooms. The distribution of choices for each question was divided into quintiles for each classroom. Each child was then assigned a score ranging from one to five, depending on the fifth of the distribution in which lay the number of times that child's name was chosen.

The two questions from the fall questionnaire requiring choices on who was "best at math and science'' and who was "a best friend'' made up the measure of status. In both data sets, there was a high level of correlation between being chosen on one of these criteria and being chosen on the other. In data set I, the correlation for the fall measures was .50 ($p<.001$); in data set II, the correlation coefficient was .64 ($p<.001$). In other settings, measures of peer status may or may not be positively associated with academic status (Cohen 1984a).

The specific status characteristic of ability in mathematics and science was the one most directly relevant to the learning materials. The question on "best friends'' was used as an indicator of the status characteristic of unattractiveness/popularity; it represents peer status. In order to derive a single measure of status in a multi-characteristic setting, the two quintile scores were added together. This measure is referred to as the co-status score. The rationale for the construction of this index was the combining principle that theoretically operates in a multi-characteristic setting (Humphreys and Berger 1981). According to this principle the actor combines all units of status information to form aggregated expectation states for the self and the other. If the information is inconsistent, such that there are both positive and negative expectations for the competence of an actor, then these can cancel each other out.

Analysis of the sociometric data in data set I showed a high level of correlation among all the sociometric indexes (see Cohen 1984b). Even being chosen as best in games and sports was highly correlated with being chosen as best in reading. One should not assume that there is a generalization from academic status characteristics to nonacademic status characteristics. In some cases the generalization appears to operate from attractiveness/popularity to perceived academic ability; some children with limited English proficiency who were perceived as attractive were given high ratings on the academic criteria despite low objective scores on achievement tests. In general, however, there is a relationship between classmate selection as best in an academic subject and objective test scores; for example, the quintile score on "best at math and science'' showed a significant correlation with scores on the achievement tests in mathematics ($r=.41$, $p<.001$ in fall; $r=.60$, $p<.001$ in spring).

Observed behavior. Observers visited classrooms once a week to obtain timed observations of the task-related behavior of target children working at learning centers. They used a device for scoring interaction that measured performance outputs of the child relevant to the task. Measures of interaction were closely related to the small-group scoring system developed on the basis of status characteristics and expectation states theory and used on small-group interaction in more controlled settings (Cohen 1982). During each 30-second interval of a three-minute period, the observer recorded the frequency of task-related talk and of selected nonverbal behaviors: working alone or together on the curriculum, behavior not related to the task, and behavior not directly relevant to this analysis.

In order to assess the reliability of the target-child instrument, each classroom observer was paired with a supervisor who acted as a criterion scorer. The supervisor scored alongside the observer. No observer was allowed to score independently until a satisfactory level of agreement with the supervisor's scoring was reached. A percentage agreement was calculated by comparing the total number of checks made by the observer and by the supervisor for each category on the scoring instrument during the scoring period. If 90 percent of the judgments were in agreement, the level of reliability was deemed satisfactory. During the data collection, each observer received visits from one of the supervisors. Reliability checks were made at that time. The average percentage agreement for this instrument was 90 percent over the 24 times reliability was assessed for data set I. For data set II, the average percentage agreement was also 90 percent over the 26 times reliability was assessed.

The two variables of interest here are the rates of task-related talk with peers and the observed frequency of working together on the curriculum with peers. A task-related speech was scored by a single check as long as it was not interrupted by another student talking or by a change to a subject that was not related within the 30-second interval. If the speech extended to the next time interval, the observer recorded another check. To calculate an average rate of talking across observations, the total frequency of these speeches was divided by the number of observations for that child.

In order to be sure that there was sufficient stability in the measures taken of a given child to justify this aggregation procedure, an analysis of variance was carried out on frequency of talk for different observations taken on the same child. This analysis showed that in both data sets, there was a substantial difference between observations taken on different children as compared with the set of observations taken on the same child; the value of F was statistically significant for this analysis on each data set.

The other critical variable was the rate of working together with peers. As with rate of talking, the child was a significant source of variance in the frequency of this behavior per observation ($F = 1.28$; $p < .033$). Rate of talking and working together is an indicator of task-related interaction in an interdependent work relationship. (For details of the information of this index, see

Cohen 1984b). This index of talking and working together has the effect of weighting talk by the frequency with which it occurs in an interdependent context. Because young children quite frequently talk to themselves about the task, not all talk takes place in an interdependent context.

Achievement data. The achievement test data consisted of fall and spring scores on the CTBS (Comprehensive Test of Basic Skills) math concepts and application and reading subscales. The spring testing took place after students had all experienced a substantial number of curriculum units. Only those students who took the English CTBS in the fall *and* in the spring were included in the sample for achievement analysis. Thus, those students who moved away during the school year, those who transferred into the school after the fall testing date, those whose English was judged insufficient to take the examination in the fall, and those who were absent on either test day were omitted. The achievement data are in national percentile scores in both data sets.

Data set I also included two additional tests. One, called the Mini-Test, was given orally in English and in Spanish; it was specifically constructed to reflect the content of the curriculum. This test was used to measure the relationship between status, interaction, and learning in the initial documentation on the effects of status in *Finding Out* (Cohen 1984b). The other test, the Language Assessment Scale, was a measure of English proficiency developed by De Avila and Duncan.

PART I

Documentation of Status Problems in Data Set I

Data set I contains nine bilingual classrooms (grades 2–4) from five districts in the San Jose, California, area; there were nine teachers who were volunteers and 307 children. Classes were largely composed of children of Hispanic background with a small proportion of Anglos, blacks, and Asians. Parental background was working class and lower white collar, with a few children from families on welfare. There was great diversity of academic skills as measured by the Comprehensive Test of Basic Skills, with many students functioning far below grade level.

The data used for this analysis were the behavioral observations, sociometric questionnaires, and test scores collected on two sets of target classroom within each of the nine classrooms (grades 2–4). One set was selected for varying levels of proficiency in English and Spanish; the other set was selected by the teacher as likely to have the most difficulty in activities requiring mathematics and science. All students filled out a sociometric questionnaire (the source of the measures of status) in the fall of the experimental year. Achievement data for this first analysis included scores on a content-referenced test (the Mini-Test) especially constructed to measure learning outcomes of this curriculum. Test scores on this instrument were used as the dependent variable. In addition, the score on the reading subscales from the Comprehensive Test of Basic Skills was used as a control variable along with a measure of English proficiency from the Language Assessment Scale developed by DeAvila and Duncan. Both of these tests were administered in the fall. The behavioral measures of target children consisted of the talking and working together index described above and a simple notation for each three-minute observation period as to whether or not the child was seen reading or writing (a 0, 1 variable).

Analysis of Collective Task Conditions in Data Set I

Unlike previous work on expectation states with schoolchildren, the method of instruction in 1979–80 rarely required children to work together to produce a joint product or to make joint decisions. Instead, children worked in shifting groups at learning centers. They were individually responsible for completion of the task and worksheet at each learning center.

However, there were some special features that produced brief interdependencies between the students. Teachers gave the following two rules: You have the right to ask anyone at your learning center for help; you have the duty to assist anyone at your learning center who asks for help. Since the tasks from *Finding Out* are highly challenging, uncertain, and always novel, and the students are compelled to complete their tasks and worksheets, there was strong motivation for students to look to one another as resources.

Grouping was temporary and heterogeneous. After finishing one center, a student would select a new center that did not already have the posted limit of students working at it. Over time, each student had the chance to work with practically every other student in the class.

Path Model Analysis of Status, Interaction, and Learning

The path model depicting the relations between status, interaction, and learning is presented in Figure 9.1 (see also Cohen 1984b). All of the paths in this model have statistically significant path coefficients. The data show a clear relationship between status characteristics and peer interaction, even when the amount of knowledge about the curriculum prior to its start is controlled. The statistically significant path coefficient between interaction and learning is particularly important in light of the multiple controls; other significant predictors of the post-test score on the criterion-referenced test are the pre-test score on this same instrument, the CTBS Reading pre-test score, and the observed frequency of reading and writing.

Cohen interpreted these results as follows:

At the same time that the path model depicts the favorable effects of peer interaction on learning, it shows the negative effects of status. In this interactional system, those children with high social status have more access to peer interaction that, in turn, assists their learning. In other words, the rich get richer. This is the dilemma of using peer

Figure 9.1
Path Model of Relations between Status, Interaction, and Learning

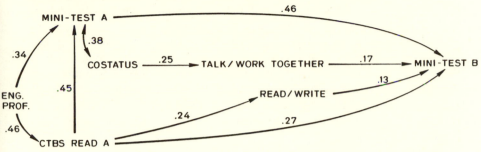

interaction; at the same time that it increases engagement and provides a strong potential for learning, it makes the status structure of the classroom salient and allows it to become the basis of the prestige and power order within the interacting classroom group. (Cohen 1984b; 184)

This analysis documents status problems among children who have been allowed and encouraged to work interdependently. The fact that some of the low-status children fail to have equal access to the interaction constitutes a barrier to their learning. Some low-status children who have inadequate reading skills are particularly dependent on peers for help in understanding the nature of the task; it is therefore critical to prevent situations in which there are children who never really understand what is expected of them because they cannot ask peers for assistance.

PART II

Moderating Status Effects

Despite gains in achievement test scores in the 1979–80 study (data set I), there was much room for improvement, particularly in training teachers to work with children at multiple learning centers. Teachers needed more help in delegating authority than they received in the three-day workshop that we held prior to the start of school in the summer of 1979. The failure of some teachers to delegate authority and to allow multiple learning centers to function without constant supervision limited opportunities for children to talk and work together and thus limited their opportunities for learning. An analysis of these problems led to the introduction of a more elaborate teacher training program and a new system of classroom management.

Revision of Rules and Roles: 1982–83 Study

In 1982–83, although we used the same curriculum materials, we made substantial changes in the way children worked at the learning centers. Teachers assigned children to heterogeneous groups (mixed as to academic achievement, language proficiency, and sex) and to particular learning centers. A child could not move on to a new learning center until the whole group had finished the task, thus increasing interdependence of group members.

We introduced a new system of group management in a two-week workshop for teachers. Teachers learned how to inculcate a set of cooperative norms in the children by means of a series of training games played prior to initiation of the curriculum. These norms of cooperation included asking questions, listening to others, helping another person without actually performing the task, explaining to others, showing other people how things work, and giving other people what they need.

In addition to new behavioral norms, children were assigned specific roles to play in the group. An important role was that of facilitator, a person who sees to it that all members of the group get the help that they need. Other roles were that of checker, who makes sure that everyone finishes the worksheet; reporter, who discusses what the group learned during the wrap-up session held at the end of every learning center session; clean-up supervisor; and safety officer. Each child had a role to play, and the roles were rotated.

To increase the achievement of low-status children, we sought to increase their opportunities for talking and working together and to treat the status problems documented in the 1979–80 data set. The purposes of the norms and roles were to help teachers delegate authority and to ensure that children were using each other as resources so that everyone might participate fully in the learning activities. Obviously, this approach would increase the probability of children talking and working together. The teaching of norms that encourage cooperation has been shown to prevent dominance by high-status members of the group (Morris 1977). When a group believes that everyone ought to participate, it will force members to share materials and will not permit one member to do all the talking. The use of such norms to equalize participation, however, does not alter expectations for competence.

The 1982–83 teacher training program gave emphasis to the use of multiple ability treatments, in which teachers attempt to modify competence expectations by convincing students that many different abilities are relevant to the tasks at hand (Tammivaara 1982; Rosenholtz 1985). In *Finding Out,* teachers discuss with students the many different abilities that are needed for the learning centers of each unit of the curriculum. They explain that reading and computational ability are only two of the relevant abilities and state specifically: "No one is going to be good at all these abilities; everyone is going to be good on at least one." The goal is for each student to have a mixed set of expectations for competence, some high, some low, for the multiple abilities relevant to the task. The multiple ability treatment is an adaptation of the laboratory study of Tammivaara (1982) and of the classroom experiment of Rosenholtz (1985). In these studies, the assignment of a set of competence expectations, some of which were high and some of which were low, substantially weakened status effects. In 1979 a brief but unsuccessful attempt was made to train teachers to use this approach. Persuading teachers to perceive tasks in terms of multiple abilities and to believe that every student will be good on some of these abilities is a difficult strategy to implement; it appears to run counter to some persistent beliefs. There is a tendency among teachers to believe that students are either competent or incompetent to perform a wide range of tasks.

Evaluation of the operation of learning centers in 1982–83 showed that teachers consistently maintained multiple and different learning centers in simultaneous operation (Cohen and DeAvila 1983). In data set II, the average percentage of children observed in small groups was 93.65 percent, whereas the average percentage in data set I was only 38.21 percent. The average percentage of students talking and manipulating the materials was increased to 32 percent in data set II from 24 percent in data set I.

Results: Comparison of Data Sets I and II

Did the introduction of the new system of classroom management weaken the relationship between status and interaction? Did low-status children interact more with their peers under the new system? These are particularly important questions because many low-status children were poor readers or nonreaders who needed the assistance of peers to understand the instructions on the activity card and on the worksheets. If they did not ask for help or if peers did not voluntarily help them, their access to the excellent learning materials was limited.

If the new system was successful, then low-status children should have higher rates of interaction in 1982–83 than in 1979–80. If we were successful in improving expectations for competence during the school year in 1982–83, then we could expect a direct effect of improved expectations for competence reflected in test scores as well as the indirect effects mediated through peer interaction and participation in activities designed to teach concepts. Still another question is whether teachers were successful in convincing the children that everyone had a contribution to make. If they were not, then high-status children would believe they were more expert and therefore more capable of offering assistance.

Description of Data Set II. During the school year 1982–83, 391 children in ten schools in three school districts, as well as 18 volunteer teachers and eight assistants, participated in the program. (Some of these assistants were teachers' aides and some were credentialed teachers.) Sociometric measures as well as standardized achievement tests were administered to all students in each classroom in the fall and spring. We were able to gather sociometric and achievement data for the pre- and post-test for 176 children in 13 classrooms of grades 2–5. Observational data were collected on a subsample of target children chosen to produce variability in academic achievement and in English language

Table 9.1

Comparison of Mean Rates* of Task-Related Talk and of Offering Assistance, 1979–80 versus 1982–83

	1979/80		1982/83	
	Mean (N=111)	S.D.	Mean (N=131)	S.D.
Peer Task-Related Talk	2.170	1.303	3.998	1.707
Offering Assistance	0.425	0.426	0.629	0.581

* Rate = Frequency per 3 minute observation period

proficiency. There were 131 target children on whom we had a sufficient number of observations as well as sociometric data.

Changes in the relationship of status to interaction and learning. Table 9.1 presents observational data from the subsample of target children. It gives the mean rates of task-related talk that the target children directed to their peers in 1979–80 and 1982–83 and the mean rates of offering assistance to peers in those two years. With the introduction of norms and roles, the mean rate of talk increased sharply from 2.17 times per three minutes to four times per three minutes ($t=4.83$; $p<.001$). There was also a statistically significant increase in the rate of offering assistance ($t=7.05$; $p<.001$).

Table 9.2 gives the mean rates of task-related talk for three categories of the co-status scores in the two data sets. The distribution of co-status scores is divided into three groups, with approximately a third of the distribution falling

Table 9.2

Mean Rates of Task-Related Talk for High-, Medium-, and Low-Status Students, 1979–80 and 1982–83

CoStatus*	Task-Related Talk			
	1979/80		1982/83	
	Mean	S.D.	Mean	S.D.
Low (2 - 4)	2.075 (N = 32)	1.257	3.662 (N = 44)	1.605
Medium (4-7)	1.879 (N = 48)	1.061	4.046 (N = 40)	1.492
High (8-10)	2.720 (N = 31)	1.541	4.272 (N = 47)	1.936

* Costatus = Quintile of Choice Distribution for "Best in Math and Science" + "Best Friend".

Table 9.3
Correlation of Co-status with Rates of Talk, Offering Assistance, and Gain Scores in Achievement Test, 1979–80 and 1982–83

	Correlations with CoStatus 1979/80			1982/83		
	N	r	p	N	r	p
Task–Related Talk*	111	.195	(.041)	131	.165	(.060)
Z Scores of Talk + Works Together	111	.175	(.067)	131	.181	(.039)
Offers Assistance	111	.152	(.110)	131	.257	(.003)
Gain Score in Math Concepts and Application	153	.278	(.001)	176	.151	(.0449)

* Because of skewness, this correlation was computed with square roots of the original rates of talk.

into each group. In 1979–80, the low- and medium-status students talked less than the high-status students, but the former two groups were not significantly different from each other. The comparison of mean rates of low- and high-status students' talk in 1979–80 yielded a t value of 1.14 ($p < .05$); the comparison of mean rates of medium- and high-status students' talk yielded a t value of 2.65 ($p < .005$).

A comparison of the two data sets by status group allows an estimate of how much the new system changed rates of interaction. One important finding is that each group in data set II talked significantly more than its counterpart in data set I. The increases in rates of talk between 1979–80 and 1982–83 were much greater for the medium- and high-status groups than for the low-status group. Moreover, there were no significant differences between the status groups in data set II, while in data set I, significant differences were found (as reported above). This is one measure of our success in equalizing rates of interaction for students participating in the 1982–83 implementation.

We examined the effects of status on three behavioral measures and test scores in the two data sets using correlational techniques. The original index scores for the behavioral measure of talking and working together were transformed to z-scores. Table 9.3 presents the correlations of the co-status score with task-related talk, with the z-score of talking and working together, with the rate of offering assistance, and with the individual's gain in achievement test score on a subscale of the Comprehensive Test of Basic Skills called Math Concepts and Application. This particular subscale is closely related to the problem-solving focus of the curriculum and has proven to be very sensitive to opportunities for interaction in the classroom. For example, the average gain per classroom in test scores on this subscale significantly correlates with the average percentage of students talking and manipulating materials, a measure of opportunities to interact in the classroom ($r = .72$ in data set II).

The correlation between co-status and task-related talk fell from .195 in 1979–80 to .165 in 1982–83. Whereas the first correlation coefficient was statistically significant, the second only reached the .06 level of significance. However, the *difference* between these two correlation coefficients is not statistically significant. The correlation of co-status with the z-score of talking and working together did not show the same pattern. The correlation was, if anything, slightly stronger in 1982–83. Most noticeable is the relatively strong correlation between co-status and rate of offering assistance in 1982–83 ($r = .257$; $p = .003$). The same correlation was much lower and not statistically significant in 1979–80. Examination of the difference between these two correlation coefficients shows that one is barely within the confidence interval of the other; thus the correlations are not significantly different.

The correlation between the co-status and gain scores in Math Concepts and Application fell from .278 in 1979–80 to .151 in 1982–83 (a nonsignificant difference). The correlation in data set II was still statistically significant ($p < .05$). We also examined the relationship of the co-status score to the achievement test score by performing regression analyses of the post-test scores from Math Concepts and Application on the pre-test scores and on the co-status scores. This analysis, for which we used data from the entire sample, not just the subsample of target children, revealed that co-status was a statistically significant predictor of the post-test scores in data set I but not in data set II (see Table 9.4). The beta weight for the co-status score as a predictor of post-test scores in 1979–80 was 1.54; in 1982–83 it was .069.

Interpretation. Introduction of the new classroom management system in 1982–83 resulted in significant increases in rates of interaction and of offering assistance. These changes reflect the fact that groups were responsible for seeing to it that everyone received the help needed and did not move on to the next learning center until the whole group had finished. New norms for interaction had the desired effect: everyone's interaction rate increased, regardless of status. Because low-status students were significantly more active in 1982–83 than in 1979–80, they probably were more likely to gain access to the learning materials by discussing the instructions on activity cards. In one second-grade classroom where the teacher stressed reading the activity cards, the conversation turned largely on what these cards instructed them to do (Navarrete 1985).

In 1982–83 the increased rates of interaction weakened the effect of status on interaction, but by no means did it disappear. Whether this was in fact the result partly depends on the index used. The relatively strong correlation in Table 9.3 between offering assistance and co-status ($r = .257$) in 1982–83 reveals the continuing operation of status characteristics; high-status children were more likely to offer assistance than low-status children. High-status children probably perceived themselves as more competent and, in terms of skills mea-

Table 9.4
Regression of Post-test Scores of Achievement Test on Co-status: 1979–80 and 1982–83

1979/80

N = 151

Dependent Variable:	Math Concepts and Applications, Post-Test		
Predictors	Beta	T	P
Pre-Test	.584	3.26	<.001
CoStatus	1.540	5.51	<.001

$R^2 = .512$

1982/83

N = 176

Dependent Variable:	Math Concepts and Applications, Post-Test		
Predictors	Beta	T	P
Pre-Test	.693	10.21	<.000
CoStatus	.069	1.02	<.310

$R^2 = .496$

sured by the standardized achievement tests in mathematics and reading, many of them were. Even if low-status children were expected by classmates to possess some of the skills required at the learning centers, continued effects of the co-status variable might be anticipated because expectations based on the original status distinctions and those stemming from the new status characteristics relevant to the curriculum would combine. On the average, expectations for competence of high-status children would still be higher.

The effect of status on learning was much weaker in 1982–83. This is a highly desirable result because, from an educational point of view, the major disadvantage of allowing status to affect interaction is that it indirectly affects learning. In an absolute sense, the sizable learning gains in 1982–83 show that the teaching methods and materials were highly effective. Furthermore, we did much to remove the inequalities in interaction that prevented the low-status students from learning as much as the high-status students.

It is ironic that learning problems should be easier to treat than status problems. One explanation is that these learning materials are extraordinarily well engineered to facilitate the understanding of math concepts and the solution of word problems. They consist of many different media so that, for example, children who understand things spatially or who can visually grasp abstract concepts are not deprived of learning because they may not understand as well by listening or by reading. Assuming that the management system helped to solve the problem of giving non-readers access to the materials, the materials themselves are capable of teaching in a powerful fashion.

Results: Change in Status over Time within Data Set II

In addition to comparing the relationship between status and interaction for two years, another way to tell whether status treatments attempted in 1982–83 were at all successful is to examine changes in perceived status at the classroom level from fall to spring of that school year. Sociometric data were collected in the fall and in the spring of 1982–83. One can compare the choices received by the group of children who were classified as "low status" by the sociometric questionnaire given in the fall to choices received by the low-status group in the spring. Did the low-status group receive more choices in the spring on the two sociometric items of "best friend" and "being good in math and science" than in the fall?

The sociometric data presented a considerable challenge for analysis. There were marked classroom differences in the number of choices in response to the sociometric questions. We had to find a measure that standardized for the variable number of choices made in different classrooms and at two points in time. Moreover, the measure had to provide us with a way to look at choices received by high-status students versus choices received by low-status students within the same classroom.

Changes in classroom climate. Analysis of data at the classroom level revealed some important changes in the pattern of choosers and the recipients of choices on the two sociometric questions used for the co-status scores. We examined the percentage of choosers who directed their choices to the lowest third of the distribution of co-status scores in the fall and in the spring. The average percentage of all possible choosers in the classroom who chose children in the lowest third of the co-status score distribution with regard to either criterion question rose from 22.65 in fall to 35.24 in spring. In contrast, a smaller percentage of classmates chose high-status students in the spring (74.25) than in the fall (79.62). Both of these changes were statistically significant. Stated differently, in every classroom but one there was an average gain in the percentage of classmates choosing low-status children; in 10 out of 13 classrooms there was an average loss in the percentage of classmates choosing high-status students.

We should emphasize that this analysis focuses on classroom rather than on individual effects. We are not examining the change in number of choices received by individuals who were in the extremes of the distribution in the fall measures. Rather, we are examining all those who received relatively fewer choices at either of these points in time. They may or may not be the same individuals. This analysis avoids the danger of over-interpreting changes that may simply be regression toward the mean of initially extreme scores.

Another critical finding is that the distributions of choices had less of a variance in the spring than in the fall, a consequence of having more choices directed at the low-status end of the distribution and fewer choices directed at the high end of the status distribution. This change is measured by a statistic called the coefficient of variation, which is the standard deviation of a distribution divided by its mean. The average value for this statistic, calculated across all classrooms, was 57.3 for the pre-test and 50.5 for the post-test. This decline in the coefficient of variation between fall and spring was found in every classroom but two.

This analysis is similar to that of Hallinan (1976) who examined the average mean and variance of the number of choices received on a friendship question in open and traditional classrooms. She argued that a larger variance in the distribution of choices might imply the presence of more sociometric stars and isolates. In support of her argument she found that the variance of the distribution was markedly lower in open classrooms than in traditional classrooms.

Similar to Hallinan's findings, there was evidence in data set II for the association between a reduction in the variance of the choice distribution between fall and spring and opportunities for interaction in the classroom. We correlated the difference between the coefficient of variation in the fall and the spring for each classroom with a measure of the quality of implementation of the program. This measure consists of the percentage of students found talking or talking while manipulating the materials. The relationship between these variables yielded a Pearson r of .48 ($p < .05$). In other words, those classrooms where teachers fostered more talking and working together tended to be the same classrooms that developed fewer underchosen and overchosen students over time.

A friendlier place. What is the meaning of these changes? And how do they relate to the status treatments? We interpret these findings to mean that these classrooms were friendlier places, where the supply of esteem was less likely to be the exclusive property of a few students in the spring than it was in the fall. This is a well-documented effect in classrooms in which there is a high level of peer interaction, especially cooperative interaction (Hallinan 1976; Epstein and Karweit 1983; Slavin 1983).

Such a favorable change in climate does not mean that all status-generated problems have been eliminated, however. Status characteristics can continue to operate in cooperative groups whose members enjoy friendly relationships. Two factors can affect the number of times a given student's name is chosen in response to a sociometric question about "best friend": the general friendliness of the classroom and the relative popularity of the student. The increase in the number of those choosing a low-status student is more likely to be explained by a change in the friendliness of the classroom than by a change in the student's relative popularity. The analysis above does not take into account the relative position of high- and low-status students in a given classroom. The results are, nonetheless, worth reporting because low-status students in these classrooms certainly had more friends in the spring than did low-status students in the fall. The changes in classroom social structure described here did succeed in improving the social situation of the low-status child in comparison to what it would have been in a more traditional classroom.

Change in status advantage. Because we sought a way to measure status changes that (1) would be less affected by the increasing friendliness of these classrooms and (2) would indicate the *relative* status differences within classrooms, we decided to use an index of status advantage. In laboratory work on status characteristics and expectation states theory, a similar index, called the expectancy advantage, is typically calculated by subtracting the aggregated expectations held for the low-status actor from those held for the high-status actor. In applied research on free interaction in mixed-status, four-person groups, Cohen has interpreted expectancy advantage as an indicator of the status effect *at the group level* and has calculated it by subtracting the mean influence or interaction rate of all low-status actors from that of all high-status actors (Cohen 1982). The index of status advantage is an extension of the expectancy advantage to the classroom level; this is justified on the assumption that at some time during the school year each student performed a collective task with every other student at least once. (Teachers were instructed to compose groups to this end.) Thus it is possible to compare high-status and low-status students at the classroom level and to talk about the status advantage of high-status students over that of low-status students in the performance of collective tasks *at the classroom level.*

The data in this case were responses to the sociometric question asking which classmates were the best in math and science. This was one of the two items making up the co-status score; it was much less reflective of general friendliness than the other item, the choice of best friend. The status advantage was based on the *average percentage of all choices* made, in a given classroom, naming children who were classified as low or high status according to the fall sociometric data. The percentage of *choices* rather than *choosers* avoids the problem of classroom differences and differences over time on the number of choices made. Since children had an unlimited number of choices in answering the sociometric questions, in many classrooms the total number of choices made by all children was very large. It ranged from 80 to 265 in the fall and from 98 to 335 in the spring in response to the question about who was best in math and science. (There were more respondents in the spring than there were in the fall.)

To make the initial determination of status in the fall, we divided the distribution of percentages of choices made in response to the math and science question into thirds, with low status defined as being in the lowest third and high status defined as being in the highest third. Next we calculated the status advantage for each classroom using the average percentage of all choices made—that is, an average percentage of all choices made by all classrooms. Since the denominator of this figure can be as large as 335, the average percentage tends to be a small number. The status advantage is calculated as follows. The average percentage of choices of children who were initially classified as low status was subtracted from the average percentage of choices of children who were initially classified as high status. Table 9.5 presents the status advantages for fall and spring for each of 13 classrooms. Because we selected high- and low-status groups on the fall distribution of choices, all status advantages in the fall were, by definition, positive. As it turned out, the fall status advantages were large in many classrooms. By spring, the status advantage for each classroom was smaller than it had been in the fall.

Table 9.5 also includes descriptive statistics derived by creating a grand mean across classrooms of the average percentage of choices naming high- and low-status target children. The average percentage of choices naming high-status children in the fall was 5.98; low-status children were named in only 0.99 percent of the choices, on the average. By spring, the comparable figures were 5.18 percent for high-status children and 1.93 percent for low-status children. The overall difference, obtained by subtracting the average percentage of all choices naming low-status students from the average percentage naming high-status students, was 4.99 percent in the fall and 3.25 percent in the spring. This difference was statistically significant ($p = .001$) according to the Mann-Whitney U test.

The decrease in status advantage over time was produced by an increase in the percentage of choices naming low-status children and a decrease in the percentage of choices naming high-status children. In all probability, this means that some low-status children were perceived as more competent as the school year progressed.

Status advantage: sociometric data versus observed behavior. A final question concerns the relationship of questionnaire evaluations of competence on a relevant status characteristic and observed behavior of mixed-status collective task groups. To answer this question, we examined the relationship of status advantages calculated from sociometric data to status advantages calculated from data on task-related talk at the classroom level.

The only children for whom we had both sets of data were the target children. To derive a status advantage from the data on task-related talk, we defined low- and high-status groups as previously described, according to the lowest and highest third of the percentage distribution of choices in response

Table 9.5

Status Advantage of High- over Low-Status Students in Percentage of Choices as Best in Math and Science, Fall versus Spring Measures for Treated Classrooms

Class	FALL Status+ Advantage	SPRING Status Advantage
1	4.47	4.14
2	6.64	4.79
3	4.06	2.81
4	5.31	4.53
5	4.45	4.06
6	4.91	2.99
8	3.42	1.62
9	6.92	2.66
10	5.17	4.30
11	4.21	2.67
12	3.99	2.12
13	6.25	3.88
14	5.94	1.55

ALL CLASSROOMS Mean Status Advantage	4.99	3.25**

+ Status Advantage = Mean % of all Choices on Math/Science Given to High Status Students − Mean % of all Choices on Math/Science Given to Low Status Students.

** $p < .001$ for difference between Spring and Fall status advantage:Mann-Whitney U Test.

to the question on math and science in the fall sociometric questionnaire. We then subtracted the average rate of talk for the low-status group from that for the high-status group. (In four classrooms there were too few target children defined as low or high status to be included in the analysis.) The Pearson correlation coefficient between the spring sociometric status advantage and the status advantage based on peer talk was .58 ($p < .01$).

Interpretation of change in status advantage. In all classrooms, status advantages were smaller in the spring than in the fall. From this it can be inferred that some children who were not perceived as best in math and science prior to the experience of *Finding Out* were likely to be perceived as very competent by at least some of their classmates at the end of the instruction. Since the regular math program in these classrooms was taught in ability groups, in which there are few mechanisms that enable the low-achieving student to display competence, and since science was not taught outside the *Finding Out* curriculum, we can presume that something about the *Finding Out* experience brought about this change in perception. But this change should not be taken to mean that the differential competence initially perceived had disappeared. Although the status advantages were smaller in the spring, they remained positive.

The correlation between status advantage based on peer talk and that based on sociometric choices in the spring suggests that this change in perception is related to the prestige and power order of small groups engaged in collective tasks. Thus we have some confidence that the sociometric analysis partly reflects the extent to which status differences were successfully treated in the classroom.

An alternative explanation for the decreased percentage of choices received by high-status students and the increased percentages of choices received by low-status students is that the changes are caused by a statistical artifact, a regression toward the mean of initially extreme values of the variable. Without a control group of sociometric measures taken on comparable classrooms that did not experience this intervention, we cannot rule out such an interpretation.

Nevertheless we have strong grounds for arguing that this observed change is unlikely to be a product of measurement error. The reduced status advantages in the spring are correlated with observed status advantages based on peer talk, an entirely independent behavioral measure. Second, the shape of the distributions changed between fall and spring showing a reduced variance, an occurrence that cannot be attributed to measurement error. Moreover, these changes in the distribution, as measured by the coefficient of variation, are correlated significantly with a measure of program implementation: the proportion of students talking or talking while manipulating the materials. We argue that insofar as the changes in status advantages are related to changes in the shape of the distribution and insofar as they have a demonstrated association with independent measures, they are unlikely to be a product of measurement error.

DISCUSSION

The discussion of results centers on two questions: (1) Why does it appear to be easier to treat learning problems than status problems? and (2) Why are expectations for competence relatively resistant to change in classroom situations and what, if anything, can be done to alter them?

Treatment of Learning Problems

Although the consistency of classroom implementation resulted in stronger gains in achievement in data set II, low and high achievers made highly significant gains in both years. Analyses of the correlation of status with learning gains should not obscure this fact. The children in data set II consistently improved their standing in comparison to that of the nationally normed population across all the subscales of the Comprehensive Test of Basic Skills. This improvement brought the average of many of the classrooms up to the fiftieth percentile even though most of them had started out far below grade level (Cohen and DeAvila 1983).

This analysis thus focuses, in part, on the results of using a powerful set of instructional materials. The study shows that if a teacher allows children to work together on these materials and encourages them to use each other as resources, scores on standardized achievement tests can be considerably improved. The high-status students in data set I gained more than the low-status students, as indicated by scores on the Math Concepts and Applications test. In 1979–80, lateral relations between students were permitted but not required. A student who was too inhibited to ask for assistance might well be excluded from the instructional activity. Teachers did not then hold regular orientation sessions to explain the learning centers and activity cards. Furthermore, teachers in some of the classrooms were using only a few learning centers attended by larger groups at each of them. This situation would make it particularly difficult for some children to "get their hands on" the learning materials.

In 1982–83 the introduction of cooperative norms and roles solved both the problem of helping teachers to encourage children to work together on their own at the learning centers and the problem of making sure that all children had access to the learning materials and activities. The norms of cooperation increased the level of interaction and taught children how to ask for and give assistance. The role of facilitator was designed to prevent children from being left out either intellectually or physically. The role of checker enforced the rule that each child had to complete the worksheet. In addition, teachers regularly held orientations and wrap-up sessions at which they explained the activities to the students. When ensured access to the learning materials low-status students made dramatic learning gains. In contrast, it is not uncommon for the standardized achievement scores of low achievers in conventional classrooms to decline between fall and spring.

Learning problems will not always be easier to treat than status problems. The results obtained in this study can be ascribed to instructional activities that enable students to learn through doing. We also utilized an elaborate system of classroom management that requires extensive teacher training and provides teachers with organizational support (Cohen and DeAvila 1983). Given the highly motivating nature of the materials, once we had solved the problem of ensuring access to the learning materials and activities, we could begin to remove the effects of status on learning outcomes.

There were several features of the new management system that increased the rates of interaction of all students. Whatever else the students did, they were supposed to play their roles. Each role led to interaction with other members of the group. The norms of cooperation included standardized ways of asking for and giving help; each child took turns practicing these new behaviors during the training period. In the scoring of interaction, no distinction was made between procedural talk that was specifically related to norms and roles, and talk that was more directly relevant to the task. When one considers the interaction arising from prescribed talk and from the responsibility that the children took for each other's performance, it is not surprising that the correlation between status and task-related talk was weaker under the new system. This does not necessarily mean that competence expectations were changed. What probably happened was that differential competence expectations no longer prevented children from interacting. In this way we solved the problem of the differential access of low-status students to the learning materials and activities.

The Challenge of Changing Competence Expectations

Can we change expectations for competence in a classroom situation where children differ on at least one status characteristic that is directly relevant to the activity we are trying to treat? The children in this study differed on the status characteristic of ability in math and science, which was seen as directly relevant to the math and science activities of the *Finding Out* curriculum. A direct path of relevance between a status characteristic and a new set of tasks should, from a theoretical point of view, have maximum power to affect behavior (Humphreys and Berger 1981).

Despite the salience of the status characteristic, there were several features of the activities and the teaching techniques that encouraged the students to see themselves as competent on intellectual abilities that were distinct from traditionally defined ability in math and science. The activities presented excellent opportunities for children to display previously hidden intellectual abilities. The multiple abilities treatment, utilized by teachers in 1982–83, also helped children to see themselves as competent on some of the intellectual abilities required by the learning activities. After discussing the different abilities required by each new set of learning centers, teachers specifically explained to the students that reading and computational skills were only two of the relevant skills required. Teachers stated that everyone could expect to be good on at least one of the required abilities.

To some extent we were successful in changing the perceptions of children's competence in math and science; status advantages of high-status students were reduced although by no means eliminated. Nonetheless high-status children were more likely to offer assistance than low-status children in data set II. This suggests that children who initially had better test scores and were perceived as more competent in the fall were more likely to adopt a tutorial role. Even if expectations for competence for low-status children were raised by the multiple abilities treatment, we might still expect that the initially high-status children would have an advantage because of a combining effect.

We were dealing with a specific status characteristic on which the children received many evaluations in connection with daily instruction in mathematics. In many of these classrooms, ability grouping was used for the teaching of math outside of *Finding Out*. Thus, to some extent, the status order we were trying to modify was probably being reconstructed as fast as we weakened it.

In addition, we were trying to change the teachers' and students' ideas about academic ability: we were introducing a multidimensional view of ability in mathematics and science. The majority of teachers have difficulty accepting the idea that children from lower social classes who show limited proficiency in English and Spanish and whose reading and writing skills in either language are minimal might have multiple intellectual abilities, such as reasoning, hypothesizing, and visual and spatial thinking. Perhaps this was the underlying source of the resistance to change of competence expectations for low-status students.

IMPLICATIONS FOR COOPERATIVE LEARNING

The major implication of this work is the realization that the implementation of cooperative learning should consider the status problems that have been described. Fostering interdependence may activate these very status problems, so that failure to deal with them may shut off access to interaction for low-status children.

The Use of Norms and Roles

The use of training for cooperative behaviors such as listening to each other and giving everyone a chance to talk in combination with the assigning of rotating roles to each member of the group will do much to solve the problem of access of low-status students to interaction. If the learning materials are sufficiently stimulating and well-related to the criterion test, then this in itself will do much to equalize the learning gains for low- and high-status students.

Curricula for Cooperative Learning

Another implication is the importance of the curricular materials that are used in conjunction with cooperative learning. They should be rich and not entirely dependent on reading so that different children are able to make different kinds of contributions. In the case of *Finding Out,* the activities themselves presented excellent opportunities for children to display previously unrecognized intellectual abilities; the activities were certainly far richer in required intellectual abilities than any set of school activities labeled as science or math. Even for adults, these activities create uncertainty and require aptitudes far beyond what is tested in ordinary achievement tests.

Multiple Ability Treatment Required

However, rich curriculum materials will not, by themselves, prevent status problems from arising. Unless they are used in conjunction with a multiple ability treatment, students will view the new tasks as requiring the same academic abilities as other school tasks. In 1982–83 teachers were trained to introduce each set of activities as requiring multiple abilities. After discussing the different abilities involved, they specifically explained to the students that reading and computational skills were only two of the relevant skills required. The point here is that if the children are persuaded by the teacher that the tasks involve multiple abilities, rich and stimulating materials can do much to equalize learning gains as a consequence of the cooperative curriculum for low- and high-status students.

Consistency of Implementation

The implementation of cooperative learning techniques is a great challenge for the in-service developer. The inclusion of techniques to deal with status problems requires special attention to teacher training and organizational support for the teacher. Teachers need to have a fundamental understanding of what status problems are and how their actions in the classroom affect those problems. Furthermore, the changes in behavior for most teachers are sufficiently great that there must be careful follow-up and feedback on exactly how consistently they are utilizing the recommended strategies. The initial workshops must be followed up by a systematic concern with how well treatments for status problems are being implemented in each classroom.

Potential of Changed Expectations for Competence

If the effects of status on learning can be weakened by equalizing participation and access, then why is it important to continue attempts to alter competence expectations? The low-status children we selected were socially isolated and were not perceived as especially competent in any academic endeavor. The public educational system is typically least successful with these children. Being defined as unattractive and incompetent in a highly evaluative setting and forced to participate five days a week is not an enviable fate for any human being. Theoretically, such children would be better if they were free of general expectations for their incompetence. Although status has indirect effects on learning as a result of students' interactions with peers, there are other ways in which expectations based on status affect learning. High-status students are more likely to initiate interaction with the teacher; this probably is a source of their superior test performance. As a result of low expectations for competence, low-status students are more likely to show low levels of effort in performing school tasks; and this behavior is a barrier to their academic success. If general expectations for competence could be raised, we should see an even greater improvement in oral proficiency and in academic achievement, to say nothing of improved social acceptance and self-esteem.

A new status treatment in which teachers assign competence to low-status children has been developed that can be integrated with the multiple-ability treatment described here. The teacher is a high-status source of evaluations for students. If teachers make evaluations of students, students are likely to believe those evaluations. Theoretically, this treatment ensures that competence expectations for low-status children are raised because they will accept the teacher's evaluation of themselves as competent on relevant skills. These evaluations must be both specific and public. For example, the teacher will specifically describe how competent a low-status student is in reasoning, in skills requiring spatial ability, or in activities requiring precision. This is a difficult set of skills to learn. Video techniques can help teachers learn to identify and to analyze student reasoning, visual and spatial thinking, and precision, and to rehearse the giving of evaluations. The advantage of continuing to try to change expectations for competence lies in the tremendous potential that cooperative learning in combination with successfully treated expectations for competence has in academically heterogeneous classrooms. We have the potential to help the most unsuccessful students to achieve.

REFERENCES

Berger, J., Cohen, B. P., and Zelditch, M., Jr. (1966) "Status characteristics and expectation states." In *Sociological Theories in Progress,* Vol. 1, edited by J. Berger and M. Zelditch, Jr. Boston, MA: Houghton-Mifflin.
———— (1972) "Status characteristics and social interaction." *American Sociological Review* 37:241–55.
Berger, J., Rosenholtz, S. J., and Zelditch, M., Jr. (1980) "Status organizing processes." *Annual Review of Sociology* 6:479–508.
Cohen, E. G. (1982) "Expectation states and interracial interaction in school settings." *Annual Review of Sociology* 8:209–35.
———— (1984a) "The desegregated school: Problems in status power and interethnic climate." In *Desegregation: Groups in Contact: Psychology of Desegregation,* edited by N. Miller and M. B. Brewer. San Diego, CA: Academic Press.
———— (1984b) "Talking and working together: status, interaction and learning." In *The Social Context of Instruction: Group Organization and Group Processes,*

edited by P. L. Peterson, L. C. Wilkinson, and M. Hallinan. San Diego, CA: Academic Press.

———— (1986) "On the sociology of the classroom." In *The Contributions of the Social Sciences to Educational Policy and Practice: 1965–1985*, edited by J. Hannaway and M. E. Lockheed. Berkeley, CA: McCutchan.

Cohen, E. G., and DeAvila, E. (1983) *Learning to Think in Math and Science: Improving Local Education for Minority Children*. Final Report to the Johnson Foundation. Stanford, CA: Stanford University, School of Education.

Cohen, E. G., and Intili, J. K. (1981) *Interdependence and Management in Bilingual Classrooms*. Final Report, NIE Grant. Stanford, CA: Center for Educational Research, Stanford University, School of Education.

Cohen, E. G., Lockheed, M. L., and Lohman, M. (1976) "The center for interracial cooperation: a field experiment." *Sociology of Education* 49:47–58.

DeAvila, E. A., and Duncan, S. E. (1980) *Finding Out/Descubrimiento*. Corte Madera, CA: Linguametrics Group.

Epstein, J. L., and Karweit, N. (1983) *Friends in School: Patterns of Selection and Influence in Secondary Schools*. New York: Academic Press.

Hallinan, M. (1976) "Friendship patterns in open and traditional classrooms." *Sociology of Education* 49:254–65.

Hoffman, D., and Cohen, E. G. (1972) "An exploratory study to determine the effects of generalized performance expectations upon activity and influence of students engaged in a group simulation game." Paper read to the American Educational Research Association, Chicago.

Humphreys, P., and Berger, J. (1981) "Theoretical consequences of the status characteristics formulation." *American Journal of Sociology* 86:953–83.

Johnson, D. W., Maruyama, G., Johnson, R. T., Nelson, D., and Skon, L. (1981) "Effects of cooperative, competitive and individualistic goal structures on achievement." *Psychological Bulletin* 89:47–62.

Maruyama, G., and N. Miller (1981) "Physical attractiveness and personality." *Progress in Experimental Personality Research* 10:203–80.

Morris, R. (1977) "A normative intervention to equalize participation in task-oriented groups." Ph.D. dissertation. Stanford, CA: Stanford University.

Navarrete, C. (1985) "Problem-resolution in small group interaction: a bilingual classroom study." Ph.D. dissertation. Stanford, CA: Stanford University.

Rosenholtz, S. J. (1985) "Treating problems of academic status." In *Status, Rewards, and Influence*, edited by J. Berger and M. Zelditch, Jr. San Francisco, CA: Jossey-Bass.

Sharan, S. (1980) "Cooperative learning in small groups: recent methods and effects on achievement, attitudes and ethnic relations." *Review of Educational Research* 5:241–71.

Slavin, R. E. (1983) *Cooperative Learning*. New York: Longman.

Tammivaara, J. (1982) "The effects of task structure on beliefs about competence and participation in small groups." *Sociology of Education* 55:212–22.

Webster, M. and Driskell, J. (1983) "Beauty as status." *American Journal of Sociology* 89:140–65.

10

Cooperative Learning as Part of a Comprehensive Classroom Program Designed to Promote Prosocial Development

DANIEL SOLOMON, MARILYN WATSON, ERIC SCHAPS, VICTOR BATTISTICH, AND JUDITH SOLOMON

Cooperative learning has many guises and has been directed toward many goals. In this chapter we discuss cooperative learning as one major element in a more extensive longitudinal program designed to enhance children's "prosocial" development: the Child Development Project (CDP). The project's major aim is to determine whether a comprehensive, long-term program, delivered primarily by teachers in elementary classrooms (but also with consistent school-wide policies and practices, family activities, and parental support), can significantly strengthen children's prosocial orientations, without harming their academic achievement. By "prosocial orientation" we mean an attitude of concern for others, a commitment to the values of fairness and social responsibility, and the ability and inclination to act on these values in everyday life.

The overall CDP program was derived from theory and research on the origins of prosocial behavior in children (e.g., Staub 1979; Mussen and Eisenberg-Berg 1977). Its basic premises are that children's prosocial characteristics can best be enhanced in a school milieu where children (a) see themselves as part of a caring and just community in which prosocial values are emphasized and exemplified; (b) have opportunities to both act on and think about those values; and (c) have opportunities to gain an understanding of the feelings, situations, and perspectives of others. With intensive guidance and assistance from CDP staff, and with support from parents and school administrators, teachers have attempted to create and maintain this milieu through the use of five mutually consistent program "components." Two of these components, cooperative learning and developmental discipline, incorporate all of the above aspects and are pervasively integrated into the school day. They are therefore seen as the central elements of the program. The other three components—helping activities, highlighting prosocial values, and promoting social understanding—play a more limited, supportive role, and help to extend the scope of the program beyond the classroom environment. For an earlier description of the project's rationale and plan, see Solomon et al. (1985). An account of the project's theoretical underpinning is presented in Battistich et al. (in press, b).

We will first describe the overall CDP program, focusing on cooperative learning and developmental discipline, but providing sufficient information about the other program components to convey the general context in which cooperative activities occurred. We then describe the processes of program training and adoption, and the problems encountered by teachers in trying to implement cooperative learning activities. Finally, we present empirical data on the degree to which teachers implemented the program, student perceptions of several aspects of classroom activities (including the goals and benefits of cooperative learning), and the project's major effects to date on children's social attitudes, motives, and behavior.

THE FIVE PROGRAM COMPONENTS

Helping activities. Children are encouraged to give help to others, and are given opportunities to do so, through doing chores and helping their classmates, participating in school-wide projects that involve helping younger students, and participating in occasional community service activities such as providing help to needy families at holiday times. Teachers are encouraged to stress the importance and value of helping others in general and as part of these activities.

Highlighting prosocial values. Central prosocial values in addition to helping are also demonstrated, explained, and emphasized. Extensive use is made of literature and other media in which such values as kindness, living up to one's responsibilities, or truthfulness are central elements. Children's books, selected for literary quality and relevance to these prosocial values, are provided to the teachers. The teachers are also encouraged to point out naturally occurring prosocial behavior, to emphasize the importance of such behavior, and to help the children understand the values exemplified.

Promoting social understanding. Literature is also an important vehicle for helping children to develop their understanding of other people. Stories that explore the motives, feelings, needs, and perceptions of various characters are read in the classroom, sometimes aloud and sometimes silently. Teachers follow up the reading with writing, art, and discussion activities to help the children comprehend the various perspectives represented in the stories. To emphasize the importance of understanding other people in all settings, not just the classroom, many books are used that portray people of diverse cultures, ages, situations, and roles in the community. Class meetings and discussions of various classroom events, including group processes during cooperative activities, are also used to help students better understand themselves, their teachers, and their classmates.

Developmental discipline. Cooperative learning activities must be managed, and current approaches to cooperative learning differ in the management systems they advocate or imply, some making heavy use of points and/or rewards (e.g., Slavin 1980), while others put more emphasis on intrinsic motivators (e.g., Cohen 1987; Graves and Graves 1985; Sharan and Hertz-Lazarowitz 1980). We have developed a management system that applies not just to the operation of cooperative activities but to the total class in which such activities are embedded. This system stresses intrinsic motivation for prosocial as well as academic activities. We ask teachers to assume that children in general are well intentioned and motivated to please others and to learn the values of their social system, but lacking in self-control, conceptual and behavioral skills, and understanding. To attain long-range socialization goals and short-term classroom compliance, children are given active roles in helping to create a caring, just, and productive classroom community, and are allowed sufficient autonomy to practice making responsible choices.

This system is characterized more by an attitude than a series of techniques, an attitude of trust in the good will of children and a sense of responsibility for maintaining the social supports necessary for children to be able to function well. At the same time, however, several techniques are useful for providing this social support and maintaining this attitude. They include:

building a personal bond with each child and helping the children build bonds with each other;

involving children in establishing class norms and rules;

teaching children techniques for self-control and conflict resolution;

increasing children's awareness of particular values in situations where those values are especially relevant;

using nonpunitive techniques when external control is necessary;

helping children see the reasons for doing the tasks they are asked to perform;

adjusting demands to children's abilities; and

taking a teaching and problem-solving approach to misbehavior.

Developmental discipline avoids using promises of rewards or threats of punishments to control children's behavior. It is a system whose primary goal is socializing children, who are seen as active, willing partners in their socialization.

Cooperative learning. Although in recent years much of the interest in cooperative learning has resulted from its demonstrated effects on academic achievement (as reviewed by Slavin 1983; Johnson et al. 1981; Sharan 1980), cooperative approaches to education have their roots in attempts to understand

and influence social attitudes and behaviors (Allport 1954; Deutsch 1949; Dewey 1966; Cook 1978), and most current cooperative learning systems also embrace social goals, such as improving interpersonal or inter-group relations or preparing for democratic citizenship (Aronson 1978; Cohen 1987; Graves and Graves 1985; Johnson and Johnson 1975; Sharan and Sharan 1976; Slavin and Hansell 1983). In the Child Development Project, the social outcomes of cooperative learning are valued in themselves, and not merely because they can help to promote academic growth.

Our approach to cooperative group activities is designed both to achieve explicit social and academic goals and to be consistent with our view of the developing nature of the child. It has been derived, in part, from the approaches of Johnson and Johnson (1975) and of Cohen (1987), but diverges from each in significant ways. Like the Johnsons, we stress the importance of building interdependence into each cooperative activity and of directly teaching the interpersonal skills needed for successful cooperation. Our approach differs from theirs in that it more directly and explicitly fosters children's intrinsic task motivation, emphasizes the acquisition and application of general social values (in addition to more specific social skills) in the group situation, and avoids both individual and group grades or rewards for the group's social or academic performance. Our approach is similar to that of Cohen in its emphasis on intrinsic motivation and the use of roles to counter status differences within groups, but differs in that its tasks are more explicitly differentiated across grades according to developmental considerations, and are developed to meet more specific interaction and interdependence requirements. When cooperative activities are done in our system, in contrast to that of Cohen, all groups in a class usually work on the same task, with the members of each group working toward a single group product.

In addition to providing varied and powerful learning opportunities, cooperative activities in the CDP approach are used to give children:

1. an awareness of the importance of prosocial values—specifically, fairness, consideration, helpfulness, and social responsibility;
2. opportunities to act in accord with those values;
3. the experience of being part of a caring, just, and responsible group;
4. opportunities to understand and consider the perspectives of others; and
5. opportunities to reflect on their own behavior and on the expression of values in the group situation.

Cooperative activities provide a kind of "learning laboratory" for practicing and experiencing prosocial values and social skills, while also pursuing academic content.

We recommend that teachers create a wide variety of formal and informal opportunities for children to work collaboratively. At the beginning of the school year, the children participate in setting class norms. They are encouraged to see these norms—which are based on the values of helpfulness, consideration, fairness, and responsibility—as the basic requirements of good citizenship and as applicable to all their interactions. Following this, we recommend that formal cooperative lessons be conducted daily so that children have frequent experiences in applying these norms or values. The lessons are carefully designed to benefit from collaborative effort, to be intrinsically interesting, and to provide challenging opportunities to apply one or more of these prosocial values.

At the start of a lesson, the teacher describes the task and helps children to see intrinsic reasons for engaging in it, talks about the prosocial values that will be most relevant to performing it, assigns interdependent roles to the group members, and explains the specific skills that will be necessary for achieving the relevant academic and social goals. The children are then left to work on the task in their groups. The teacher's role at this point is to observe and to provide guidance only when group members seem unable to solve their problems by themselves. At the end of the lesson, the teacher helps the children to think about and discuss their academic and social learning, and to plan for improvement.

Students work in pairs for their first few cooperative learning activities, and for later ones that have particularly demanding academic or social requirements. We have developed a number of paired activities that provide a simplified context in which to practice complex collaboration skills such as giving reasons for ideas or elaborating on the ideas of others. When children progress to groups larger than two, they are assigned differentiated roles (e.g., "facilitator," "reporter," "recorder") to minimize the possible effects of status differences, and to help ensure the involvement of all group members.

We have developed several cooperative learning formats, and teachers are encouraged to repeat each one several times so that the students can consolidate their learning. For example, a format called "vocabulary guesswork" requires that children work together to deduce word meanings from sentence context. The first time this format is used, considerable time and energy are devoted to learning how to do the task. On succeeding days the same task is repeated with different words, until the children have become familiar with the format. The teacher then introduces a new format, for example, collaborative story completion. Each learned format is returned to periodically throughout the year.

While developing children's commitment to and ability to act upon prosocial values is an important goal for the cooperative lessons, academic goals are also stressed. Because we ask teachers to rely on intrinsic motivation and to incorporate cooperative learning into the teaching of their regular academic content, we have tried to devise activities that children find inherently interesting, and for which cooperation is likely to be seen as natural and advantageous. These include:

1. challenging, open-ended activities in which multiple perspectives are helpful;
2. multifaceted activities in which children are likely to appreciate the efficiency of a collaborative effort as they plan and integrate their individual contributions;
3. activities in which the contributions of all group members are necessary to the success of the group (e.g., peer editing, science and math activities that require different simultaneous measurements or actions); and
4. activities that stimulate children's curiosity.

For children younger than seven or eight we take a less structured approach to cooperative learning, and recommend that activities that require children to coordinate their behavior be done in pairs (e.g., making a joint tower). When larger groups are used with young children, we recommend either that the coordination of behavior be optional (as in playing with blocks or painting a mural), or that the coordination be structured by the situation (as in playing a game with known rules). The cooperative forms we have developed for students of this age are generally loosely structured. They do not involve the use of differentiated roles, but approach the problem of achieving full and equal participation indirectly by controlling the nature and complexity of the task, the composition of the group, or the task instructions. A description of the CDP approach to cooperative learning with young children can be found in Watson, Hildebrandt, and Solomon (in press).

The Child Development Project tries to promote a cooperative orientation in the classroom as a whole, not limited to the times when the students are organized into cooperative learning groups. We believe that this consistency is important, particularly for the attainment of the project's social objectives, because it allows the experiences children have in cooperative groups and those they have during other aspects of classroom life to reinforce and supplement each other (rather than undermine or contradict each other, as might be the case if, for example, children were given much autonomy when in cooperative groups, but little during other classroom activities). The whole program is thus designed to provide children with mutually supportive experiences in autonomy, self-direction, community participation, responsible decision making, being helpful to others, learning to understand and appreciate others, and learning to collaborate with others. It is our hope that these experiences will help children in program classrooms learn to feel commitment to and responsibility for the groups in which they participate, and for the class as a whole.

DESIGN OF THE PROJECT

The CDP program has been provided to children in three elementary schools in a suburban, middle- to upper-middle-class district near San Francisco. Three equivalent schools in the same district have served as a "comparison" group, and have participated in the project's research activities, while not receiving the program. The six schools were initially formed into two "matched" groups of three that were similar in terms of faculty and parent interest in the program, student achievement scores, and community sociodemographic characteristics. One group was then randomly selected to receive the program and the other to serve as the comparison. Enrollment ranges from about 350 to 650 students per school. The project has concentrated on a longitudinal cohort of children that entered kindergarten in the fall of 1982. Intensive work has been done each year to help teachers at the cohort grade levels in the three program schools learn and implement the classroom program. The evaluation research has followed the same cohort, including children at the same grade levels in both program and comparison schools. Data presented in this report cover kindergarten through fourth grade.

THE PROCESS OF PROGRAM TRAINING AND ADOPTION

Because this program is complex and represents a fundamental departure from most current teaching approaches, helping teachers to master it and make it an integral part of their teaching turned out to be a very ambitious task. We worked with a variety of teachers; some had natural teaching styles that were quite consistent with the program, others had initial beliefs that were quite inconsistent with it. The teachers also varied in their willingness to try the program and in their ability to implement it successfully.

Teachers at each cohort grade were introduced to the program through a one-day workshop during the spring before their year with the cohort children and a week-long workshop late in the summer. Throughout their cohort year, the teachers at the three program schools attended all-day workshops approximately once a month. "Coaching" arrangements were also employed whereby each program teacher's classroom would be visited about once a week by a designated project staff member who would later discuss with the teacher what had been observed during program implementation.

Problems Encountered in Implementing Cooperative Learning

Although the teachers, on the whole, ultimately reached satisfactory levels of program implementation (as will be shown presently), there were several areas that caused difficulties as they attempted to master the program. With the exception of the kindergarten teachers, for whom socialization has traditionally been a major classroom goal, most of the teachers did not fully embrace the program or begin conducting cooperative activities on a regular basis until they were several months into the year in which they were teaching the cohort children. Even when teachers became committed to the importance of cooperative learning, some of them had significant problems implementing one or more of the major aspects of a successful cooperative lesson. Following is a description of the major problems areas encountered by teachers in learning to conduct cooperative lessons.

Developing appropriate lessons. When teachers developed their own cooperative lessons they sometimes selected learning tasks that were unsuitable for cooperation. Some were unsuitable because they allowed children to be academically disengaged while waiting their turn; some because they were cumbersome to accomplish collaboratively (e.g., four children trying to draw on one small piece of paper); some because they provided too few ways for children to contribute.

Introducing the lesson. Teachers found two aspects of lesson introduction difficult: (a) identifying intrinsically interesting learning goals (as opposed to pragmatic ones, such as ''finishing the worksheet''); and (b) selecting social goals that were clearly related to general prosocial values and were also appropriate to the given task. In recent years we have been helping teachers with these aspects by suggesting specific learning and social goals that met the above criteria (e.g., ''being sure everyone is included in the group's discussions'' as a way of achieving fairness in a task involving group decision making).

Monitoring the lesson. Some teachers had problems with the monitoring role when the children were working in groups. They found it difficult to learn to focus their observations so that they would be useful for later decisions or discussion. Learning to guide rather than control children's behavior was also a difficult aspect of lesson monitoring. Sometimes teachers ignored or failed to notice problems that required their guidance, and sometimes they intervened too soon or with too much direction in problems that the children might have solved themselves. Some teachers also found it difficult to facilitate children's social learning through the careful use of suggestions, questions, or demonstrations.

Lesson wrap-up/reflection. The wrap-up was perhaps the most difficult part of the cooperative learning lesson for the teachers to master. When time was short, it was likely to be omitted altogether. But even when it was done, teachers often failed to make the process interesting and meaningful. In many cases the teachers did not succeed in getting children seriously to discuss and think about their behavior and learning during the group session.

A final problem that some teachers evidenced during both the introduction and the wrap-up of the lesson was a tendency to be repetitive or formulaic in their presentations and responses. Although this is a common occurrence when one is learning a new skill, it presents a special problem for cooperative learning because formulaic introductions are not likely to engage children's intrinsic interest in the task, and formulaic questions tend to evoke stereotyped responses.

In addition to trying to master cooperative learning, the teachers in this project were also making efforts to learn a new classroom management system, to increase children's opportunities to be helpful to others, and to acquire new techniques for using literature to highlight prosocial values and enhance interpersonal understanding. There were difficulties in implementing these other aspects of the program as well, particularly when they called for similar attitudes and skills on the part of teachers. For example, in their work with developmental discipline, some teachers found it difficult to learn to use indirect methods (suggesting, demonstrating, asking questions) rather than direct ones when attempting to get children to change their behavior, or to allow children to solve minor problems themselves (but to intervene when needed). These issues were quite similar to those they struggled with in learning to monitor cooperative groups.

The difficulties teachers had in implementing cooperative learning may have been heightened by the fact that they were simultaneously trying to learn the other complex strategies of the program. However, the separate strategies were all highly related in that they sprang from a consistent view of child learning and made use of an overlapping set of skills. It is possible that this consistent and supportive framework facilitated rather than interfered with the acquisition of this version of cooperative learning.

By the spring of each cohort year a few teachers were implementing cooperative learning quite well, using some lessons that we provided them and some that they developed from existing formats; and a few teachers were conducting cooperative lessons poorly and infrequently (some no more than once a week); but most of them were conducting reasonably successful cooperative lessons three or so times a week. We had still not succeeded in having teachers develop a range of daily classroom opportunities for cooperation, nor did we feel that most teachers were knowledgeable enough about cooperative learning to create their own lesson formats or to maintain high-quality implementation without support. Nevertheless, with weekly guidance and prepared materials, most teachers were implementing cooperative learning reasonably well.

EVALUATION METHODS AND FINDINGS

Evaluation of such an extensive attempt at changing the traditional classroom environment has required an equally comprehensive program of research. Although a thorough description of our research activities is beyond the scope of this chapter (for more details, see Solomon et al. 1985, 1987), we should note that our major assessments have focused on: (a) assessment of program implementation during each year of the program through classroom observations in each of the cohort-grade classrooms in each of the six schools; (b) assessment of behavioral effects of the program through observations of children in the classrooms, on the playgrounds, and in structured small-group tasks; and (c) assessment of motivational, attitudinal, and cognitive effects of the program through administration of interviews and questionnaires to cohort-grade children each year in each of the schools.[1]

In this section we will present the major findings of our evaluation of CDP over the first five years of implementation. We should note, initially, that an extensive baseline assessment of children's social attitudes, motives, and behavior conducted in the year prior to the start of the CDP program did not reveal any large or consistent differences between children in the program and comparison schools, indicating that the two school populations were quite comparable before the start of the program. (We did not assess teachers' classroom practice or childrens' classroom behavior before the start of the program.)

Assessment of Program Implementation

Our primary measures of program implementation were derived from an extensive series of structured observations conducted each year. (A detailed description of the observation instruments and procedures can be found in Solomon et al., in press.) A total of 67 classrooms were observed during the first five years of the project: 37 in the program schools and 30 in the comparison schools. Observers, who were "blind" to the program status of the schools, visited each classroom (at unannounced times) for a total of 16 hours (eight separate two-hour visits) each year. Two structured observation instruments were used: a "sign" system (with which behaviors or activities observed during successive two-minute periods were tallied) and a global rating form (which was used to register observations and impressions from the total two-hour visit). Scores derived from these instruments that represent the degree of implementation of each of the five program components across the full five years are presented in Figure 10.1. The scores for each component were significantly higher in the program schools. Thus, although the data (as well as the informal observations discussed above) also indicate that there was substantial variability in the adequacy of implementation among the program teachers, this evidence indicates that, as a group, their classrooms could be clearly differentiated from those in the comparison schools.

The observation-based index of cooperative learning was composed of five subcomponents. In order to focus more specifically on the implementation of these various aspects of cooperative learning, the differentiation of the program and comparison classrooms with respect to these subcomponents was also investigated. The relevant mean standard scores are graphed in Figure 10.2. Significant programs versus comparison differences were found for four of the subcomponents. The largest difference was obtained with Teacher Facilitation of Cooperative Activities (which included the following items: helps group with group/interpersonal skills, acknowledges group effort or product, states value and/or describes effects of cooperation, tells or encourages students to work together toward common goal, and sets up groups to work cooperatively). The other significantly differentiated subcomponents were Student Cooperative Group Activities (including: students working toward group goal, and students taking different interdependent roles); Collaborative Within-Group Discussion (containing items that refer to the internal dynamics of the group, including: suggesting or giving reasons for plans, strategies, opinions or suggestions; seeking

Figure 10.1
Implementation of CDP Program Components, Grades K–4 Combined

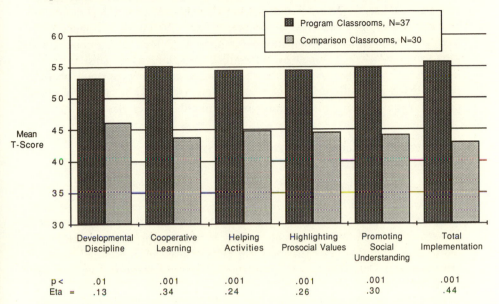

| p < | .01 | .001 | .001 | .001 | .001 | .001 |
| Eta = | .13 | .34 | .24 | .26 | .30 | .44 |

Figure 10.2
Cooperative Learning Subcomponents in Program and Comparison Classrooms, Grades K–4 Combined

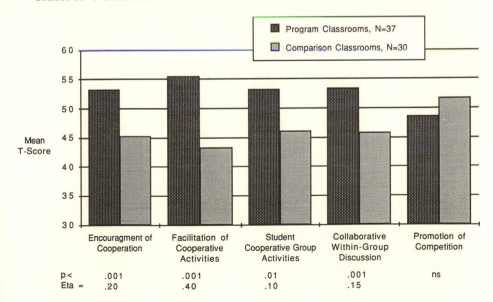

| p < | .001 | .001 | .01 | .001 | ns |
| Eta = | .20 | .40 | .10 | .15 | |

out others' ideas; supporting/elaborating on others' ideas; polling of members' opinions; reaching solutions by informal general agreement; and orienting or reorienting others to the task); and Teacher Encouragement of Cooperation (including: encouraged students to cooperate, and discouraged competition). Teachers' Promotion of Competition (composed of four items: competitive intra-group structure, competitive inter-group structure, whole-class competitive activity, and tells/encourages students to compete) was the only subcomponent that was undifferentiated between groups. (It should be noted that competitive activities occurred quite infrequently in either set of classrooms.)

Student Perceptions of Cooperative Learning and Classroom Organization

Further information about the cooperative learning activities in these classrooms was provided by an interview given to children toward the end of third grade. The interview included a series of open-ended questions about students' perceptions of and attitudes about various events and practices in the classroom, including group activities and, for classes in which it occurred, cooperative learning. Data showing student responses to these questions are shown in Table 10.1.

All of the students said that they had worked in groups in their classrooms. We did not ask explicitly about *cooperative* groups, but since the observation data showed clearly higher mean scores for the cooperative learning indices, it can be assumed that the program students were more likely than the comparison students to be referring to cooperative groups in their responses to these questions. In general, the responses indicate that the program students saw both academic and social goals and benefits in cooperative activities (perhaps in part reflecting what had been communicated to them by their teachers). They were more likely than comparison students to report that they worked on academics in groups and that they learned more in groups (than alone). The academic benefits they saw included getting help, and the speed and amount of work accomplished. The program students also saw more arguing over answers in groups, however, perhaps reflecting the fact that their groups sometimes engaged in active discussion and controversy as part of the group process. Among the perceived social benefits were: learning how to work in groups, learning to be cooperative, learning to understand and appreciate others, and "preparing for adulthood." There were three responses that were given more frequently by comparison schoolchildren: they were more likely to say that they liked group activity because it is "fun," that their teacher had them work in groups so the "work will be done better" (rather than for more specific academic or social goals), and that they learned more by themselves than in groups.

Another set of questions in this third-grade interview asked students about the rules in their classrooms. Responses to these questions, shown in the second part of Table 10.1, indicate that: (a) students in the program classrooms

Table 10.1

Student Perceptions and Attitudes Concerning Classroom Activities

Questions and Responses	Percent Giving Response		Chi² Value
	Program Students	Comparison Students	
A. Cooperative/Group Activities			
Do you ever work in groups?			
Yes	100.0	100.0	
Group N	(196)	(162)	
What do you do in groups?			
Academics	85.3	67.7	16.01****
Art/Music/Crafts	24.4	29.9	1.42
Games and Play	10.2	14.4	1.51
Group N	(197)	(167)	
Do you like working in groups?			
Yes	83.3	85.4	1.20
Group N	(192)	(158)	
What do you like about working in groups?			
You get the benefit of everyone's ideas.	25.9	22.2	.69
You learn how to work in groups.	10.2	5.4	2.88*
You get help with problems, mistakes.	29.9	18.0	7.15***
Work gets done faster, more gets done.	19.8	9.0	8.69***
It's nice for everyone to help each other.	25.4	14.4	6.91***
Fun, makes you feel good, be with friends.	38.1	50.9	6.04**
Opportunity to talk.	11.2	15.6	1.52
Group N	(197)	(167)	

Table 10.1 *continued*

Questions and Responses	Percent Giving Response		
	Program Students	Comparison Students	Chi² Value
What <u>don't</u> you like about working in groups?			
People get distracted, talk, fool around.	25.4	19.2	2.02
People argue about answers.	20.3	8.4	10.63***
People are bossy.	19.3	15.0	1.19
Some don't do their share.	4.6	5.4	.13
Bad effect on quality or quantity.	6.6	3.6	1.70
No fun.	2.5	5.4	1.99
Nothing child doesn't like.	21.8	25.7	.77
Group N	(197)	(167)	
Do you learn more working with others or by yourself?			
With others.	72.3	61.5	8.86**
By self.	22.1	35.4	
Sometimes one, sometimes the other.	3.6	2.5	
Makes no difference.	2.1	.6	
Group N	(195)	(161)	
Why do you think your teacher has you work together?			
So work will be done better.	8.1	16.8	6.37**
To develop academic skills.	6.6	5.4	.24
To prepare for adulthood.	13.2	3.6	11.30****
So each can benefit from the others.	22.3	16.8	1.78
To learn to be cooperative.	39.6	20.4	16.06****
To learn to understand and appreciate others.	21.3	7.8	13.62****
To learn to be helpful and kind.	5.6	6.6	.16
Pragmatic (get the job done).	15.2	18.6	.72
Group N	(197)	(167)	

Table 10.1 *continued*

Questions and Responses	Percent Giving Response		Chi² Value
	Program Students	Comparison Students	

B. Class Rules

Example of a class rule (academic, behavioral, or prosocial)

Academic (related to school work)	2.7	2.5	
Behavioral (social conventions, expectations)	87.5	94.4	6.72**
Prosocial/moral/ethical (higher-level values)	9.8	3.1	
Group N	(197)	(167)	

How were the class rules made?

Authority made and announced	33.8	75.6	
Students and teacher discussed and all decided	51.9	11.1	
Students discussed and decided themselves	4.5	1.1	50.23****
Authority announced some, students made up others	4.5	4.4	
Tradition, part of school, left over from before	5.3	7.8	
Group N	(197)	(167)	

What happens if a student breaks a rule?

Punishment	51.0	64.7	6.91***
Temporary separation	26.4	13.8	9.04***
Warning, name on board, etc.	32.5	43.7	4.85**
Reparation	11.7	3.6	8.66***
Discussion with teacher and/or other adults	10.7	5.4	3.43*
Group N	(197)	(167)	

*p<.10; **p<.05; ***p<.01; ****p<.001

Note. The children were allowed multiple responses to most of the above questions; the percentages therefore generally total to more than 100%. Because the program school children gave more responses to most of the questions, it seemed possible that some of the above differences might merely be a function of differences in the amount of speech. The analyses were therefore redone, limiting the sample to children who gave no more than one response to any given question. The same pattern of results was obtained.

were much more likely than those in the comparison classrooms to say that they had participated in the development of the classroom rules (almost 60 percent of the program students said that they had developed the rules in collaboration with the teacher or by themselves, compared with about 12 percent of the comparison students); (b) although the rule examples given by students in both sets of classrooms referred predominantly to social conventions and expectations, the proportion of these was higher in the comparison classrooms, while the proportion of rules referring to higher-level values was higher in the program classrooms; and (c) rule infractions were seen as more likely to be responded to with warnings and punishments in the comparison classrooms, and with temporary separation, reparation, or discussions with adults in the program classrooms. All of these differences are consistent with the approach to classroom management advocated by this project, emphasizing student autonomy and the development of a cooperative classroom community to which students will feel responsible and committed. A corroborative finding was obtained with a questionnaire given to students in fourth grade, with program students scoring higher than comparison students on a scale representing student participation in classroom decision-making (Prog. & Comp. $Ms = 1.99$ & 2.14; $F[1,290] = 10.11$; $p < .002$).

Teacher Perceptions of Cooperative Learning and Classroom Organization

Questionnaires asking about various aspects of classroom organization and activities have been given to the cohort-grade teachers in the program and comparison schools near the end of each school year. These provide further information about the use of cooperative activities in the classrooms, as well as more general approaches to classroom management. Responses to some parts of these questionnaires are shown in Table 10.2. (The questionnaire has changed somewhat over time; not all questions have been asked in all years. The grades and numbers of teachers covered by each included item or scale are indicated in the table.)

The first part of the table refers to cooperative activities. Program students were described (by their teachers) as spending significantly more time than comparison students in cooperative groups where students helped each other with individual tasks. (While they also reported that their students spent more time in groups working on group products, this difference was not significant.) Program teachers also attached significantly greater weight to learning of academic materials, learning of group interaction skills, and improvement of interpersonal understanding as goals of group activities than did comparison teachers.

The other parts of Table 10.2 refer to aspects of teachers' classroom management that are consistent with our approach to cooperative learning, with specific reference to their control orientations, use of extrinsic versus intrinsic incentives, and provision for student autonomy and participation in classroom decision making. For four of the five years covered in this report, the questionnaire included a measure of teachers' "control ideology," adapted from one developed by Deci et al. (1981). Teachers with high scores on this measure express greater reliance on maximizing student autonomy in the classroom, those with low scores, greater reliance on the use of power assertion and other forms of external control. The program teachers consistently scored substantially higher on this measure than the comparison teachers. They also reported less use of prizes and rewards as incentives, and greater use of praise. Similar to the report by students, the program teachers also described their students as more directly involved in the development of class rules. Several other differences also indicate greater student autonomy and self-determination in the program classrooms. Program teachers were more likely to report that students in their classrooms were involved in class discussions about classroom problems, solved their own minor conflicts, decided about their own learning and problem-solving methods, had fewer and less explicit rules to deal with, and had more time in which they were free to interact with one another in class.

Effects of the Program

As indicated above, a broad range of student outcomes had been assessed each year, through interviews, questionnaires, and observations in classrooms, on the playgrounds, and in structured task sessions. A number of variables from each of these sources have shown scattered differences between program and comparison schoolchildren—generally favoring the former—but most of these differences have not been strong enough or consistent enough across years to warrant definitive conclusions. A few variables, however, have shown clear and strong differences that were maintained consistently across years. We will direct most of our attention to these.

Interpersonal behavior in the classroom. The classroom observers spent part of their time observing student interpersonal behavior in the classroom. Four scales were derived from these observations: supportive and friendly behavior, negative behavior, spontaneous prosocial behavior, and harmoniousness. Analyses of these data have consistently indicated that student behavior is more positive in program than in comparison classrooms.

The strongest and most consistent program effect was found for spontaneous prosocial behavior (a measure based on observers' ratings of students' spontaneous helpfulness, concern for others, and cooperation). Significant program versus comparison differences were also found for supportive and friendly behavior (a combination of a number of sign-system items, including gives support/encouragement, shows affection, invites others to join activity, thanks or praises other student, etc.) and for harmoniousness (based on ratings of harmoniousness, apparent interest and involvement, and apparent student happiness).

Table 10.2
Teacher Descriptions of Classroom Activities and Teaching Practices and Goals

Questions and Responses	Grade Levels	Mean Score Program Teachers	Mean Score Comparison Teachers	t Value
A. Time Students Spend in Groups:				
Doing individual work, with help provided by teacher	K-3	3.27	3.38	.04
Doing individual work, with help provided by students	K-3	3.43	2.68	2.53**
Working on a group product	K-3	3.00	2.61	1.47
N for group:		25	24	
B. Teacher Goals for Group Activities:				
To learn academic material more thoroughly & effectively	2-4	4.58	3.92	3.21***
To learn group interaction skills	2-4	4.82	4.15	3.33***
To improve interpersonal understanding & concern for others	2-4	4.68	4.21	1.82*
To provide experience in competition between groups	2-4	1.32	1.83	1.86*
To make it easy for students to monitor each other and enforce classroom rules	2-4	2.97	2.23	1.47
To provide experience in cooperating with others	2-4	4.74	4.55	1.02
To make the class and learning more interesting	2-4	4.50	4.73	1.04
N for group:		18	14	
C. Teacher Control and Use of External and Internal Incentives				
Teacher control ideology	1-4	9.44	5.89	2.98***
N:		26	24	
Frequency of giving awards or prizes to students in class	2-4	2.27	3.97	2.91***
Frequency of giving awards or Frizes to class as a whole	2-4	2.30	3.54	2.28**

Table 10.2 *continued*

| Questions and Responses | Grade Levels | Mean Score | | t Value |
		Program Teachers	Comparison Teachers	
Rewards to individuals for performance in groups	2-4	1.37	2.64	3.55****
Rewards to groups for group performance	2-4	2.24	2.90	1.35
Praise to individuals for performance in groups	2-4	3.61	3.29	.63
Praise to groups for group performance	2-4	4.63	3.63	3.47***
N for group:		18	16	

D. Student Autonomy and Participation in Classroom Decision-Making

Questions and Responses	Grade Levels	Program Teachers	Comparison Teachers	t Value
Explicitness/pervasiveness of classroom rules	K-3	1.55	2.03	1.80*
Reliance on students to solve minor conflicts/arguments	K-3	4.06	3.39	2.91***
Time students spend interacting freely in class	K-3	3.76	3.10	2.41**
Student decision-making about learning & problem-solving methods to use	K-3	2.78	2.32	2.60***
N for group:		26	24	
Student decision-making about class activities, projects, trips, etc.	K-4	2.35	2.33	.10
Student participation in development of class rules	K-4	3.75	2.29	4.87****
Joint planning sessions with teacher & students	K-4	2.69	2.49	.55
Class discussions to solve classroom problems	K-4	4.30	3.35	3.54****
N for group:		33	30	

*p<.10; **p<.05; ***p<.01; ****p<.001

Figure 10.3
Student Social Behavior in Program and Comparison Classrooms,
Grades K–4 Combined

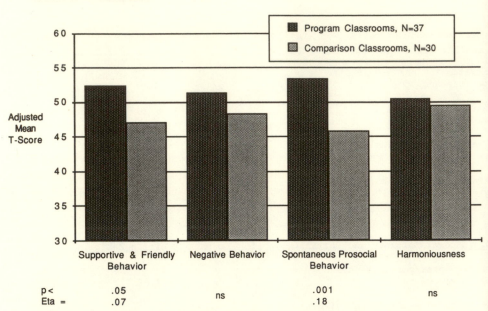

The Ns for the data points represented in this figure are: K program, 190; K comparison, 152; grade 2 program, 182; grade 2 comparison, 178; grade 4 program, 162; grade 4 comparison, 155.

Because teacher competence (a scale based on observers' ratings of teachers' enthusiasm, confidence, "withitness," clarity, smoothness and efficiency, anticipation of problems, and effectiveness of control) was found to be strongly related to classroom harmoniousness ($r = .85$, $p < .0001$) and was also marginally higher for the program than the comparison teachers ($Ms = 51.75$ and 47.84 respectively; $t = 1.66$, $p < .11$), we decided to partial its effect out of the analysis of program effects on students' classroom behavior. In addition, because cooperative activities provided a greater opportunity for student interaction in the classroom (and thus possibly a greater potential for either positive or negative interpersonal behavior), we decided to partial out the effect of student participation in cooperative activities as well. A multivariate analysis of covariance, with these two effects removed, produced an $F(4, 60)$ of 3.64 ($p < .02$, eta$^2 = .06$). The program effect of harmoniousness disappeared completely, but the other two indices of positive student classroom behavior were still significantly higher in the program classrooms. The adjusted program and comparison means, combined across years, are shown in Figure 10.3. It can be seen that the effect is still strongest for spontaneous prosocial behavior. Within-year analyses showed that students in the program classrooms scored significantly higher on this measure than those in the comparison classrooms in four out of the five years, more than with any of the other student classroom behavior measures. A fuller exposition of these results can be found in Solomon et al. (in press).

Responses to questions asked in the fourth-grade student questionnaire and in the yearly teacher questionnaires have provided some corroborative evidence that student interpersonal behavior is more positive in program than in comparison classrooms. Program students' responses indicated that they saw their classmates as more supportive (e.g., being willing to go out of their way to help others, working together to solve problems, caring about other students' work as well as their own) than did comparison students (prog. and comp. $Ms = 1.99$ and 1.85, respectively; $F[1,209] = 6.63$, $p < .01$). The program teachers also have reported more positive behavior among their students than have the comparison teachers (with respective program and comparison means, across the four years, of 3.74 and 3.47), although this difference is not statistically significant.

Behavior during small-group interactions outside of the classroom. The findings reported above are consistent with a large body of literature indicating that cooperative learning enhances interpersonal attitudes and behavior in the classroom (Aronson, Bridgeman, and Geffner 1978; Johnson, Johnson, and Maruyama 1983; Sharan, 1980; Slavin, 1983). Surprisingly, however, only a few attempts have been made to examine the extent to which the positive social attitudes and skills developed during cooperative learning activities affect childrens' interpersonal behavior outside of the classroom. While the studies that have examined this issue have generally found positive effects on children's prosocial behavior, the implications for generalization have been limited either by the use of the same groups that worked together in the classroom (Ryan and Wheeler 1977), groups drawn from members of the same classroom (Sharan et al. 1984), or by the use of academic-like tasks similar to those used in the classroom (e.g., Hertz-Lazarowitz, Sharan, and Steinberg 1980). Consequently, it is as yet still unclear to what extent and under what conditions the positive social effects of cooperative learning generalize to peer relationships in other settings (cf., Miller, Brewer, and Edwards 1985).

As one approach to examining social behavior during non-academic peer interactions outside of the classroom, the cohort children in both sets of schools have participated in a series of small-group tasks each spring. The tasks were done in four-person, same-sex groups (composed of two children from each of two different classrooms) when the children were in grades K, 2, and 4, and in dyadic, same-sex groups (composed of two children from the same classroom) when they were in grades 1 and 3. Three of the tasks assessed various aspects of collaborative behavior, and thus are particularly relevant to cooperative activity. These included the "Pep board" (a four-person group construction task adapted from Pepitone 1980), a four-person *discussion* task, and a dyadic *referential communication* task. In the Pep board task, which was used in kindergarten and second and fourth grades, children were given a large number of parquetry blocks of different shapes and colors. There were two task phases, one with general and vague instructions (so that spontaneous collaboration could be assessed), the other with instructions to build something together (so that the quality of collaboration could be assessed). In the discussion task, used in the second and fourth grades, the children were asked to reach consensus on the best solution to a hypothetical interpersonal problem. In the referential communication task, used in the first and third grades, one child was given a complex model that the other child could not see, and was instructed to help the other child reproduce the model (from provided materials) by giving verbal directions. The four-person task sessions were videotaped and later scored from the videotapes; the dyadic task sessions were scored live.

Analyses of children's behavior during these tasks did show some significant status effects, all of which favored groups from the program schools. However, the differences were generally of small magnitude and were limited to the lower grades (kindergarten through second grade).

A multivariate analysis of variance involving three composite Pep board variables (spontaneous collaboration, quality of collaboration, and use of praise) showed a borderline program effect ($F[3,77] = 2.20$, $p < .10$) at kindergarten but not at second or fourth grade. Groups from the program schools scored higher than those from the comparison schools with respect to spontaneous collaboration ($Ms = 2.35$ and 1.77, t $[79] = 1.82$, $p < .07$) and use of praise ($Ms = .14$ and $.03$, t $[78] = 1.64$, $p < .11$) during this task in kindergarten, but showed no significant differences on any of the Pep board measures at second or fourth grades.

Four composite variables were derived from the discussion task:

1. discussion engagement/equality (composed of three variables—involvement in discussion, number of members stating opinions, and equality of participation);
2. use of reason/explanation (composed of three variables—active support or elaboration of another's opinion, reasoned disagreement, and explicit comparing/contrasting of different solutions);
3. striving for consensus (composed of three variables—explicit polling of members' opinions, use of "we" statements, and length of discussion); and
4. raucousness of discussion (composed of two items—berating/denigrating/ridiculing, and orderliness of discussion [reflected]).

Although the multivariate difference was not significant, there was a borderline program effect ($t[80] = 1.80$, $p < .08$) for discussion engagement/equality (with respective program and comparison group means of 4.79 and 4.24) at second grade. However, no significant differences were found between program and comparison groups at fourth grade.

The referential communication task produced a significant multivariate program effect at first grade ($F[3,174] = 4.29$, $p < .01$), with program groups scoring higher than comparison groups on members' supportiveness of one another

Figure 10.4
Conflict Resolution Scores for Program and Comparison Students, Kindergarten and Second and Fourth Grades

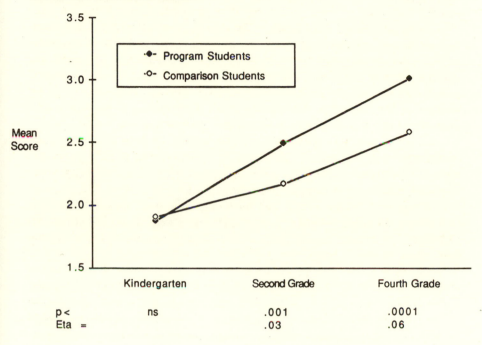

$(Ms = .41$ and $.28$, $t[176] = 2.69$, $p < .01)$, and scoring lower on irritability $(Ms = .97$ and 1.11, $t[176] = 1.88$, $p < .07)$. (A third variable, quality of communication, did not show a significant difference.) When the same task was done with the third-graders, however, no significant differences were found.

Social problem solving. Two different measures of social problem solving included in the child interviews have shown strong and consistent program effects. One measure, administered as part of the kindergarten, second-, and fourth-grade interviews, presented the children with hypothetical interpersonal conflict situations and asked them to state how the problem could be resolved. The other measure, given to the children in the first and third grades, was adapted from one developed by Elias (Elias et al. 1978), and asked about possible solutions to hypothetical problems concerned with gaining access to an attractive toy and of gaining entry into a group.

A single score was derived from the conflict responses, taking into account both the degree to which the solution showed consideration of both persons' needs and the content of the suggested solutions (with "prosocial" solutions given the highest weights). The mean conflict resolution scores in grades K, 2, and 4, for program and comparison children, are shown in Figure 10.4. While the scores increase with increasing grade for both groups of schools, the increase is greater for the program schoolchildren. There was no difference between groups at kindergarten, a substantial (and significant) difference favoring the program children at second grade, and a still greater difference at fourth grade.

The results obtained with the Elias measure were similar. There were four major measures: interpersonal sensitivity (referring to the child's understanding of characters' situations in the hypothetical problem), problem resolution strategy (referring to the content of the proposed solution, with more reasonable and ''prosocial'' strategies given greater weight), outcome expectancy (a combination of the expectation that the outcome will be favorable and that it will result from the exercise of personal initiative), and means-ends cognitive problem solving (referring to the complexity and sophistication of the child's suggested steps toward problem resolution). The latter three of these showed significant differences favoring the program schoolchildren in first grade (with respective program and comparison means of 4.88 and 4.59, 4.69 and 4.31, and .46 and .27), while the first and fourth did so at third grade (with means of 3.07 and 2.77 and .70 and .52)—all differences were significant at $p < .01$ or better. For a fuller description of these findings, see Battistich et al. (in press, a).

Democratic values. Several findings have indicated a greater concern for democratic values on the part of the program schoolchildren. On the student questionnaire administered in third grade, program children scored significantly higher (prog. and comp. $Ms = 3.26$ and 2.99, $F = 9.44$, $p < .01$) in one aspect of democratic values—assertion responsibility (the responsibility to state one's position, even if it seems unlikely to prevail). With a similar questionnaire given the following year, the program children scored higher than the comparison children on the same measure of assertion responsibility ($Ms = 3.33$ and 3.14, $F = 6.44$, $p < .05$), and on a measure of equality of participation and representation ($Ms = 3.19$ and 2.92, $F = 16.66$, $p < .001$), and on total democratic values ($Ms = 3.31$ and 3.12, $F = 15.30$, $p < .001$)—a measure combining assertion responsibility and equality of participation/representation with a consistent and marginally significant [$Ms = 3.40$ and 3.30, $F = 2.48$, $p < .12$] measure of willingness to compromise.

Greater concern for equality of participation and equality of outcomes on the part of program students was also reflected in observers' ratings of children's behavior during several of the small-group tasks administered each spring. This occurred with respect to free-play behavior during a four-person dart-board task in the kindergarten assessment ($p < .05$), in both the discussion task described above and a prize distribution task in the second-grade assessment ($p < .10$), and in a mixed-motive (cooperative-competitive) ''bridge-crossing'' dyadic task at third grade ($p < .05$). These findings are presented more fully in Solomon et al. (1987).

Academic achievement. Scores on the California Achievement Test, administered to all fourth-graders by the school district, revealed generally high scores, which were undifferentiated between program and comparison children in the fourth grade. This held both for all the children enrolled in fourth grade that year and for just the fourth-graders who had been with the project since kindergarten (165 children). Similar achievement tests administered in the same schools the year before the start of the project also showed generally high scores, with no differences between these two sets of schools, at either fourth or sixth grade. We conclude that pursuit of the CDP program did not impede academic progress, as indexed by standard achievement tests.[2]

DISCUSSION AND CONCLUSIONS

The CDP program was conceived as a broad-ranging attempt to influence children's social development. It was expected that the program experience would have effects on children's prosocial motives, attitudes, skills, inclinations, perceptions, and behaviors. The general model for these expectations was presented in Solomon et al. (1985). In order to assess effects in all these areas, a similarly comprehensive set of measures and procedures was developed and/or adapted.

The analyses conducted thus far have revealed strong and consistent program effects in several of the many areas assessed; these have been the focus of the data presentation in the present paper. To summarize:

1. There has been clear observational evidence that the program was more closely approximated in the program than the comparison school classrooms.

2. Students' interview responses indicated that they were aware of several of the social goals and values involved in cooperative group activities.

3. Data from teacher questionnaires, student questionnaires, and student interviews all corroborated observational evidence of greater provision of student autonomy and participation in classroom decision making in the program classrooms.

4. Students' interpersonal behavior was more prosocial in the program than the comparison school classrooms (this was also corroborated by student questionnaire responses, and was independent of group differences in either general teacher competence or the frequency of cooperative activities in the classroom).

5. Program students' behavior in small-group tasks was more prosocial according to some measures in the early grades, but these differences were not maintained in the third- and fourth-grade assessments.

6. Students' social problem-solving skill (assessed through interviews) was strongly enhanced by the program (and consistently, across years).

7. Students' endorsement of democratic values (particularly assertion responsibility and concern for equality) appeared to be increased by the program experience.

The overall impression conveyed by this combination of effects is that participation in the program enhanced both social competence and concern for others in students. Program students have consistently demonstrated a better understanding of common interpersonal problems, and a more thoughtful and sophisticated approach to solving such problems than comparison students. Their approach to problem resolution also was more prosocial; program students were more likely than comparison students to consider the other person's needs as well as their own, and to suggest a mutually beneficial solution to the problem. Similarly, while program students were more likely than comparison students to feel that it is important to state one's own position in a disagreement, they also were more concerned about fairness and equality. These findings, we believe, reflect a *self–other balance:* an inclination to be concerned about the needs of others without discounting one's own needs, and to achieve solutions that optimize both in situations where they conflict.

The program was presented as a whole; we are thus unable to assess the relative importance of different aspects of the program to these outcomes. (We plan to conduct additional "natural variation" analyses to explore differences in the effects of different program components.) Certain aspects of the program, however, seem at the least to be logically consistent with these outcomes. The opportunity for interpersonal interaction provided by cooperative learning gives children experience at negotiating, stating positions, compromising, and working together. As it is implemented in the program classrooms, children are encouraged to attend to each other's needs and feelings and to help one another. It is reasonable to expect that this experience would help to produce the blend of social competence and interpersonal concern that seems, so far, to be the major effect of this program. Similar effects of interpersonal interaction have been proposed by Youniss (1980), in an integration of the theories and observations of Sullivan and Piaget.

Our particular approach to cooperative learning explicitly emphasizes and draws children's attention to the social values relevant to group activity, and tries to help them focus on the intrinsic merits and goals of the activity by avoiding or minimizing external controls or incentives. It was expected that these practices would promote children's intrinsic orientation to the group activity (similar predictions, with substantial supporting evidence, are made by Lepper 1983; and Ryan, Connell, and Deci 1985). The fact that the program children expressed awareness of the social goals and values of the group activity is consistent with this expectation. Other aspects of the program were also designed to promote children's intrinsic orientation to prosocial values and interpersonal concern. For example, external control is also de-emphasized in teachers' discipline practices, while student autonomy and participation in rule setting and classroom decision making are encouraged.

Although the program does appear to have influenced children's social development in some of the areas that we expected, there are other areas in which anticipated effects either were not found, or were not as large or consistent as we would wish. We are particularly puzzled by the findings obtained with the small-group behavioral data, which showed some program effects in the lower grades but none in the upper ones, as contrasted with the classroom observational data, which showed program students behaving in a more positive way toward each other at all grade levels. As we pointed out above, there have been only a few prior attempts to assess generalization of the behavioral effects of cooperative learning beyond the immediate group or classroom setting. The present findings suggest that such generalization may be difficult to achieve. One aspect of our approach to cooperative learning was expected to be important for promoting generalization—involving students in frequent discussions (before and after cooperative sessions) about the relevance and importance of general prosocial values to their group experience during cooperative activities, and about the skills and behaviors needed to apply those values. Unfortunately, as noted earlier, while the importance of such discussions was emphasized in our training, our informal observations of typical cooperative activities in the program classrooms left us feeling that the discussions were often superficial and did not sufficiently engage students in reflection about the social, personal, or academic implications of the cooperative experience. Furthermore, no explicit attempts were made to show students how the same values and behaviors apply to interpersonal relationships outside the classroom. Generalization may require clear discussions about cross-situational relevance, as well as repeated cooperative experiences in varied settings. Thus, while program students clearly engaged in more cooperative interactions in the classroom than comparison students, and were apparently aware of some of the social goals and purposes of the cooperative activities (as indicated in their interview responses), their experiences do not as yet appear to have resulted in as strong or consistent positive effects on interpersonal behavior outside of the classroom as within it.

More generally, it seems probable that program effects would have been more widespread if "deeper" and more consistent program implementation had been achieved by more of the program teachers. Our retrospective judgment is that it would have been better to train teachers at a whole-school rather than a single-grade level, and to have given them more time to learn the program before assessing its implementation and effects (not doing so, as we did, in the teachers' first year with the program). We plan to conduct further analyses to determine whether students who received the most adequate program implementation show broader ranges of program effects.

The initial research strategy on this project was to include a broad net of variables representing the variety of areas in which we thought program effects were either likely or possible. The sets of findings on which we have focused in this paper are those that have shown sufficiently strong and consistent program effects, across years, to give us confidence that they are "real." These findings are helping to shape our further analyses of these data, further data collection efforts, and continuing program development and refinement activities. We are now in the process of extending this program to the fifth and sixth grades in the same district, and to a different district with a heterogeneous, working-to-middle-class student population. We will be exploring ways to achieve deeper and more consistent program implementation, determining whether any changes are necessary to carry out the program in the new district, and investigating the generality of the effects found thus far.

NOTES

The research and writing for this project have been funded by the William and Flora Hewlett Foundation. Its initial formulation was a direct result of the ideas and efforts of Dyke Brown (see Brown and Solomon 1983).

1. We would like to acknowledge important contributions to the initial specification of the program and the design of the evaluation by Nancy Eisenberg and Joel Moskowitz, and by an advisory panel consisting of Paul Mussen, Ervin Staub, Marian Radke-Yarrow, Marilynn Brewer, and Martin Hoffman (and later joined by David Johnson, Roger Johnson, David Weikart, and Thomas Lickona, who have also made very helpful contributions). Work on adaptation or development of instruments and procedures, training of research workers, coordination of data collection, and collection and coding of data has been provided by Jane Deer, Allyson Rickard, Marc Rosenberg, Carol Stone, and Margaret Tauber, plus numerous observers, task administrators, interviewers, and coders. Work on specifying and refining the program components, developing specific program activities and approaches, and helping teachers, principals, and parents to understand, support, and implement the program has been provided by Carole Cooper, Patricia Tuck, Wendy Ritchey, Sylvia Kendzior, Carolyn Hildebrandt, Stefan Dasho, and Gail Mandella. Kevin Delucchi has been responsible for substantial portions of the data analysis.

2. These tests do not assess higher-level cognitive skill and understanding, which are the aspect of achievement that we would expect most likely to be enhanced by the CDP approach to cooperative learning. Such findings have in fact been reported in studies by Sharan (e.g., Sharan and Shachar 1988) and the Johnsons (Johnson, Skon, and Johnson 1980).

REFERENCES

Allport, G. (1954) *The Nature of Prejudice*. Reading, MA: Addison-Wesley.

Aronson, E. (1978) *The Jigsaw Classroom*. Beverly Hills, CA: Sage.

Aronson, E., Bridgeman, D. L., and Geffner, R. (1978) "The effects of a cooperative classroom structure on student behavior and attitudes." In *Social Psychology of Education*, edited by D. Bar-Tal and L. Saxe, pp. 257–72. New York: Hemisphere.

Battistich, V., Solomon, D., Watson, M., Solomon, J., and Schaps, E. (in press, a) "Effects of an elementary school program to enhance prosocial behavior on children's cognitive social problem-solving skills and strategies." *Journal of Applied Developmental Psychology*.

Battistich, V., Watson, M., Solomon, D., Schaps, E., and Solomon, J. (in press, b) "The Child Development Project: A comprehensive program for the development of prosocial character." In *Moral Behavior and Development: Advances in Theory, Research, and Application, (Vol. 1)*, edited by W. M. Kurtines and J. L. Gewirtz. Hillside, NJ: Erlbaum.

Brown, D., and Solomon, D. (1983) "A model for prosocial learning: An in-progress field study." In *The Nature of Prosocial Development*, edited by D. Bridgman, pp. 273–307. New York: Academic Press.

Cohen, E. G. (1987) *Designing Group Work: Strategies for the Heterogeneous Classroom*. New York: Teachers College Press.

Cook, S. W. (1978) "Interpersonal and attitudinal outcomes of cooperating interracial groups." *Journal of Research and Development in Education* 12:97–113.

Deci, E. L., Schwartz, A. J., Sheinman, L., and Ryan, R. M. (1981) "An instrument to assess adults' orientation toward control versus autonomy with children: Reflections on intrinsic motivation and perceived competence." *Journal of Educational Psychology* 73:642–50.

Deutsch, M. (1949) "A theory of cooperation and competition." *Human Relations* 2:129–52.

Dewey, J. (1966) *Democracy and Education*. New York: Free Press.

Elias, M. J., Larcen, S. W., Zlotow, S. F., and Chinsky, J. M. (1978). "An innovative measure of children's cognitions in problematic interpersonal situations." Paper presented at the meeting of American Psychological Association, Toronto, August.

Graves, N. B., and Graves, T. D. (1985) "Creating a cooperative learning environment: An ecological approach." In *Learning to Cooperate, Cooperating to Learn*, edited by R. Slavin, S. Sharan, S. Kagan, R. Hertz-Lazarowitz, C. Webb, and R. Schmuck. New York: Plenum.

Hertz-Lazarowitz, R., Sharan, S., and Steinberg, R. (1980) "Classroom learning style and cooperative behavior of elementary school children." *Journal of Educational Psychology* 72:97–104.

Hoffman, M. L. (1970) "Moral development." In *Carmichael's Manual of Child Psychology*, 3rd edn, edited by P. H. Mussen, pp. 261–360. New York: Wiley.

Johnson, D. W., and Johnson, R. T. (1975) *Learning Together and Alone: Cooperation, Competition, and Individualization*. Englewood Cliffs, NJ: Prentice-Hall.

Johnson, D. W., Johnson, R. T., and Maruyama, G. (1983) "Interdependence and interpersonal attraction among heterogeneous and homogeneous individuals: A theoretical formulation and a meta-analysis of the research." *Review of Educational Research* 53:5–54.

Johnson, D. W., Maruyama, G., Johnson, R. T., Nelson, D., and Skon, L. (1981) "Effects of cooperative, competitive, and individualistic goal structures on achievement: A meta-analysis." *Psychological Bulletin* 89:47–62.

Johnson, D. W., Skon, L., and Johnson, R. T. (1980) "The effects of cooperative, competitive and individualistic goal structures on student achievement on different types of tasks." *American Educational Research Journal* 17:83–93.

Lepper, M. R. (1983) "Extrinsic reward and intrinsic motivation: Implications for the classroom." In *Teacher and Student Perceptions*, edited by J. M. Levine and M. C. Wang, pp. 281–317. Hillsdale, NJ: Lawrence Erlbaum.

Miller, N., Brewer, M. B., and Edwards, K. (1985) "Cooperative interaction in desegregated settings: A laboratory analogue." *Journal of Social Issues* 41:63–79.

Mussen, P. H., and Eisenberg-Berg, N. (1977) *Roots of Caring, Sharing and Helping*. San Francisco, CA: Freeman.

Pepitone, E. A. (1980) *Children in Cooperation and Competition*. Lexington, MA: D. C. Heath.

Ryan, F., and Wheeler, R. (1977) "The effects of cooperative and competitive background experiences of students on the play of a simulation game." *Journal of Educational Research* 70:295–99.

Ryan, R. M., Connell, J. P., and Deci, E. L. (1985) "A motivational analysis of self-determination and self-regulation in education." In *Research on Motivation in Education. Vol. 2: The Classroom Milieu,* edited by C. Ames and R. Ames, pp. 13–51. New York: Academic Press.

Sharan, S. (1980) "Cooperative learning in small groups: Recent methods and effects on achievement, attitudes, and ethnic relations." *Review of Educational Research* 50:241–71.

Sharan, S., and Hertz-Lazarowitz, R. (1980) "A group-investigation method of cooperative learning in the classroom." In *Cooperation in Education,* edited by S. Sharan et al., pp. 14–46. Provo, UT: Brigham Young University Press.

Sharan, S., Raviv, S., Kussell, P., and Hertz-Lazarowitz, R. (1984) "Cooperative and competitive behavior." In *Cooperative Learning in the Classroom: Research in Desegregated Schools,* edited by S. Sharan et al., Chapter 3. Hillsdale, NJ: Erlbaum.

Sharan, S., and Shachar, H. (1988) *Language and Learning in the Cooperative Classroom.* New York: Springer-Verlag.

Sharan, S., & Sharan, Y. (1976) *Small-Group Teaching.* Englewood Cliffs, NJ: Educational Technology Publications.

Slavin, R. E. (1980) *Using Student Team Learning.* Baltimore, MD: Center for Social Organization of Schools, Johns Hopkins University.

———. (1983) *Cooperative Learning.* New York: Longmans.

Slavin, R. E., and Hansell, S. (1983) "Cooperative learning and intergroup relations: Contact theory in the classroom." In *Friends in School,* edited by J. Epstein and N. Karweit. New York: Academic Press.

Solomon, D., Watson, M. S., Battistich, V., Schaps, E., Tuck, P., Solomon, J., Cooper, C., and Ritchey, W. (1985) "A program to promote interpersonal consideration and cooperation in children." In *Learning to Cooperate: Cooperating to Learn,* edited by R. Slavin, S. Sharan, S. Kagan, R. Hertz-Lazarowitz, C. Webb, and R. Schmuck, pp. 371–401. New York: Plenum.

Solomon, D., Schaps, E., Watson, M. S., and Battistich, V. (1987). "Promoting prosocial behavior in schools: A second interim report on a five-year longitudinal project." Paper presented at meetings of American Educational Research Association, Washington, D.C., March.

Solomon, D., Watson, M. S., Delucchi, K. L., Schaps, E., and Battistich, V. (in press) "Enhancing children's prosocial behavior in the classroom." *American Educational Research Journal.*

Staub, E. (1979) *Positive Social Behavior and Morality. Vol. 2: Socialization and Development.* New York: Academic Press.

Watson, M. S. (1982) "Classroom control: To what ends? At what price?" *California Journal of Teacher Education* 9:75–95.

Watson, M., Hildebrandt, C., and Solomon, D. (in press) "Cooperative learning for kindergarten and early primary grade children." *International Journal of Social Education.*

Youniss, J. (1980) *Parents and Peers in Social Development.* Chicago, IL: University of Chicago Press.

11
Comprehensive Cooperative Learning Models: Embedding Cooperative Learning in the Curriculum and the School

ROBERT E. SLAVIN

From its beginnings cooperative learning has been an application of social psychology to education. Not surprisingly, the emphasis of these methods was on interpersonal processes, incentives, task structures, and so on. Such methods as student teams achievement divisions (Slavin 1986), jigsaw teaching (Aronson et al. 1978), group investigation (Sharan and Sharan 1976), and the Johnsons' techniques (Johnson and Johnson 1986) are generic methods applicable to a wide range of subjects and grade levels. This wide applicability probably accounts for much of the current popularity of cooperative learning. However if cooperative learning is to fulfill its potential for enhancing student achievement, it is arguably necessary to design methods that are uniquely designed to teach particular kinds of content to students of particular ages. To do this, cooperative learning methods must be embedded in comprehensive models that accomplish curricular goals of schooling and which confront such problems of instruction as adaptation to individual differences. In addition to the possibility of increasing the achievement effects of cooperative learning, embedding cooperative learning within the curriculum may solve a critical problem of implementation: maintenance of cooperative learning beyond its current peak of popularity.

Fundamental change in schools comes about (when it does occur) through comprehensive changes in curriculum and school and classroom organization, which may be closely tied to changes in instructional methods. When schools set out to undertake comprehensive reform, they are unlikely to do so by grafting innovative teaching methods onto existing curriculum; rather, they are likely to look toward methods that accomplish the fundamental goal of schooling, transmission of curriculum to students.

Programs that integrate cooperative processes with particular curricula are appearing in many areas. One is Elizabeth Cohen and Edward DeAvila's Finding Out/Descubrimiento program (see Cohen 1986), which is a comprehensive discovery-oriented approach to teaching mathematics and science in bilingual classes. Another is Marilyn Burns' (1981) Groups of Four program in mathematics. Writing process models (e.g., Graves 1983; Calkins 1983) apply peer response groups to teaching of writing. Writing process models have so transformed the teaching of writing that they may ultimately be the most durable form of cooperative learning.

At Johns Hopkins University we have been working on comprehensive cooperative learning approaches to the three major curriculum areas in the elementary school curriculum: reading, writing, and mathematics. This chapter describes our research and development efforts in these areas. Most recently, we have begun working to integrate our comprehensive approaches within the same elementary schools and to apply principles of cooperative learning throughout the school, among teachers and administrators as well as students. At the end of this chapter the elements of these cooperative elementary schools are described, and the implications of the research on curriculum-embedded and school-embedded forms of cooperative learning are discussed.

TEAM-ASSISTED INDIVIDUALIZATION

The first comprehensive cooperative learning model we developed and researched was team-assisted individualization—mathematics, a program that combines cooperative learning with individualized instruction to meet the needs of diverse classrooms.[1]

TAI was developed for several reasons. First, it was hoped that TAI would provide a means of combining the motivational power and peer assistance of cooperative learning with an individualized instructional program capable of giving all students materials appropriate to their levels of skill in mathematics and allowing them to proceed through these materials at their own rates. It was felt that such a program would enable students to move more rapidly in mathematics than in traditional classes or group-paced cooperative learning programs. Low-achieving students could gain the prerequisite skills for each successive unit and would not be left behind by the pace of instruction, while average and high-achieving students could move through mathematics at a rate limited only by their ability to understand mathematical concepts.

Second, TAI was developed to apply cooperative learning techniques to solve many of the problems of programmed instruction. In the 1960s programmed instruction and related methods were expected to revolutionize instruction, especially in mathematics. However, reviews of the research on programmed instruction methods in mathematics have consistently concluded that these methods are no more effective than traditional instruction (e.g., Miller 1976; Horak 1981). Several problems inherent to programmed instruction have been cited as contributing to these disappointing findings (see Kepler and Randall 1977; Schoen 1976). Among these are too much time spent on management rather than teaching, too little incentive for students to progress rapidly through the programmed materials, and an excessive reliance on written instruction rather than instruction from a teacher. It was felt that by combining programmed instruction with cooperative learning and turning most of the management functions (e.g., scoring answers, locating and filing materials, keeping records, assigning new work) over to the students themselves, these problems could be solved. If students could handle most of the checking and management, the teacher would be free to teach individuals and small, homogeneous teaching groups. Students working in learning teams toward a cooperative goal could help one another study, provide instant feedback to one another, and encourage one another to proceed rapidly and accurately through the materials.

Finally, TAI was developed as a means of producing the well-documented social effects characteristic of cooperative learning (Slavin 1983a) while meeting diverse needs. The principal concern here was with mainstreaming. It was felt that mainstreaming of academically handicapped students in mathematics was limited by a feeling on the part of regular-class teachers that they were unprepared to accommodate the instructional needs of these students (Gickling and Theobold 1975). Further, studies of attitudes toward academically handicapped students consistently find that these students are not well accepted by their non-handicapped classmates (Gottlieb and Leyser, 1981). Since cooperative learning methods have had positive effects on social relations of all kinds, and specifically on relationships between handicapped and non-handicapped students (Ballard et al. 1977; Cooper et al. 1980; Johnson and Johnson 1982; Madden and Slavin 1983b), it was felt that the best possible mathematics program for the mainstreamed classroom, or indeed for any classroom containing a heterogeneous group of students, would be one that combined cooperative learning with individualized instruction (Madden and Slavin 1983a).

Principal Features of TAI

TAI is primarily designed for grades 3 through 6, but has also been used at higher grade levels. It is almost always used without aides, volunteers, or other assistance. The principal elements of TAI are as follows (adapted from Slavin, Leavey, and Madden 1986):

Teams. Students are assigned to four- to five-member teams. Each team consists of a mix of high, average, and low achievers, boys and girls, and students of any ethnic groups in the class. Every eight weeks students are reassigned to new teams.

Placement test. Students are pretested at the beginning of the program on mathematics operations. They are placed at the appropriate point in the individualized program based on their performance on the placement test.

Curriculum materials. Following instruction from the teacher (see "Teaching Groups," below), students work in their teams on self-instructional curriculum materials covering addition, subtraction, multiplication, division, numeration, decimals, fractions, word problems, statistics, and algebra. Word problems are emphasized throughout the materials. The units are in the form of books. Each unit has the following subparts:

- A guide page that reviews the teacher's lesson, explaining the skill to be mastered and giving a step-by-step method of solving the problems
- Several skill practice pages, each consisting of 16 problems. Each skill practice page introduces a subskill that leads to a final mastery of the entire skill
- Two parallel sets of ten items, formative tests A and B
- A unit test of 15 items
- Answer sheets for the skill practice pages and formative tests (located at the back of student books) and answers for unit tests (located in a separate "monitor book")

Teaching groups. Every day the teacher gives lessons to small groups of students drawn from the heterogeneous teams who are at the same point in the curriculum. Teachers use specific concept lessons provided as part of the program. The purpose of these sessions is to introduce major concepts to the students. Teachers make extensive use of manipulatives, diagrams, and demonstrations. The lessons are designed to help students understand the connection between the mathematics they are doing and familiar, real-life problems. While the teacher works with a teaching group, the other students continue to work in their teams on their self-instructional units. This direct instruction to teaching groups is made possible by the fact that students take responsibility for almost all checking, materials handling, and routing.

Team study method. Following the placement test, the students are given a starting place in the sequence of mathematics units. They work on their units in their teams, using the following steps:

1. Students locate their units within their books and read the guide page, asking teammates or the teacher for help if necessary. Then the students begin with the first skill practice page in their unit.

2. Each student works the first four problems on his or her own skill practice page and then has a teammate check the answers against an answer sheet printed upside-down at the back of each student book. If all four are correct, the student may go on to the next skill practice page. If any are incorrect, the student must try the next four problems, and so on, until he or she gets one block of four problems correct. If they run into difficulties at this stage, the students are encouraged to ask for help within their teams before asking the teacher for help.

3. When a student gets four in a row on the last skill practice page, he or she takes

Formative Test A, a ten-item quiz that resembles the last skill practice page. Students work alone on the test until they are finished. A teammate scores the formative test. If the student gets eight or more of the ten problems correct, the teammate signs the student's paper to indicate that the student is certified by the team to take the unit test. If the student does not get eight correct (this is rare), the teacher is called in to respond to any problems the student is having. The teacher would diagnose the student's problem, briefly reteach the skill, and then may ask the student to work again on certain skill practice items. The student then takes Formative Test B, a second ten-item test comparable in content and difficulty to Formative Test A.

4. When a student passes Formative Test A or B, he or she takes the test paper to a student monitor from a different team to get the appropriate unit test. The student then completes the unit test, and the monitor scores it. Two different students serve as monitors each day. If the student gets at least 12 items correct (out of 15), the monitor posts the score on the student's team summary sheet. Otherwise, the test is given to the teacher, who meets with the student to diagnose and overcome the student's problems. Again, because students have already shown mastery on the skill practice pages and formative tests, they rarely fail a unit test.

Team scores and team recognition. At the end of each week the teacher computes a team score. This score is based on the average number of units covered by each teammember and the accuracy of the unit tests. Criteria are established for team performance. A high criterion is set for a team to be a "superteam," a moderate criterion is established for a team to be a "greatteam," and a minimum criterion is set for a team to be a "goodteam." The teams meeting the "superteam" and "greatteam" criteria receive attractive certificates.

Facts tests. Twice each week the students are given three-minute facts tests (usually multiplication or division facts). The students are given fact sheets to study at home to prepare for these tests.

Whole-class units. After every three weeks the teacher stops the individualized program and spends a week teaching lessons to the entire class covering such skills as geometry, measurement, sets, and problem-solving strategies.

RESEARCH ON TAI

Seven field experiments have been conducted to evaluate the effects of TAI on student achievement, attitudes, and behavior (Slavin 1985a, 1985b). The principal features and results of these studies are summarized in Table 11.1 (from Slavin 1985b) and discussed in more detail in the following section. To avoid confusion, the studies will be referred to as "Experiment 1," "Experiment 2," and so on; the actual references for the studies appear in Table 11.1.

Research Strategies

All of the TAI studies used either random assignment of classes (Experiment 1) or matched experimental and control classes (Experiments 2 and 3). In all

Table 11.1
Summary of Research on Team-Assisted Individualization

Study and Major Reports	Setting and Design Characteristics					Measures and Results [1]		
	No. of Students	Grade Levels	Duration (weeks)	Kinds of Schools	Experimental Design	Mathematics Achievement	Attitudes	Behavior Ratings
Experiment 1: Full Sample (Slavin, Leavey, and Madden 1984)	506	3-5	8	Surburban	Randomly Assigned Schools	CTBS Computations +	Liking of Math + Class; Self-Concept + in Math	Classroom Behavior +; Self-Confidence +; Friendships +; Neg. Peer Behavior +
Experiment 1: Academically Handicapped Students (Slavin, Madden, and Leavey 1984a)	117	3-5	8	Surburban	Randomly Assigned Schools	CTBS Computations 0	Liking of Math (+) Class; Self-Concept 0 in Math; "Best Friend" + Choices; "Rejection" + Choices	Classroom Behavior +; Self-Confidence 0; Friendships +; Neg. Peer Behavior +
Experiment 2 (Slavin, Leavey, and Madden 1984)	320	4-6	10	Surburban	Matched Schools	CTBS Computations +	Liking of Math + Class; Self-Concept 0 in Math	Classroom Behavior 0; Self-Confidence +

Experiment 3: Full Sample (Slavin, Madden, and Leavey 1984)	1371	3-5	Surburban	Matched Schools	CTBS Computations + CTBS Concepts & Applications +	
Experiment 3: Academically Handicapped Students (Slavin, Madden, and Leavey 1984)	113	3-5	Surburban	Matched Schools	CTBS Computations + CTBS Concepts & Applications +	
Experiment 4 (Oishi, Slavin, & Madden 1983)	160	4-6	Urban	Randomly Assigned Classes	CAT Computations 0 CAT Concepts & Applications 0	Cross Race: Friends + Rejects + Nice 0 Not Nice + Smart 0 Not Smart (+)
Experiment 5 (Oishi, 1983)	120	4-6	Urban	Randomly Assigned Classes		Cross Race: Friends 0 Playmates + Nice 0 Not Nice + Smart + Not Smart 0

267

Table 11.1 *continued*

Study and Major Reports	Setting and Design Characteristics					Measures and Results <1>		
	No. of Students	Grade Levels	Duration (weeks)	Kinds of Schools	Experimental Design	Mathematics Achievement	Attitudes	Behavior Ratings
Experiment 6 (Slavin & Karweit, 1985)	354	4-6	18	Urban	Randomly Assigned Classes	CTBS Computations + CTBS Concepts & Applications	0 Liking of Math + Class Self-Concept + in Math	
Experiment 7 (Slavin & Karweit, 1985)	480	3-5	16	Rural	Randomly Assigned Classes	CTBS Computations + CTBS Concepts & Applications	0 Liking of Math + Class Self-Concept 0 in Math	

<1> + = TAI students scored significantly higher than control students on the indicated measure, p < .05 or better.

(+) = Same as above, but p < .10.

From Robert E. Slavin, "Team-Assisted Individualization: Combining Cooperative Learning and Individualized Instruction in Mathematics." In *Learning to Cooperate, Cooperating to Learn.* edited by Robert Slavin, Shlomo Sharan, Spencer Kagan, Rachel Hertz-Lazarowitz, Clark Webb, and Richard Schmuck (New York: Plenum.)

Source: Slavin (1985a).

cases, teachers who had volunteered to use TAI were either assigned to use TAI immediately or to serve as a control group and use TAI later. Analyses of covariance or equivalent multiple regression procedures were used to control for any initial differences between students and to increase statistical power. In three of the studies (Experiments 3, 6, and 7) the numbers of teachers involved were large enough to allow for nested analyses of covariance, which are essentially equivalent to conservative class-level analyses. In Experiment 6 the "control group" was the Missouri Mathematics Program, or MMP (Good, Grouws, and Ebmeier 1983), a whole-class instructional method that emphasizes a high ratio of active teaching to seatwork and other principles derived from direct instruction research. Experiment 7 compared TAI both to the MMP and to an untreated control group. All other studies compared TAI and untreated control groups only. Teacher training for each experiment involved a three-hour workshop, followed by classroom visits to ensure faithful implementation. The settings for the studies ranged from inner-city Baltimore and Wilmington, Delaware, to suburban and rural Maryland, and grade levels from three to six. Implementation periods varied from 8 to 24 weeks (median = 16 weeks).

Academic Achievement

Academic achievement outcomes were assessed in six of the seven studies. In Experiment 5 our original intention was to assess achievement outcomes, but the departure of a teacher upset the comparability of the experimental and control groups in terms of prior achievement, so achievement was not assessed. The post-test achievement data were district-administered California Achievement Tests (CAT) in Experiment 4, but in all other studies the Comprehensive Test of Basic Skills (CTBS) was used. CTBS scores were also used as covariates to control for initial performance level in Experiments 1 and 2, and district-administered CAT scores served this purpose in Experiments 3, 4, 6, and 7. The Mathematics Computations scale was used in all studies, and in all but the first two, Mathematics Concepts and Applications scales were also given.

In five of the six achievement studies, TAI students significantly exceeded control students in Computations. Similar effects were found for Concepts and Applications in only one of the four studies in which this variable was assessed (Experiments 3), but in all four studies means for Concepts and Applications favored the TAI group. The one study in which statistically significant effects on neither achievement measure were found was Experiment 4 (Oishi, Slavin, and Madden 1983), which took place in a Baltimore city public school. Poor implementation (particularly failure to use teaching groups) may account for this anomalous finding. In the five studies in which the treatment effects for Computations were statistically significant, they were also quite large. Even in the relatively brief Experiments 1 and 2, the TAI classes gained twice as many grade equivalents as did control students. The TAI-control differences were 42 percent of a grade equivalent in Experiment 3, and in Experiment 6 TAI exceeded the Missouri Mathematics Program (MMP) by 93 percent of a grade equivalent. In Experiment 7 TAI exceeded MMP by 30 percent of a grade equivalent and exceeded the control group by 75 percent of a grade equivalent. The remarkable effects found in Experiments 6 and 7 (in only 18 and 16 weeks, respectively) may be due in part to a complete revision of the curriculum materials just before Experiments 6 and 7, and perhaps more importantly to an increased emphasis on regular use of teaching groups for concept instruction in these studies.

Searches for interactions between treatment of various student attributes failed to find any consistent patterns. Experiments 1 and 3 failed to find any interactions between academically handicapped/non-handicapped status and treatment effect. There was an interaction between ability (pre-test) and treatment in Experiment 1 favoring TAI effects for low achievers, but this was almost certainly due to a ceiling effect on the tests used; no such interactions were found in Experiments 2, 3, 6, or 7. An exhaustive search for interactions was conducted in Experiments 6 and 7; no significant interactions were found between treatment and absolute prior performance level, prior performance relative to class means, sex, or (in Experiment 7) race.

Attitudes

Two general attitude scales were used in Experiments 1, 2, 6, and 7. These were eight-item experimenter-made scales, Liking of Math Class and Self-Concept in Math. Statistically significant effects favoring TAI were found for Liking of Math Class in Experiments 1, 6, and 7, but not in Experiment 2. For Self-Concept in Math, positive effects were found in Experiments 1 and 6 but not Experiments 2 or 7. However, in no case did means for these variables favor a control treatment.

Behaviors

In Experiments 1 and 2 teachers were asked to rate a subset of their students (all academically handicapped students plus six randomly selected non-handicapped students) on six scales: Classroom Behavior, Self-Confidence Behavior, Friendship Behavior, and Negative Peer Behavior (e.g., fighting). In Experiment 1 statistically significant effects favoring TAI students were found on all four scales. Experiment 2 replicated these findings for Self-Confidence and Friendship behaviors, but not for the other two scales (though the means were in the same direction).

Race Relations

The primary purpose of Experiments 4 and 5 was to assess the effects of TAI on race relations, to discover whether the frequently found positive effects of cooperative learning in general on attitudes between blacks and whites (Slavin 1985c) would also be found for TAI. In Experiment 4 positive effects of TAI were found on cross-racial nominations on two sociometric scales, "Who are your friends in this class?" and "Who would you rather *not* sit at a table with?" No effects were found on cross-racial ratings of classmates as "nice" or "smart," but TAI students made significantly fewer cross-racial ratings as "not nice" and marginally fewer as "not smart." In Experiment 5 no effects were found on cross-racial "friendship" nominations, but TAI students named significantly more students of another race as playmates at recess than did control students. Positive effects were also found on cross-racial ratings as "smart" and on reductions in ratings as "not nice." Interestingly, the effect on "smart" ratings was due primarily to increases in whites' ratings of black classmates.

Effects on Academically Handicapped Students

One principal impetus for the development of TAI was to develop a means of meeting the instructional needs of academically handicapped students in the context of the regular class while providing these students with the cooperative experiences found in earlier research to improve the acceptance of academically handicapped students by their non-handicapped classmates (Madden and Slavin 1983a, 1983b). Effects of TAI on academically handicapped students have been positive on several dimensions. No achievement differences for the academically handicapped subsample were found in Experiment 1, which involved an eight-week intervention, but significant and strong achievement effects were found in the longer (24 weeks) Experiment 3, where academically handicapped students gained 52 percent of a grade equivalent more in Computations than did their control counterparts. In Experiment 1 academically handicapped students in TAI gained more than control students in sociometric choices as "best friends" or as "o.k." They were also rated much more positively than control students on all four behavior rating scales.

COOPERATIVE INTEGRATED READING AND COMPOSITION

Following the success of the TAI mathematics program, we turned our development efforts toward reading and writing/language arts, the two subjects which, with mathematics, constitute the core of the elementary school program. Because these subjects are very different from mathematics, our approach to applying cooperative learning to reading and writing was very different from our approach to mathematics. For one thing, reading, writing, and language arts subsume a set of subskills, each of which demands a different approach. For example, optimal procedures for teaching reading comprehension or vocabulary would certainly be different from those for teaching decoding, spelling, writing, or language mechanics.

The program we ultimately developed and researched is called Cooperative Integrated Reading and Composition, or CIRC (Madden, Slavin and Stevens 1986). The overall development plan focused on cooperative learning as a vehicle by which to introduce practices identified in recent research on reading and writing into routine classroom practice, and to embed cooperative learning within the fabric of the elementary reading and writing program. The major elements of CIRC and rationales for each are presented in the following section.

Principal Features of CIRC

The CIRC program consists of three principal elements: basal-related activities, direct instruction in reading comprehension, and integrated language arts/writing. In all of these activities, students work in heterogeneous learning teams. All activities follow a cycle that involves teacher presentation, team practice, peer pre-assessment, additional practice, and testing.

Reading groups. Students are assigned to two or three reading groups (8–15 students per group) according to their reading level, as determined by their teachers.

Teams. Students are assigned to pairs (or triads) within their reading groups. The pairs are then assigned to teams composed of partnerships from two different reading groups. For example, a team might be composed of two students from the top reading group and two from the low group. Mainstreamed academically handicapped and remedial reading students are distributed among the teams.

Many of the activities within the teams are done in pairs, while others involve the whole team; even during pair activities, however, the other pair is available for assistance and encouragement. Most of the time, the teams work independently of the teacher, while the teacher either teaches reading groups drawn from the various teams or works with individuals. One of the most important aspects of the reading component of CIRC is the provision of meaningful, cooperative activities during follow-up times (i.e., times when the teacher is working with one of the reading groups). Research on follow-up time has found the usual seatwork activities provided to students to be of very little value (Anderson et al. 1985; Osborn 1984). Students follow a weekly schedule of activities, and their partners initial "assignment record form" as students complete each of the week's tasks.

Students' scores on all quizzes, compositions, and book reports are contributed to form a team score. Teams that meet an average criterion of 90 percent on all activities in a given week are designated "superteams" and receive attractive certificates; those that meet an average criterion of 80 to 89 percent are designated "greatteams" and receive less elaborate certificates.

Basal-related activities. Students use their regular basal readers. Basal stories are introduced and discussed in teacher-led reading groups that meet for approximately 20 minutes each day. During these sessions, teachers set a purpose for reading, introduce new vocabulary, review old vocabulary, discuss the story after students have read it, and so on. Presentation methods for each segment of the lesson are structured. For example, teachers are taught to use a vocabulary presentation procedure that requires a demonstration of understanding of word meaning by each individual, a review of methods of word attack, repetitive oral reading of vocabulary to achieve automaticity, and use of the meanings of the vocabulary words to help introduce the content of the story. Story discussions are structured to emphasize such skills as making and supporting predictions about the story and understanding major structural components of the story (e.g., problem and solution in a narrative).

After stories are introduced, students are given a series of activities to do in their teams when they are not working with the teacher in a reading group. The sequence of activities is as follows:

a. *Partner reading.* Students read the story silently first, and then take turns reading the story aloud with their partners, alternating readers after each paragraph. As their partner reads, the listener follows along and corrects any errors the reader makes. Repeated reading has been found in previous research to contribute to decoding and to comprehension of narratives (Dahl 1979). Partner reading also gives students a great deal of oral reading practice, and enables the teacher to assess student performance by circulating and listening without having to take the time of all students in the reading group to allow individual students to read aloud.

b. *Story structure and story-related writing.* Students are given questions related to each narrative story emphasizing the story grammar. Halfway through the story, they are instructed to stop reading and to identify the characters, the setting, and the problem in the story, and to predict how the problem will be resolved. At the end of the story students respond to the story as a whole and write a few paragraphs on a topic related to the story (for example, they might be asked to write a different ending to the story). Research on reading comprehension has indicated the importance of students' understanding of the structure of stories (Fitzgerald and Spiegel 1983; Short and Ryan 1982) and of making predictions based on partial information about stories (Palincsar and Brown 1984).

c. *Words out loud.* Students are given a list of new or difficult words used in the story that they must be able to read correctly in any order without hesitating or stumbling. These words are presented by the teacher in the reading group, and then students practice their lists with their partners or other teammates until they can read them smoothly. This activity is designed to help students gain automaticity in decoding critical words, an essential prerequisite for comprehension (Rosenshine and Stevens 1986; Samuels 1981).

d. *Word meaning.* Students are given a list of story words that are new in their speaking vocabularies and asked to look them up in a dictionary, paraphrase the definition, and write a sentence for each that shows the meaning of the word (e.g., "An *octopus* grabbed the swimmer with its eight long legs," not "I have an *octopus*.").

e. *Retelling stories.* After reading the story and discussing it in their reading groups, students summarize the main points of the story to their partners. The partners have a list of essential story elements that they use to check the completeness of the story summaries. Summarizing recently read material for a peer has been found to be an effective means of enhancing comprehension and retention of the material (Doctorow, Wittrock, and Marks 1978).

f. *Spelling*. Students pre-test one another on a list of spelling words each week, and then work over the course of the week to help one another master the list. Students use a "disappearing list" strategy in which they make new lists of missed words after each assessment until the list disappears and they can go back to the full list, repeating the process as many times as necessary.

Partner checking. After students complete each of the activities listed above, their partners initial a student assignment form indicating that they have completed and/or achieved the criterion on that task. Students are given daily expectations as to the number of activities to be completed, but they can go at their own rate and complete the activities earlier if they wish, creating additional time for independent reading (see below).

Tests. At the end of three class periods, students are given a comprehension test on the story, are asked to write meaningful sentences for each vocabulary word, and are asked to read the word list aloud to the teacher. Students are not permitted to help one another on these tests. The test scores and evaluations of the story-related writing are major components of students' weekly team scores.

Direct instruction in reading comprehension. One day each week, students receive direct instruction from the teacher in reading comprehension skills such as identifying main ideas, drawing conclusions, and comparing and contrasting ideas. A special step-by-step curriculum was designed for this purpose. After each lesson, students work on reading comprehension worksheets and/or games as a whole team, first gaining consensus on one set of worksheet items, then practicing independently, assessing one another's work, and discussing any remaining problems on a second set of items. Recent research indicates that reading comprehension can be effectively taught as a skill separately from basal instruction (e.g., Palincsar and Brown 1984; Paris, Lipson, and Wixson 1983; Stevens, 1988).

Independent reading. Every evening, students are asked to read a trade book of their choice for at least 20 minutes. Parents initial forms indicating that students have read for the required time, and students contribute points to their teams if they submit a completed form each week. Students complete at least one book report every two weeks, for which they also receive team points. Independent reading and book reports replace all other homework in reading and language arts. If students complete their basal-related activities or other activities early, they may also read their independent reading books in class.

Integrated language arts and writing. During language arts periods, teachers use a specific language arts/writing curriculum especially developed for the project. Students work on language arts in the same teams as in reading. During three one-hour sessions each week, students participate in a writer's workshop, writing at their own pace on topics of their choice. Teachers present ten-minute mini-lessons at the beginning of each period on writing process, style, or mechanics, for example brainstorming for topics, conducting a peer revision conference, eliminating run-on sentences, or using quotations. Students spend the main part of the period planning, drafting, revising, editing, and publishing their writing. Informal and formal peer and teacher conferences are held during this time. Ten minutes at the end of the hour are reserved for sharing and "celebration" of student writing. Teacher-directed lessons on specific aspects of writing, such as organizing a narrative or a descriptive paragraph, using specific sensory words in a description, and ensuring noun–verb agreement, are conducted during two periods each week, and students practice and master these skills in their teams. Writing process models using peer response groups and a sequence of planning, drafting, editing, and revision have been found to be effective in previous research (Hillocks 1984), although very little of this research has been done at the elementary level. Also, previous research on teaching of language mechanics has found positive effects of cooperative learning methods (e.g., Slavin and Karweit 1985).

Involvement of special education resource teachers and reading teachers. One key concern in the design of the CIRC program was to fully integrate the activities of special education resource teachers and remedial reading teachers with those of the regular classroom teachers. "Remedial reading" refers here both to reading programs involving the mainstreaming of handicapped students and to LEA-funded remedial programs. This integration was done differently in the two evaluations of the full CIRC program. In the twelve-week pilot study (Madden, Stevens, and Slavin 1986), resource and remedial reading teachers removed students from their reading classes for part or all of the reading period, and implemented the CIRC program in separate areas. However, in a 24-week full-scale evaluation (Stevens et al 1987; Madden et al. 1986), the schools involved scheduled resource and remedial reading pullouts at times other than reading or language arts/writing periods. Special and remedial reading teachers attended the CIRC training sessions but did not use CIRC methods or materials in their pullout programs, except that they occasionally helped students with problems they were encountering in the CIRC program being used in the regular class.

RESEARCH ON CIRC

As of this writing, two studies have evaluated the impact of the full CIRC program, and a third study has investigated the effects of the cooperative reading comprehension component separately. These are described in the following sections.

Study 1

The first study (Madden, Stevens, and Slavin 1986; Stevens, Madden, Slavin, and Farnish 1987) evaluated the full CIRC program over a 12-week period. A total of 461 third- and fourth-grade students in 21 classes in a suburban Maryland school district participated in the study; eleven experimental classes were matched on standardized reading scores with ten control classes.

Overall, the effects of the CIRC program on student achievement were quite positive. After adjusting for pre-tests, analyses of variance using class means on the California Achievement Test (CAT) indicated that CIRC classes gained significantly more (30 to 36 percent of a grade equivalent more) than control students in reading comprehension and reading vocabulary, 52 percent of a grade equivalent more than control in language expression, and 72 percent of a grade equivalent more in spelling. Only in language mechanics were experimental–control differences not significant, and even here, the CIRC students gained a quarter of a grade equivalent more than control students. On writing samples CIRC students outperformed control on ratings of organization, ideas, and mechanics, but these differences were only statistically significant for organization ratings, with an effect size of more than half of an individual-level standard deviation.

Tests for interactions with pre-test levels indicated that the effects of CIRC were equal for students at all levels of prior achievement, high, average, and low. However, probably because of the small samples involved, effects computed separately for special education and remedial reading students were not statistically significant in this study (Madden et al. 1986).

Study 2

The second study (Stevens et al. 1987b; Madden et al. 1986) was designed to evaluate the CIRC program over a full school year, incorporating changes suggested by the experience of the pilot study. In addition to refinements in methods and materials, Study 2 changed the program for special education and remedial reading students. In Study 1 these students were pulled out of class (as usual) during reading times and experienced part or all of their exposure to the CIRC procedures in the pull-out class (this was not our preference, but was an accommodation to school district policies). In Study 2, special education and remedial students were left in the regular class, and were either pulled out for corrective instruction at other times or were not given additional instruction.

Study 2 was conducted in a suburban school district different from the one involved in the first study. Four hundred and fifty students in 22 third- and fourth-grade classes participated; nine experimental classes were matched with control classes on standardized reading and language scores. The CIRC program was implemented from October to March, a total of 24 weeks.

For the total samples involved, the results of Study 2 were even more positive than those of Study 1. On California Achievement Test reading comprehension, language expression, and language mechanics scales, class-level analyses of variance indicated that CIRC students gained significantly more than control students, averaging gains of almost two-thirds of a grade equivalent more than control students. Differences of 20 percent of a grade equivalent on reading vocabulary were not significant, however. On writing samples, CIRC students again outperformed controls on organization, ideas, and mechanics ratings, but in this case the class-level analyses indicated significant differences only on ratings of ideas. Study 2 added informal reading inventories as measures of students' oral reading skills. CIRC students scored significantly higher than controls on word recognition, word analysis, fluency, error rate, and grade placement measures of the Durrell Informal Reading Inventory (Durrell and Catterson 1980), with effect sizes ranging from 44 to 64 percent of a standard deviation.

As in Study 1, tests for interactions indicated that the CIRC program produced equal gains for students who were initially high, average, and low in reading skills.

Probably because of the longer duration and the fact that students were not pulled out of their reading classes, effects of the CIRC program on the reading achievement of special education and remedial reading students were much more positive than in Study 1. Mainstreamed special education students gained 1.92 grade equivalents more than special control students in reading comprehension and 1.44 grade equivalents more in reading vocabulary. Both of these differences were statistically significant using individual-level analyses of covariance. Remedial reading students gained significantly more in CIRC than in traditional methods on measures of reading comprehension, language expression, and language mechanics, with experimental–control differences ranging from 66 to 80 percent of a grade equivalent. On the informal reading inventory scales, students in the lowest third of their classes gained as much as 1.38 standard deviations more than control students in oral reading fluency, and made other outstanding gains in word recognition, word analysis, and overall grade placement.

Study 3

The next step in program development and evaluation was to study the major components that make up the program (Slavin 1984b). The first of these component analyses to be completed was a study of cooperative learning and direct instruction in reading comprehension (Stevens et al. 1987b). In this study, 30 grade 3 and 4 classes in a primarily lower-class urban school district in Pennsylvania were randomly assigned to three treatments: cooperative learning and direct instruction, direct instruction only, and control. The cooperative learning and direct instruction treatment was the same as that used one day each week in CIRC; teachers gave lessons on a reading comprehension objective, students worked in mixed-ability teams to gain consensus on a set of items related to the objective, and then students worked independently, compared answers, and helped one another resolve any misunderstandings. Finally, students took a quiz on the reading comprehension objective, and teams received certificates based on the sum of their members' scores. In the direct instruction treatment teachers taught the same lessons and students used the same materials as individual worksheets. Control teachers were asked to work toward the same reading comprehension objectives during their basal instruction but were otherwise untreated.

Class-level analyses of covariance indicated strong, statistically significant positive effects of direct instruction in reading comprehension, both on main idea skills similar to those taught in the reading comprehension curriculum and, to a lesser degree, on inference skills that were not specifically taught. The cooperative learning classes exceeded controls by 82 percent of a standard deviation on main ideas and 31 percent of a standard deviation on inferences, and the corresponding percentages were 58 percent and 20 percent for the direct instruction treatment. Individual-level analyses indicated that the addition of cooperative learning to the direct instruction model significantly enhanced the effects for main idea. As in the studies of the full CIRC program, this study found that the positive effects were equal for students who were high, average, and low in prior performance.

THE COOPERATIVE SCHOOL

The development and successful evaluation of the comprehensive TAI and CIRC models has created an exciting new possibility. With cooperative learning programs capable of being used all year in the three R's, it is now possible to design an elementary school program based upon a radical principle: that students, teachers, and administrators can work *cooperatively* to make the school a better place for working and learning. Recently we have begun working with a small number of schools toward a vision of a *cooperative elementary school,* an organizational plan in which cooperative activities take place at the school level as well as at the classroom level. Each school working toward this vision is proceeding differently, and there may be many ways to structure a cooperative school. However, the major components of the plan we are currently pursuing are as follows.

Cooperative learning in the classroom. Clearly, a cooperative elementary school would have cooperative learning methods in use in most classrooms, and in more than one subject. Students and teachers should feel that the idea that students can help one another learn is not just applied on occasion, but is a fundamental principle of classroom organization. Students should see one another as resources for learning, and there should be a school-wide norm that every student's learning is everyone's responsibility, that every student's success is everyone's success.

Integration of special education and remedial services with the regular program. In the cooperative elementary school, mainstreaming should be an essential element of school and classroom organization. Special education teachers may team-teach with regular teachers, integrating their students in teams with non-handicapped students and contributing their expertise in adapting instruction to individual needs to the class as a whole. Similarly, Chapter I or other remedial services should be provided in the regular classroom. If we take seriously the idea that all students are responsible for one another, this goes as much for students with learning problems as for anyone else. Research on use of TAI and CIRC to facilitate mainstreaming and meet the needs of remedial readers has found positive effects on the achievement and social acceptance of these students (Slavin 1984a; Slavin, Stevens, and Madden, 1988).

Peer coaching. In the cooperative elementary school, teachers should be responsible for helping one another to successfully use cooperative learning methods and to implement other improvements in instructional practice. Peer coaching (Joyce, Hersh, and McKibbin 1983) is perfectly adapted to the philosophy of the cooperative school. In peer coaching, teachers learn new methods together and are given release time to visit one another's classes to give assistance and exchange ideas as they begin using the new programs.

Cooperative planning. Cooperative activities among teachers should not be restricted to peer coaching. In addition, teachers should be given time to plan goals and strategies together, to prepare common libraries of instructional materials, and to make decisions about cooperative activities involving more than one class.

Building-level steering committee. In the cooperative elementary school, teachers and administrators should be able to work together to determine the direction the school takes. A steering committee composed of the principal, teacher representatives, representatives of other staff (e.g., special education, Chapter I, aides), and one or more parent representatives meets to discuss the progress the school is making toward its instructional goals and to recommend changes in school policies and practices designed to achieve these goals.

Cooperation with parents and community members. The cooperative school should invite the participation of parents and of members of the community in which the school is located. Development of a community sense that children's success in school is everyone's responsibility is an important goal of the cooperative school.

As of this writing, we are working most intensively with five schools, one in Alexandria, Virginia, three in Anne Arundel County, Maryland, and one in Bay Shore, New York. However, many other schools are also moving toward a vision of the cooperative school. A major element in this movement is the beginning of dissemination of the CIRC program; reading, writing, and language arts are so central to the elementary school curriculum that any school that adopts CIRC on a substantial scale is already well on the way to implementing the classroom elements of the cooperative school plan.

It is unclear at this point whether large numbers of schools will begin to work toward becoming cooperative schools in the coming years. If they do, this will represent what is perhaps the best chance for cooperative learning to survive beyond the current enthusiasm. In a cooperative school it is far more likely that teachers will continue to pursue cooperative learning indefinitely, and that changes in staff, including changes in building or district administration, will not disable the program. In a cooperative school new teachers are likely to be selected according to their interest in cooperative learning and then socialized to a set of pro-cooperative norms and expectations. As long as cooperative learning remains primarily an activity in which just a few teachers engage within any given school, its survival over the long term is in doubt.

Of course, it may be enough to offer the field of education a set of cooperative instructional methods that can be applied to a variety of subjects and situations. But if we take seriously the idea that cooperative learning may produce a lasting revolution in education, it is likely that we must work with schools, not just individual teachers, and that we must confront curricular and school and classroom organizational concerns beyond the classroom process.

NOTES

Preparation of this chapter was supported by a grant from the Office of Educational Research and Improvement, U.S. Department of Education (no. OERI-G-86-0006). However, any opinions expressed are mine, and do not represent OERI policy.

1. TAI is currently published under the title *Team-Accelerated Instruction* by Mastery Education Corporation, 85 Main Street, Watertown, MA 02171.

REFERENCES

Anderson, L. M., Brubaker, N. L., Alleman-Brooks, J., and Duffy, G. G. (1985) "A qualitative study of seatwork in first-grade classrooms." *Elementary School Journal* 86:123–40.

Aronson, E., Blaney, N., Stephan, C., Sikes, J., and Snapp, M. (1978) *The Jigsaw Classroom.* Beverly Hills, CA: Sage.

Ballard, M., Corman, L., Gottlieb, J., and Kauffman, M. (1977) "Improving the social status of mainstreamed retarded children." *Journal of Educational Psychology* 69:605–11.

Burns, M. (1981) "Groups of four: Solving the management problem." *Learning* (September): 46–51.

Calkins, L. M. (1983) *Lessons from a Child: On the Teaching and Learning of Writing.* Exeter, NH: Heinemann.

Cohen, E. G. (1986) *Designing Groupwork: Strategies for the Heterogeneous Classroom.* New York: Teachers College Press.

Cooper, L., Johnson, D. W., Johnson, R., and Wilderson, F. (1980) "Effects of cooperative, competitive, and individualistic experiences on interpersonal attraction among heterogeneous peers." *Journal of Social Psychology* 111:243–52.

Dahl, P. R. (1979) "An experimental program for teaching high-speed word recognition and comprehension skills." In *Communication Research in Learning Disabilities and Mental Retardation,* edited by J. E. Button, T. C. Lovitt, and T. D. Rowland. Baltimore, MD: University Park Press.

Doctorow, M., Wittrock, M. C., and Marks, C. (1978) "Generative processes in reading comprehension." *Journal of Educational Psychology* 70:109–18.

Durrell, D., and Catterson, J. (1980) *Durrell Analysis of Reading Difficulty.* New York: The Psychological Corporation.

Fitzgerald, J., and Spiegel, D. (1983) "Enhancing children's reading comprehension through instruction in narrative structures." *Journal of Reading Behavior* 14:1–181.

Gickling, E., and Theobold, J. (1975) "Mainstreaming: Affect or effect." *Journal of Special Education* 9:317–28.

Good, T., Grouws, D., and Ebmeir, H. (1983) *Active Mathematics Teaching.* New York: Longman.

Gottlieb, J., and Leyser, Y. (1981) "Friendship between mentally retarded and nonretarded children." In *The Development of Children's Friendships,* edited by S. Asher and J. Gottman. Cambridge: Cambridge University Press.

Graves, D. (1983) *Writing: Teachers and Children at Work.* Exeter, NH: Heinemann.

Hillocks, G. (1984) "What works in teaching composition: A meta-analysis of experimental treatment studies." *American Journal of Education* 93:133–70.

Horak, V. M. (1981) "A meta-analysis or research findings on individualized instruction in mathematics." *Journal of Educational Research* 74:249–53.

Johnson, D. W., and Johnson, R. T. (1986) *Learning Together and Alone,* 2d edn. Englewood Cliffs, NJ: Prentice-Hall.

Johnson, R., and Johnson, D. W. (1982) "Effects of cooperative and competitive learning experiences on interpersonal attraction between handicapped and nonhandicapped students." *Journal of Social Psychology* 116:211–19.

Joyce, B. R., Hersh, R. H., and McKibbin, M. (1983) *The Structure of School Improvement.* New York: Longman.

Kepler, K., and Randall, J. W. (1977) "Individualization: Subversion of elementary schooling." *Elementary School Journal* 77:348–63.

Madden, N. A., and Slavin, R. E. (1983a) "Mainstreaming students with mild academic handicaps: Academic and social outcomes." *Review of Educational Research* 53:519–69.

——— (1983b) "Cooperative learning and social acceptance of mainstreamed academically handicapped students." *Journal of Special Education* 17:171–82.

Madden, N. A., Slavin, R. E., and Stevens, R. J. (1986) *Cooperative Integrated Reading and Composition: Teacher's Manual.* Baltimore, MD: Johns Hopkins University, Center for Research on Elementary and Middle Schools.

Madden, N. A., Stevens, R. J., and Slavin, R. E. (1986) *Reading Instruction in the Mainstream: A Cooperative Learning Approach,* Technical Report no. 5. Baltimore, MD: Center for Research on Elementary and Middle Schools, Johns Hopkins University.

Miller, R. L. (1976) "Individualized instruction in mathematics: A review of research." *The Mathematics Teacher* 69:354–51.

Oishi, S. (1983) *Effects of Team Assisted Individualization in mathematics on the cross-*

race and cross-sex interactions of elementary school children. Doctoral dissertation. College Park: University of Maryland.

Oishi, S., Slavin, R. E., and Madden, N. A. (1983) "Effects of student teams and individualized instruction on cross-race and cross-sex friendships." Paper presented at the annual meeting of the American Educational Research Association, Montreal, April.

Osborn, J. (1984) "The purposes, uses, and contents of workbooks and some guidelines for publishers," In *Learning to Read in American Schools,* edited by R. C. Anderson, J. Osborn, and R. J. Tierney, pp. 45–112. Hillsdale, NJ: Erlbaum.

Palincsar, A. S., and Brown, A. L. (1984) "Reciprocal teaching of comprehension fostering and comprehension monitoring activities." *Cognition and Instruction* 2:117–75.

Paris, S., Lipson, M., and Wixson, K. (1983) "Becoming a strategic reader." *Contemporary Educational Psychology* 8:293–316.

Rosenshine, B., and Stevens, R. J. (1986) "Teaching functions." In *Handbook of Research of Teaching,* 3rd edn, edited by M. C. Wittrock. New York: Macmillan.

Samuels, S. J. (1981) "Some essentials of decoding." *Exceptional Education Quarterly* 2:11–25.

Schoen, H. L. (1976) "Self-paced mathematics instruction: How effective has it been?" *Arithmetic Teacher* 23:90–96.

Sharan, S., and Sharan, Y. (1976) *Small-Group Teaching.* Englewood Cliffs, NJ: Educational Technology Publications.

Short, E., and Ryan, E. (1982) "Remediating poor readers' comprehension failures with a story grammar strategy." Paper presented at the annual meeting of the American Educational Research Association, New York.

Slavin, R. E. (1983a) *Cooperative Learning.* New York: Longman.

––––––– (1984a) "Team-assisted individualization: Cooperative learning and individualized instruction in the mainstreamed classroom." *Remedial and Special Education* 5, no. 6:33–42.

––––––– (1984b) "Component building: A strategy for research-based instructional improvement." *Elementary School Journal* 84:255–69.

––––––– (1985a) "Team-assisted individualization: Combining cooperative learning and individualized instruction in mathematics." In *Learning to Cooperate, Cooperating to Learn,* edited by R. E. Slavin, S. Sharan, S. Kagan, R. Hertz-Lazarowitz, C. Webb, and R. Schmuck, pp. 177–209. New York: Plenum.

––––––– (1985b) "Team-assisted individualization: A cooperative learning solution for adaptive instruction in mathematics." In *Adapting Instruction to Individual Differences,* edited by M. C. Wang and H. Walberg. Berkeley, CA: McCutchan.

––––––– (1985c) "Cooperative learning: Applying contact theory in desegregated schools." *Journal of Social Issues* 41, no. 3:45–62.

––––––– (1986) *Using Student Team Learning,* 3rd edn. Baltimore, MD: Johns Hopkins University, Center for Research on Elementary and Middle Schools.

Slavin, R. E., and Karweit, N. (1985) "Cognitive and affective outcomes of an intensive student team learning experience." *Journal of Experimental Education* 50:29–35.

Slavin, R., Leavey, M., and Madden, N. (1984) Combining cooperative learning and individualized instruction: Effects on student mathematics achievement, attitudes and behaviors. *Elementary School Journal* 84, 409–22.

Slavin, R., Madden, N., and Leavey, M. (1984) Effects of cooperative learning and individualized instruction on the social acceptance, achievement and behavior of mainstreamed students. *Exceptional Children* 50, 434–43.

Slavin, R. E., Leavey, M. B., and Madden, N. A. (1986) *Team-Accelerated Instruction—Mathematics.* Watertown, MA: Mastery Education Corporation.

Slavin, R. E., Stevens, R. J., and Madden, N. A. (1988) "Accommodating student diversity in reading and writing instruction: A cooperative learning approach." *Remedial and Special Education* 9:60–66.

Stevens, R. J. (1988) "The effects of strategy training on the identification of the main idea of expository passages." *Journal of Educational Psychology* 80:21–26.

Stevens, R. J., Madden, N. A., Slavin, R. E., and Farnish, A. M. (1987a) "Cooperative integrated reading and composition: Two field experiments." *Reading Research Quarterly* 22:433–54.

Stevens, R. J., Slavin, R. E., Farnish, A. M., and Madden, N. A. (1987b) *Effects of Cooperative Learning and Direct Instruction in Reading Comprehension Strategies on Main Idea and Inference Skills.* Baltimore, MD: Johns Hopkins University, Center for Research on Elementary and Middle Schools.

12
Cooperative Learning: A Perspective on Research and Practice

SHLOMO SHARAN

WHY DOES COOPERATIVE LEARNING APPEAL TO TEACHERS?

Research and development on cooperative learning methods and their effects on pupils in classrooms has its roots in work done decades ago. Nevertheless, systematic research in substantial quantity and with the required degree of controls and sophistication has been published only during the past 15 years. Within this relatively short period of time, cooperative learning underwent a renaissance and has generated considerable interest among educators responsible for the daily work of instruction, as well as among researchers concerned with a wide range of educational, psychological, and social issues. Foremost among these issues are the improvement of student academic achievement and promotion of high-level thinking as well as positive interpersonal and inter-group relations among students in school. Hence, much research conducted on the effects of cooperative learning was motivated by the desire of researchers to cope with the problems confronting public education in many countries today. This fact probably lends the research in this field a certain sense of urgency and relevance that is not always evident in some other domains of educational and social-psychological research. Because of its status as an innovation that frequently is perceived as a potential solution to several unresolved challenges that schools face, cooperative learning research is often expected to be more responsive to the needs of ongoing educational practice than other areas of academic research on education. Many of these same questions have not yet received satisfactory replies from the large body of research performed within the context of traditional instruction as it is conducted daily in the majority of classrooms today. Research on cooperative learning has been remarkably extensive, considering its relatively recent emergence as an alternative instructional method in public education. Some of that research has also striven to penetrate the more complex and recalcitrant social-psychological issues related to classroom instruction.

What accounts for the relatively rapid dissemination of cooperative learning among thousands of educators and for the strong appeal that cooperative learning holds for research? The following factors appear to account, at least in part, for this phenomenon albeit without any claim to constitute a definitive reply. The first factor deals with the social nature of the classroom setting and of cooperative learning methods. Classrooms are, first and foremost, social settings inhabited by relatively large groups of students. Typical classes in Western countries range from 20 or 25 to 40 or more students located in a room where a single adult serves as the instructor. The fact that the same teacher meets with the same large group of students, for most of the school day in elementary schools or for one or two periods in secondary schools, and usually for an entire academic year, poses many serious challenges for teachers and schools. The main challenge is to manage such a large number of young people who meet each other five or six days a week confined to that space called a classroom, while ensuring that their time is spent productively in the pursuit of learning. Moreover, one must manage the class within a set of constraints that limit the teachers' time span for instruction, their physical and instructional resources, and the nature of the activities that can be carried out within the allotted space and in accordance with the nature of the social roles dictated by the setting. Astute observers of the process of schooling have challenged the need for these often debilitating constraints and have lamented the terrible price that students and society pay for conducting schools in the way we ordinarily do (Goodlad 1984; Sarason 1982, 1983). However, it seems that these basic conditions of schooling will not change radically in the near future. The challenge now is to design the instructional process for the existing classroom setting in order to reap optimum benefits for all of the people involved, adults and children.

By basing the learning process on the interaction among small groups of students formed within existing classrooms, cooperative learning incorporates the social dimension of the classroom as a component of its basic procedures. In this fashion it deals directly with the entire classroom population in terms of management (all students collaborate directly with peers in small groups) and learning (the groups are focused on academic content). Other instructional methods either enjoin teachers to treat all of the students in the class as belonging to a single undifferentiated unit, expecting each and every one to learn the same material at the same pace in the same way, or to treat each student as an individual unrelated to the other students in the class, *as if* the others weren't there. Both of the latter approaches consider the social dimension of the classroom as potentially disruptive of effective instruction and learning. Cooperative learning is effective precisely because it finds an active role for everyone by creating small aggregates of students as interacting units, rather than attempting to relate to each individual separately while disregarding their relationship to their peers around them.

The peer-interactive nature of cooperative learning also appeals to educators as fulfilling an important function in the socialization of students. Teachers frequently voice concern about the socialization of our youth but often do not know how to cultivate the students' social skills as part of their instructional procedures. In the case of the ethnically heterogeneous classroom, for example, the socializing role of cooperative learning is particularly prominent in filling an obvious need. It enhances mutual exchange and assistance among peers, thereby promoting mutual support and acceptance among classmates on the basis of their common task orientation rather than on the basis of their cultural background. These kinds of peer interaction are obviously needed in classrooms where the ethnic or cultural diversity of the students can be socially divisive.

Another factor that should be mentioned here that contributes to the appeal of cooperative learning is the high degree of students' engagement in the task that is apparent in the operation of cooperative learning groups. This active involvement in learning is almost always accompanied by a distinct decline in students' disruptive behavior, at least some of which can be explained as stemming from being bored! Consequently, teachers generally feel released in large measure from the need to discipline students and to comment constantly on their need to pay attention, stop talking to one another, and so on. The sharp decline in student boredom and in the need for discipline in the cooperative classroom was elegantly documented in the study reported in this volume by Hertz-Lazarowitz and Shachar as part of their assessment of teachers' verbal behavior in traditional and cooperative instruction. To be constrained to listen to teachers' talk several hours every day, and in the formalistic manner typical of whole-class instruction, is inevitably boring for large numbers of students (Sarason 1983; Wells, Chang, and Maher, this volume). The more personal, intimate, and supportive relationship established by teachers (and by the *same* teachers in the case of this particular study) with their students in the cooperative classroom, along with the interest generated by direct interaction with peers, appears to dispel a good deal of this boredom and the students' disruptive behavior. The subject of student boredom in school in general, and under varying instructional conditions in particular, has yet to be studied systematically. It is almost as if this topic was purposely shunned by educational researchers! The study by Hertz-Lazarowitz and Shachar is a valuable addition to the small body of research reported thus far on teachers in the cooperative classroom. (For earlier research on teachers and cooperative learning see Sharan and Hertz-Lazarowitz 1982; Talmage, Pascarella, and Ford 1984.)

Another approach to understanding the role of cooperative learning in arousing students' interest in learning, and, consequently, reducing boredom, is the study of students' motivation in cooperative versus traditional classrooms by Sharan and Shaulov. Cooperative learning positively affected student motivation to learn far more than did whole-class instruction. From this perspective as well, cooperative learning can be seen as making school learning more engaging and less boring for students, to the point where they will be prepared to remain in the classroom and continue working on learning tasks rather than taking a recess and going outside to play. Students' motivation to learn in cooperative learning classes is frequently very evident to teachers, who often comment upon it with no small degree of surprise as if their expectation is that school learning is generally boring and any other reaction is unanticipated. (For a detailed presentation of ways in which cooperative learning can affect motivation, see Johnson and Johnson 1985a.)

Thus, the appeal of cooperative learning appears to stem from its "face validity," from those features that almost at a glance can be seen by teachers to deal successfully with the major challenges they confront in today's typical classroom. Generally, a teaching method does not appeal to practicing educators because of research findings about relatively subtle effects. The benefits must be seen to be appreciated.

However, it is more than apparent to the research community that the "face validity" and widespread appeal that cooperative learning holds for educators do not necessarily constitute confirmation that this approach actually results in the effects ascribed to it, appearances notwithstanding. Moreover, there are many potential effects of cooperative learning, particularly in the cognitive-intellectual realm, that teachers may not appreciate intuitively and which are not immediately obvious even to the practiced eye. Nor can we claim to understand as yet just how the effects that have been documented occur. Without these bodies of knowledge, cooperative learning will continue to function on the basis of personal preference rather than on reliable information, as does a good deal of instructional practice in schools. It seems fair to say that researchers of cooperative learning, in addition to contributing to the accumulation of reliable knowledge about the processes of teaching and learning in school, would prefer to base support of cooperative learning on a solid foundation of objective knowledge so that official bodies at all levels of the educational enterprise can make enlightened and well-documented policy decisions. We hope that the work presented in this volume is a step in that direction.

Cooperative Learning Effects on Achievement

There are several themes that dominate the research reported in this book along with its obvious diversity. One of those themes is: How does cooperative learning contribute to pupils' learning and academic achievement? The potentially positive effects of cooperative learning on students' achievement have been documented many times in the existing research literature on cooperative learning. The chapters in this volume give complete bibliographical references to this work. In addition, the relevant chapters in this book raise several questions about cooperative learning effects on achievement and how they should be studied. They also provide some thoughts and data about achievement that deserve attention here.

Few studies published heretofore treated the effects of cooperative learning in high school classrooms. Lazarowitz and Karsenty implemented cooperative learning (a combination of jigsaw with group investigation) in tenth-grade biology classes and evaluated many different potential effects of cooperative learning on the students. By all accounts, high schools are far more regimented and conservative, pedagogically, than elementary schools. Indeed, the Rand Corporation's study of educational innovations (Berman and McLaughlin 1978) listed the concentration on elementary schools as one of the factors predicting potential success of educational change projects. Lazarowitz and Karsenty showed that cooperative learning in high school is feasible and potentially productive. Moreover, the wide range of variables assessed in their work, particularly those variables concerned with the students' laboratory and study skills, emphasize that cooperative learning fosters pupils' knowledge about *how* to study and not only about *what* they learned. Frequent claims were made through the years that students would derive benefits from cooperative learning in the realm of "learning how to learn." This study supports that claim empirically, demonstrating that positive effects of cooperative learning on student achievement can be documented in the realm of their thought processes and not only in the realm of having accumulated quantities of information.

The contribution of cooperative learning to children's thinking is also treated in the ethnographic study by Wells, Chang, and Maher that, like the Lazarowitz and Karsenty work, was conducted in a science class. Wells and colleagues carefully recorded the children's conversations as they worked together to find the answer to questions that puzzled them as they observed the behavior of various insects. The conversations revealed how each child built his/her thinking on the other children's comments, and how this conversation led them to various conclusions and to "construct" the meaning of the experience for themselves instead of being told by the teacher what they were to learn and understand. Again, we are informed about the way in which cooperative learning affects pupils' thinking in the wake of their collective engagement in the learning task. The features of cooperative learning that Wells and his colleagues describe include some of the elements that Johnson and Johnson (this volume) point to as the critical components of cooperative group work that enhance achievement.

A next step in research is to study the link between thinking processes and achievement, and how the two are affected by variation in instruction. In earlier studies, my colleagues and I distinguished between lower- and higher-level thinking as part of the assessment of student achievement following their exposure to cooperative learning (Sharan, Hertz-Lazarowitz, and Ackerman 1980; Sharan et al. 1984). However, that research did not actually document the manner in which pupils engaged in logical thinking during or following their experiences in cooperative small groups. Nor is it obvious by any means that higher achievement scores necessarily reflect logical or critical thought or even better understanding of subject matter. The meaning of the term "achievement" is vague, at best, often without any clear implications beyond the simple fact that the students remember more or fewer details about a topic.

From the point of view of actually learning about what the students understand, the ethnographic approach employed in the study reported here by Wells et al. is invaluable. Furthermore, when students who studied with a cooperative or whole-class method were compared for the extent to which they employed various cognitive strategies in their speech, some were found to have benefited from cooperative learning and others did not differ from their peers who studied with the whole-class method (Sharan and Shachar 1988). To determine why this was so requires further study. It seems that, as is the case with other methods of instruction, the effects of cooperative learning on students' thinking, quite apart from effects on achievement, await extensive investigation. The research presented in this book or mentioned here indicates that this can be a fruitful area of investigation. The wealth of research on cooperative learning and achievement published thus far demonstrates the academic benefits of cooperative learning compared to whole-class instruction (individualistic). Just what features of the cooperative learning method produce these effects is a question that researchers will continue to study for many years to come. The possibilities appear to be many, such as: the goal structure, the use of group rewards and/or individual accountability, the heightened sense of group members' responsibility for reaching the group goal, the nature of the interaction among the group members during the group learning activity, increased motivation to learn as a member of a cooperative group, and so on. The chapter by Johnson and Johnson (this volume) spells out these components clearly and precisely, citing research support relevant to each component. (See also Johnson, Johnson & Holubec 1986.)

A carefully prepared list of the many facets of cooperative learning that could explain how it affects student achievement appears in the chapter by Knight and Bohlmeyer. Clearly, there are many possible answers to such a complex problem. For example, the Sharan and Shaulov study reported here shows that cooperative learning groups contribute to increased motivation to learn, and that motivation to learn accounted for 38 percent of the variance in the achievement scores of the sixth-grade pupils ($n = 553$) in that study. What part of the achievement scores can be explained by pupils' better understanding of, or thinking about, the subject matter? To what extent did the peer interaction in the groups contribute to their achievement? Even when we arrive at the point where the achievement variance can be reliably subdivided into the portions explained by different factors (motivation, cognitive strategies, interaction within groups, etc.), that will not illuminate how the individual student is affected by peers in the small learning group. More careful microanalytic work on students' exchanges in cooperative learning groups can enhance our understanding of this process. The internal dynamics of cooperative learning groups is a recurrent theme in cooperative learning research (see the chapters in Part II of Slavin et al. 1985). We will return to that topic as a key to explaining the effects of cooperative learning when we discuss the subject of interpersonal relations in the multi-ethnic classroom.

The chapter by Knight and Bohlmeyer emphasizes the need to employ a research strategy that will enable investigators to reach clear conclusions about the causal relations between factors in cooperative learning methods that affect student achievement or other variables. The detailed table prepared by Knight and Bohlmeyer of factors in cooperative learning methods that reputedly affect student achievement in itself suggests an entire research agenda. If researchers would adopt the strategy described by Knight and Bohlmeyer, it could lead to considerable progress in the theoretical clarity of research in the field of cooperative learning. Researchers would be required to specify much more carefully the precise relationship between the variables in their study. For example, variables heretofore considered to be dependent variables in some studies could be conceived as mediating or moderating variables. Such changes require basic theoretical reconceptualizing of research work. This line of thought directed the design of the experiment reported here by Sharan and Shaulov.

Thus, it seems that two avenues of research converge upon the question of how cooperative learning affects achievement—one way leads to the microanalytic (Sharan and Shachar 1988; Webb 1985) and ethnographic (Wells, Chang, and Maher, this volume) approaches that, in detective fashion, look for the clues in students' utterances and interactions that lead to improved problem solving, cognitive strategies, understanding, and achievement. The second road is to determine when the amount of variance in achievement scores explained by cooperative learning declines significantly after the effect of a particular mediating variable on those scores has been removed. Since Knight and Bohlmeyer provided a formidable list of potential mediating variables gleaned from the research literature, such a research agenda could sustain several careers. Both lines of investigation are needed, provide different kinds of information, and can be mutually enriching.

Cooperative Learning and Interpersonal and Inter-Ethnic Relations

Since its inception, cooperative learning has been employed to foster positive relations among students in the multi-ethnic classroom (Sharan 1980; Sharan et al. 1984; Sharan and Rich 1984; Slavin 1983; Slavin and Madden 1979; Slavin et al. 1985). Generally, Allport's "contact theory" for reducing inter-group prejudice served as the theoretical basis for explaining the positive effects of cooperative learning on inter-ethnic relations in the classroom (Allport 1954). The two chapters in this volume on cooperative learning and ethnic relations, one by Norman Miller and Hugh Harrington, the other by Cohen, Lotan, and Catanzarite, extend the theoretical and empirical base for the application of cooperative learning methods to inter-group relations in the ethnically hetero-geneous classroom.

Chapter 3 in this book by Miller and Harrington is the latest in a series in which Norman Miller and associates explore in depth the various theories and facets of inter-group relations in the multi-ethnic classroom. They carefully set forth the features of, and conditions under which cooperative learning can best contribute to positive relationships between pupils from different ethnic/racial groups (Brewer and Miller 1984; Miller and Brewer 1986; Miller and David-son-Podgorny 1987). Miller and co-workers have accomplished precisely what Knight and Bohlmeyer said was needed for the study of achievement, namely, specification of variables that mediate between cooperative learning methods on the one hand and improved inter-ethnic relations on the other so that re-search can gradually ascertain how the positive effects of cooperative learning occur. But they have done even more than that: Miller has contrasted the the-oretical alternatives for explaining the reduction of social categorization, and has specified the conditions obtaining in cooperative learning methods that can reduce social categorization and enhance relationships based on the students' personal rather than group characteristics. In these penetrating chapters, Miller has paved the way to more theoretically sound and productive research on how cooperative learning affects inter-ethnic relations.

The research done in California by Cohen, Lotan, and Catanzarite and by Huber and Eppler in Germany highlights the important contribution of group management techniques and skills to the regulation of peer interaction within the small learning groups. In both studies, cultivation of social management skills among the students was shown to contribute to a range of important consequences for the students. These include the students' own satisfaction from participating in the groups, and the chance for lower-class and low-status pupils to participate in, and derive both social and academic benefits from, their membership in small mixed-ethnic groups.

The work by Cohen et al. demonstrated the distinct difference in effects on the pupils' behavior of groups that functioned with and without the use of such techniques as role differentiation and norms of cooperative interaction. These norms and roles eliminate the competitive nature of traditional instructional practices that cultivate interpersonal antagonism instead of mutual acceptance. In the multi-ethnic classroom, such competition can only work at cross pur-poses to the express goals of ethnic integration. Clearly, the multi-ethnic setting must be designed and conducted differently from the procedures typical of the traditional classroom (Cohen 1980; Miller and Brewer 1984; Sharan et al. 1984; Sharan and Rich 1984).

Huber and Eppler also point out how important it can be to ask the students themselves how they perceive the way their groups are functioning. The students reveal great sensitivity to their experiences in small groups, and if we ask them they will tell us much about what we as educators need to know if we are to help student groups operate more effectively and with greater satisfaction for their members. Student groups will not function well automatically! Students need management techniques and skills to be able to reach their goals. The authors of cooperative learning textbooks have consistently taken that position from the start. Yet, probably because such management and team-building techniques, largely taken from the group dynamics literature, are not ordinarily part of teachers' professional repertoire, students are often placed in groups and expected to function reasonably well without any preparation for assuming such a role. When this approach fails, teachers can become disenchanted with cooperative learning as too difficult for the students to cope with, or too complex to implement, "unless you start with kids at a young age." The study by Huber and Eppler, as well as the experiment by Lazarowitz and Karsenty, shows that junior and senior high school students can acquire the necessary management and interaction skills relatively easily, and that, with appropriate guidance from the teacher, they can achieve important academic and social goals at the secondary school level.

Huber and Eppler observed that different cooperative learning methods have different levels of requirements for group skills. Teachers can use the methods in sequence so that the students will experience the "easier" methods early and gradually acquire the experience and skill that will enable them to function in the manner appropriate for the methods that stress problem solving and systematic investigation of subject matter. Guidelines for distinguishing the cognitive and social-interactive requirements of the various cooperative learning methods appear in the literature on cooperative learning and group dynamics in the classroom (Graves and Graves 1985; Kagan 1985; Johnson and Johnson 1987; Schmuck and Schmuck 1988; Sharan and Sharan 1976).

COOPERATIVE LEARNING AND THE TOTAL INSTRUCTIONAL PROGRAM

Most of the research on cooperative learning in the classroom treated a given subject or small set of subjects for a relatively limited amount of time, from several weeks to several months or even, on occasion, an entire academic year. To the best of this author's knowledge, nowhere except in work reported by the San Ramon (California) group (see the chapter by Solomon, Watson, Schaps, Battistich, and Solomon) was an attempt made to have cooperative learning methods encompass the entire school experience of students, at any given grade level or in an entire school. For that matter, few if any authors have raised the possibility of having cooperative learning supplant, rather than supplement, traditional whole-class instruction for the entire school day or week. Indeed, the question of the extent to which cooperative learning methods could, or should, be used with a given class of students has hardly been discussed in print. It is clear, therefore, that there is little specific information available about how such a school might function, what it would demand from administrators and teachers, and what would be its possible effects on the students. Would students find it possible to pursue an entire day of school study in that fashion? Or, perhaps it might not be advisable because it is not advisable to use *any* given approach to instruction exclusively for many hours at a time. Apart from the San Ramon project, we do not have any notion of the effort needed or requirements for transforming an entire school into one that conducts the bulk of its instruction with cooperative learning methods.

In the same vein one might ask: If we seriously intended to foster genuine ethnic integration in multi-ethnic schools, or if we felt it to be of paramount importance to cultivate prosocial behavior among students, wouldn't we be well advised to expose students to cooperative activities for prolonged periods of time, and not just for a class period now and then for a few hours during the week? How can we hope to change pupils' relationships and behavior toward one another through cooperative experiences when they are exposed to such experiences in short spurts? The school is a community that convenes every day for five or six hours, for a total of 25 to 30 hours a week. How can cooperative learning practiced for three, four, or even five hours a week affect the relationship among students from different ethnic groups in a given class, when they are in a competitive relationship with one another for the other 20 or 25 hours a week they spend in the classroom together? And what impact would cooperative learning have on students, in all domains of school life, if it were practiced in various forms for half the time pupils spend in school instead of for three or four hours per week? Not many researchers have asked, or undertaken to respond, to such questions. Nor do educators ordinarily ask such questions because rarely do schools or school systems consider making such policy decisions. Schools are very eclectic organizations that typically lack clear educational goals other than purposely vague declarations such as "striving for academic excellence." Usually, change agents external to the school are interested in promoting a particular policy or method, and they try to convince the school of the merits of their program. In that situation, rarely is it feasible, or even considered, to change the entire instructional and curricular program of the school to meet the needs of the new approach or policy, and rarely is it possible to provide the in-service training needed to have the staff adopt and implement the new program extensively. Most often the change agents are gratified when they succeed in implementing their program a few hours a week in one or two subject areas.

It is against this background that we can appreciate all the more the two chapters in this volume that address the problem of making cooperative learning a central feature of the school's instructional and educational policy. The chapter by Solomon, Watson, Schaps, Battistich, and Solomon and the chapter by Robert Slavin are noteworthy for addressing themselves, albeit in distinctly different ways, to the problem of disseminating cooperative learning throughout the school. The authors of both chapters are concerned with expanding cooperative learning into a comprehensive school-wide program that encompasses many subjects or even all of the students' learning and social experience in school. The Prosocial Development Program in San Ramon is based on the assumption that the teaching and learning processes in school must be conducted in a cooperative manner if we wish to influence children's social behavior in school. Such an ambitious goal cannot be achieved by an extracurricular activity added on to the existing instructional program, or by devoting an hour or so a week to discussing social values with the students. Schools socialize students primarily through their instructional activities, which occupy the bulk of the time they spend in school. Hence, programs designed to cultivate moral or prosocial behavior that seek to transmit their message for an hour or two a week almost inevitably will yield very lean results. Therefore, one of the main problems facing research in cooperative learning is the question of the degree to which the innovation is implemented, and the San Ramon group devoted considerable attention to that question. Their chapter presents what seems to be the most extensive documentation in the existing research literature of the extent and domains in which their program for promoting prosocial behavior was actually implemented in three experimental and three comparison schools.

The San Ramon study is also noteworthy for its longitudinal dimension. Few investigators ever have the opportunity to create an integrated instructional policy and program where students are exposed to a theoretically coherent set of educational experiences over the course of their years in school. The findings regarding the consistent effects of cooperative experiences in the experimental schools reported by Solomon and colleagues are a unique contribution to our knowledge about the potential outcomes of the cooperative learning approach to instruction. In substance they contribute much support to the claim that cooperative learning can produce long-term positive effects if implemented consistently over the years.

One of the findings to emerge from the data on program implementation was that the comparison schools implemented similar practices to almost 50 percent of the extent to which the same methods were carried out in the experimental program. In light of this fact it comes as no surprise to learn that no differences were found between the treatment and control groups on some of the dependent measures. This state of affairs means that the results should not be generalized to other situations where the control schools frequently practice whole-class instruction only and do not conduct cooperative activities as part of regular classroom teaching. In such cases, the impact of cooperative learning and other prosocial activities employed in the San Ramon project would probably yield even more striking results than the many positive effects that did emerge.

An important feature of the work reported by Slavin in his chapter on comprehensive cooperative learning models is that cooperative learning can be viewed as a dynamic set of paradigms from which we can continue to devise new and different techniques for coping with the wide variety of instructional needs of schools. We should not rest content with existing ''methods'' as if they were inviolable, but use them as building blocks for new combinations of procedures as the need arises. A second message of Slavin's chapter is that, granted the merits of the generic cooperative learning models developed heretofore, the methods must be adapted to the specific needs of particular curricular materials because each subject has its own special requirements. We are indebted to Slavin for emphasizing this point. Perhaps investigators of cooperative learning would prefer to ignore the message that sooner or later we will have to cope with the need to consider the problems of adapting curricular contents to the demands of cooperative learning, and that teachers, with their limited time and resources, cannot be expected to perform that service themselves. That message will inevitably dampen the enthusiasm of some investigators because of the enormity of the task that lies ahead. Of course it is easier to transfer responsibility to professionals who deal with curriculum development and for whom the process of instruction is secondary. Slavin shows us that the investigator/ school consultant role can be combined in the figure of one person, that that person should shoulder the responsibility for both elements of the task—designing the curricular materials and the instructional procedures, as well as evaluating the effects of the teaching methods—and that he/she is probably the best qualified person to do that. One way or the other, what is sorely needed is an integrated approach to planning the *process and content* of instruction before significant progress can be made in improving teaching and learning in today's schools.

SOME TOPICS FOR FUTURE RESEARCH

This volume could not possibly encompass all of the many areas of research on the various methods and potential effects of cooperative learning in the classroom. Also, new avenues of research remain to be explored that were not mentioned in this book. Without presuming to develop these themes, it is worthwhile to give some examples of topics about which we know relatively little, or which remain to be explored.

Only a few studies have appeared thus far on the effects of cooperative learning on students' thinking. Yet, authors of the earliest cooperative learning textbooks pointed to the potentially positive effects of this approach on children's thinking that could emerge from the interchange of ideas and perspectives among peers in the classroom. There have been studies of changes in perspective taking (Bridgeman 1981) as a function of students' participation in cooperative learning, as well as of children's problem-solving behavior (Skon, Johnson, and Johnson 1981). My colleague and I studied children's cognitive strategies during group discussions with students who had studied in classes taught with the group investigation approach to cooperative learning compared with those from classes taught with the whole-class method (Sharan and Shachar 1988).

These studies indicate that important changes do occur in students' thinking following their experiences in cooperative learning classes, but the existing research only touched the surface of this important topic.

As noted earlier in this chapter, the study of students' academic achievement should be extended to include investigation of the cognitive processes affected by cooperative learning that can explain how achievement is enhanced. Until this step is taken, the concept of achievement will remain vague and largely synonymous with the accumulation of additional information, as it is still widely understood by many educators. We will not learn how cooperative learning promotes student achievement if we remain content with the assessment of achievement as an intellectual "black box" that fails to specify how and what the learner gained from this approach to instruction.

One aspect of the study of cooperative learning effects on students' thinking should derive from the seminal work by the Johnsons on the role and effects of controversy on learning (Johnson and Johnson 1979, 1985b; Johnson, Johnson and Smith 1986). Controversy can arouse a critical approach to a topic, and the effect of controversy within cooperative learning groups on students' critical thinking is a natural development of the existing research. However, it seems unlikely that all intellectual controversy will arouse critical thinking in our students (Nijhof and Kommers 1985). The features and conditions of cognitive controversy that can stimulate critical thinking remain to be studied. This topic stands at the intersection of several research traditions in developmental, cognitive, and educational psychology, and its study can produce critically important knowledge for all of these fields and for instructional practice in the classroom.

These are only some examples of new or still underdeveloped arenas of research on the methods and effects of cooperative learning that were not treated in this volume. Many more topics in the field of cooperative learning that are worthy of intensive study, and which were not referred to in this book, will surely continue to emerge as new research is published.

WHAT WAS LEARNED ABOUT WHOLE-CLASS TEACHING

Research on cooperative learning is most often read from the point of view of its effects on students and teachers. What receives less prominence in research reports is the generally covert, and only occasionally explicit criticism that this body of research presents of traditional whole-class instruction. The whole-class, recitation and presentation method predominates in the majority of classrooms in the Western world, and certainly comes close to being almost the exclusive form of instruction in most academic subjects in high schools (except for laboratory and workshop sessions, music and gym). Hence, criticism of this approach to teaching has important implications for a very large number of people and schools.

A theme running through most of the cooperative learning research, including the chapters in this book, states that traditional instruction is less than satisfactory for most pupils of almost any age, and often produces many negative consequences for teachers and pupils alike, not all of which are immediately apparent to the players themselves. Some of these negative consequences, in both the academic and social domains, are serious enough to lead to the conclusion that whole-class instruction should be retired as the primary mode of teaching, and, at best, should occupy a fraction of the time it presently occupies in the instructional repertoire of teachers. It contributes more than its share to the boredom, rote learning, thoughtlessness, and lack of motivation that is rampant in school learning, although admittedly it cannot be cited as the only source of those phenomena (Sarason 1983).

We are not trying to argue that the teaching method operates totally independent of the teacher that uses it. No method, in and of itself, guarantees high-quality instruction. My interpretation is that the research on cooperative learning should be understood as saying, *inter alia,* that the competent implementation of cooperative learning creates conditions more conducive to higher-level student motivation to learn, higher-level achievement for all students, and more positive social relations with peers from one's own and from other ethnic groups in the classroom, by comparison with the whole-class method. Moreover, not only does cooperative learning foster more *positive* educational experiences and results than whole-class teaching, but the latter often generates *undesirable* outcomes. Among these are: social distance between peers in the classroom and between those from different ethnic groups in particular, insidious social comparison processes, more tightly knit cliques in classrooms, and many more students at the lower levels of achievement. We have also read in this volume about the formalistic, impersonal nature of teachers' interaction with students in the traditional classroom setting, a pattern that changes with the change in instructional method without a change in teaching personnel. The schools continue to employ an instructional technology that often is at cross purposes to its expressed goals.

The fact is that cooperative learning can be implemented only to the extent that traditional whole-class teaching is supplanted, not just altered! Since the instructional time in schools remains fixed, more or less, choices must be made. We cannot keep doing what we have been doing all along and still allow room for change, at least not in this particular instance. A change is sorely needed to revitalize teaching and learning in schools. Research on cooperative learning provides a relatively firm basis for concluding that the direction of the change is known and is feasible within the existing organizational structure of today's classrooms. The key to adoption of cooperative learning methods lies in the professional competence of the teachers. That is another topic not discussed in this book. It must await treatment in future volumes.

REFERENCES

Allport, G. (1954) *The Nature of Prejudice.* Cambridge, MA: Addison-Wesley.

Berman, P., and McLaughlin, M. (1978) *Federal Programs Supporting Educational Change. Vol. 8: Implementing and Sustaining Innovations.* Santa Monica, CA: Rand Corporation.

Brewer, M., and Miller, N. (1984) "Beyond the contact hypothesis: Theoretical perspectives on desegregation." In *Groups in Contact,* edited by N. Miller and M. Brewer, pp. 77–96. Orlando, FL: Academic Press.

Bridgeman, D. (1981) "Enhanced role taking through cooperative interdependence: A field study." *Child Development* 52:1231–39.

Cazden, C. (1986) "Classroom discourse." In *Handbook of Research on Teaching,* 3rd edn, edited by M. Wittrock, pp. 432–63. New York: Macmillan.

Cohen, E. (1980) "Design and redesign of the desegregated school: Problems of status, power and conflict." In *School Desegregation,* edited by W. Stephan and J. Feagin, pp. 251–80. New York: Plenum.

——— (1986) *Designing Groupwork: Strategies for the Heterogeneous Classroom.* New York: Teachers College Press.

Goodlad, J. (1984) *A Place Called School.* New York: McGraw-Hill.

Graves, N., and Graves, T. (1985) "Creating a cooperative learning environment: An ecological approach." In *Learning to Cooperate, Cooperating to Learn,* edited by R. Slavin, S. Sharan, S. Kagan, R. Hertz-Lazarowitz, C. Webb, and R. Schmuck, pp. 403–36. New York: Plenum.

Johnson, D., and Johnson, R. (1979) "Conflict in the classroom: Controversy and learning." *Review of Educational Research* 49:51–61.

——— (1985a) "Motivational processes in cooperative, competitive and individualistic learning situations." In *Research on Motivation in Education. Vol. 2: The Classroom Milieu,* edited by C. Ames and R. Ames, pp. 249–86. Orlando, FL: Academic Press.

——— (1985b) "Classroom conflict: Controversy versus debate in learning groups." *American Educational Research Journal* 22:237–56.

——— (1987) *Learning Together and Alone,* 2d edn. Englewood Cliffs, NJ: Prentice-Hall.

Johnson, D., Johnson, R., and Holubec, E. (1986) *Circles of Learning.* Edina, MN: Interaction Book Co.

Johnson, D., Johnson, R., and Smith, K. (1986) "Academic conflict among students: Controversy and learning." In *The Social Psychology of Education,* edited by R. Feldman, pp. 199–231. New York: Cambridge University Press.

Kagan, S. (1985) "Dimensions of cooperative classroom structures." In *Learning to Cooperate, Cooperating to Learn,* edited by R. Slavin, S. Sharan, S. Kagan, C. Webb, R. Hertz-Lazarowitz, and R. Schmuck, pp. 67–96. New York: Plenum.

——— (1986) *Cooperative Learning Resources for Teachers.* Riverside, CA: University of California.

Miller, N., and Brewer, M. (eds) (1984) *Groups in Contact: The Psychology of Desegregation.* Orlando, FL: Academic Press.

——— (1986) "Social categorization theory and team learning procedures." In *The Social Psychology of Education,* edited by R. Feldman, pp. 172–98. Cambridge: Cambridge University Press.

Miller, N., and Davidson-Podgorny, G. (1987) "Theoretical models of intergroup relations and the use of cooperative teams as an intervention for desegregated settings." In *Group Processes and Intergroup Relations,* edited by C. Hendrick, pp. 41–67. Newbury Park, CA: Sage Publications.

Nijhof, W., and Kommers, P. (1985) "An analysis of cooperation in relation to cognitive controversy." In *Learning to Cooperate, Cooperating to Learn,* edited by R. Slavin et al., pp. 125–45. New York: Plenum.

Sarason, S. (1982) *The Culture of the School and the Problem of Change,* 2d edn. Boston, MA: Allyn and Bacon.

——— (1983) *Schooling in America: Scapegoat and Salvation.* New York: The Free Press.

Schmuck, R., and Schmuck, P. (1988) *Group Processes in the Classroom,* 5th edn. Dubuque, IA: Wm. C. Brown.

Skon, L., Johnson, D., and Johnson, R. (1981) "Cooperative peer interaction versus individual competition and individualistic efforts: Effects on the acquisition of cognitive reasoning strategies." *Journal of Educational Psychology* 73:83–92.

Sharan, S. (1980) "Cooperative learning in small groups: Recent methods and effects on achievement, attitudes and ethnic relations." *Review of Educational Research* 50:241–71.

Sharan, S., and Hertz-Lazarowitz, R. (1982) "The effect of an educational change project on teachers' perceptions, attitudes and behavior." *Journal of Applied Behavioral Science* 18:185–201.

Sharan, S., Hertz-Lazarowitz, R.; and Ackerman, Z. (1980) "Academic achievement of elementary school children in small group versus whole-class instruction." *Journal of Experimental Education* 48:125–29.

Sharan, S., Kussell, P., Hertz-Lazarowitz, R., Bejarano, Y., Raviv, S., and Sharan, Y. (1984) *Cooperative Learning in the Classroom: Research in Desegregated Schools.* Hillsdale, NJ: Lawrence Erlbaum and Associates.

Sharan, S., and Rich, Y. (1984) "Field experiments on ethnic integration in Israeli schools." In *School Desegregation: Cross-Cultural Perspectives,* edited by Y. Amir and S. Sharan, pp. 189–217. Hillsdale, NJ: Erlbaum.

Sharan, S., and Shachar, H. (1988) *Language and Learning in the Cooperative Classroom.* New York: Springer.

Sharan, S., and Sharan, Y. (1976) *Small-Group Teaching.* Englewood Cliffs, NJ: Educational Technology Publications.

Slavin, R. (1983) *Cooperative Learning.* New York: Longman.

Slavin, R., and Madden, N. (1979) "School practices that improve race relations." *American Educational Research Journal* 16:169–80.

Slavin, R., Sharan, S., Kagan, S., Hertz-Lazarowitz, R., Webb, C., and Schmuck, R. (eds) (1985) *Learning to Cooperate, Cooperating to Learn.* New York: Plenum.

Talmage, H., Pascarella, E., and Ford, S. (1984) "The influence of cooperative learning strategies on teacher practices, students' perceptions of the learning environment, and academic achievement." *American Educational Research Journal* 21:163–79.

Webb, N. (1985) "Student interaction and learning in small groups: A research summary." In *Learning to Cooperate, Cooperating to Learn,* edited by R. Slavin et al., pp. 147–72. New York, Plenum.

Selected Bibliography

Ames, C., and Ames, R. (eds) (1985) *Motivation in Education. Vol. 2: The Classroom Milieu.* Orlando, FL: Academic Press.

Aronson, E., Blaney, N., Stephan, C., Sikes, J., and Snapp, M. (1987) *The Jigsaw Classroom.* Beverly Hills, CA: Sage Publications.

Cohen, E. (1987) *Designing Group Work: Strategies for the Heterogeneous Classroom.* New York: Teachers College Press.

DeCharms, R. (1976) *Enhancing Motivation: Change in the Classroom.* New York: Irvington (Halsted-Wiley).

Deutsch, M. (1949) "A theory of cooperation and competition." *Human Relations* 2:129–52.

——— (1949) "An experimental study of the effects of cooperation and competition upon group process." *Human Relations* 2:199–232.

Graves, N., and Graves, T. (1985) "Creating a cooperative learning environment: An ecological approach." In *Learning to Cooperate, Cooperating to Learn,* edited by R. Slavin, S. Sharan, S. Kagan, R. Hertz-Lazarowitz, C. Webb, and R. Schmuck, pp. 403–36. New York: Plenum.

Hertz-Lazarowitz, R., and Sharan, S. (1984) "Enhancing prosocial behavior through cooperative learning in the classroom." In *Development and Maintenance of Prosocial Behavior: International Perspectives,* edited by E. Staub, D. Bar-Tal, J. Karylowski, and J. Reykowski, pp. 423–43. New York: Plenum.

Johnson, D., and Johnson, R. (1974) "Instructional goal structure: Cooperative, competitive or individualistic?" *Review of Educational Research* 44:213–40.

——— (1975) *Learning Together and Alone.* Englewood Cliffs, NJ: Prentice-Hall.

——— (1979) "Conflict in the classroom: Controversy and learning." *Review of Educational Research* 49:51–70.

—— (1985) "Motivational processes in cooperative, competitive and individualistic learning situations." In *Research on Motivation in Education. Vol. 2: The Classroom Milieu,* edited by C. Ames and R. Ames, pp. 249–86. Orlando, FL: Academic Press.

Johnson, D., Johnson, R., Holubec, E., and Roy, P. (1984) *Circles of Learning.* Alexandria, VA: Association for Supervision and Curriculum Development.

Johnson, D., Johnson, R., and Maruyama, G. (1983) "Interdependence and interpersonal attraction among heterogeneous and homogeneous individuals: A theoretical formulation and a meta-analysis of the research." *Review of Educational Research* 53:5–54.

Johnson, D., Maruyama, G., Johnson, R., Nelson, D., and Skon, L. (1981) "Effects of cooperative, competitive and individualistic goal structures on achievement: A meta-analysis." *Psychological Bulletin* 89:47–62.

Kagan, S. (1985) "Dimensions of cooperative classroom structures." In *Learning to Cooperate, Cooperating to Learn,* edited by R. Slavin, S. Sharan, S. Kagan, R. Hertz-Lazarowitz, C. Webb, and R. Schmuck, pp. 67–96. New York: Plenum.

—— (1986) *Cooperative Learning Resources for Teachers.* Riverside, CA: University of California.

Miel, A. (1952) *Cooperative Procedures in Learning.* New York: Teachers College.

Miller, N., and Brewer, M. (eds) (1984) *Groups in Contact: The Psychology of Desegregation.* New York: Academic Press.

—— (1986) "Social categorization theory and team learning procedures." In *The Social Psychology of Education,* edited by R. Feldman, pp. 172–98. Cambridge: Cambridge University Press.

Miller, N., and Davidson-Podgorny, G. (1987) "Theoretical models of intergroup relations and the use of cooperative teams as an intervention for desegregated settings." In *Group Processes and Intergroup Relations,* edited by C. Hendrick, pp. 41–67. Newbury Park, CA: Sage Publications.

Pepitone, E. (1980) *Children in Cooperation and Competition.* Lexington, MA: D. C. Heath.

Ryan, R., Connell, J., and Deci, E. (1985) "A motivational analysis of self-determination and self-regulation in education." In *Research on Motivation in Education, Vol. 2: The Classroom Milieu,* edited by C. Ames and R. Ames, pp. 13–51. Orlando, FL: Academic Press.

Sarason, S. (1982) *The Culture of the School and the Problem of Change,* 2d edn. Boston, MA: Allyn and Bacon.

—— (1983) *Schooling in America: Scapegoat and Salvation.* New York: The Free Press.

Schmuck, R., and Schmuck, P. (1988) *Group Processes in the Classroom,* 5th edn. Dubuque, IA: Brown and Co.

Sharan, S. (1980) "Cooperative learning in small groups: Recent methods and effects on achievement, attitudes and ethnic relations." *Review of Educational Research* 50:241–71.

Sharan, S., Hare, P., Webb, C., and Hertz-Lazarowitz, R. (eds) (1980) *Cooperation in Education.* Provo, UT: Brigham Young University Press.

Sharan, S., and Hertz-Lazarowitz, R. (1980) "A group-investigation method of cooperative learning in the classroom." In *Cooperation in Education,* edited by

S. Sharan, P. Hare, C. Webb, and R. Hertz-Lazarowitz, pp. 14–46. Provo, UT: Brigham Young University Press.

―――― (1982) "Effects of an instructional change program on teachers' behavior, attitudes and perceptions." *Journal of Applied Behavioral Science* 18:185–201.

Sharan, S., Kussell, P., Hertz-Lazarowitz, R., Bejarano, Y., Raviv, S., and Sharan, Y. (1984) *Cooperative Learning in the Classroom: Research in Desegregated Schools*. Hillsdale, NJ: Lawrence Erlbaum Associates.

Sharan, S., and Shachar, H. (1988) *Language and Learning in the Cooperative Classroom*. New York: Springer.

Sharan, S., and Sharan, Y. (1976) *Small Group Teaching*. Englewood Cliffs, NJ: Educational Technology Publications.

Sharan, Y., and Sharan, S. (1987) "Training teachers for cooperative learning." *Educational Leadership* 45:20–25.

Slavin, R. (1983) *Cooperative Learning*. New York: Longman.

―――― (1983) "When does cooperative learning increase student achievement?" *Psychological Bulletin* 94:429–45.

―――― (1984) "Team assisted individualization: Combining cooperative learning and individualized instruction in mathematics." In *Learning to Cooperate, Cooperating to Learn*, edited by R. Slavin, S. Sharan, S. Kagan, R. Hertz-Lazarowitz, C. Webb, and R. Schmuck, p. 177–209. New York: Plenum.

―――― (1986) *Using Student Team Learning*, 3rd edn. Baltimore, MD: Johns Hopkins University, Center for Research on Elementary and Middle Schools.

Solomon, D., Watson, M., Battistich, V., Schaps, E., Tuck, P., Solomon, J., Cooper, C., and Ritchey, W. (1985) "A program to promote interpersonal consideration and cooperation in children." In *Learning to Cooperate, Cooperating to Learn*, edited by R. Slavin, S. Sharan, S. Kagan, R. Hertz-Lazarowitz, C. Webb, and R. Schmuck, pp. 371–401. New York: Plenum.

Steiner, I. (1972) *Group Process and Productivity*. New York: Academic Press.

Thelen, H. (1981) *The Classroom Society*. New York: John Wiley.

Thew, D. (1975) "The classroom social organization category system." *Classroom Interaction Newsletter* 11:18–24.

Webb, N. (1985) "Student interaction and behavior in small groups: A research summary." In *Learning to Cooperate, Cooperating to Learn*, edited by R. Slavin, S. Sharan, S. Kagan, R. Hertz-Lazarowitz, C. Webb, and R. Schmuck, pp. 147–72. New York: Plenum.

Index

About the Editor and Contributors

SHLOMO SHARAN, Ph.D., moved to Israel from the United States. He is Professor of Educational Psychology at the School of Education, Tel-Aviv University in Israel, where he has been teaching since 1966. Since 1972 he has been actively involved in research and development work on cooperative learning in small groups and on cooperative staff organization and management in schools, carrying out extensive field experiments at all levels of public schooling. He is one of the founders of the International Association for the Study of Cooperation in Education, and served as its president from 1982 to 1988. Among his books in English are *Small Group Teaching* (with Yael Sharan, 1976), *Cooperative Learning in the Classroom: Research in Desegregated Schools* (with P. Kussell, R. Hertz-Lazarowitz, Y. Bejarano, S. Raviv and Y. Sharan, 1984), and *Language and Learning in the Cooperative Classroom* (with Hana Shachar, 1988). Along with colleagues he has edited *Cooperation in Education* (1980), *School Desegregation* (1984) and *Learning to Cooperate, Cooperating to Learn* (1985).

VICTOR BATTISTICH, Ph.D., is Senior Research Associate, Developmental Studies Center in San Ramon, California. His main interests are in personality development and personality influences on social cognition and behavior.

ELAINE MORTON BOHLMEYER, Ph.D., is School Psychologist, Phoenix, Arizona. Her major areas of research are cooperative learning, prosocial behavior, and learning strategies.

LISA CATANZARITE is a graduate student at Stanford University, Stanford, California.

GEN LING M. CHANG is Senior Research Officer, Ontario Institute for Studies in Education in Toronto, Ontario. She is interested in literacy and writing development, the language of learning and instruction, and means of educational change.

ELIZABETH G. COHEN, Ph.D., is Professor of Education and Sociology, Stanford University, Stanford, California, where she directs the Program for Complex Instruction. Her main interests are in the organization of schools and teaching, and the application of expectation states theory. Among her recent publications is *Designing Groupwork: Strategies for Heterogeneous Classrooms* (1986).

RENATE EPPLER, Ph.D., is Teacher, State school administration, Rottweil, West Germany.

HUGH JORDAN HARRINGTON, Ph.D., is Program Manager of Social Research for Corporate Human Resources, Hughes Aircraft Co., Los Angeles, California.

RACHEL HERTZ-LAZAROWITZ, Ph.D., is Senior Lecturer, School of Education, Haifa University, Haifa, Israel. Her research interests include cooperative learning, prosocial behavior, and planned change in schools. She is co-author (with Shlomo Sharan) of two volumes on cooperative learning that emerged from their joint field projects and research, and co-author (with Ina Fuchs) of a textbook on cooperative learning (all of these in Hebrew). She also co-edited *Cooperation in Education* (1980) and *Learning to Cooperate, Cooperating to Learn* (1985). Hertz-Lazarowitz is one of the founders of the International Association for the Study of Cooperation in Education.

GÜNTER L. HUBER, Ph.D., is Professor of Educational Psychology, University of Tubingen, Tubingen, West Germany.

DAVID W. JOHNSON, Ph.D., Professor of Educational Psychology, and ROGER T. JOHNSON, Ph.D., Professor of Curriculum and Instruction, are both at the University of Minnesota, Minneapolis, Minnesota, where they are co-directors of the Cooperative Learning Center. Among their many books are *Learning Together and Alone* (1987, 2nd edition), *Circles of Learning* (with Edythe Johnson Holubec, 1986), and *Creative Conflict* (1987).

GABBY KARSENTY, Ph.D., is Senior Instructor in Biology in high school and Supervisor of Biology Instruction, Israel Ministry of Education, Haifa, Israel.

GEORGE P. KNIGHT, Ph.D., is Associate Professor, Department of Psychology, Arizona State University, Tempe, Arizona. His major research interests are the development of cooperative, competitive, and individualistic social values, prosocial development, and the development of ethnic identity.

REUVEN LAZAROWITZ, Ph.D., is Associate Professor of Science Education, Department of Education in Technology and Science, the Technion, Israel Institute of Technology, Haifa, Israel. His research interests focus on the cognitive and affective aspects of biology instruction in individualized and cooperative settings.

RACHEL LOTAN, Ph.D., is Associate Director, Program for Complex Instruction, Stanford University.

ANN MAHER is Teacher, Board of Education of the City of Toronto in Toronto, Ontario.

NORMAN MILLER, Ph.D., is Mendel B. Silberberg Professor of Psychology, University of Southern California, Los Angeles, California. His research interests include attitude change, inter-group relations, school desegregation, cooperation, and helping. He edited *School Desegregation* (with H. Gerard, 1975) and *Groups in Contact: The Psychology of Desegregation* (with M. Brewer, 1984). He has been a Guggenheim, Cattell, Fulbright, Haynes and USPHS Fellow.

ERIC SCHAPS, Ph.D., is President of the Developmental Studies Center, San Ramon, California. His primary interests are in prosocial development, educational improvement, and program evaluation.

HANA SHACHAR, Ph.D., is Lecturer, Department of Education, and is also at the Institute for Promotion of Social Integration in Schools, both at Bar Ilan University, Ramat Gan, Israel. She directs the implementation of cooperative learning projects in schools. With Shlomo Sharan she is co-author of *Language and Learning in the Cooperative Classroom* (1988) and *Participative Management in Schools* (1990, in Hebrew).

ADA SHAULOV is a graduate student, School of Education, Tel-Aviv University, Tel-Aviv, Israel. She teaches in the Beit Berl Teachers College, Kfar Sava.

ROBERT E. SLAVIN, Ph.D., is Director, Elementary School Program, Center for Research on Elementary and Middle Schools, The Johns Hopkins University, Baltimore, Maryland. He has published extensively on cooperative learning, school and classroom organization, desegregation, mainstreaming, ability grouping, and research review. Among his many books are *Cooperative Learn-*

ing (1983), *Educational Psychology* (1986), and *Classroom Organization* (1989). He is one of the founders of the International Association for the Study of Cooperation in Education.

DANIEL SOLOMON, Ph.D., is Director of Research, Developmental Studies Center, San Ramon, California. His interests are in child social development and the social psychology of education. He is the author (with Arthur Kendall) of *Children in Classrooms: An Investigation of Person-Environment Interaction* (Praeger, 1979).

JUDITH SOLOMON, Ph.D., is Lecturer, Department of Psychology, San Francisco State University. Her interests are in the study of attachment, parent-child relationships, and social development.

MARILYN WATSON, Ph.D., is Program Director, The Child Development Project at the Developmental Studies Center, San Ramon, California. Her research interests are in social and moral development, parent-child relationships, and the application of evolutionary theory to the understanding of human development.

GORDON WELLS, Ph.D., is Professor of Education, Ontario Institute for Studies in Education, Toronto, Ontario. He teaches and does research on literacy, language, and learning, including research in schools with multilingual students. Before moving to Canada in 1984, he was director of the Bristol Study of Language at Home and in School that led to the publication of *The Meaning Makers* (1986) and *Language Development in the Pre-School Years* (1985).